Advanced XML Applications from the Experts at The XML Guild

Members of The XML Guild

THOMSON™
COURSE TECHNOLOGY
Professional ■ Technical ■ Reference

THOMSON

COURSE TECHNOLOGY

Professional ■ Technical ■ Reference

Educational facilities, companies, and organizations interested in multiple copies or licensing of this book should contact the Publisher for quantity discount information. Training manuals, CD-ROMs, and portions of this book, are also available individually or can be tailored for specific needs.

ISBN-10: 1-59863-214-0

ISBN-13: 978-1-59863-214-9

Library of Congress Catalog Card Number: 2006923271

Printed in the United States of America

07 08 09 10 11 PH 10 9 8 7 6 5 4 3 2 1

Thomson Course Technology PTR, a division of Thomson Learning Inc.
25 Thomson Place
Boston, MA 02210
http://www.courseptr.com

Publisher and General Manager, Thomson Course Technology PTR:
Stacy L. Hiquet

Associate Director of Marketing:
Sarah O'Donnell

Manager of Editorial Services:
Heather Talbot

Marketing Manager:
Mark Hughes

Acquisitions Editor:
Mitzi Koontz

Marketing Assistant:
Adena Flitt

Project Editor:
Kezia Endsley

PTR Editorial Services Coordinator:
Erin Johnson

Copy Editor:
Kezia Endsley

Interior Layout Tech:
Digital Publishing Solutions

Cover Designer:
Mike Tanamachi

Indexer:
Kelly Dobbs Henthorne

Proofreader:
Sandi Wilson

About the Authors

The authors of this book are members of the XML Guild (http://www.xmlguild.org/).

Ronald Bourret

Ronald Bourret is a consultant, writer, and researcher specializing in how XML and databases work together. As a consultant, he focuses on high-level projects, such as reviewing XML application architectures, designing features for XML/database tools, and introducing clients to XML and how it applies to their specific situation. His writing includes *XML and Databases,* often considered the standard introduction to the subject, the XML Namespaces FAQ, and an IBM Redbook about XML support in DB2. He also maintains a website with descriptions of more than 200 XML/database and XML data-binding products at http://www.rpbourret.com.

Anthony B. Coates

Anthony B. Coates (Tony) is a London-based consultant who works with financial and enterprise clients on the design and mapping of data models, especially the production of enterprise message models based on industry standard XML or other message models. Tony is actively involved in numerous standards groups including ISO, UN/CEFACT, OASIS, MDDL, and FpML.

Betty Harvey

Betty Harvey is President of Electronic Commerce Connection, Inc. Ms. Harvey has participated with many government and commercial enterprises in planning and executing their migration to structured information. She is involved in the ebXML initiative and is the co-author of *Professional ebXML Foundations,* published by Wrox, August 2001, as well as many other publications. She started and coordinates the Washington, D.C. Area SGML/XML Users Group. Prior to starting ECC, Inc., Betty worked in Scientific and Engineering Computing at David Taylor Model Basic, NSWC. In her capacity with the US Navy, she participated in the development of US DoD CALS standards including IETMs, SGML, and Internet protocols.

G. Ken Holman

G. Ken Holman is the Chief Technology Officer for Crane Softwrights Ltd., current international secretary of the ISO subcommittee responsible for the SGML family of standards, an invited expert to the W3C and member of the W3C Working Group that developed XML from SGML, the founding chair of the two OASIS XML and XSLT Conformance Technical Committees and current chair of the UBL FPSC subcommittee. He is also the former chair of the Canadian committee to the ISO, the author of electronically published and print-published books on XML-related technologies, and a frequent conference speaker.

Michael Kay

Michael Kay is the developer of the Saxon XSLT and XQuery processor. He is the editor of the XSLT 2.0 specification and is also a member of the XQuery working group in W3C. He wrote the Wrox Press book *XSLT Programmers Reference*, widely accepted as the definitive reference on XSLT, which is now in its third edition, and he has delivered a wide variety of papers, articles, and seminars on subjects related to XSLT and XQuery. He is based in the UK, and has 30 years' experience in the industry working with a wide variety of information management technologies. He founded Saxonica Limited in 2004 to continue the development of the Saxon technology and to provide services to Saxon integrators and users. Assignments undertaken include customized training courses and seminars, strategic advice on technology selection and application architecture, project mentoring, code reviews and performance tuning, and integration of Saxon into third-party tools.

Michael Kay is the joint winner (together with Norman Walsh) of the XML Cup 2005 awarded for services to the XML community.

Evan Lenz

Evan Lenz is an independent XML consultant specializing in XSLT. He is author of O'Reilly's *XSLT 1.0 Pocket Reference*, co-author of *Office 2003 XML*, and contributor to *Word Hacks*. He has written articles, spoken at conferences, and served as invited expert on the W3C XSL Working Group. He lives in Seattle with his wife and three children.

Benoît Marchal

Benoît Marchal is a Belgian consultant. He is the author of *XML by Example*, Second Edition and other XML books. He has also published close to 200 articles on XML, Web services, and related technologies.

Nikita Ogievetsky

Nikita Ogievetsky is a New York-based consultant. He is an expert in Information Architecture, Data Modeling, and Knowledge Sharing and Interoperability.

He leads the community in finding simple solutions for real-life problems on the enterprise scale. Nikita contributed to the XTM 1.0 specification and is a funding member of TopicMaps.Org. He presented and published papers on the subjects of XML, XSLT, Knowledge Technologies, Physics, and general computer science. As an author he has contributed to both *XML Topic Maps* (Addison-Wesley) and *XSLT Cookbook* (O'Reilly).

Zarella Rendon

Zarella Rendon is the Managing Director and Principal Consultant at XML-Factor. Her focus is implementing end-to-end customer solutions for document and data transformation, management, and reuse. She works with XML and related standards, and applies her specific talents of connecting XML concepts with real-world applications. She works within the XML community to influence the direction of emerging technology standards. She is a member of OASIS, the W3C XSL Working Group, and several industry groups where she strives to help further the development, support, and use of standards in vertical markets.

Eric van der Vlist

Eric van der Vlist is CEO and founder of Dyomedea. He has, before starting Dyomedea, managed technical teams for six years at Sybase. At Sybase, he has also developed an intranet to facilitate team operations and access to the technical support legacy system. This engineer, graduated from Ecole Centrale de Paris (1981), has also managed development teams for small companies and worked for six years at Philips. He has a passion for technique (especially for Internet, XML, and open source software) and, open-minded, has developed a global knowledge of the different activities of a company.

Introduction

The foundations of XML are found in two World Wide Web Consortium (W3C) recommendations: Extensible Markup Language and Namespaces in XML. Using just these foundations, it is very simple and straightforward to express a set of information in a labeled hierarchy. The hierarchy has simple parent, child, and sibling relationships, and the labels used for the information items found therein can be made globally unique and universally identifiable.

Layered on top of the foundations are many and varied other W3C Recommendations and International Organization for Standardization (ISO) Standards used to implement text processing and information manipulation tasks. These tasks can be used in tandem to solve both simple and very challenging publishing and interchange problems.

Standardized in 1998, XML has been around long enough that the worldwide community of XML users has created a sufficient oral tradition of use and a plethora of freely-available examples of application to solve simple markup problems.

Without guidance, however, it can be difficult to see how such a simple technology can be used to meet some of the challenges faced in information publishing and interchange. But these challenges are being faced and are being overcome with expert application of the layered technologies. Tips and techniques have been honed with the real-world deployments of such technology by seasoned users of markup tools and standards.

The collective experience of the members of the XML Guild brings together some of these solutions in this book of guidance on the advanced application of XML-based technologies to meet challenging tasks. Incorporating these approaches and techniques in your solutions can help you harness some of the advantages of using markup.

The XML Guild

This book's authors are current and past members of the XML Guild, a consortium of some of the best independent XML consultants in the world. Our members have extensive experience in XML and markup technologies. We are involved in the establishment of standards and best practices. We are authors of numerous books, articles, and papers, and are well-known presenters and speakers.

The XML Guild currently has members in Belgium, Canada, France, the United Kingdom, and the United States of America, all of whom are willing to work with customers in other locations.

Advanced XML Applications

This book assumes the reader is already familiar with, indeed intimate with, the use of XML syntax as described by the XML Recommendation. This is not the place to learn about angle brackets and the escaping of markup characters with which to create well-formed XML documents. Well-formed documents are streams of marked-up information that do not violate the productions and rules of the XML Recommendation. Starting with your use of well-formed XML, you can build on your knowledge with the more advanced tips and techniques we offer here than are typically found in how-to books for markup-based applications.

We begin by presenting the role and advanced use of XML Namespaces, with which one disambiguates the labels used in their XML structures. The labels used for the information items in a hierarchy, or any collection of information for that matter, are critically important for it is by these labels that processing applications recognize, or identify, the information being processed. Without being able to identify the information, or by being confused by the ambiguity of the identity of the information, an application is unable to produce trusted results. As this is often not an issue in a closed environment, where a community of users does not influence others nor is influenced by the presence of information from others, using one's information in an open context requires careful consideration of the fully-qualified labels used in XML documents.

Ensuring your information is structured in the way suitable for your processing applications requires you to express the constraints of your structures in ways in which those constraints can be tested for having been violated. One expresses those constraints as a schema or a document model of the use of the structures and their labels in an XML document. The document schema constraints are expressed using an XML schema language, from which there are a number of choices one can make. Each choice of language gives the user a different set of constraint semantics with which the model is limited. Many users of XML are unfamiliar with some of the constraint semantics available by choosing or combining validation technologies designed for XML. We present some of the techniques available to describe co-occurrence constraints, constraints on repeated elements, and the use of microformats to describe the structure rules for document models.

The Extensible Stylesheet Language Transformations language has for a long time been a commonly-applied technology for constructing new structures of information from existing structures of XML documents. An exciting new revision to XSLT delivers more functionality, remains substantially compatible with the original standard, and provides access to the information provided by document models described using the W3C XML Schema Recommendation. We present some of the features that make this new language very powerful.

Many users of XML already have some experience with the use of one, or possibly two application programming interfaces to XML (XML APIs). There are, in fact, many interfaces from which programmers can choose the most appropriate method that fits their tasks at hand. And, surprisingly to some, performance is not the only benchmark used to measure fit for purpose. We overview the pros and cons and applicability of a number of approaches to accessing our structured information from within our applications.

Making a decision regarding storing information expressed in XML in databases has a long-term impact on the choices available to access the information that has been stored. It is important to think about the long-term requirements and how your information will be stored in a medium for which XML was not designed. We review different database approaches to managing the information found in XML documents to help you choose which method makes sense for your objectives.

The XQuery language provides a tool for programmers to access structured information stored not only in XML documents, but also database stores and XML streams. This pervasive and orthogonal approach to obtaining information allows one to synthesize results from accessing heterogeneous sources, yet producing homogeneous results. As more and more information is created and maintained in XML and stored using various methods and used differently by different users, we show you how XQuery has the power to bring it all together.

Not all XML is created from within programs. When asking people to express the information they have, which is often free-form and unstructured, in strictly structured arrangements, how these people approach the XML authoring task will dictate whether they succeed or flounder. Members of the XML Guild have been helping customers create systems that work well with people responsible for entering information into structured systems. We present important steps to be considered in planning for success of this critical phase after which all other publishing and production phases will succeed or fail.

Finally, we look more deeply at advanced publishing issues when it comes to paginating information found in XML documents. The same working group that brought XSLT to our markup community has published the Extensible Stylesheet Language Formatting Objects (XSL-FO) Recommendation, itself an XML vocabulary expressing pagination semantics for the production of PDF and other final-form printed documents. Nuanced situations requiring careful analysis and decision-making are presented so that published results can best present to the final consumers your information that has been modeled, labeled, authored, accessed, processed, and published.

All together in this book the members of the XML Guild bring the power of XML to light to help you think about your XML in new ways and with advanced applications of old and new technologies.

TABLE OF Contents

1 XML Namespaces

by Evan Lenz

This chapter is about XML namespaces, the standard mechanism for assigning expanded-names to elements and attributes. The first part, "Understanding Namespaces," looks at what their purpose is and how the mechanism itself works. The second part, "Namespaces in XSLT," presents an in-depth look at how XSLT handles namespaces, including coverage of features that are new in XSLT 2.0.

Understanding Namespaces

Namespaces are used heavily across many XML applications, tools, and technologies. Even if you decide not to use them for your own custom XML vocabularies, you will need to learn how they work. For example, XSLT uses namespaces to disambiguate between code and data. All of XSLT's elements are in the XSLT namespace, whereas other elements are taken to be literal result elements, that is, elements that are copied to the result as data rather than interpreted as code.

Motivation for Using XML Namespaces

The "Namespaces in XML 1.0" recommendation cites two primary reasons you might want to use XML namespaces: to avoid name collisions and to facilitate name recognition.

> **Note**
> See "Namespaces in XML 1.0" at http://www.w3.org/TR/xml-names/.

Avoiding Name Collisions

Namespaces allow you to use multiple markup vocabularies within the same document without having to worry about name collisions. For example, you might have an XML document that contains two different elements named `title`. One of them might describe the title of a bibliographic reference, whereas the other might describe a person's professional title. It's not really an issue if you control the definition of both elements; you can tell the difference by their context within the document. But the possibility for name collisions becomes a bigger problem when you don't control both definitions—perhaps because they were defined as part of distinct schemas by different parties. XML namespaces address that problem by supplementing the name `title` (in this case) with a universally unique *namespace name*, also called a *namespace URI*.

Facilitating Name Recognition

Avoiding collisions is the most common rationale that's given for using XML namespaces, but an even stronger (and more positive) motivation for using them is that they facilitate recognition of elements or attributes based only on their namespace URI. For example, software modules that are designed for processing elements in a given vocabulary, such as UBL (Universal Business Language) orders, can be automatically invoked as soon as an element in the UBL namespace appears in a document that you're processing. In that case, your code might not need to know anything about UBL orders except that their namespace URI is as follows:

```
urn:oasis:names:specification:ubl:schema:xsd:Order-1.0
```

When you come across any element in that namespace, you can then dispatch to the appropriate module that knows how to process UBL orders and let it do the work.

Using Namespaces for Versioning

When defining a custom XML vocabulary that is likely to evolve over time, one option you have is to use the namespace URI as a versioning mechanism, updating it for each version of the schema that is released. The UBL folks, for example, are considering this option. However, this is not the most common approach, as it is likely to inhibit name recognition for existing software (unless that software already knows what future versions of the namespace will look like). XSLT takes the more common approach: retain the same namespace URI for both the 1.0 and 2.0 versions of the language, and instead use a version attribute to make the distinction. Whichever approach you take, you will need to plan ahead from the start, keeping in mind that changing the namespace of an element is tantamount to changing its name. An evolving draft published by the W3C Technical Architecture Group (TAG) lends more insight into versioning issues, including a section devoted to namespaces. See http://www.w3.org/2001/tag/doc/versioning.

Namespaces Grafted into the Foundation

Namespaces in XML were defined as a layer on top of XML 1.0. But in practice, that layer has become a required layer. Now, when people say "XML," they usually mean "XML 1.0 + Namespaces". That doesn't mean you must always use namespaces. It just means that if you don't want to use namespaces, you must ensure that you:

- **Don't use colons (:) in your element and attribute names**
- **Don't use the xmlns attribute**

Colons are reserved for namespace prefixes, and the **xmlns** attribute is reserved for namespace declarations. If you avoid both of those, your XML can peacefully coexist with namespace-aware XML parsers. If your only purpose for reading this chapter is figuring out how to avoid namespaces, you can stop here! But because you probably won't be able to avoid them anyway, and because namespaces are in fact quite useful, I suggest you read on and take a look at how they work.

A Namespaces Primer

This section is a tutorial that explains how the XML namespaces mechanism assigns expanded-names to elements and attributes. It concludes with a brief FAQ that ties up some loose ends not addressed by the examples.

A Simple Example

An example of using namespaces is the Atom Syndication Format (RFC 4287), which is an XML vocabulary used for describing blog content. Take a look at the following example Atom feed:

```
<feed xmlns="http://www.w3.org/2005/Atom"
      xmlns:xhtml="http://www.w3.org/1999/xhtml"
      xmlns:my="http://xmlportfolio.com/xmlguild-examples">

  <title>Example Feed</title>
  <rights type="xhtml"
          my:type="silly">
    <xhtml:div>
      You may not read, utter, interpret, or otherwise
      <xhtml:strong>verbally process</xhtml:strong> the words
      contained in this feed without <xhtml:em>express written
      permission</xhtml:em> from the authors.
    </xhtml:div>
  </rights>

  <!-- ... -->

</feed>
```

At the top of this document are three *namespace declarations*—one for Atom, one for XHTML, and one for a custom extension namespace that I made up. The one for Atom is called a *default namespace declaration*, because it applies to unprefixed elements:

```
xmlns="http://www.w3.org/2005/Atom"
```

It declares that all unprefixed element names in the document (in this case, **<feed>**, **<title>**, and **<rights>**) have the namespace URI http://www.w3.org/2005/Atom. In other words, these elements are "in the Atom namespace". Default namespace declarations like this one apply only to element names; they do *not* apply to attributes. That means, for example, that the unprefixed **type** attribute on the **<rights>** element is considered to be *not* in a namespace, even though it is defined by the Atom specification.

The next namespace declaration denotes that all elements and attributes prefixed with `xhtml:` (namely, **<xhtml:div>**, **<xhtml:strong>**, and **<xhtml:em>**) are a part of the XHTML namespace:

```
xmlns:xhtml="http://www.w3.org/1999/xhtml"
```

If it were not for that declaration, the document would not be well-formed with respect to namespaces, and a namespace-aware XML parser would complain with a message like "The prefix `xhtml` is not bound." Any time you use a colon in an element or attribute name, you must include a corresponding namespace declaration that binds that prefix to a non-empty namespace URI.

Atom allows you to extend its vocabulary by defining elements or attributes in your own namespace. That's what the third namespace declaration is for:

```
xmlns:my="http://xmlportfolio.com/xmlguild-examples"
```

In this case, I added my own **my:type** attribute to the **<rights>** element. This attribute has the same *local name* as Atom's built-in **type** attribute, but it has a different namespace URI, as indicated by the `my` prefix. More accurately, because **my:type** has a prefix, you know that it is in a namespace. On the other hand, you know that the naked **type** attribute is *not* in a namespace, because it does not have a prefix. Sometimes people say that elements or attributes that are not in a namespace have the "null" or "empty" namespace URI. Either way, it means the same thing.

When Should You Namespace-Qualify Attributes?

Attributes don't take on the default namespace, and, as with Atom's **type** attribute, are not usually placed in a namespace (using a prefix), because they are traditionally thought to be "owned" by their parent element. In most cases, placing an attribute in a namespace adds no value. The exception is the case of "global attributes," which are generally meant to be attached to *any* element, perhaps as an annotation mechanism. For example, W3C XML Schema's **xsi:type** attribute is a global attribute; it can be added to any XML element in any instance document as an assertion about that element's schema type. It is placed in a namespace to ensure that it does not collide with any of the element's other attributes. The W3C

> TAG's findings are consistent with this advice regarding global attributes. See http://www.w3.org/TR/webarch/#xml-namespaces.

An Equivalent Example

The following is an alternative representation of the same Atom document. Before reading further, see what else you can conclude about how namespace declarations work, based on comparing these two examples.

```
<feed xmlns="http://www.w3.org/2005/Atom">

  <title>Example Feed</title>
  <rights type="xhtml"
          example:type="silly"
          xmlns:example="http://xmlportfolio.com/xmlguild-examples">
    <div xmlns="http://www.w3.org/1999/xhtml">
      You may not read, utter, interpret, or otherwise
      <strong>verbally process</strong> the words
      contained in this feed without <em>express written
      permission</em> from the authors.
    </div>
  </rights>

  <!-- ... -->

</feed>
```

Did you notice the differences? This example reveals some additional features of namespaces:

- You can put a namespace declaration on any element, not just the document element. That binding is said to be *in scope* for that element and its descendants.
- You can override an in-scope namespace declaration. For example, the **<div>** element overrides the default namespace declaration, so that unprefixed element names among **<div>** and its descendants will be in the XHTML namespace, not the Atom namespace.
- It doesn't matter what prefix you use. All that matters is that the namespace URI is the correct one. For example, we used `example` as the prefix instead of **my** this time around, but the **example:type** attribute still has the same *expanded-name* as the **my:type** attribute in the previous example. The expanded-name has two parts: the local part (`type`) and the namespace URI (`http://xmlportfolio.com/xmlguild-examples`).

Disabling the Default Namespace Declaration

A namespace-qualified attribute is easy to spot. If it has a prefix, it's namespace-qualified. If it doesn't, it's not. Unprefixed elements, on the other hand, sometimes are namespace-qualified and sometimes aren't. That depends on whether a default namespace declaration is in scope. Consider the following simple XSLT stylesheet:

```
<xsl:stylesheet version="1.0"
  xmlns:xsl="http://www.w3.org/1999/XSL/Transform">

  <xsl:template match="/">
    <html>
      <head>
        <title>My Web Page</title>
      </head>
      <body>
        <!-- ... -->
      </body>
    </html>
  </xsl:template>

</xsl:stylesheet>
```

As mentioned earlier, XSLT uses namespaces to distinguish between XSLT instructions and literal result elements. In this stylesheet, **<html>**, **<head>**, **<title>**, and **<body>** are the literal result elements. These unprefixed elements are *not* in a namespace, because the stylesheet doesn't have a default namespace declaration. As you can see, using namespaces isn't an all-or-nothing proposition. A document can contain some elements that are namespace-qualified and some that are not.

This stylesheet uses the conventional `xsl` prefix for XSLT elements. What would happen if you decided that you didn't want to use a prefix at all? In that case, you would need to use a default namespace declaration:

```
<stylesheet version="1.0"
  xmlns="http://www.w3.org/1999/XSL/Transform">
```

This associates unprefixed elements with the XSLT namespace. The only problem with that is that the stylesheet includes elements that aren't in a namespace at all. You don't want **<html>**, for example, to be interpreted as an XSLT instruction (causing an XSLT error). You need some way of *disabling* the default namespace declaration. Fortunately, the authors of the namespaces recommendation thought of that scenario. Here's the full stylesheet example again, using only default namespace declarations (no prefixes):

```
<stylesheet version="1.0"
  xmlns="http://www.w3.org/1999/XSL/Transform">

  <template match="/">
    <html xmlns="">
      <head>
        <title>My Web Page</title>
      </head>
      <body>
        <!-- ... -->
      </body>
    </html>
  </template>

</stylesheet>
```

As in the previous example, the **<stylesheet>** and **<template>** elements are in a namespace, but all the other elements are not. The `xmlns=""` declaration on the **<html>** element disables the default namespace declaration for that branch of the document tree.

Primer FAQ

The rest of this primer is formatted as a FAQ, as a quick way to fill in the missing pieces and to clear up any misconceptions you might have at this point.

You showed examples of redefining the default namespace. Can you also override namespace declarations that use a prefix, binding the prefix to a different namespace URI?

Yes. In this example, **<my:foo>** and **<my:bar>** are in different namespaces:

```
<my:foo xmlns:my="http://example.com/uri1">
  <my:bar xmlns:my="http://example.com/uri2"/>
</my:foo>
```

Does the parser retrieve the namespace URI from the Web?

No. Consider the namespace URI as nothing more than a case-sensitive string.

Are http://example.com/ and http://EXAMPLE.COM/ the same namespace URI?

No. Even though they're the same logical URI, they are different namespace URIs. An XML parser will not treat them as equivalent. They're only the same if they're the same string, character-for-character.

Is it okay to use a relative URI reference as a namespace name?

It's strongly discouraged, although chances are it will just be treated like any other string. The Namespaces recommendation does not forbid the use of relative URI references, but because of inconsistent stories on whether or not they should be resolved into absolute URIs during namespace processing, the W3C decided to officially deprecate them. You can (and should) sidestep the whole issue by always using absolute URI references for namespace names. For more background on the decision to deprecate them, see http://www.w3.org/2000/09/xppa.

*What about the **xml:lang** and **xml:space** attributes? I've seen those used without a corresponding namespace declaration.*

This is the one exception to the rule that names with a colon must have a corresponding namespace declaration. The namespaces recommendation defines a fixed binding between the **xml** prefix and this namespace URI:

```
http://www.w3.org/XML/1998/namespace
```

Both the prefix and the namespace URI are reserved, which means you can't override this binding or bind a different prefix to this namespace name. Although it's legal to explicitly declare the implicit binding using **xmlns:xml**, it's never necessary to do so.

I see how to determine what namespace an element or attribute belongs to. Is there a way to determine which elements or attributes belong to a given namespace?

No, there is no standard mechanism nor requirement for "registering" a namespace. Some might object, claiming that W3C XML Schemas' notion of "target namespace" (which associates a namespace URI with the elements in a given schema) does in fact provide a way to do this. Although that's true, no one is required to use that technology. Namespaces are ripe for the picking. If you can type a namespace declaration, you can use a namespace. Thus, when we say an element is "in a namespace," we really mean that it *has* such-and-such a namespace URI.

I see that you can disable a default namespace declaration using `xmlns=""`. Can you also disable a namespace declaration that uses a prefix?

No, you can't in XML 1.0. But you can in XML 1.1. It looks like `xmlns:foo=""`.

> **Note**
> See "Namespaces in XML 1.1" at http://www.w3.org/TR/xml-names11/.

But if a prefixed name is invalid without a corresponding declaration, why would you ever need to do this?

Excellent question. You're right that such an "undeclaration" of a prefix binding does nothing to aid the representation of element and attribute names. That's because prefixed elements and attributes must be associated with a non-empty namespace URI. Unfortunately, things are more complicated than this: namespace declarations are now used for more than just representing element and attribute names. They are also used to qualify names that appear in XML content. Before you can fully understand the answer to this question, you must consider the topic of QNames in content.

QNames in Content

In an ideal world, XML namespaces would have a simple, cohesive purpose: the representation of element and attribute names in an XML document. The details of where you put your namespace declarations, which prefixes you use, and whether or not you use a default namespace would be mere lexical details. In that world, an XML processor could throw away those details and report just the expanded-names of elements and attributes to the application.

Alas, that ideal world never really existed. That's because core XML technologies, including XSLT and W3C XML Schemas, use namespace declarations to not only expand the names of elements and attributes, but also to expand *QNames* that appear in attribute values or document content (character data).

You'll see an example of this shortly. But first I'll define what I mean by QName. Remember that an expanded-name describes a pair of strings: the local part and the namespace URI. Well, a QName (short for "qualified name") is the syntactic construct for representing an expanded-name. It's an XML name with an optional colon (:) character. For example, both `foo` and `my:foo` are QNames. The QName by itself doesn't tell you what the expanded-name is. You have to consult the in-scope namespace declarations to determine that. (The one exception, of course, is an unprefixed attribute name; in that case, you know that the local part is the QName itself and that the namespace URI is null.)

One of the most common uses of QNames in content is in XSLT, as shown in this example:

```
<xsl:stylesheet version="1.0"
  xmlns:xsl="http://www.w3.org/1999/XSL/Transform"
  xmlns:x="http://www.w3.org/1999/xhtml">

  <xsl:template match="/">
    <x:html>
      <x:head>
        <x:title>
```

```
          <xsl:value-of select="/x:html/x:head/x:title"/>
        </x:title>
      </x:head>
      <x:body>
        <!-- ... -->
      </x:body>
    </x:html>
  </xsl:template>

</xsl:stylesheet>
```

In this example, the stylesheet is using the XHTML namespace declaration not only for element names but also for expanding names in the XPath expression `/x:html/x:head/x:title` (for extracting the title value from the input document). In the ideal world I alluded to, you would be able to change the lexical details of a namespace declaration without breaking a thing. In this example, I've changed the `x` prefix to `xhtml`:

```
<xsl:stylesheet version="1.0"
  xmlns:xsl="http://www.w3.org/1999/XSL/Transform"
  xmlns:xhtml="http://www.w3.org/1999/xhtml">

  <xsl:template match="/">
    <xhtml:html>
      <xhtml:head>
        <xhtml:title>           <!-- broken -->
          <xsl:value-of select="/x:html/x:head/x:title"/>
        </xhtml:title>
      </xhtml:head>
      <xhtml:body>
        <!-- ... -->
      </xhtml:body>
    </xhtml:html>
  </xsl:template>

</xsl:stylesheet>
```

Now the elements still have the same expanded-names and the document is perfectly well-formed, but the stylesheet breaks. Specifically, the XPath expression can't be evaluated, because there's no way to determine what namespace the x prefix binds to. You might be wondering why this is really a problem. Why didn't I just update the XPath expression to use the **xhtml** prefix instead? Admittedly, that would be easy enough to do since I was just editing the XML document by hand. Having to make one more edit is not the issue. The real problem is the additional burden this dependency places on general XML processors. No longer is it safe for an XML processor to merely report the expanded-names of elements and attributes, throwing away the details of how the namespaces are declared. Instead, the XML processor must now preserve the set of in-scope namespace bindings for each element—all because document content (or attribute values as in the previous example) *might* depend on that information.

Using QNames in Content Within Your Own Custom Schema

When defining your own XML vocabulary, you do have the option of using QNames in content, and W3C XML Schemas even defines the **xs:QName** datatype for you. However, you should use QNames only when it really makes sense to do so—such as when the values in your document refer to actual element or attribute names or when you need to embed XPath expressions in your XML. Unless you're defining another schema or transformation language for XML, you most likely won't need to use QNames in content, and you'll be saving yourself from potential trouble by avoiding them. The W3C TAG offers more food for thought in its own meditation on QNames in content. See http://www.w3.org/2001/tag/doc/qnameids.html.

Although this puts an additional complexity burden on everyone—whether beginners who are learning XML, developers writing XML processing tools, or writers of specifications that depend on XML—the good news is that it's a one-time cost. All you have to remember is that, when writing generic XML processing tools, the namespace prefix bindings are significant too, not just the element and attribute names they help define. More precisely, for each element, you must preserve its set of *in-scope namespaces*, a property that is formalized in the XML infoset specification.

Note

See "XML Information Set (Second Edition)" at http://www.w3.org/TR/xml-infoset/.

Misusing the Namespace Context

You've now seen that because QNames might appear in content, namespace context must be preserved, including the prefixes. But just because you can get the value of a namespace prefix doesn't mean you should let any of your application code depend on it.

At a client site, I recently used an internally developed tool for generating HTML documentation for W3C XML Schema documents. I ran it against some sample .xsd files and was dismayed to see this error message: `No xs:schema element found`. Well, the problem was that my input .xsd files used the `xsd` prefix rather than the `xs` prefix—a perfectly acceptable choice, as would be any other prefix (or no prefix, using a default namespace declaration) as long as it's bound to the right namespace URI. The problem was that this application was hard-coded to only recognize the `xs` prefix. What it should have been doing is looking for the W3C XML Schemas namespace URI and ignoring the prefix. There are only a few practices that I would describe as universally bad, and this is one of them.

XSLT doesn't prevent you from making this same mistake. See the section entitled "Perils of the name() Function" later in this chapter.

Overloading QName

Although QName is defined as an XML name with an optional colon (:) character, more recent usage has complicated things a bit. In XML Schema Part 2: Datatypes, the value space of the **xs:QName** datatype is the set of all possible expanded-names (that is, tuples of local part and namespace URI), whereas the lexical space is the set of all strings that match the QName production of the Namespaces recommendation (that is, a name with an optional prefix). In XPath 2.0 and XQuery 1.0, the datatype **xs:QName** is actually a triple consisting of the namespace URI, local part, and prefix.

The upshot is that you have to be careful to note the context when someone uses the term "QName". The person might be referring to a simple, self-contained string consisting of a name with an optional prefix, or otherwise to an "object" from which you can also extract the namespace URI.

Un-Declaring Namespaces

Now I can finally answer that last question from the Primer FAQ, earlier in this chapter. Here it is again, in a nutshell:

Why does Namespaces in XML 1.1 allow `<my-element xmlns:foo="">`?

The first thing to keep in mind is that Namespaces in XML 1.1 applies only to XML 1.1, so you might not find yourself directly using this very often (if ever). But you might see it output from XML 1.1-aware tools.

> **Note**
> See "Extensible Markup Language (XML) 1.1 (Second Edition)" at http://www.w3.org/TR/xml11/.

The reason it's needed is that it allows you to embed an XML fragment into another document, using technologies such as XInclude, without cluttering the in-scope namespaces property of the elements in that fragment.

> **Note**
> See "XML Inclusions (XInclude) Version 1.0" at http://www.w3.org/TR/xinclude/.

For example, the following document uses XInclude to embed another document (doc2.xml) inside it:

```
<my:doc xmlns:my="http://xmlportfolio.com/xmlguild-examples">
<xi:include href="doc2.xml"
            xmlns:xi="http://www.w3.org/2001/XInclude"/>
</my:doc>
```

Let's say that the content of doc2.xml looks like this:

```
<simple>
  <remark>We don't use namespaces.</remark>
</simple>
```

Namespaces aren't used in doc2.xml, so the only in-scope namespace that is present for the **<simple>** and **<remark>** elements is the implicit one that binds the reserved prefix **xml**. But the situation changes when you perform the inclusion:

```
<my:doc xmlns:my="http://xmlportfolio.com/xmlguild-examples">
<simple>
  <remark>We don't use namespaces.</remark>
</simple>
</my:doc>
```

Now the **<simple>** and **<remark>** elements have an additional namespace binding—for the `my` prefix, which is inherited from their ancestor. The embedded document has effectively been altered simply by being included inside another document. To be sure, the *names* of the elements have not changed, but their set of in-scope namespaces has been augmented. The only way the XInclude processor can avoid making this alteration is if it is able to *un-declare* that namespace binding. And the only way it can do that is if it supports XML 1.1 as its output format:

```
<?xml version="1.1"?>
<my:doc xmlns:my="http://xmlportfolio.com/xmlguild-examples">
<simple xmlns:my="">
  <remark>We don't use namespaces.</remark>
</simple>
</my:doc>
```

Although that might *look* more cluttered, it's actually less cluttered with respect to the set of in-scope namespaces for each element. The `xmlns:my=""` declaration (or rather *un*declaration) has the effect of *removing* the `my` namespace binding from the scope of **<simple>** and its descendants.

What is the practical import of all this? Why does it matter? The negative impact of unwanted namespaces is really only felt when you later go to extract that same document out of its containing envelope. For example, in XSLT, you could use an instruction like this to perform a deep copy of the **<simple>** element:

```
<xsl:copy-of select="//simple"/>
```

If your input was of the XML 1.0 flavor (without namespace undeclarations), the serialized result of that copy will look like this:

```
<simple xmlns:my="http://xmlportfolio.com/xmlguild-examples">
  <remark>We don't use namespaces.</remark>
</simple>
```

All you wanted to do was get back the contents of the original doc2.xml file, but instead you see that a namespace has "bled through" as an artifact of the document's processing history. That's almost certainly not what you intended. You have no use for that namespace declaration, but there's no getting around it. It must be present in order to accurately represent the in-scope namespaces of the **<simple>** and **<remark>** elements as they occurred in the input document.

On the other hand, if the input was of the XML 1.1 variety and it used a namespace undeclaration to keep **<simple>** and its descendants pristine (free from unwanted namespaces), you'll get the uncluttered result that you wanted:

```
<simple>
  <remark>We don't use namespaces.</remark>
</simple>
```

Also, you can see that the namespace undeclaration isn't present anymore, now that **<simple>** has been extracted from the containing document. The `my` prefix binding is no longer present on an ancestor element, so there's no need to disable it.

SOAP, which uses XML "envelopes" as a transport mechanism for other XML documents, has the same problem as XInclude. In XML 1.0, this simply cannot be done in a clean way—any SOAP-related namespace prefixes will bleed through into the embedded document. The real kicker was described in the requirements document for Namespaces in XML 1.1:

> Even worse, the inability to round trip an infoset through XML accurately prevents accurate canonicalization, and the security features based upon it (like XML digital signatures and XML encryption).

> **Note**
> See "Namespaces in XML 1.1 Requirements" at http://www.w3.org/TR/xml-names11-req/.

So does that mean we should all be using XML 1.1? Hardly. First of all, the addition of namespace undeclarations is a small change compared to other changes in XML 1.1 (such as the expanded set of allowed Unicode characters in element names). Secondly, although it's possible that most of the world will eventually migrate to XML 1.1, the most likely situation is that XML 1.0 will continue to be used alongside XML 1.1 for a long time. XML 1.0 is firmly entrenched and meets the needs of most applications. Use XML 1.1 (and supporting tools) only when XML 1.0 does not meet your needs–such as when you absolutely must have the ability to un-declare namespace prefix bindings.

Using Namespaces in XSLT

Namespace concerns in XSLT can be broadly divided into two categories:

- Dealing with namespaces in the input document, or *processing namespaces*.
- Dealing with namespaces in the output document, or *constructing namespaces*.

The next two sections cover each of these in turn.

Processing Namespaces

This section covers how namespaces are represented in the XPath data model and how the XPath language allows you to access the information in that data model. In this section, when I say "XPath", I am talking about both the 1.0 and 2.0 versions of the language. When I need to make a distinction, I use "XPath 1.0" or "XPath 2.0". Also, unless I'm talking specifically about XSLT features, all of the XPath observations in this section are also applicable to XQuery, which is an extension of XPath 2.0.

> **Note**
> See "XQuery 1.0: An XML Query Language" at http://www.w3.org/TR/xquery/.

Selecting Elements and Attributes by Name

In XPath, to select an element named foo, you (unsurprisingly) use the name test `foo`. A namespace-qualified element can be selected with an expression such as `xyz:foo`. For this to work without error, the XPath context must be initialized to include a binding between the `xyz` prefix and a non-empty namespace URI. Different XPath APIs have their own ways of initializing expression context. But when XSLT is the host language, the namespace context is determined by the namespace bindings that are in scope where the XPath expression appears in the XSLT document. You saw an example of this earlier in the chapter, in the "QNames in Content" section, where the **x** prefix was bound to the XHTML namespace.

The key point to remember is that what prefix is (or isn't) used in the source document is completely independent of what prefix you use in your stylesheet. When selecting an element or attribute by name, only its local name and namespace URI are considered.

XSLT 2.0: xpath-default-namespace

In XPath 1.0, an unprefixed name in an expression always means "not in a namespace". For example, the expression `foo` always means "select all child elements that have local name `foo` and that are not in a namespace". In other words, the default namespace is *not* used for XPath 1.0 expressions. If you want to select a namespace-qualified element or attribute, you must use a prefix (and include a corresponding namespace declaration for that prefix).

This turns out to be quite a pain if one day you decide to start using namespaces when you haven't been using them previously. First, you update all your input documents. This could be as simple as manually typing a default namespace at the top of your files:

```
<doc xmlns="http://example.com">
...
```

Next, you update all your stylesheets. Because your stylesheets were designed to process non-namespace-qualified elements, none of your XPath expressions use namespace prefixes. And because you can't declare a default namespace for XPath 1.0 expressions, that means you have to go through and update each and every XPath expression so that it uses namespace prefixes.

Fortunately, XPath 2.0 provides a remedy; it allows you to apply a default namespace to unprefixed element names in expressions. Now, to update your stylesheets, you won't have to touch every XPath expression. Provided that you're using XSLT 2.0, all you have to do is add the **xpath-default-namespace** attribute on the document element of each stylesheet:

```
<xsl:stylesheet version="2.0"
  xmlns:xsl="http://www.w3.org/1999/XSL/Transform"
  xpath-default-namespace="http://example.com">
...
```

Now, a bare `foo` expression in this stylesheet will only select elements in the `http://example.com` namespace. Note that an XPath default namespace, like a default namespace in XML itself, applies only to elements names, not to attribute names.

Accessing Element and Attribute Names

XPath defines the local name and namespace URI as properties of the element or attribute node itself and provides functions for accessing those properties. Specifically, the **local-name()** function returns the local part of the expanded-name, and the **namespace-uri()** function returns the universal part.

For example, consider this document:

```
<my:doc xmlns:my="http://example.com" id="abc123"/>
```

Table 1.1 shows what's returned by these functions for the **<my:doc>** element and the id attribute.

Table 1.1 The local-name() and namespace-uri() Functions

Expression	Value Returned (String)
local-name(/*)	doc
namespace-uri(/*)	http://example.com
local-name(/*/@id)	id
namespace-uri(/*/@id)	empty string

Notice that the prefix `my` doesn't appear anywhere in this table. That's because XPath does not directly expose the prefix that's used in an element or attribute name. The only way you can get to that is by way of the **name()** function, which you'll read about later, in "Perils of the name() Function".

Name Wildcards

Name tests in XPath 1.0 can be grouped into three categories, as shown in Table 1.2. These examples assume that `x` is bound to `http://example.com`.

Table 1.2 Name Tests in XPath 1.0

Description	Name Test	Equivalent To
Match any name	*	*
Match a particular expanded-name	x:foo	*[local-name() = 'foo' and namespace-uri() = 'http://example.com']
Match a particular namespace	x:*	*[namespace-uri() = 'http://example.com']

XPath 2.0: Namespace Wildcards

XPath 2.0 adds an additional category, shown in Table 1.3.

Table 1.3 Syntax for Namespace Wildcards

Description	Name test	Equivalent to
Match a particular local name	*:foo	*[local-name() = 'foo']

The `*:foo` expression matches any element whose local name is foo, regardless of its namespace URI. This syntax is only legal in XPath 2.0. In XPath 1.0, you must instead use `*[local-name() = 'foo']`.

Namespace Nodes

Consider the following XML document:

```
<foo xmlns="http://example.com"
     xmlns:my="http://xmlportfolio.com/xmlguild-examples">
  <bar>
    <bat/>
  </bar>
</foo>
```

A naive XPath user might try getting this document's default namespace URI by directly accessing the namespace declaration attribute using an expression like `//@xmlns`. But this expression will never return a result, because namespace declarations are *not* exposed as attributes in the XPath data model. Even though namespace declarations use XML 1.0's syntax for attributes, they're not attributes as far as XPath is concerned.

So if namespace declarations aren't attributes, what are they? There's actually no direct representation for namespace declarations in the XPath data model. Instead, each element has a set of one or more namespace nodes attached to it that represents the set of namespace prefix/URI bindings that are in scope for that element. Even if you don't use namespaces, each element will at least have the implicit `xml` namespace node attached to it.

Given that knowledge, how many namespace nodes do you think are in the document? Two? Three? The answer is nine. Each of the three elements has three namespace nodes attached to it—a default namespace, the `xml` namespace, and the namespace bound to the prefix `my`. This might become more clear when you consider that an equivalent representation of this document can be expressed using nine namespace declarations:

```
<foo xmlns="http://example.com"
     xmlns:my="http://xmlportfolio.com/xmlguild-examples"
     xmlns:xml="http://www.w3.org/XML/1998/namespace">
  <bar xmlns="http://example.com"
       xmlns:my="http://xmlportfolio.com/xmlguild-examples"
```

```
        xmlns:xml="http://www.w3.org/XML/1998/namespace">
    <bat xmlns="http://example.com"
         xmlns:my="http://xmlportfolio.com/xmlguild-examples"
         xmlns:xml="http://www.w3.org/XML/1998/namespace"/>
  </bar>
</foo>
```

This is more like what XPath sees when it looks at the document. It gets past the syntax sugar that allows you to type a namespace declaration once on an ancestor element. Instead, for each element, XPath sees a namespace node for each in-scope namespace, not unlike what we see in this much more verbose (but perfectly valid) serialization.

Like other XPath node types, each namespace node has an expanded-name and a string-value. The name of a namespace node is the prefix, and the string-value is the URI that the prefix is bound to. (The namespace URI part of a namespace node's name is always empty.) Table 1.4 lists the value of these properties for the three namespace nodes that appear on each element shown previously.

Table 1.4 Namespace Node Properties

Expanded-Name		**String-Value**
Local Part	**Namespace URI Part**	
xml	*[always empty]*	http://www.w3.org/XML/1998/namespace
empty	*[always empty]*	http://example.com
my	*[always empty]*	http://xmlportfolio.com/xmlguild-examples

The Namespace Axis

To access namespace nodes in XPath, you use the *namespace axis*. For example, this expression will select the namespace node attached to the document element that binds the `my` prefix:

```
/*/namespace::my
```

And this expression returns the string-value of the node, that is, the namespace URI that's bound to the `my` prefix:

```
string(/*/namespace::my)
```

In practice, it's usually not necessary to access namespace nodes directly like this, unless you're performing some sort of namespace surgery on the document. The most common use case is creating additional namespaces in the result document.

> **Note**
> One example of such surgery is the "Namespace declaration normalizer" stylesheet I wrote several years ago. See http://xmlportfolio.com/namespaces/.

Perils of the name() Function

In addition to the **local-name()** and **namespace-uri()** functions, XPath provides the **name()** function. The **name()** function returns a QName string that represents the expanded-name of the given argument node with respect to the namespace declarations that were in effect on the argument node in the source document. In regards to XPath 2.0's **name()** function, consider this simpler description: it returns the lexical QName used for the element or attribute name in the source document. In XPath 1.0, the **name()** function usually behaves the same, but it *could* return a different QName than the one that's used in the document. The easiest way to explain this distinction is by example. Consider the following document, which has two namespace declarations for the same namespace URI:

```
<my:foo xmlns:my="http://example.com" xmlns:my2="http://example.com"/>
```

In XPath 2.0, `name(/*)` will always return the string `my:foo`. In XPath 1.0, it could return either `my:foo` or `my2:foo`. That's because the XPath 1.0 data model doesn't include the actual prefix that's used on an element or attribute node. To find an appropriate prefix, the applicable namespace nodes must be queried. In this case, there are two choices, so it could use either one. That said, XPath 1.0 implementations are allowed to preserve what QName is actually used, even though it's not part of the data model, and always return it. The difference in XPath 2.0 is that the prefix of an element or attribute now *is* part of the data model and the **name()** function is *required* to use that prefix in its result.

Ultimately, this is pretty inconsequential, because it turns out you should avoid using the **name()** function most of the time anyway. Recall that earlier in this chapter, in "Misusing the Namespace Context," you saw how dependence on the use of a particular namespace prefix was a bad thing. Well, in XSLT, here's how you'd make the same mistake. The following is a naïve but legal way of matching an **atom:feed** element:

```
<xsl:template match="*[name() = 'atom:feed']">
  <!-- ... -->
</xsl:template>
```

This will work as long as your documents use the string `atom` as the namespace prefix. But it won't work, for example, for the Atom documents you looked at earlier in this chapter, which instead used a default namespace (no prefix). To ensure that your template rule works for *all* Atom documents, you'll want to write it this way instead:

```
<xsl:template match="atom:feed">
  <!-- ... -->
</xsl:template>
```

Then you would just need to declare `xmlns="http://www.w3.org/2005/Atom"` at the top of your document so that the XSLT processor knows what namespace you're referring to when you use the `atom` prefix. At that point, what prefix you choose to use is a mere detail of how you wrote your stylesheet, *not* an external contract that requires people to use a particular prefix. The only requirement is that input documents use the correct namespace URI.

In most cases, you should avoid using the **name()** function and instead use **local-name()** and **namespace-uri()** to access the two parts of an expanded-name. I can think of a few cases where using the **name()** function is okay:

- When you're inserting diagnostic or debugging information in the result about which element was matched, via `<xsl:value-of select="name(.)"/>`.
- When the argument node is a node other than an element or attribute, in which case the result of **name()** will always be the same as the result of **local-name()**.
- When you're testing for **xml:space** or **xml:preserve**, as in `@*[name() != 'xml:space']`. This is safe because the `xml` prefix is fixed 1:1 to that namespace.
- When you're testing for an attribute that is not in a namespace, as in `@*[name() != 'id']`. This is safe because an unprefixed attribute name always means "not in a namespace". That's because the default namespace is not in effect for attribute nodes.
- When you're creating a node using `<xsl:element name="{name(.)}" namespace="{namespace-uri(.)}">`. This is safe (as is an analogous use of **<xsl:attribute>**), because a prefix that might be present in the **name** attribute won't be used to look up the namespace URI as long as you provide it explicitly using the **namespace** attribute. The reason this usage of **name()** is handy is that the XSLT processor can then use that prefix in the element name that it creates in the result tree. (In XSLT 1.0, using the prefix is optional. In XSLT 2.0, it's required, barring any conflicts.)

I'll leave it up to you to decide whether to try to remember these cases or just follow the blanket rule of using **local-name()** instead.

Constructing Namespaces

You've seen how to deal with namespaces on the input side, using XPath. This section looks at how to control namespaces on the output side, using XSLT. Your choices for controlling output namespaces in XSLT 1.0 were fairly limited. Much was left for the implementer to decide. XSLT 2.0 introduces several new features designed to transcend those limitations and give more control to the stylesheet writer.

This section takes up a good portion of the chapter, and many of the XSLT 2.0 features I'll introduce here were designed for some admittedly arcane use cases. But the only way to be truly ready for a real problem when it arises is to have a comprehensive understanding upfront. Besides, there's a certain satisfaction that comes from being able to control exactly what namespace declarations appear in your resulting document.

Namespace Nodes: A Mostly Covert Operation

Most of the time, in XSLT, you will not directly cross paths with namespace nodes. They just get copied along with the element nodes that you copy from the source tree or stylesheet. You saw an example of this behavior earlier, in the "Un-declaring Namespaces" section. When either the **<xsl:copy-of>** or **<xsl:copy>** instruction is applied to an element node, it copies all of the element's namespace nodes along with it, thereby ensuring that the same namespace bindings are in scope in the result tree as were in scope for that element in the source tree.

Similarly, whenever you use a literal result element in your stylesheet, it is treated as an instruction to copy that element from the stylesheet into the result tree. In that case, the namespace nodes are copied along with that element into the result tree.

Finally, whenever you create an element or attribute using the explicit XSLT instructions for doing so (**<xsl:element>** and **<xsl:attribute>**), the XSLT processor will automatically create the necessary namespace nodes in the result tree (and corresponding namespace declarations in the serialized result) to ensure that the result is namespace-well-formed.

The bottom line is that when you're just using namespaces for the purpose of qualifying element and attribute names—regardless of how you create the element or attribute in the result—you don't have to do anything special to ensure that the appropriate namespace nodes will be generated. The XSLT processor takes care of this for you.

Just to drive this point home, imagine you want to start using namespaces in your documents. If there are only a few documents to update, you could just open the files in a text editor and manually add an `xmlns` declaration to the top of each one. But what if you have a thousand files to update? XSLT can do the trick, but in XSLT you approach the problem much differently than you would if you were editing the files manually. That's because the `xmlns` declaration is *not* an attribute as far as XPath and XSLT are concerned. Instead, it's a short-hand way of qualifying all the element names in the document. Accordingly, the essence of your task is to update all the element names in the document. The stylesheet for doing that looks like this:

```
<xsl:stylesheet version="1.0"
  xmlns:xsl="http://www.w3.org/1999/XSL/Transform">

  <!-- copy these nodes as is -->
  <xsl:template match="@* | comment() | processing-instruction()">
    <xsl:copy/>
```

```
  </xsl:template>

  <!-- but rename the elements -->
  <xsl:template match="*">
    <xsl:element name="{local-name()}"
                 namespace="http://example.com/new-namespace">
      <xsl:apply-templates select="@* | node()"/>
    </xsl:element>
  </xsl:template>

</xsl:stylesheet>
```

The task is thus a matter of naming elements. You don't have to worry about namespace nodes; they are automatically created as a by-product of the names you give your elements.

So when *do* you have to worry about namespace nodes? Broadly speaking, there are two scenarios when namespace nodes will appear on your radar screen:

- The result has too many namespaces.
- The result doesn't have enough namespaces.

In the first case, the result has extraneous namespace declarations that you don't need, because you're not using any QNames in content. In the second case, the result doesn't include enough namespace context to expand all the QNames that you're using in character data or attribute values. Again, in both of these cases, I'm not talking about namespace declarations that are needed to expand element and attribute names. Those will *always* be present, and you can't (nor would you want to) prevent them from appearing.

Too Many Namespaces

There are generally two situations in which you might end up with more namespace nodes in the result than you want or need:

- When copying an element from the stylesheet, that is, when using a literal result element.
- When copying an element from the source tree, using **<xsl:copy>** or **<xsl:copy-of>**.

In the first case (literal result elements), there is one relevant feature available in both XSLT 1.0 and 2.0 to help filter undesired namespaces from the result: the **exclude-result-prefixes** attribute.

In the second case (copying elements from the source tree), XSLT 2.0 introduces a new feature to help filter undesired namespaces from the result, the **copy-namespaces** attribute, which is an optional attribute on the **<xsl:copy>** and **<xsl:copy-of>** instructions.

A third feature, also introduced in XSLT 2.0, is the **inherit-namespaces** attribute, which allows you to disable XSLT's default behavior of automatically copying namespace nodes to descendant elements in the result tree.

Let's take a more detailed look at each of these features.

XSLT 1.0: exclude-result-prefixes

The following stylesheet uses a literal result element to create the **<html>** document element in the resulting tree:

```
<xsl:stylesheet version="1.0"
  xmlns:xsl="http://www.w3.org/1999/XSL/Transform"
  xmlns:my="http://example.com">

  <xsl:template match="/*">
    <html>
      <xsl:apply-templates select="my:section"/>
    </html>
  </xsl:template>

  <!-- ... -->

</xsl:stylesheet>
```

The `xmlns:my` namespace declaration is included so you can select nodes in that namespace from the input document, using XPath expressions like `my:section`. But this declaration has another effect that you might not want. Because the `my` namespace is in scope on the **<html>** literal result element, the XSLT processor will copy that namespace node along with the **<html>** element into the result tree. Without any further changes to the stylesheet, the result will look like this:

```
<html xmlns:my="http://example.com">
  <!-- ... -->
</html>
```

Fortunately, XSLT (both 1.0 and 2.0) provides an easy way to avoid this. If you have no use for the `my` namespace in the result, you can use the **exclude-result-prefixes** attribute to list what namespaces you want to exclude from the result:

```
<xsl:stylesheet version="1.0"
  xmlns:xsl="http://www.w3.org/1999/XSL/Transform"
  xmlns:my="http://example.com"
```

```
  exclude-result-prefixes="my">
...
```

I have been referring to namespaces by their prefix, as in "the `my` namespace," but remember that this is just a shorthand that refers (in this case) to the `http://example.com` namespace. The prefix itself is immaterial, so long as there's a corresponding namespace declaration for it. So it goes with `exclude-result-prefixes="my"`. (If you don't include a namespace declaration for the `my` prefix, the XSLT processor won't know what namespace you're referring to and will signal an error.) In this case, the XSLT processor knows to disable copying of the `http://example.com` namespace nodes. Now the result looks like this:

```
<html>
  <!-- ... -->
</html>
```

Note that you didn't have to explicitly include the `xsl` namespace in that list. It's the one exception for literal result elements: the XSLT namespace is *not* automatically copied to the result. If for some reason you need the XSLT namespace in the result (and if you aren't already generating an element or attribute in the XSLT namespace), you would have to explicitly copy a namespace node for the XSLT namespace. You'll see an example of how to copy namespace nodes in the "Not Enough Namespaces" section, later in this chapter.

In addition to the **exclude-result-prefixes** attribute, any namespaces listed in the **extension-element-prefixes** attribute will also be excluded from the result (again, provided they're not necessary to qualify element or attribute names).

XSLT 2.0: copy-namespaces

Consider the following input document:

```
<doc xmlns:my="http://example.com" my:id="AAA">
  <p>This is the first paragraph.</p>
  <p>This is the second paragraph.</p>
</doc>
```

The only purpose of the `my` namespace in this case is to qualify the **my:id** attribute. The elements are not in a namespace. Now, let's say you want to copy the paragraphs from this document into the result tree. Start with a stylesheet like this:

```
<xsl:stylesheet version="1.0"
  xmlns:xsl="http://www.w3.org/1999/XSL/Transform">

  <xsl:template match="/doc">
    <new-doc>
```

```
      <xsl:apply-templates/>
    </new-doc>
  </xsl:template>

  <xsl:template match="p">
    <xsl:copy>
      <xsl:apply-templates/>
    </xsl:copy>
  </xsl:template>

</xsl:stylesheet>
```

Here's the result of the transformation:

```
<new-doc>
  <p xmlns:my="http://example.com">This is the first paragraph.</p>
  <p xmlns:my="http://example.com">This is the second paragraph.</p>
</new-doc>
```

As you can see, the result is cluttered with namespace nodes from the original document. That's because the default behavior of **<xsl:copy>** (and **<xsl:copy-of>**) when copying elements is to copy all the namespace nodes along with that element. In XSLT 1.0, this is always the case. (You might think that **exclude-result-prefixes** could be used, but that only applies to literal result elements in the stylesheet, *not* to elements that are copied from the source tree.)

XSLT 2.0, however, provides a new **copy-namespaces** attribute that can be used to prevent unnecessary namespace nodes from being copied into the result. Its default value is `yes`. If you're using an XSLT 2.0 processor, you can override the default behavior like this:

```
  <xsl:template match="p">
    <xsl:copy copy-namespaces="no">
      <xsl:apply-templates/>
    </xsl:copy>
  </xsl:template>
```

Now the result looks more pristine:

```
<new-doc>
  <p>This is the first paragraph.</p>
  <p>This is the second paragraph.</p>
</new-doc>
```

XSLT 1.0: Dodging Unwanted Namespace Nodes

Even though XSLT 1.0 doesn't have the **copy-namespaces** attribute, there are other ways to get the result that you want. One way is to use a literal result element instead of **<xsl:copy>**, like this:

```
<xsl:template match="p">
  <p>
    <xsl:apply-templates/>
  </p>
</xsl:template>
```

A more generic approach (which can be extended to match more than just **<p>** elements) uses the **<xsl:element>** instruction to "replicate" rather than copy the element, using the same local name and namespace URI:

```
<xsl:template match="*">
  <xsl:element name="{name()}" namespace="{namespace-uri()}">
    <xsl:apply-templates/>
  </xsl:element>
</xsl:template>
```

This rule ensures that the resulting element will have the same local name and namespace URI as the context element in the source tree, but it won't end up with any unnecessary namespaces, because it's not actually copying the element from the source tree.

XSLT 2.0: inherit-namespaces and undeclare-prefixes

Recall the XInclude example from earlier, in the "Un-Declaring Namespaces" section. XSLT 2.0 introduces a couple of new features that allow you to effectively implement an XInclude processor in XSLT, complete with support for XML 1.1 and namespace undeclarations.

Let's augment the original XInclude example slightly. Here, I've added an additional, unused default namespace at the top of the document:

```
<my:doc xmlns:my="http://xmlportfolio.com/xmlguild-examples"
        xmlns="http://example.com">
<xi:include href="doc2.xml"
            xmlns:xi="http://www.w3.org/2001/XInclude"/>
</my:doc>
```

And let's say the content of doc2.xml does use a namespace now:

```
<s:simple xmlns:s="http://example.com/simple">
  <s:remark>We *do* use namespaces.</s:remark>
</s:simple>
```

In XSLT 1.0 or 2.0, a simple XInclude implementation might look like this:

```
<xsl:stylesheet version="2.0"
  xmlns:xsl="http://www.w3.org/1999/XSL/Transform"
  xmlns:xi="http://www.w3.org/2001/XInclude">

  <!-- by default, copy all nodes -->
  <xsl:template match="@* | node()">
    <xsl:copy>
      <xsl:apply-templates select="@* | node()"/>
    </xsl:copy>
  </xsl:template>

  <!-- but replace XInclude elements with the referenced content -->
  <xsl:template match="xi:include">
    <xsl:apply-templates select="document(@href)"/>
  </xsl:template>

</xsl:stylesheet>
```

Here's the result of applying that stylesheet to the original document:

```
<my:doc xmlns:my="http://xmlportfolio.com/xmlguild-examples"
        xmlns="http://example.com">
<s:simple xmlns:s="http://example.com/simple">
  <s:remark>We *do* use namespaces.</s:remark>
</s:simple>
</my:doc>
```

The inclusion worked fine, but the included document is now muddied with namespace nodes inherited from the <my:doc> ancestor. Extracting the contents of doc2.xml again later would yield a cluttered result:

```
<s:simple xmlns:s="http://example.com/simple"
          xmlns:my="http://xmlportfolio.com/xmlguild-examples"
          xmlns="http://example.com">
  <s:remark>We *do* use namespaces.</s:remark>
</s:simple>
```

To avoid this, you need a way to prevent those namespace nodes from being inherited. In other words, you want to prevent them from being automatically copied to all descendant elements

when the document inclusion takes place. XSLT 2.0 provides the **inherit-namespaces** attribute for just that purpose. Its default value is `yes`, so you want to change it to **no**. It can appear on **<xsl:element>**, **<xsl:copy>**, or any literal result element. (When attached to a literal result element, it must use the XSLT namespace; in that case it would be named **xsl:inherit-namespaces**.) In this case, you want to use it on the **<xsl:copy>** element, like this:

```
<!-- by default, copy all nodes -->
<xsl:template match="@* | node()">
  <xsl:copy inherit-namespaces="no">
    <xsl:apply-templates select="@* | node()"/>
  </xsl:copy>
</xsl:template>
```

This has the effect that, when this template rule is invoked for the **<my:doc>** element, the XSLT processor is instructed to *not* copy the resulting element's namespace nodes to its descendant elements, which is otherwise the default behavior. (Unfortunately, **inherit-namespaces** is a bit of a misnomer. If I pass something down to my descendants, I'm not inheriting anything; they are. It might better have been called **propagate-namespaces**, or even more fun: **bequeath-namespaces**. But as of this writing, the XSLT 2.0 recommendation is being finalized, so that's not going to change. My current way of coping with this is to think of **inherit-namespaces** not so much as a property of the element, but instead as an imperative that's issued by the element: "My dear children and grandchildren, inherit from me!".)

When you reapply the stylesheet, things look better, but the serialized result is still not quite what you want:

```
<my:doc xmlns:my="http://xmlportfolio.com/xmlguild-examples"
        xmlns="http://example.com">
<s:simple xmlns:s="http://example.com/simple" xmlns="">
  <s:remark>We *do* use namespaces.</s:remark>
</s:simple>
</my:doc>
```

Specifically, while the default namespace was un-declared (using `xmlns=""`), the `my` namespace was not. You want to see `xmlns:my=""` in there too. But this is a feature that's only available in XML 1.1. That's the problem. You need to tell the XSLT processor that you want XML 1.1 as output. Also, because namespace undeclarations (other than for the default namespace) are such a newfangled thing, you need to explicitly tell the processor that, yes, you want those in the serialized result too. At the top level of the stylesheet (as a child of the **<xsl:stylesheet>** element), you must make one more addition:

```
<xsl:output version="1.1" undeclare-prefixes="yes"/>
```

If we apply our updated stylesheet one last time, we now get the result we wanted:

```
<?xml version="1.1"?>
<my:doc xmlns:my="http://xmlportfolio.com/xmlguild-examples"
        xmlns="http://example.com">
<s:simple xmlns:s="http://example.com/simple" xmlns:my="" xmlns="">
  <s:remark>We *do* use namespaces.</s:remark>
</s:simple>
</my:doc>
```

Now, both the `my` namespace and the default namespace are explicitly disabled on the included **<s:simple>** element, which is to say that those namespace nodes are *not* inherited. The upshot is that, when you extract the **<s:simple>** element again, you'll get back exactly the same data as was in the original doc2.xml file, including the same namespace nodes—no more, no less.

It turns out that including the **<xsl:output>** declaration as shown previously is the only way to ensure that an XML 1.1 document can be fully round-tripped through XSLT. Specifically, `undeclare-prefixes="yes"` ensures that not only will the presence of namespace nodes be preserved, but so will their absence.

Not Enough Namespaces

The opposite situation (not enough namespace declarations in the result) is not nearly as common a problem. It can happen though. For example, if your result document uses QNames in content or attribute values, you need to make sure that the corresponding namespace declarations for those QNames will appear in the result. Even then, this usually isn't a problem, because you can rely on the XSLT processor to copy the namespace nodes for you automatically—either from the source document when you use **<xsl:copy>** or **<xsl:copy-of>**, or from the stylesheet when you use a literal result element.

So when *do* you have to go out of your way to get a namespace into the result document? The answer, of course, is when the namespace nodes you need are not copied for you automatically. The most common case of that happening is when you use **<xsl:element>** to generate the result element. In that case, no additional namespace nodes will be generated other than the one that's needed to qualify the element name itself (when the element is in a namespace).

There are two ways to explicitly make a namespace node appear in the result. When the first is not possible, you can use the second way:

- By explicitly copying existing namespace nodes (using XPath's `namespace` axis).
- By generating a new namespace node, using XSLT 2.0's **<xsl:namespace>** instruction.

This section contains examples of both of these techniques.

XSLT 1.0: Copying Namespace Nodes Using the Namespace Axis

It might seem counterintuitive, but sometimes you want to add a namespace node so that your result document will have *fewer* namespace declarations. Recall the example document you saw earlier, in the section named, "XSLT 2.0: copy-namespaces". Before you added `copy-namespaces="no"` to the stylesheet, this is the result you were getting:

```
<new-doc>
  <p xmlns:my="http://example.com">This is the first paragraph.</p>
  <p xmlns:my="http://example.com">This is the second paragraph.</p>
</new-doc>
```

Let's say now that you *don't* want to strip this namespace from the result, but instead you want it to be declared on the document element, so that it doesn't have to be declared on each and every `<p>` element, which isn't so nice looking. You can do that when you create the `<new-doc>` element, by explicitly copying all the namespace nodes from the source tree's `<doc>` element, like this:

```
<xsl:template match="/doc">
  <new-doc>
    <xsl:copy-of select="namespace::*"/>
    <xsl:apply-templates/>
  </new-doc>
</xsl:template>
```

This causes the in-scope namespaces of `<doc>` to also be in-scope for the `<new-doc>` element. Now the result tree, when serialized, only needs one namespace declaration at the top, which is much nicer looking:

```
<new-doc xmlns:my="http://example.com">
  <p>This is the first paragraph.</p>
  <p>This is the second paragraph.</p>
</new-doc>
```

This goes to show you that having more namespace *nodes* does not necessarily mean having more namespace *declarations*.

XSLT 2.0: Creating Namespace Nodes Using <xsl:namespace>

XSLT 2.0 filled an obvious gap in the XSLT 1.0 recommendation: the inability to create an arbitrary namespace node. Of course, this wasn't usually a problem for people, and even when you did need to dynamically create a namespace node, there were workarounds using an extension function, as shown in the next section.

Let's say you have a bunch of W3C XML Schema documents lying around that were generated from an automated tool. And let's say that the automated tool forgot to output a default namespace declaration, thereby breaking all the QName references to internal schema components. (Unlike XSLT, W3C XML Schemas *do* use the default namespace to expand QNames in attribute values.) To fix all the schemas in bulk, you need to add an `xmlns` declaration to the top of each document and set its value to the same as that of the schema's **targetNamespace** attribute.

In other words, you need to turn this:

```
<xsd:schema xmlns:xsd="http://www.w3.org/2001/XMLSchema"
            targetNamespace="http://www.example.com">
...
```

Into this:

```
<xsd:schema xmlns:xsd="http://www.w3.org/2001/XMLSchema"
            targetNamespace="http://www.example.com"
            xmlns="http://example.com">
...
```

This example might seem a bit contrived, but by gum it meets the criteria for a use case for **<xsl:namespace>**. You need to add a namespace node that's not already there; it won't be generated automatically; and you don't know what the namespace URI will be until runtime. If you already knew what namespace URI you needed to add to each document, you could just hard-code a corresponding namespace declaration into the stylesheet or secondary input document and copy it from there using the **document()** function and the `namespace::` axis. (The advantage of that approach is that it's possible to do in XSLT 1.0 without extensions.) But because you don't know what the namespace URI is going to be, you can't hard-code a namespace declaration anywhere; you must create it dynamically. That's what **<xsl:namespace>** is for.

Here's a stylesheet that does just what you need:

```
<xsl:stylesheet version="2.0"
  xmlns:xsl="http://www.w3.org/1999/XSL/Transform">

  <!-- Add a namespace node to the document element -->
  <xsl:template match="/*">
    <xsl:copy>
      <xsl:namespace name="" select="string(@targetNamespace)"/>
      <xsl:copy-of select="@* | node()"/>
    </xsl:copy>
```

```
  </xsl:template>

</xsl:stylesheet>
```

The **name** attribute determines what prefix to use. Because this one's empty, it means a default namespace node will be created. The **select** expression ensures that the **targetNamespace** value gets used as the namespace URI of the resulting namespace node.

You could have written this stylesheet a bit differently. For example, you could have explicitly created a namespace node for every element in the document (not just the document element). After all, you do need the namespace to be in scope for every element. But that approach would produce the exact same result. As you might recall from the discussion of the **inherit-namespaces** attribute, XSLT's default behavior is to copy all namespace nodes to descendant elements in the result tree. (In other words, the default value of **inherit-namespaces** is `yes`.) As long as you insert the namespace node into the document element, it will automatically be copied to the rest of the elements in the document.

XSLT 1.0: Creating Dynamic Namespace Nodes

Even though the **<xsl:namespace>** instruction is not available in XSLT 1.0, there are still ways to create dynamic namespace nodes, provided you're willing to use your processor's version of the **node-set()** extension function (for converting result tree fragments to first-class node-sets). Fortunately, most XSLT 1.0 processors provide such an extension. Not so fortunately, this approach isn't entirely reliable, because implementers aren't as constrained as they are in XSLT 2.0 to use the exact namespace prefix that you specify.

In any case, the trick is to create a temporary element whose namespace is determined at runtime. This causes a namespace node to be created, which you can then access and copy into the result tree. The following XSLT 1.0 is a solution to the schema fix-up problem introduced in the last section. It's using the EXSLT project's **node-set()** extension, which is implemented in several popular processors, including Saxon and libxslt:

```
<xsl:stylesheet version="1.0"
  xmlns:xsl="http://www.w3.org/1999/XSL/Transform"
  xmlns:exsl="http://exslt.org/common">

  <xsl:template match="/*">
    <xsl:variable name="ns-uri" select="string(@targetNamespace)"/>
    <xsl:variable name="ns-container">
      <xsl:element name="dummy" namespace="{$ns-uri}"/>
    </xsl:variable>
    <xsl:copy>
```

```
      <xsl:copy-of select="exsl:node-set($ns-container)
                              /*/namespace::*[. = $ns-uri]"/>
      <xsl:copy-of select="@* | node()"/>
    </xsl:copy>
  </xsl:template>

</xsl:stylesheet>
```

This stylesheet works perfectly in Saxon. Unfortunately it doesn't do so well in libxslt. Although it's perfectly conformant, libxslt auto-generates a prefix when you don't specify one in the **name** attribute of **<xsl:element>**. The result has an `xmlns:ns1` declaration instead of the `xmlns` declaration that you were hoping for. Saxon, on the other hand, takes the absence of a prefix to mean that you want to generate a default namespace declaration, which in fact *is* what you want. Both implementations are correct according to the XSLT 1.0 recommendation. Only with XSLT 2.0's **<xsl:namespace>** instruction do you have full assurance that the namespace node that's created will use exactly the prefix (or absence of a prefix) that you specify.

Generating XSLT Using xsl:namespace-alias

The final namespace-related use case considered in this chapter is the use of "meta-stylesheets," that is, using XSLT to generate XSLT. The following example shows a naïve attempt at using XSLT to generate another stylesheet:

```
<xsl:stylesheet version="1.0"
  xmlns:xsl="http://www.w3.org/1999/XSL/Transform">

  <xsl:template match="/">
    <xsl:stylesheet version="1.0"> <!-- wrong -->
      ...
    </xsl:stylesheet>
  </xsl:template>

</xsl:stylesheet>
```

The presumed intention here was to generate an **xsl:stylesheet** element in the result, but the XSLT processor will just choke when it sees that and say, "Hey, that's not allowed here." That's because it has no way of knowing that you want **<xsl:stylesheet>** copied to the result, rather than interpreted as an XSLT instruction. One way to get around this is to use the **<xsl:element>** instruction instead:

```
  <xsl:template match="/">
    <xsl:element name="xsl:stylesheet">
```

```
      <xsl:attribute name="version">1.0</xsl:attribute>
      ...
    </xsl:element>
  </xsl:template>
```

Now it's clear that you want to create an element in the result. Problem solved. The only nagging thing is that this stylesheet is going to start looking pretty verbose pretty fast if you're going to use **<xsl:element>** for every element (and consequently **<xsl:attribute>** for every attribute). This is where **<xsl:namespace-alias>** comes to the rescue. It lets you define a "dummy" namespace whose only purpose is to temporarily disambiguate between literal result elements and stylesheet instructions. Here's what it looks like:

```
<xsl:stylesheet version="1.0"
  xmlns:xsl="http://www.w3.org/1999/XSL/Transform"
  xmlns:out="http://xmlportfolio.com/dummy">

  <xsl:namespace-alias stylesheet-prefix="out" result-prefix="xsl"/>

  <xsl:template match="/">
    <out:stylesheet version="1.0">
      ...
    </out:stylesheet>
  </xsl:template>

</xsl:stylesheet>
```

This is much nicer. Now all you have to do is use the `xsl` prefix for stylesheet instructions that you want executed, and use the `out` prefix for literal result elements—for the code that you want to generate. The **<xsl:namespace-alias>** element instructs the XSLT processor, after it's done generating the result tree, to convert all elements (and attributes) in the dummy `out` namespace to the actual XSLT namespace. Effectively, the resulting document will use the correct XSLT namespace.

Summary

My goal when writing this chapter was to be unbiased about how you should use namespaces (if indeed you choose to use them). I did this on the theory that you are the best person to make your own design choices, as long as you're equipped with a solid understanding of the technology, the general conventions that are used, and the stickiest issues that can arise.

Ironically, by focusing exclusively on XSLT's handling of namespaces, I've probably come off as anything but unbiased. It's true, XSLT is my XML processing tool of choice. And you will find that XML APIs do not always treat namespaces the same way. For example, depending on how you configure your parser, the SAX API can expose namespace declarations as attributes (in addition to expanding element and attribute names for you). But XSLT, especially with version 2.0, makes about as many distinctions with regard to namespaces as you can hope for, and I didn't want to skimp on that coverage. After tackling XSLT's handling of namespaces, I suspect that getting up to speed on the namespace policies of a given XML API will be a walk in the park.

2 XML Schema Languages

by Eric van der Vlist

You need to read this chapter if you're already familiar with XML schema languages and want to become an advanced user. Being familiar with XML schema languages probably means that you know the basics of W3C XML Schema and have never had an opportunity to work with other schema languages.

This chapter looks at common problems that are difficult or impossible to use with W3C XML Schema and discusses how you can work around them with W3C XML Schema, as well as using other schema languages either together with or instead of W3C XML Schema.

By the end of the chapter, you should have a much better idea of what you can do when you hit a wall using your favorite schema language!

XML Schema Technology Overview

Schema languages have the reputation for being a complex matter and this, by itself, is enough to make me wonder if the name "schema" is well chosen.

In plain English, a "schema" is a simpler description of an object. When I draw the schema of a car, this schema is simpler to read than a photograph of the car.

With XML the documents are simpler than the schemas to the point that documentations of most XML vocabularies include XML snippets to make their schemas easier to understand!

The reason is that XML schemas are not schemas in the common sense of the term: their main goal isn't about describing XML documents, but about "validating" them.

Why is validation more complex than description?

A real schema or description can be very concise yet accurate. The art of a good cartoonist is to use a minimum of traits and yet produce a drawing that really looks like the object that is drawn.

A map of the ground is often highly simplified and very different from what an aerial picture would be and yet this map is clear and useful.

When we start speaking of validation we can't afford these simplifications any longer: when you omit a detail in a schema, most XML schema languages will simply refuse this detail in XML documents.

And when you think about it, "validating" a XML document can mean pretty much everything... XML validation can include things as different as:

- Validating the structure of a document; checking that elements and attributes are embedded as you expect them to be.
- Validating the values of attributes and text nodes independently (often referred as "datatype" checking).
- Validating keys and references.
- Checking "business rules" such as the fact that a start date must be smaller than an end date or that the sum of item prices is equal to the total price.
- Checking good practices such as the fact that a new concept is introduced in a book before being referred to.
- Any other thing, including spell checking!

With all these tasks to perform, it shouldn't be a surprise that XML schema languages are complex and diverse.

To perform a whole set of different tasks, there are always two possible options:

- The Swiss army knife approach that tries to do its best with a single tool.
- The toolbox approach that uses a specialized tool for each task.

In the XML world, the W3C has chosen the Swiss army knife approach with its schema language that tries to be both a description tool and a validation tool covering structure, datatype, and keys and references checks. The ISO has chosen the toolbox approach with a set of highly specialized languages federated under the DSDL project.

In this chapter, you will start using W3C XML Schema (after all, you probably have an old Swiss army knife somewhere and that's a good start) and spot some of the most common situations where this tool shows its limitations.

Facing these limitations, you have two choices:

- Cope with the limitations and see how to make them less disturbing while still using only W3C XML Schema.
- See how you can either replace the W3C XML Schema Swiss army knife with the ISO DSDL toolbox or find a place for the Swiss army knife within the ISO DSDL toolbox.

ISO DSDL is still a work in progress and you'll mainly see its two most stable parts: RELAX NG, which focuses on structure validation, and Schematron, which is unique at validating any type of business rules, including keys and references.

Other tools can be added to your validation toolbox and you'll see that XSLT can help you too.

People are often disappointed to discover that they are not able to define all their validation rules with W3C XML Schema, confused to learn that there are many other schema languages, and angry at what they perceive as pointless competition between standards.

That shouldn't be the case: getting more than one tool to perform a difficult task is always a good thing!

Co-Occurrence Constraints

Co-occurrence constraints are the top one FAQ in mailing lists and I would find it difficult to name a single of my projects where I have not met them.

Note that I will use it to introduce most of the concepts that you will use again in the other sections and I encourage you to read this section even if you're not interested in this specific issue.

The Use Case (Example)

To take a simple yet meaningful example, say you are creating a schema to represent a person. A person has a first name, a last name, a gender, and, at least in our western societies, a person can also have a given name but only if her gender is "female".

The fact that you want to allow a **givenName** element if and only if the gender is "female" is a co-occurrence constraint.

In angle brackets, that means that the following **person** elements will be valid:

```
<person>
  <firstName>Charly</firstName>
  <lastName>Brown</lastName>
  <gender>male</gender>
</person>
<person>
  <firstName>Sally</firstName>
  <lastName>Brown</lastName>
  <gender>female</gender>
</person>
<person>
  <firstName>Jenny</firstName>
  <lastName>Smith</lastName>
```

```
  <givenName>Brown</givenName>
  <gender>female</gender>
</person>
```

Whereas the following one is invalid:

```
<person>
  <firstName>Charles</firstName>
  <lastName>Smith</lastName>
  <givenName>Brown</givenName>
  <gender>male</gender>
</person>
```

In real life, there are two domains where you'll find it very difficult to avoid co-occurrence constraints:

- When describing inter-application messages, most people will include a "message type" somewhere and expect to get different content models depending on this type value.
- Microformats are a kind of XHTML high-jacking that attach different meaning and content models to XHTML elements depending on one of their attributes (the **class** attribute being the most commonly used).

> **Note**
> You will see that co-occurrence constraints are not the only difficulty that you have when validating microformats.

W3C XML Schema

Let's first see what you can do with only a Swiss army knife in your pocket...

Impossible to Express

There is no special feature in W3C XML Schema to express co-occurrence constraints and people try all kind of interesting things to express these constraints.

In this specific case, an ingenious schema designer could try the following:

(Note: the following schema is invalid, don't use it!)

```
<?xml version="1.0" encoding="UTF-8"?>
  <xs:schema xmlns:xs="http://www.w3.org/2001/XMLSchema"
      elementFormDefault="qualified">
```

```
  <xs:element name="person">
    <xs:complexType>
      <xs:sequence>
        <xs:element name="firstName" type="xs:token"/>
        <xs:element name="lastName" type="xs:token"/>
        <xs:choice>
          <xs:element name="gender">
            <xs:simpleType>
              <xs:restriction base="xs:token">
                <xs:enumeration value="male"/>
              </xs:restriction>
            </xs:simpleType>
          </xs:element>
        <xs:sequence>
          <xs:element name="givenName" type="xs:token" minOccurs="0"/>
            <xs:element name="gender">
              <xs:simpleType>
                <xs:restriction base="xs:token">
                  <xs:enumeration value="female"/>
                </xs:restriction>
              </xs:simpleType>
            </xs:element>
          </xs:sequence>
        </xs:choice>
      </xs:sequence>
    </xs:complexType>
  </xs:element>
</xs:schema>
```

If you keep to the logic of each W3C XML Schema compositors (the **xs:sequence** and **xs:choice**) being used there, this schema should work (and you'll see that this is how you express the constraint with RELAX NG). This schema says that you want either a **gender** element with a value **male** or an optional **givenName** element followed by a **gender** element with a value **female**. This should effectively rule out males with given names. This schema is illustrated by Figure 2.1, generated by the oXygen XML.

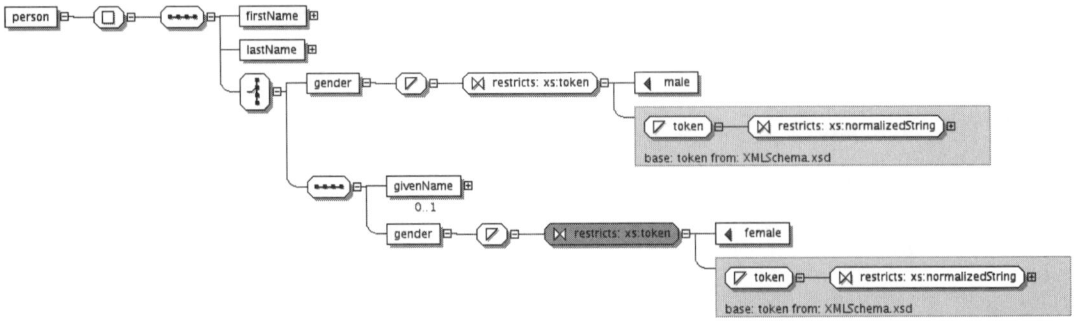

Figure 2.1 *Graphical view of the first schema.*

Unfortunately, as mentioned, this schema is invalid and, if you try it, you'll get an errors such as:

```
Description: cos-element-consistent: Error for type '#AnonType_person'.
         Multiple elements with name 'gender', with different types,
         appear in the model group.
URL: http://www.w3.org/TR/xmlschema-1/#cos-element-consistent

Description: cos-nonambig: gender and gender (or elements from their
   substitution group) violate "Unique Particle Attribution". During
   validation against this schema, ambiguity would be created for those
   two particles.
URL: http://www.w3.org/TR/xmlschema-1/#cos-nonambig
```

The Xerces-J parser is kind enough to give us the URL of the W3C XML Schema validation where these errors are documented and if you're brave enough, you can have a look. However, this recommendation isn't really fun to read and I'll try to explain the motivation behind these two W3C XML Schema restrictions that you've probably hit quite a few times if you've been working with this language.

To understand these restrictions, you must know that there are two main algorithms to implement grammar based schema languages such as W3C XML Schema and RELAX NG:

- Finite State Automatons or Machines (FSA or FSM) can be used. The idea here is to compile the schema into an automaton in which attributes, elements, and text nodes trigger transitions between validation steps represented as states.
- The Brzozowski derivatives method in which schemas are "derived" by documents. In a nutshell, the idea is that for each attribute, element, and text node, you recursively remove the corresponding description from the schema. When you reach the end of the document and haven't reached any errors, your document is valid if and only if all what is remaining in your schema is optional.

The derivative method is an adaptation of works previously done for implementing regular expressions and was already known when the W3C XML Schema recommendation was being written. Its application to XML schema languages was quite new and the Working Group has decided that W3C XML Schema had to be simple to implement as an automaton.

One of the main problems with implementing a schema language as an automaton is to keep the number of states and transitions as low as possible and the two errors that we've seen come from this requirement.

The first error says that, with the content of an element (in this case, the **person** element), the type of each sub-element should be the same. The definition of the **gender** element violates this rule since you've defined it once with a type accepting only the **male** value and a second time with a type accepting the **female** value.

The second error is often associated with the first one and says that when a processor sees a **gender** element without having seen a **givenName**, it doesn't know in advance the type of this **gender** element.

This second error can be suppressed by making the **givenName** element mandatory when the **gender** element is female. That wouldn't be very elegant (you would have to provide an empty **givenName** element for women when they don't have one), but the second error would disappear because the presence of a **givenName** element would be enough to tell a schema processor which definition of the **gender** element should be used. However, the first error would remain and this compromise wouldn't help much.

The problem would have been slightly different if **gender** was an attribute instead of an element. In that case, attributes can't be embedded in a **xs:choice** and the logical (and invalid) solution would have been to embed two definitions of the **person** element in an **xs:choice**. Here again, I have seen various very astute attempts to workaround W3C XML Schema limitations, such as:

```
<?xml version="1.0" encoding="UTF-8"?>
<xs:schema xmlns:xs="http://www.w3.org/2001/XMLSchema"
           elementFormDefault="qualified">
<xs:group name="person">
  <xs:choice>
    <xs:element name="person">
      <xs:complexType>
        <xs:sequence>
          <xs:element name="firstName" type="xs:token"/>
          <xs:element name="lastName" type="xs:token"/>
        </xs:sequence>
        <xs:attribute name="gender">
          <xs:simpleType>
```

```
          <xs:restriction base="xs:token">
            <xs:enumeration value="male"/>
          </xs:restriction>
        </xs:simpleType>
      </xs:attribute>
    </xs:complexType>
  </xs:element>
  <xs:element name="person">
    <xs:complexType>
      <xs:sequence>
        <xs:element name="firstName" type="xs:token"/>
        <xs:element name="lastName" type="xs:token"/>
        <xs:element name="givenName" type="xs:token" minOccurs="0"/>
      </xs:sequence>
      <xs:attribute name="gender">
        <xs:simpleType>
          <xs:restriction base="xs:token">
            <xs:enumeration value="female"/>
          </xs:restriction>
        </xs:simpleType>
      </xs:attribute>
    </xs:complexType>
  </xs:element>
 </xs:choice>
</xs:group>
<xs:element name="root">
 <xs:complexType>
  <xs:sequence>
   <xs:group ref="person"/>
  </xs:sequence>
 </xs:complexType>
</xs:element>
</xs:schema>
```

Note: the preceding schema is invalid, don't use it!

This schema is represented in Figure 2.2.

In that case, the attempt is to define a choice between a person with a **male** content and a person with a **female** content. Unfortunately, you just move the two errors that you had before in the **person** element a level above within the element that does now contain the **person** elements (in this example, this element is named **root**):

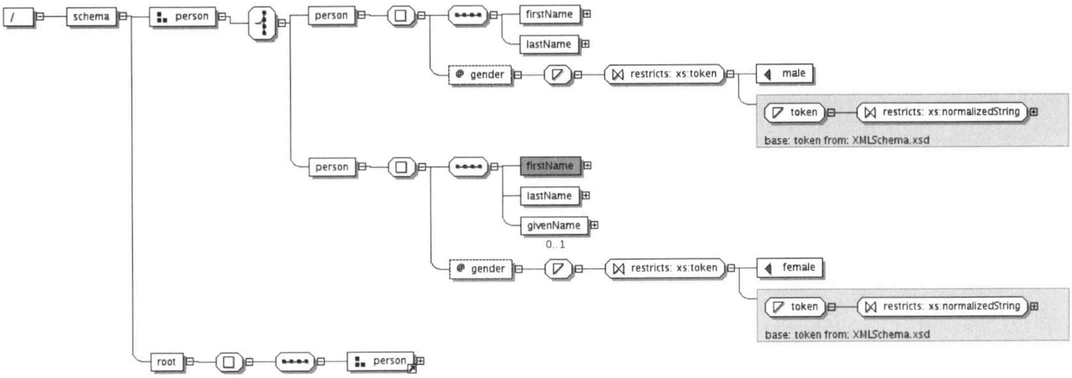

Figure 2.2 *Graphical view of the schema with a **gender** attribute.*

```
Description: cos-element-consistent: Error for type '#AnonType_root'. Multiple
elements with name 'person', with different types, appear in the model group.

URL: http://www.w3.org/TR/xmlschema-1/#cos-element-consistent


Description: cos-nonambig: person and person (or elements from their
substitution group) violate "Unique Particle Attribution". During validation
against this schema, ambiguity would be created for those two particles.

URL: http://www.w3.org/TR/xmlschema-1/#cos-nonambig
```

Workaround: Use xsi:type

You've seen that W3C XML Schema requires that the type of an element is known when the processor starts the validation of this element and that this requirement is the motivation for the errors that have blocked all your attempts to define a co-occurrence constraint up to now.

Acknowledging that, W3C XML Schema gives you a way to define this type in the instance documents. This is the purpose of the **xsi:type** attribute and this will be your first workaround.

The idea here is that, because you have a content model for males and another one for females, you use the **xsi:type** attribute to specify which one you want to use, for instance:

```
<person xmlns:xsi="http://www.w3.org/2001/XMLSchema-instance"
  xsi:type="maleType">
  <firstName>Charly</firstName>
  <lastName>Brown</lastName>
  <gender>male</gender>
</person>
```

or

```
<person xmlns:xsi="http://www.w3.org/2001/XMLSchema-instance"
  xsi:type="femaleType">
  <firstName>Jenny</firstName>
  <lastName>Smith</lastName>
  <givenName>Brown</givenName>
  <gender>female</gender>
</person>
```

The **gender** element becomes quite redundant because you already carry this information in the **xsi:type** attribute and because you do not have to use **Type** suffixes. You might as well write:

```
<person xmlns:xsi="http://www.w3.org/2001/XMLSchema-instance"
  xsi:type="male">
  <firstName>Charly</firstName>
  <lastName>Brown</lastName>
</person>
```

or

```
<person xmlns:xsi="http://www.w3.org/2001/XMLSchema-instance"
  xsi:type="female">
  <firstName>Jenny</firstName>
  <lastName>Smith</lastName>
  <givenName>Brown</givenName>
</person>
```

The **xsi:type** attribute is now playing the role of the **gender** element and that seems pretty much what you want to achieve except that, of course, the **gender** is now located in an attribute named **xsi:type**, which can be considered kind of weird.

As a reminder, to define the schema that will validate these documents, you need to define a **person** element with a type that will be a super-type of the two types used for males and females and define the male and female types as a derivation of this super-type.

Here, with a super simple example, you're lucky because **male** can be defined as a derivation by restriction of female and **female** can be defined as a derivation by extension of male.

In the first case, you would write:

```
<?xml version="1.0" encoding="UTF-8"?>
<xs:schema xmlns:xs="http://www.w3.org/2001/XMLSchema"
           elementFormDefault="qualified">
```

```
<xs:complexType name="person" abstract="true">
  <xs:sequence>
    <xs:element name="firstName" type="xs:token"/>
    <xs:element name="lastName" type="xs:token"/>
  </xs:sequence>
</xs:complexType>

<xs:complexType name="male">
  <xs:complexContent>
    <xs:extension base="person"/>
  </xs:complexContent>
</xs:complexType>

<xs:complexType name="female">
  <xs:complexContent>
    <xs:extension base="person">
      <xs:sequence>
        <xs:element name="givenName" type="xs:token" minOccurs="0"/>
      </xs:sequence>
    </xs:extension>
  </xs:complexContent>
</xs:complexType>

<xs:element name="person" type="person"/>

</xs:schema>
```

This schema is represented in Figure 2.3.

You choose the base type (**person**), which is the same than the male type and derive the male type by an empty extension and the female type by adding the **givenName** element. The **person** type is made abstract to force the use of the **xsi:type** attribute in instance documents.

Instead of that, you could find simpler to define the following schema:

```
<?xml version="1.0" encoding="UTF-8"?>
<xs:schema xmlns:xs="http://www.w3.org/2001/XMLSchema"
           elementFormDefault="qualified">
```

```
<xs:complexType name="male">
  <xs:sequence>
    <xs:element name="firstName" type="xs:token"/>
    <xs:element name="lastName" type="xs:token"/>
  </xs:sequence>
</xs:complexType>

<xs:complexType name="female">
  <xs:complexContent>
    <xs:extension base="male">
      <xs:sequence>
        <xs:element name="givenName" type="xs:token" minOccurs="0"/>
      </xs:sequence>
    </xs:extension>
  </xs:complexContent>
</xs:complexType>

<xs:element name="person" type="male"/>

</xs:schema>
```

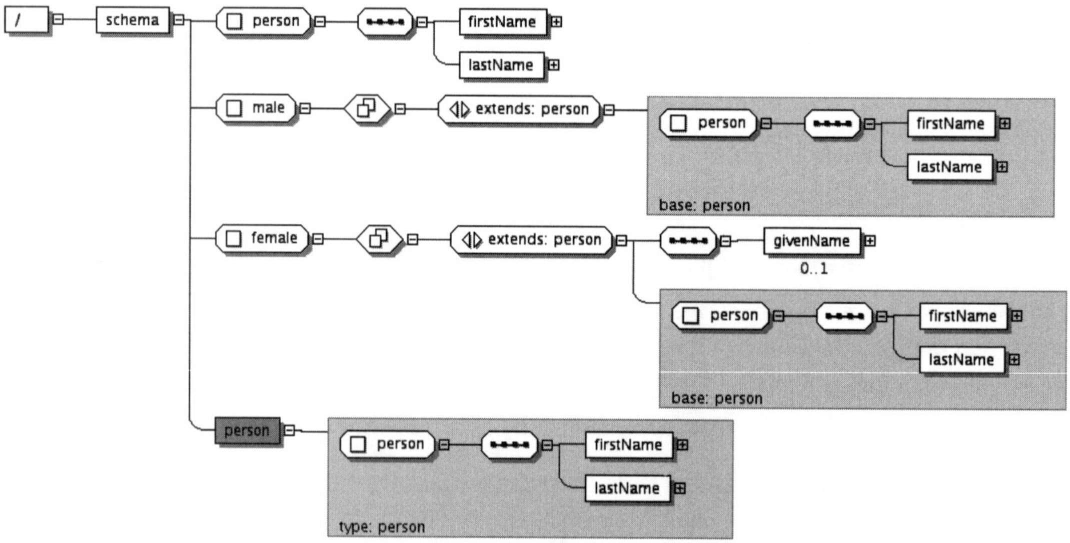

Figure 2.3 *Graphical view of the schema relying on **xsi:type**.*

This schema is almost equivalent to the previous one but it allows documents without **xsi:type** attributes that were forbidden by the preceding schema such as:

```
<person>
  <firstName>Charly</firstName>
  <lastName>Brown</lastName>
</person>
```

and considers that this is equivalent to:

```
<person xmlns:xsi="http://www.w3.org/2001/XMLSchema-instance"
        xsi:type="male">
  <firstName>Charly</firstName>
  <lastName>Brown</lastName>
</person>
```

Considering that persons are male by default is probably wrong enough so that you need to take the pain of creating an abstract type!

The two preceding schemas were using a derivation by extension to add the optional **givenName** element to the content of the **female** type. If you prefer using a derivation by restriction to remove this optional element from the content of the **male** type, you can also write:

```
<?xml version="1.0" encoding="UTF-8"?>
<xs:schema xmlns:xs="http://www.w3.org/2001/XMLSchema"
           elementFormDefault="qualified">

<xs:complexType name="person" abstract="true">
  <xs:sequence>
    <xs:element name="firstName" type="xs:token"/>
    <xs:element name="lastName" type="xs:token"/>
    <xs:element name="givenName" type="xs:token" minOccurs="0"/>
  </xs:sequence>
</xs:complexType>

<xs:complexType name="male">
  <xs:complexContent>
    <xs:restriction base="person">
      <xs:sequence>
        <xs:element name="firstName" type="xs:token"/>
        <xs:element name="lastName" type="xs:token"/>
      </xs:sequence>
```

```
    </xs:restriction>
  </xs:complexContent>
</xs:complexType>

<xs:complexType name="female">
  <xs:complexContent>
    <xs:restriction base="person">
      <xs:sequence>
        <xs:element name="firstName" type="xs:token"/>
        <xs:element name="lastName" type="xs:token"/>
        <xs:element name="givenName" type="xs:token" minOccurs="0"/>
      </xs:sequence>
    </xs:restriction>
  </xs:complexContent>
</xs:complexType>

<xs:element name="person" type="person"/>

</xs:schema>
```

This schema is illustrated in Figure 2.4.

The base type is now the same as the **female** type; you remove the **givenName** element to create the **male** type.

These derivations by restrictions are verbose, redundant, and probably not justified in this case where you can use the much simpler derivation by extension, but you will see in a next section that they can be very useful in other circumstances.

Before you leave **xsi:type** to see the next workaround, I must mention a downside of **xsi:type** that you can't see on this example that doesn't use a namespace.

To do so, imagine that you had defined the same schema with **http://ns.xmlguild.org/example/** as a target namespace. In that case, instance documents could use any prefix to refer to the datatypes and the instance document could be:

```
<x:person xmlns:xsi="http://www.w3.org/2001/XMLSchema-instance"
          xmlns:x="http://ns.xmlguild.org/example/" xsi:type="x:male">
  <x:firstName>Charly</x:firstName>
  <x:lastName>Brown</x:lastName>
</x:person>
```

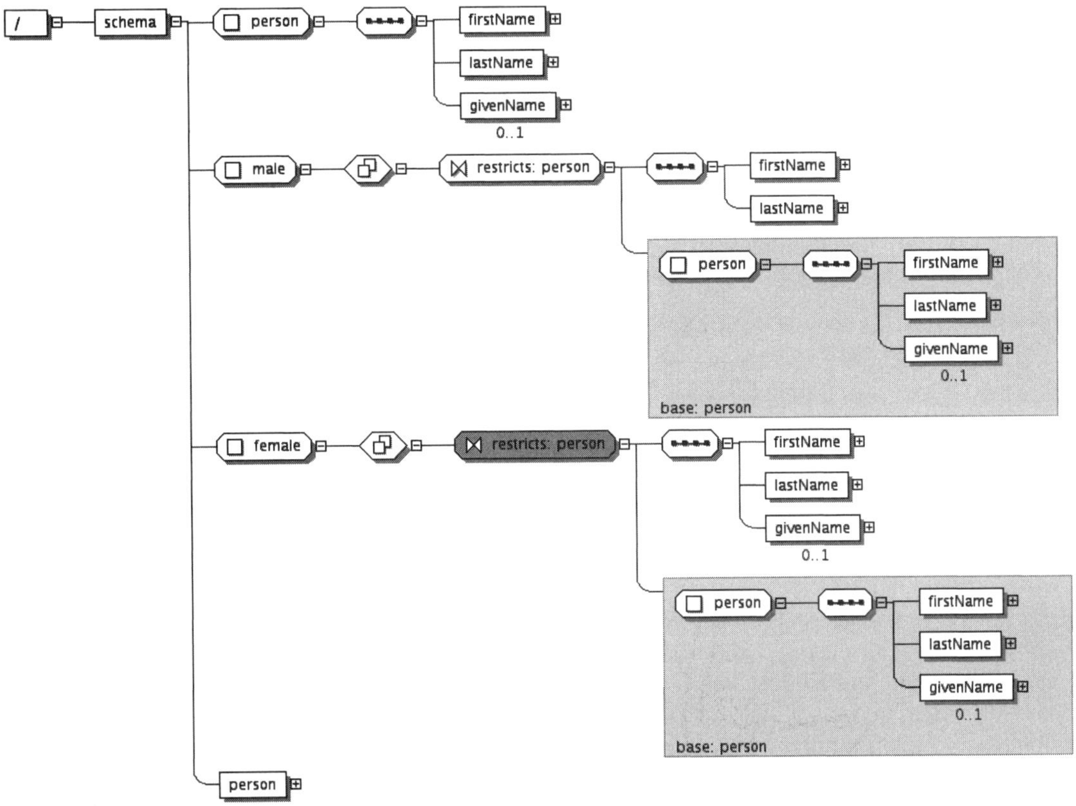

Figure 2.4 *Graphical view of the schema relying on* ***xsi:type*** *using a derivation by restriction.*

This means that applications should check the value of the **xsi:type** as a qualified name (or QName) rather than as a string and this can be quite complex if the tools that you are using do not support QNames correctly. A notorious example of a tool that will make you wish you had chosen another workaround is XSLT 1.0!

Workaround: Use Different Element Names

The second workaround that's commonly used requires that you change the structure of the XML instances. Because the type of an element needs to be known when you start validating it, the idea is that the element name itself triggers a type.

If you distinguish between men and women, most of the problems are gone:

```
<man>
  <firstName>Charly</firstName>
  <lastName>Brown</lastName>
</man>
```

```
<woman>
  <firstName>Jenny</firstName>
  <lastName>Smith</lastName>
  <givenName>Brown</givenName>
</woman>
```

You have now two different elements that could have totally different contents. The schema is very easy to write, but the downside is that you've lost the notion of **person** and you need to find a way to manipulate as simply as possible an element that's either **man** or **woman**.

This can be done very straightforwardly by replacing the occurrences of the element **person** in the schema by a choice between **man** and **woman**. If this choice comes in multiple locations in the schema, it can be located in a group:

```
<?xml version="1.0" encoding="UTF-8"?>
<xs:schema xmlns:xs="http://www.w3.org/2001/XMLSchema"
    elementFormDefault="qualified">
<xs:group name="person">
  <xs:choice>
    <xs:element name="man">
      <xs:complexType>
        <xs:sequence>
          <xs:element name="firstName" type="xs:token"/>
          <xs:element name="lastName" type="xs:token"/>
        </xs:sequence>
      </xs:complexType>
    </xs:element>
    <xs:element name="woman">
      <xs:complexType>
        <xs:sequence>
          <xs:element name="firstName" type="xs:token"/>
          <xs:element name="lastName" type="xs:token"/>
          <xs:element name="givenName" type="xs:token" minOccurs="0"/>
        </xs:sequence>
      </xs:complexType>
    </xs:element>
  </xs:choice>
</xs:group>
<xs:element name="root">
  <xs:complexType>
    <xs:sequence>
      <xs:group ref="person"/>
```

```
    </xs:sequence>
  </xs:complexType>
</xs:element>
</xs:schema>
```

This schema is represented in Figure 2.5.

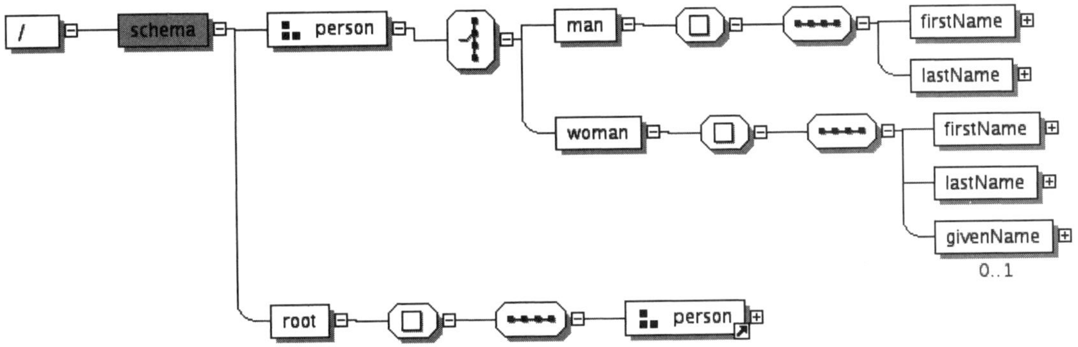

Figure 2.5 *Graphical view of the schema relying on element names.*

Another option is to use substitution groups. Substitution groups are a feature to express choices between elements in more global and extensible ways. All the different elements from a substitution group can replace the substitution group head in instance documents. A constraint of substitution groups is that all the elements from a substitution group must be explicitly derived from the element that's the head of the group.

This means that, here again, you need to explicitly define the links between the two types by derivation and, here again, you can choose between derivation by extension and derivation by restriction.

If you chose to derive by extension, you can write:

```
<?xml version="1.0" encoding="UTF-8"?>
<xs:schema xmlns:xs="http://www.w3.org/2001/XMLSchema"
           elementFormDefault="qualified">
<xs:complexType name="man">
  <xs:sequence>
    <xs:element name="firstName" type="xs:token"/>
    <xs:element name="lastName" type="xs:token"/>
  </xs:sequence>
</xs:complexType>
  <xs:complexType name="woman">
    <xs:complexContent>
```

```
      <xs:extension base="man">
        <xs:sequence>
          <xs:element name="givenName" type="xs:token" minOccurs="0"/>
        </xs:sequence>
      </xs:extension>
    </xs:complexContent>
  </xs:complexType>
<xs:element name="man" type="man"/>
<xs:element name="woman" type="woman" substitutionGroup="man"/>
<xs:element name="root">
  <xs:complexType>
    <xs:sequence>
      <xs:element ref="man"/>
    </xs:sequence>
  </xs:complexType>
</xs:element>
</xs:schema>
```

The **man** element is used as the head of the substitution group, meaning that each time a reference is made to the element **man** in the schema, it can be replaced by the **woman** element, which is the other member of the substitution group.

This schema, shown in Figure 2.6, does perfectly well what it is supposed to do: each reference to a **man** element can be replaced by a **woman** element and, in a sense, you might say that it gives equal rights to men and women. However; this isn't exactly true... With these definitions, you can impose a **woman** element somewhere but you can't impose a **man** element.

There are applications for which that can be a problem. Imagine that you want to define a couple as being composed of a man and a woman. With the current definitions, you can avoid that a couple is composed of two men but you can't avoid that it is composed of two women.

If a schema designer wants or needs to be able to impose the presence of a **man** element, he or she needs to design a better-balanced schema such as this one:

```
<?xml version="1.0" encoding="UTF-8"?>
<xs:schema xmlns:xs="http://www.w3.org/2001/XMLSchema"
           elementFormDefault="qualified">
<xs:complexType name="person">
  <xs:sequence>
    <xs:element name="firstName" type="xs:token"/>
    <xs:element name="lastName" type="xs:token"/>
  </xs:sequence>
</xs:complexType>
```

```
<xs:complexType name="woman">
  <xs:complexContent>
    <xs:extension base="person">
      <xs:sequence>
        <xs:element name="givenName" type="xs:token" minOccurs="0"/>
      </xs:sequence>
    </xs:extension>
  </xs:complexContent>
</xs:complexType>
<xs:element name="person" type="person" abstract="true"/>
<xs:element name="man" type="person" substitutionGroup="person"/>
<xs:element name="woman" type="woman" substitutionGroup="person"/>
<xs:element name="root">
  <xs:complexType>
    <xs:sequence>
      <xs:element ref="person"/>
    </xs:sequence>
  </xs:complexType>
</xs:element>
</xs:schema>
```

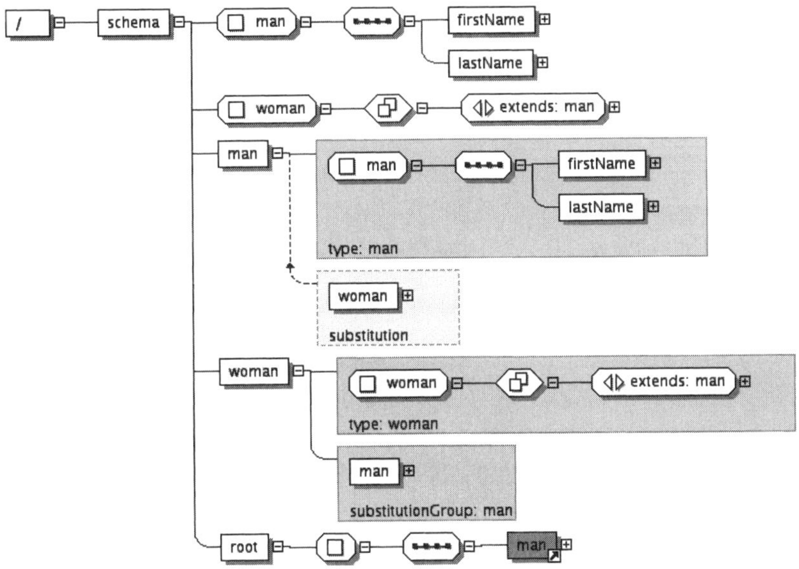

Figure 2.6
Schema using a substitution group based on the man element.

In this new schema, shown in Figure 2.7, the head of the substitution group is the **person** element. This element can be described as **abstract** like I've done in the previous example if you want to make sure you'll never get **person** elements in instance documents. The **man** and **woman** element are now two non-head elements of the substitution group. A reference to **person** will allow either **man** or **woman** while a reference to **man** or **woman** will only allow the element that's being referenced.

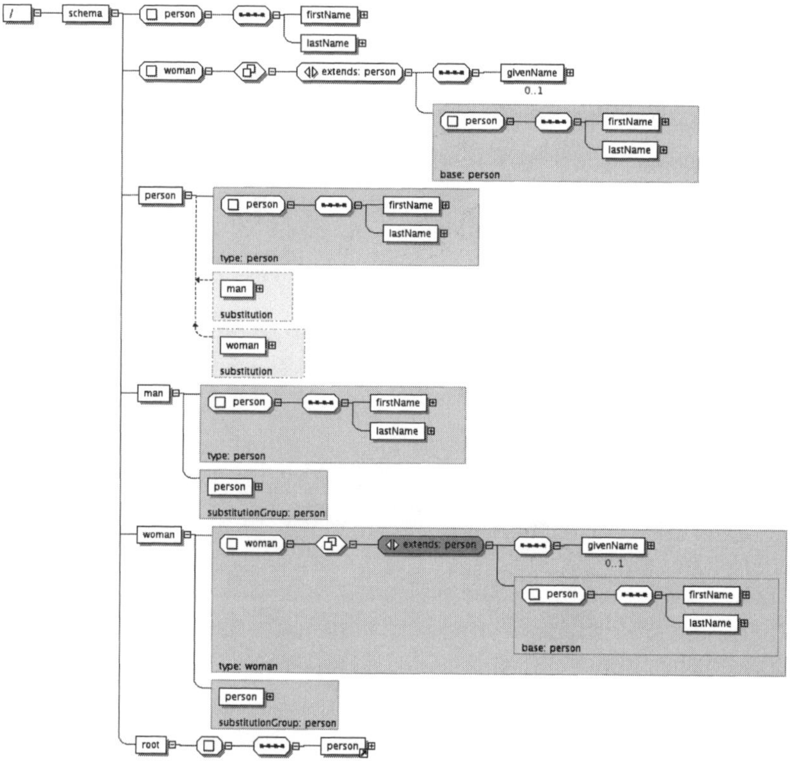

Figure 2.7
*Schema using a substitution group based on a **person** element.*

RELAX NG Alone

Within the DSDL toolbox, RELAX NG is the tool that comes closest to W3C XML Schema.

Like W3C XML Schema, RELAX NG is "grammar based," meaning its principal is to describe the structure of XML documents through descriptions called *grammars*.

Unlike W3C XML Schema, RELAX NG doesn't rule out non-deterministic schemas and has nothing similar to the "Unique Particle Attribution" or "Consistent Declaration" rules that have hit you when you've tried to define the co-occurrence constraints. This section shows you how to exploit this flexibility and just define your schemas like you've tried to with W3C XML Schema.

For those of you who are not familiar with RELAX NG, I'll start by showing how a schema for a person might look without the co-occurrence constraints.

RELAX NG has two different syntaxes. The XML syntax looks like a simpler version of the W3C XML Schema syntax:

```
<?xml version="1.0" encoding="UTF-8"?>
<grammar xmlns="http://relaxng.org/ns/structure/1.0" datatypeLibrary="">
<start>
  <ref name="person"/>
</start>
<define name="person">
  <element name="person">
    <ref name="firstName"/>
    <ref name="lastName"/>
    <optional>
      <ref name="givenName"/>
    </optional>
    <ref name="gender"/>
  </element>
</define>
<define name="firstName">
  <element name="firstName">
    <data type="token"/>
  </element>
</define>
<define name="lastName">
  <element name="lastName">
    <data type="token"/>
  </element>
</define>
<define name="givenName">
  <element name="givenName">
    <data type="token"/>
  </element>
</define>
<define name="gender">
  <element name="gender">
    <choice>
      <value>male</value>
      <value>female</value>
```

```
    </choice>
  </element>
</define>
</grammar>
```

> **Note**
> Note that any .rng files you find are RELAX NG schemas using the XML syntax. They can be opened and edited with any XML or text editor. Any .rnc files you find are RELAX NG schemas using the compact syntax and can be opened with any text editor.

The root element of the RELAX NG schema is **grammar** and you'll notice that a RELAX NG grammar has a **start**, which defines which element (or elements) can be used as a root in an XML document.

The grammar is also composed of a number of named definitions (**define**), referred through **ref** elements.

These named definitions replace the various W3C XML Schema global particles (elements, attributes, types, groups, and so on) and, in this schema, we've adopted a style where each element is described in its own global definition.

Oxygen gives you the graphical representation for this schema shown in Figure 2.8.

Figure 2.8
RELAX NG schema without co-occurrence constraints.

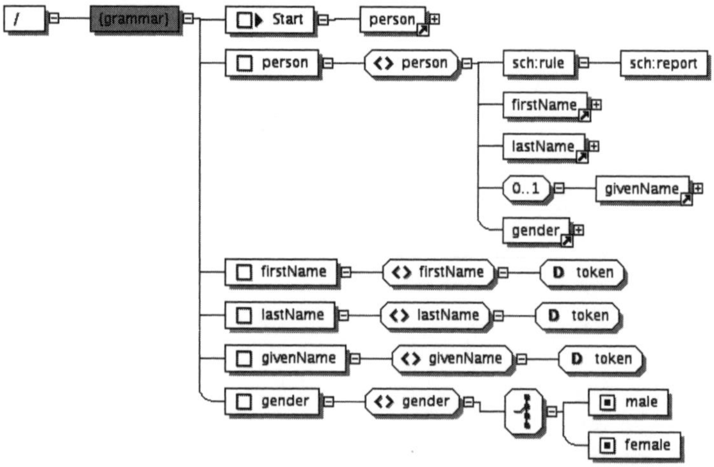

RELAX NG has also a compact, non-XML syntax that's strictly equivalent to the XML syntax. The same schema written in the compact syntax would be:

```
start = person

person = element person {
  firstName,
  lastName,
  givenName?,
gender
}

firstName = element firstName { token }

lastName = element lastName { token }

givenName = element givenName { token }

gender = element gender { "male"|"female" }
```

This compact syntax is quite straightforward to read and I won't explain it in detail but just mention how named definitions are replaced by an equals statement and referred through their names. Note also how **optional** has been translated by a trailing **?**, like in a DTD or in a regular expression (like in DTDs and regular expressions, you would also use ***** for "zero or more" and **+** for "one or more"). Note also how choices are expressed using an **or** sign (**|**) like in **"male"|"female"**.

You will use this choice operator to define the co-occurrence constraints and, depending on the way you want to express this model, you can "factorize" what you want to keep in common between the male and female models.

If you think of this model in terms of "we can either have a male or a female," you can write the schema as:

```
start = person

person = male|female

male = element person {
  firstName,
  lastName,
  element gender { "male" }
}

female = element person {
  firstName,
```

```
  lastName,
  givenName ?,
  element gender { "female" }
}

firstName = element firstName { token }

lastName = element lastName { token }

givenName = element givenName { token }
```

In this first schema, the choice is done out of the **person** element and **male** and **female** are defined as **person** elements with two different content models with the benefit that you can make reference to a male or a female. See Figure 2.9.

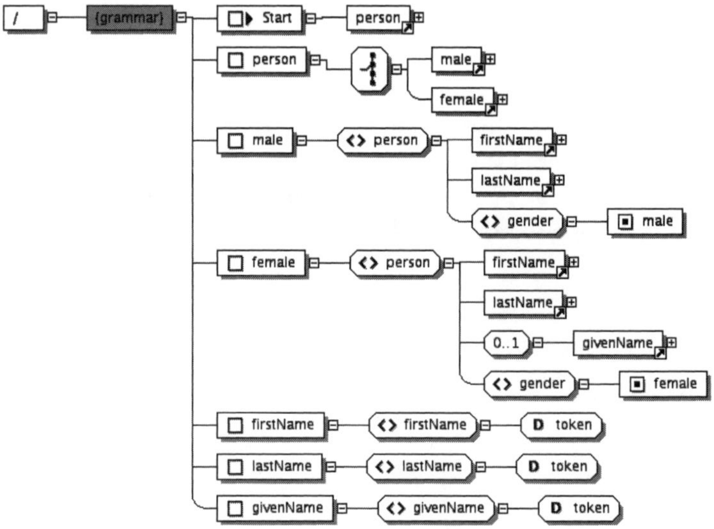

Figure 2.9
*RELAX NG schema with a choice between two definitions of the **person** element.*

You could also move the choice within the element:

```
start = person

person = element person {
  male|female
}

male =
  firstName,
```

```
  lastName,
  element gender { "male" }

female =
  firstName,
  lastName,
  givenName ?,
  element gender { "female" }

firstName = element firstName { token }

lastName = element lastName { token }

givenName = element givenName { token }
```

In this new schema, shown in Figure 2.10, which validates exactly the same set of instance documents, you have a single definition of the **person** element. Its entire content is either male or female.

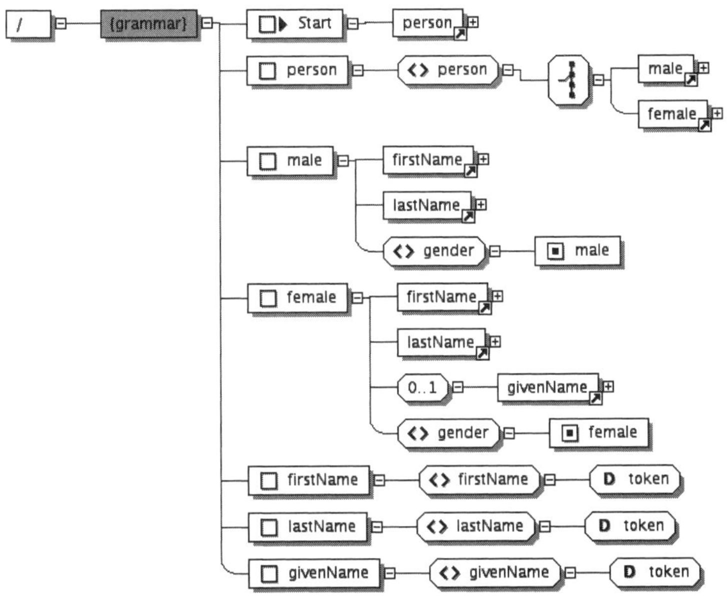

Figure 2.10
RELAX NG schema with a choice between two definitions of the full content of the ***person*** *element.*

This can be seen as a factorization of the **person** element that's now common to both content models. You might also want to factorize the **firstName** and **lastName** elements, which are common to the two cases:

```
start = person

person = element person {
  firstName,
  lastName,
  (male|female)
}

male =
  element gender { "male" }

female =
  givenName ?,
  element gender { "female" }

firstName = element firstName { token }

lastName = element lastName { token }

givenName = element givenName { token }
```

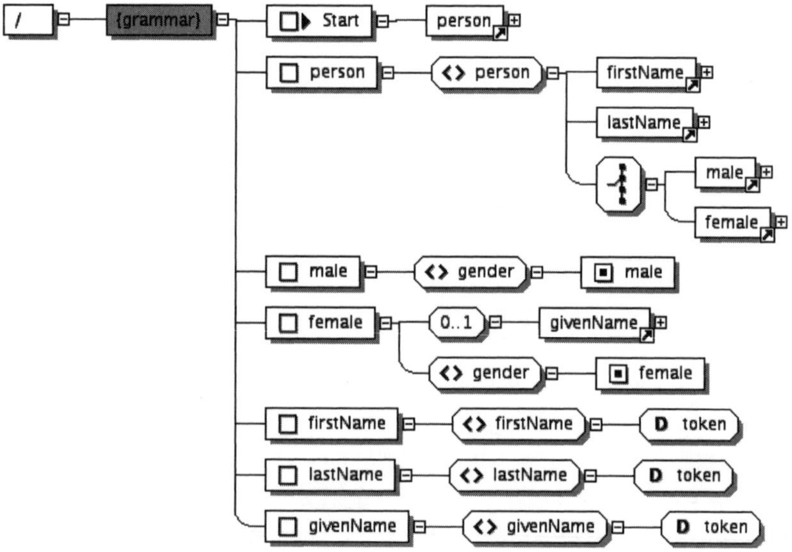

Figure 2.11 *RELAX NG schema with a choice between what is different in the content of male and female person elements.*

These three schemas are equivalent in that they validate the same set of instance documents. Note that these three schemas can be written to replace the **gender** element with an attribute, for instance:

```
start = person

person = element person {
  firstName,
  lastName,
  (male|female)
}

male =
  attribute gender { "male" }

female =
  givenName ?,
  attribute gender { "female" }

firstName = element firstName { token }

lastName = element lastName { token }

givenName = element givenName { token }
```

RELAX NG is clever enough to know that attributes belong to **start** tags and to accept them wherever you want to put them in your descriptions. Here, it will find out that the **gender** attribute belongs to the **person** element and use the **attribute** value to differentiate between male and female. See Figure 2.12.

All these schemas are "non-deterministic" because a schema processor must read the content of a **person** element before it knows which content model should be used. For this reason, they cannot be translated into the W3C XML Schema.

Note that these schemas are "non-ambiguous" because it is always possible to say which alternative of the choices have been used to validate the **person** element.

You might be interested to know that RELAX NG also supports ambiguous schema but it is important to understand that even if ambiguity and determinism are often confused, they are two different notions.

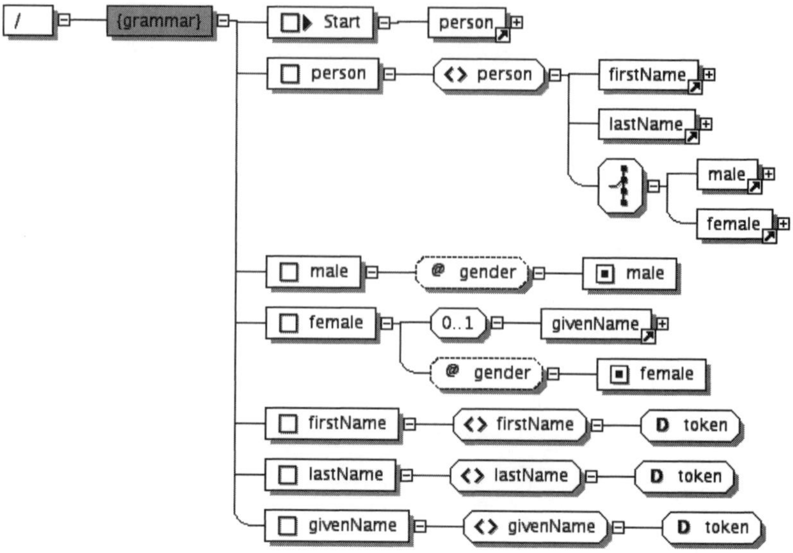

Figure 2.12
RELAX NG schema with ***gender*** *attributes instead of elements.*

People often justify W3C XML Schema limitations, saying that ambiguous schemas are a bad thing when you're using a schema language as a modeling tool. This argument is understandable: when you describe something you want to keep ambiguity as limited as possible, but the truth is that W3C XML Schema limitations have been introduced to avoid non-deterministic schemas–a very different concept.

W3C XML Schema and the Schematron Constraint

With RELAX NG, it looks like you've found the ideal tool to express co-occurrence constraints. So, why would you want to use any other one?

There can be two different answers to this question:

- The first one is that not everyone is lucky enough to be able to choose the tool he or she can use!
  Because W3C XML Schema is the dominant schema language, there is a lot of pressure and thus a lot of good reasons for using it: organizations' policies can mandate to use W3C XML Schema, the tools that you are using can support only W3C XML Schema, the developers can be trained only on W3C XML Schema, and so on.
- The second answer is that even if co-occurrence constraints can expressed with RELAX NG, this isn't necessarily the place where you want to express these constraints.
  The example you've seen here was simple enough, but these constraints can be more complex. What if I wanted to check that only married women have a given name? Because you

would be adding more conditions, the schema would become harder to read and, depending on the kind of conditions, it could become impossible to express in RELAX NG. Furthermore, the complexity you might add here makes it more difficult to understand the structure of the XML documents. That can be seen as a sign that you are mixing two kinds of validation here: you are no longer validating the structure but also co-occurrence constraints, which may be considered as business rules.

The approach you'll see in this section separates these two types of validation: it uses grammar-based schema languages (such as W3C XML Schema or RELAX NG) to validate the structure and a rule-based schema language to validate the business rules (including co-occurrence constraints).

If you try to think of this constraint as a business rule expressed in plain English, the easiest way you can say it is probably "a **person** element with a **gender** element equal to **male** must not contain a **givenName** sub-element".

The translation into Schematron can be written as:

```
<?xml version="1.0" encoding="UTF-8"?>
<schema xmlns="http://www.ascc.net/xml/schematron">
<pattern name="co-occurrence">
  <rule context="person[gender='male']">
    <report test="givenName">A person element with a gender element
       equal to male must not contain a givenName sub-element</report>
  </rule>
</pattern>
</schema>
```

In this schema, you are defining a "rule" in the context of **person** elements with **gender** sub-elements equal to **male** (the context is being expressed as a XPath expression, like it is the case with XSLT).

This rule reports an error when a **givenName** element is found. Here again, the test is expressed as an XPath expression and you'll note that I have pasted the complete text of my explanation in plain English. This is one of the nice features of Schematron: the error messages are defined in the schema itself and can be as user friendly as you'll take pain to express them!

Note that this schema makes very few assumptions on the structure of the XML documents. If there is no **person** element in a document or only **person** elements without **gender** sub-elements or only **person** elements with **gender** sub-elements having any values other than **male**, the schema will never have a chance to raise any error because its rule will never be evaluated. The one and only thing that this schema validates is the co-occurrence constraint.

Is it really worth writing a standalone schema for checking only one rule?

I could answer that in real-life applications you would rapidly find other business rules that can easily be checked with Schematron but still, it can be handy to manipulate only one schema and include your Schematron rules with a W3C XML Schema or RELAX NG schema.

This is possible through *annotations*.

With W3C XML Schema, annotations rely on xs:annotation and xs:appinfo elements. You write:

```
<?xml version="1.0" encoding="UTF-8"?>
<xs:schema xmlns:xs="http://www.w3.org/2001/XMLSchema"
           elementFormDefault="qualified"
           xmlns:sch="http://www.ascc.net/xml/schematron">
<xs:element name="person">
  <xs:annotation>
    <xs:appinfo>
      <sch:rule context="person[gender='male']">
        <sch:report test="givenName">A person element with a gender
            element equal to male must not contain a givenName
            sub-element</sch:report>
      </sch:rule>
    </xs:appinfo>
  </xs:annotation>
  <xs:complexType>
    <xs:sequence>
      <xs:element name="firstName" type="xs:token"/>
      <xs:element name="lastName" type="xs:token"/>
      <xs:element name="givenName" type="xs:token" minOccurs="0"/>
      <xs:element name="gender">
        <xs:simpleType>
          <xs:restriction base="xs:token">
            <xs:enumeration value="male"/>
            <xs:enumeration value="female"/>
          </xs:restriction>
        </xs:simpleType>
      </xs:element>
    </xs:sequence>
  </xs:complexType>
</xs:element>
</xs:schema>
```

RELAX NG considers that any element in a namespace different from its own namespace is an annotation. You would write:

```
<?xml version="1.0" encoding="UTF-8"?>
<grammar xmlns:sch=http://www.ascc.net/xml/schematron
      xmlns="http://relaxng.org/ns/structure/1.0"
datatypeLibrary="">
<start>
  <ref name="person"/>
</start>
<define name="person">
  <element name="person">
    <sch:rule context="person[gender='male']">
      <sch:report test="givenName">A person element with a gender
         element equal to male must not contain a givenName
         sub-element</sch:report>
    </sch:rule>
  <ref name="firstName"/>
  <ref name="lastName"/>
  <optional>
    <ref name="givenName"/>
  </optional>
  <ref name="gender"/>
</element>
</define>
<define name="firstName">
  <element name="firstName">
    <data type="token"/>
  </element>
</define>
<define name="lastName">
  <element name="lastName">
    <data type="token"/>
  </element>
</define>
<define name="givenName">
  <element name="givenName">
    <data type="token"/>
```

```
  </element>
</define>
<define name="gender">
  <element name="gender">
    <choice>
      <value>male</value>
      <value>female</value>
    </choice>
  </element>
</define>
</grammar>
```

The compact syntax becomes less straightforward when you start adding annotations, but this is still possible:

```
namespace sch = "http://www.ascc.net/xml/schematron"
start = person
person =
[
sch:rule [
context = "person[gender='male']"
sch:report [
test = "givenName"
"A person element with a gender element equal to male must not " ~
"contain a givenName sub-element"
]
]
]
element person { firstName, lastName, givenName?, gender }
firstName = element firstName { token }
lastName = element lastName { token }
givenName = element givenName { token }
gender = element gender { "male" | "female" }
```

You might be wondering why you are embedding rules, since the **context** attribute is kind of redundant with the context where you are adding the rule in the schema.

In these three examples, the rule context mentions that you are interested in **person** elements with a **gender** sub-element equal to **male**, whereas the context of the schema is already the definition of **person** elements.

The answer is that if you want a maximum amount of interoperability, you need to ensure that low-level tools such as an XSLT transformation can extract a Schematron schema from annotated W3C XML Schema or RELAX NG schemas. The price to pay is this redundancy. What you get in return is that you can use any schema processor to process these compounded schemas.

This means that the location where the rules are embedded in the schema isn't really important. It is recommended to embed rules where they belong for maximum readability, but the schemas would have had the same meaning if the rules had been embedded anywhere else, even in a context such as the definition of the **firstName** element!

Now, for those of you who prefer to trade convenience against interoperability, implementations such as Sun's MSV take the W3C XML Schema or RELAX NG schema context as a Schematron context rule and allow to directly embed Schematron **assert** and **report** elements as annotations.

Constraint on Repeated Elements

The first case that you saw (co-occurrence constraints) was very contrasted: the constraints can't be expressed in W3C XML Schema and you can either replace this language by RELAX NG or complement it with Schematron.

The second case that you'll see right now is less contrasted: the constraints that you want to express can't be fully expressed by either W3C XML Schema or RELAX NG, and both languages need to be complemented by Schematron.

The Use Case

This example originally came on the XMLfr main mailing list. It is a remarkable example of a simple and legitimate set of constrains that are tough to express by grammar-based schema languages.

In plain English these constrains are: "we want to enforce the fact that each article has a title in English, a title in French, and optional titles in other languages and, of course, the titles must be unique for each language".

In other words, you want to validate documents such as:

```
<?xml version="1.0" encoding="UTF-8"?>
<article xmlns:dc="http://purl.org/dc/elements/1.1/">
<dc:title xml:lang="en">
  <!-- mandatory -->
  Constraint on repeated elements</dc:title>
<dc:title xml:lang="fr">
  <!-- mandatory -->
  Contrainte sur des éléments répétés</dc:title>
```

```
<dc:title xml:lang="...">
<!--  Optional -->
...</dc:title>
</article>
```

W3C XML Schema

For W3C XML Schema, the situation is pretty much the same as the one for co-occurrence constrains: because of the "Element Declarations Consistent" rule which you hit for co-occurrence constrains, you can't define two different definitions of an element in the same context.

It is thus impossible to say that you want a **dc:title** element with an **xml:lang** attribute set to **en** followed by a **dc:title** element with an **xml:lang** attribute set to **fr** (these would be two different definitions of **dc:title** in the same context).

In fact, the only things that you can check is that you have at least two titles and that the languages are unique.

The closest schema that you can write is something such as:

```
<?xml version="1.0" encoding="UTF-8"?>
<xs:schema xmlns:xs="http://www.w3.org/2001/XMLSchema"
           elementFormDefault="qualified"
           xmlns:dc="http://purl.org/dc/elements/1.1/">
<xs:import namespace=http://purl.org/dc/elements/1.1/
      schemaLocation="dc.xsd"/>
<xs:element name="article">
  <xs:complexType>
    <xs:sequence>
      <xs:element ref="dc:title" minOccurs="2" maxOccurs="unbounded"/>
    </xs:sequence>
  </xs:complexType>
  <xs:key name="languages">
    <xs:selector xpath="dc:title"/>
    <xs:field xpath="@xml:lang"/>
  </xs:key>
</xs:element>
</xs:schema>
```

Whereby dc.xsd would be:

```
<?xml version="1.0" encoding="UTF-8"?>
<xs:schema xmlns:xs="http://www.w3.org/2001/XMLSchema"
           elementFormDefault="qualified"
           targetNamespace="http://purl.org/dc/elements/1.1/"
           xmlns:dc="http://purl.org/dc/elements/1.1/">
<xs:import namespace="http://www.w3.org/XML/1998/namespace"
           schemaLocation="xml.xsd"/>
<xs:element name="title">
  <xs:complexType mixed="true">
    <xs:attribute ref="xml:lang" use="required"/>
  </xs:complexType>
</xs:element>
</xs:schema>
```

and xml.xsd would be:

```
<?xml version="1.0" encoding="UTF-8"?>
<xs:schema xmlns:xs="http://www.w3.org/2001/XMLSchema"
           attributeFormDefault="qualified"
           targetNamespace="http://www.w3.org/XML/1998/namespace">
<xs:attribute name="lang" type="xs:language"/>
</xs:schema>
```

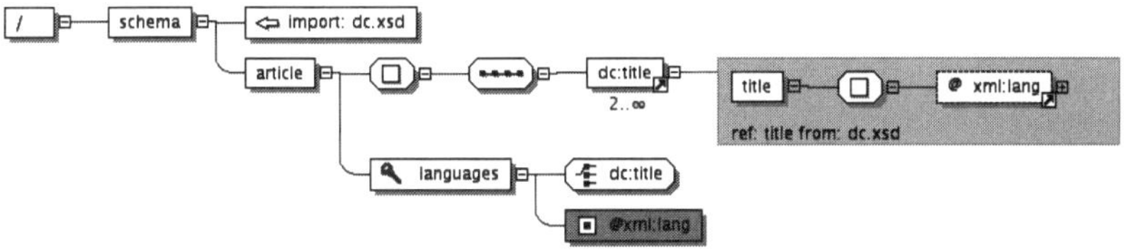

Figure 2.13
Closest W3C XML Schema for repeated element constraint.

The workarounds that you might find involve changing the structure of the instance documents and using different element names for titles in English, French, and other languages, but that sounds like a dirty hack.

RELAX NG Alone

After the flexibility shown by RELAX NG to solve co-occurrence constrains, you are probably confident that it will save the day here again. That's true as long as you stay in the scope of grammar-based languages and you can easily write that you want a title in English followed by a title in French and optional titles that are neither English nor French:

```
default namespace = ""
namespace dc = "http://purl.org/dc/elements/1.1/"

start =
element article {
element dc:title {
attribute xml:lang { "en" },
text
},
element dc:title {
attribute xml:lang { "fr" },
text
},
element dc:title {
attribute xml:lang { xsd:language - ("fr" | "en") },
text
} *
}
```

Figure 2.14
Closest RELAX NG schema for repeated element constraint.

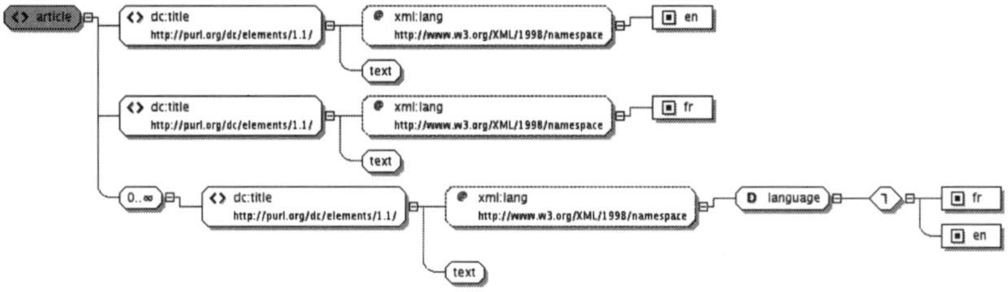

That's pretty good, but how do you check that languages are unique and that you won't have two titles in Chinese?

The answer is that you can't. Uniqueness constrains, together with keys and key references, have been considered out of the scope of RELAX NG and can't be expressed in RELAX NG.

A workaround could be to consider the **xml:lang** attribute to have a type **xs:ID**, but that would work only if you are sure that you enforce this rule only once in a single document, since **xs:ID** identifiers are global to the entire document.

W3C XML Schema or RELAX NG with Schematron

So, with W3C XML Schema you've been able to express that titles are unique. With RELAX NG, you have titles in English and French and optional titles in other languages.

For different reasons, in both cases, you have been able to express only a subset of the rules that you need to express and, in both cases, an answer was to add Schematron rules to express what has been left aside.

W3C XML Schema and Schematron

What you've missed with W3C XML Schema is the fact that the first title is in English and the second in French.

You can express these two constrains in a single Schematron rule:

```
<?xml version="1.0" encoding="UTF-8"?>
<schema xmlns="http://www.ascc.net/xml/schematron">
  <ns uri="http://purl.org/dc/elements/1.1/" prefix="dc"/>
  <pattern name="titles">
    <rule context="article">
      <assert test="dc:title[1]/@xml:lang = 'en'">The first title should be
          in English</assert>
      <assert test="dc:title[2]/@xml:lang = 'fr'">The second title should
         be in French</assert>
    </rule>
  </pattern>
</schema>
```

Unless you prefer to split these constrains in two different rules:

```
<?xml version="1.0" encoding="UTF-8"?>
<schema xmlns="http://www.ascc.net/xml/schematron">
  <ns uri="http://purl.org/dc/elements/1.1/" prefix="dc"/>
  <pattern name="titles">
    <rule context="article/dc:title[1]">
      <assert test="@xml:lang = 'en'">The first title should be
          in English</assert>
    </rule>
    <rule context="article/dc:title[2]">
      <assert test="@xml:lang = 'fr'">The second title should be
         in French</assert>
    </rule>
  </pattern>
</schema>
```

The difference between these two schemas is that the first one does check that there is a first and a second title, whereas the second one skips the corresponding test if the first or second title is missing but provides a better context information because the context nodes of its rules are directly the nodes that contain the errors.

Both are perfectly fine with the schema that we've shown that had a **minOccurs** set to 2. The choice boils down to a decision about the split between tests done by W3C XML Schema and tests done by Schematron.

The first schema introduces a redundancy between the tests performed by the two languages, whereas the second one is strictly testing only the constrains that have not been tested by W3C XML Schema.

This redundancy can be considered a good thing because tools supporting only one of the schemas will catch more errors. As any redundancy in an information system, it can also be considered a bad thing because updates have to be made in multiple locations.

A simple way to eliminate this redundancy with the first schema is to change **minOccurs** to 0 in W3C XML Schema.

RELAX NG and Schematron

With RELAX NG, what you've missed is the uniqueness of the titles for each language.

This test can be written in Schematron as:

```
<?xml version="1.0" encoding="UTF-8"?>
<schema xmlns="http://www.ascc.net/xml/schematron">
  <ns uri="http://purl.org/dc/elements/1.1/" prefix="dc"/>
  <pattern name="titles">
    <rule context="article/dc:title">
      <report test="preceding-sibling::dc:title/@xml:lang = @xml:lang">
          Titles should be unique for each language.</report>
    </rule>
  </pattern>
</schema>
```

Now, because you are using two different schema languages, you might also want to change the split between the scopes of their tests.

The RELAX NG schema that we've written isn't overly complicated, but it is still more complicated than it would be without these constrains about English and French titles. One may consider that this kind of rule belongs more to the domain of business rules, for which Schematron is known, rather than to the domain of grammar-based schema languages, in which business rules are often less readable.

In that case, you could simplify the RELAX NG schema to just be:

```
default namespace = ""
namespace dc = "http://purl.org/dc/elements/1.1/"

start =
element article {
element dc:title {
  attribute xml:lang {xsd:language},
  text
}
}
```

and add the tests that you've removed from this schema into the Schematron schema that would become:

```
<?xml version="1.0" encoding="UTF-8"?>
<schema xmlns="http://www.ascc.net/xml/schematron">
  <ns uri="http://purl.org/dc/elements/1.1/" prefix="dc"/>
  <pattern name="titles">
  <rule context="article">
    <assert test="dc:title[1]/@xml:lang = 'en'">The first title should be
       in English</assert>
    <assert test="dc:title[2]/@xml:lang = 'fr'">The second title should be
      in French</assert>
  </rule>
  <rule context="article/dc:title">
    <report test="preceding-sibling::dc:title/@xml:lang = @xml:lang">
        Titles should be unique for each language.</report>
  </rule>
</pattern>
</schema>
```

Figure 2.15 illustrates this simplified schema.

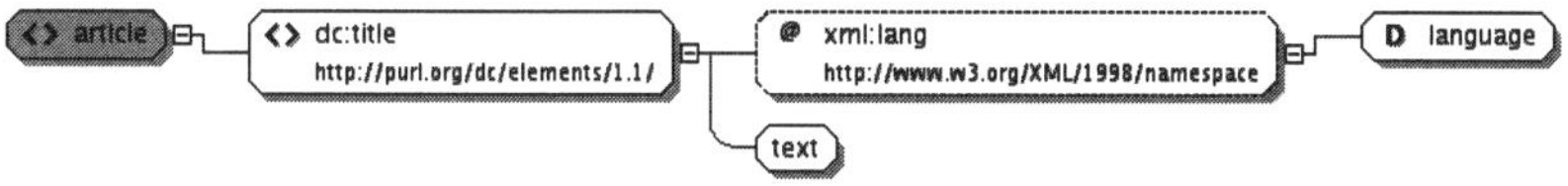

Figure 2.15
Simplified RELAX NG schema without repeated element constraint.

Microformats

So far you've seen a case in which W3C XML Schema can be replaced by RELAX NG alone or supplemented with Schematron, a case where neither W3C XML Schema nor RELAX NG was sufficient, and a third case where Schematron had to be used if you wanted to check all the rules mentioned in the use case.

Let's now raise the level of complexity a second time whereby W3C XML Schema and RELAX NG can't follow for different reasons and even Schematron begins to show its limits.

The Use Case

Microformats are one of the new buzzwords that seems pretty much impossible to ignore. I won't go into the details of microformats, but just mention what you need to know to understand why their validation is so complex. The basic principle of microformats is that they highjack existing vocabularies to use their existing features in novel ways to carry new meanings.

The most common host vocabulary is XHTML and the feature that is used most of the time is its **class** attribute: specific tokens are recognized in the **class** attributes for each microformat as its tagging system.

A simple example is worth pages of explanations. Here is a snippet copied from the site that defines **hReview**, a microformat designed for expressing reviews:

```
<?xml version="1.0" encoding="UTF-8"?>
<!DOCTYPE html PUBLIC "-//W3C//DTD XHTML 1.1//EN"
    "http://www.w3.org/TR/xhtml11/DTD/xhtml11.dtd">
<html xmlns="http://www.w3.org/1999/xhtml">
<head>
<title>test</title>
</head>
<body>
<div class="hreview">
<span><span class="rating">5</span> out of 5 stars</span>
<h4 class="summary">Crepes on Cole is awesome</h4>
<span class="reviewer vcard">Reviewer: <span class="fn">Tantek</span> -
<abbr class="dtreviewed" title="20050418T2300-0700">April 18, 2005</abbr></span>
<div class="description item vcard"><p>
<span class="fn org">Crepes on Cole</span> is one of the best little
     creperies in <span class="adr"><span class="locality">
     San Francisco</span></span>.
Excellent food and service. Plenty of tables in a variety of sizes
```

```
for parties large and small.  Window seating makes for excellent
people watching to/from the N-Judah which stops right outside.
I've had many fun social gatherings here, as well as gotten
plenty of work done thanks to neighborhood WiFi.
</p></div>
<p>Visit date: <span>April 2005</span></p>
<p>Food eaten: <span>Florentine crepe</span></p>
</div>
</body>
</html>
```

In this XHTML snippet, the **class** attributes carry information pertaining to different microformats.

You'll recognize **<div class="hreview">**, which is the root element for a review, **<span class= "rating">5</span>**, which is the rating, **<span class="fn">Tantek</span>**, which is a first name (**"fn"**), and so on.

What makes these vocabularies difficult to validate is the extraordinary flexibility left to the authors of such documents.

Information can be written in any order (a microformat doesn't care if a rating comes before or after a description), in any element (the class attribute is the only thing that matters), and at any depth in the hierarchy of XML elements (there can be as many elements to traverse between a review and a rating than the authors wants to add).

This last statement is itself carried to the extreme and in the snippet, the element **<abbr class= "dtreviewed" title="20050418T2300-0700">April 18, 2005</abbr>** is embedded within the element **<span class="reviewer vcard">** even though the date of the review (**dtreviewed**) is considered to be a property of the review itself rather than a property from the reviewer!

W3C XML Schema

Microformats can be considered an extreme case of co-occurrence constraints: all the reasons why you have not been able to use the language in the two previous examples apply to microformats.

Furthermore, I've mentioned that the content models of microformats are unordered and if all the restrictions that you've seen so far were not enough, you would hit the limitations of the W3C XML Schema **xs:all** particle.

RELAX NG

Let's see what RELAX NG can do.

If you take a tag such as **version**, you have to express the fact that the **class** attribute contains the token **version**. Class attributes are lists of tokens and that would seem natural to use the RELAX NG **list** pattern, whose purpose it is to validate lists of tokens to express this condition.

Unfortunately, you want to accept the token **version** in any position in the list of tokens and need a pattern that does not depend on the relative positions. Outside a list, you would use the **interleave** pattern, but this pattern is forbidden in a list.

The fall-back solution for this is to use W3C XML Schema datatypes and facets: although RELAX NG is focused on the validation of document structures, it allows one to use "external" datatype libraries and the most commonly used and best supported type library are W3C XML Schema datatypes.

With this type library, you can use the **pattern** facet to validate the **class** attribute using a regular expression:

```
attribute class {
  xsd:token { pattern = "(.+\s)?version(\s.+)?" }
}
```

The regular expression **"(.+\s)?version(.+\s)?"** requires a **version** token optionally preceded and followed by other characters if they are separated by a space.

Let's then use RELAX NG "name classes," which give you the ability to use wildcards in element names and to define an element that can have any name and a **class** attribute containing the token **version**. You write:

```
element * {
  attribute class {
  xsd:token { pattern = "(.+\s)?version(\s.+)?" }
  }
}
```

Of course, this model needs to be extended to accept other attributes and content, and you would end up with a definition such as:

```
element * {
  attribute class {
    xsd:token { pattern = "(.+\s)?version(\s.+)?" }
  },
  anyOtherAttributes,
  mixed { anyElements }
}
anyOtherAttributes = attribute * - class { text }*
```

```
anyElements =
  element * {
  attribute * { text }*,
  mixed { anyElements }
}*
```

Where **anyOtherAttributes** is a pattern defined as being any attributes with a name not equal to **class** and **anyElements** is defined as accepting any elements. See Figure 2.16.

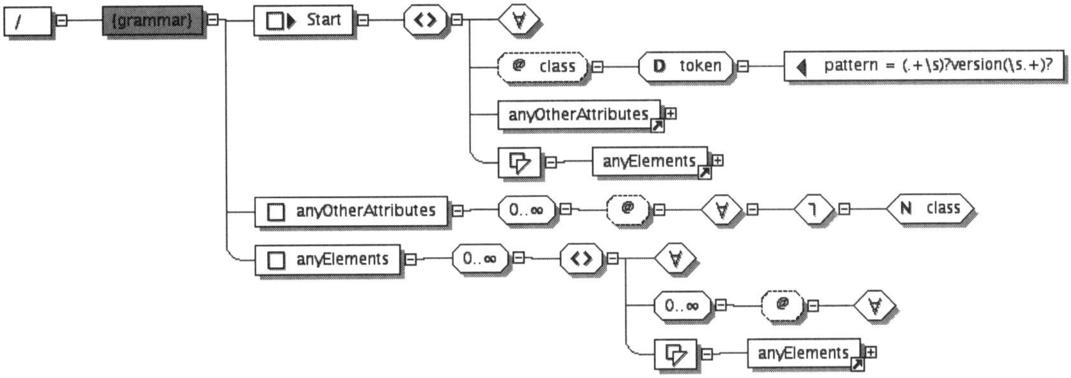

Figure 2.16 *A schema that validates any element containing the token "version" in its class attribute.*

This definition would then have to be extended to express the fact that this condition on the **class** attribute is expected not only at the current level but can be found at any level of imbrication. You can do this through a choice between the previous content and something containing the same model called recursively:

```
version =
  element * {
    (attribute class {
      xsd:token { pattern = "(.+\s)?version(\s.+)?" }
    },
    anyOtherAttributes,
    mixed { anyElements })
  | (attribute class {
    xsd:token - xsd:token { pattern = "(.+\s)?version(\s.+)?" }
  }?,
  anyOtherAttributes,
  mixed { version, anyElements })
}
```

This pattern expresses that you are looking for an element with a **class** attribute containing a token **version** at any depth in the XML hierarchy and is getting close to what you are looking for; however, you have reached a point where you can't go much further without getting into trouble. See Figure 2.17.

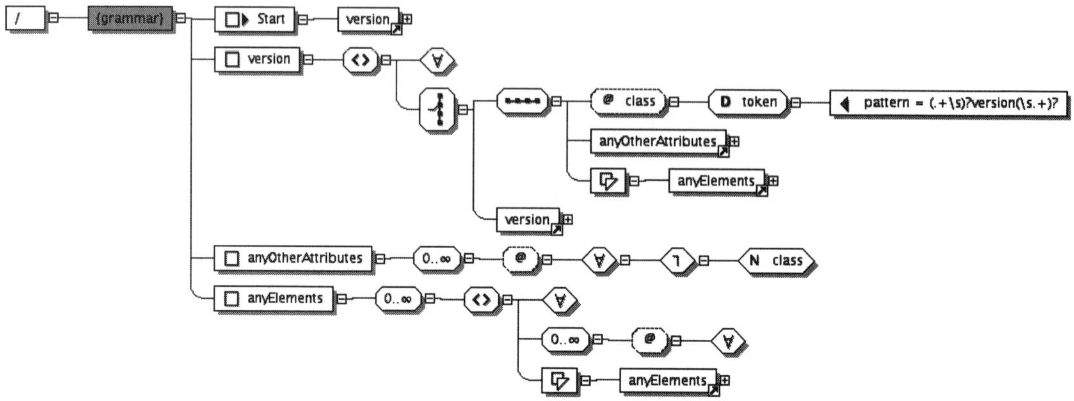

Figure 2.17 *A schema that validates an element containing, at any depth, an element containing the token "version" in its class attribute.*

Up to now, you have expressed the rules for a tag (here, the **version** tag) independently and have implicitly assumed that a whole fragment was tagged as **version** if it contained a **version** token at any level of depth.

As you have seen when I have introduced microformats, this isn't the case and, not only can a fragment contain several different tags, but you've seen in the example that the logical structure can be different from the physical structure.

Another issue is how you can assemble different patterns like the **version** pattern within their parent pattern.

The relative order of each tag is not significant for microformats and to define the parent pattern it would seem natural to use an interleave. Interleave is what comes nearer to the W3C XML Schema **xs:all** compositor in RELAX NG.

Unlike **xs:all**; **interleave** has very few restrictions but one of them will hit you very hard in this specific case: the class names of the elements combined by interleave cannot overlap. In other words, when you combine several elements by interleave, the names of these elements must be distinct. In microformats where the names of the elements don't matter, all the elements have been using wildcards and overlap and you can't use interleave.

To work around these issues, the only solution is to define a choice between all the possible combinations of the physical positions of these tags.

This is possible in theory and you could write a program that would generate a schema with these different combinations, but their number would grow very rapidly beyond what is reasonable for a RELAX NG processor.

Schematron

Now that you've exhausted the possibilities of both W3C XML Schema and RELAX NG, you need to have a look at what you can do with Schematron.

The first thing to check is how to express the fact that a **class** attribute contains a token.

With XPath 1.0, the simplest way to do so is to add a space before and after the **attribute** value, after its spaces have been normalized. By doing so, you can then check that the token value is there, preceded and followed by a space.

In XPath, this can be written as: **"contains(concat(' ', normalize-space(@class), ' '), ' version ')"**.

Now that you know this trick, you can use it over and over. For instance, you can validate the content of the **review** tag through this Schematron pattern:

```
<pattern name="hreview.hreview">
<rule context="*[contains(concat(' ', normalize-space(@class), ' '),
       ' hreview ')]">
<report
test="count(.//*[contains(concat(' ', normalize-space(@class), ' '),
       ' version ')]) &gt; 1"
>A "version" tag is duplicated.</report>
<report
test="count(.//*[contains(concat(' ', normalize-space(@class), ' '),
       ' summary ')]) &gt; 1"
>A "summary" tag is duplicated.</report>
<report
test="count(.//*[contains(concat(' ', normalize-space(@class), ' '),
       ' type ')]) &gt; 1"
>A "type" tag is duplicated.</report>
<assert test=".//*[contains(concat(' ', normalize-space(@class), ' '),
       ' item ')]">A
mandatory "item" tag is missing.</assert>
<report
test="count(.//*[contains(concat(' ', normalize-space(@class), ' '),
       ' item ')]) &gt; 1"
>A "item" tag is duplicated.</report>
<report
test="count(.//*[contains(concat(' ', normalize-space(@class), ' '),
       ' reviewer ')]) &gt; 1"
```

```
>A "reviewer" tag is duplicated.</report>
<report
test="count(.//*[contains(concat(' ', normalize-space(@class), ' '),
      ' dtreviewed ')]) &gt; 1"
>A "dtreviewed" tag is duplicated.</report>
<report
test="count(.//*[contains(concat(' ', normalize-space(@class), ' '),
     ' rating ')]) &gt; 1"
>A "rating" tag is duplicated.</report>
<report
test="count(.//*[contains(concat(' ', normalize-space(@class), ' '),
      ' description ')]) &gt; 1"
>A "description" tag is duplicated.</report>
</rule>
</pattern>
```

This should convince you that microformat validation is feasible with Schematron. So, now, consider if the code is readable? Not really. Writing such a schema is low-level and error-prone because you have to be sure that all the conditions have been correctly checked.

Transformations Needed

With W3C XML Schema and RELAX NG both failing and Schematron considered too low level for the task, you have to think differently and find a way to move out of the box. Transformations in general are great ways to change the rules of the game and XSLT can certainly help you here.

Validation is a process with two inputs (the instance document and the schema), a processor, and an output (the validation report). In such a process, you can use XSLT to transform the inputs or to replace the processor.

Transforming Instance Documents

A first possibility is to transform the instance documents into a structure easier to validate. In this case, that would mean imposing the same physical structure as the logical one and would involve replacing the element names by the tokens you're matching in the **class** attributes.

One of the issues is that we are interested only by specific tokens and should ignore the other ones. In other words, the transformation needs to know the structure of the microformat that is processed and cannot be generic.

Apart from this specific issue, this approach is very generic and could have been used in the two previous examples. In both cases (co-occurrence constrains and repeated elements), you could have transformed instance documents before validation to add **xsi:type** elements or change the element names depending on the content. And in both cases, the result of this transformation would have become easy to validate with W3C XML Schema.

A downside of this method is that schemas are applied on the result of the transformation. The error messages make reference to the transformed document rather than the original document that's known by the document author.

When the transformation does profoundly modify the structure of the document like this, as is the case with microformats, this can be a real problem. Information should probably be added by the transformation to identify where each element comes from in the original document. Even with this precaution, the error messages aren't easy to interpret.

Transforming Schemas

When the validation is possible but verbose and tedious with a schema language (like it is here with Schematron), another solution is to generate the schema through XSLT.

Even without using a meta-model as a source for the transformation, plain XSLT using named templates can be more readable than the Schematron schema to generate, as you see from this snippet:

```
<rule context="*[contains(concat(' ', normalize-space(@class), ' '),
     ' hreview ')]">
  <xsl:call-template name="check-tag">
    <xsl:with-param name="name">item</xsl:with-param>
    <xsl:with-param name="minOccurs">1</xsl:with-param>
  </xsl:call-template>
  <xsl:call-template name="check-tag">
    <xsl:with-param name="name">reviewer</xsl:with-param>
    <xsl:with-param name="maxOccurs">1</xsl:with-param>
  </xsl:call-template>
</rule>
```

XSLT as a Schema Language

You could also use XSLT as the schema language and write the validation rules as a XSLT transformation.

Schematron can be seen as a more concise way of expressing validation rules in XSLT and is generally more concise than XSLT.

However, XSLT is Turing complete and has more features than Schematron. It is thus an interesting alternative in cases where something is impossible to express with Schematron or when named templates can be used to improve the readability (such as is the case here).

In this context, you might for instance write templates such as:

```
<xsl:template match="*[contains(concat(' ', normalize-space(@class), ' '),
     ' hreview ')]">
  <xsl:call-template name="check-tag">
```

```
    <xsl:with-param name="name">item</xsl:with-param>
    <xsl:with-param name="minOccurs">1</xsl:with-param>
  </xsl:call-template>
  <xsl:call-template name="check-tag">
    <xsl:with-param name="name">reviewer</xsl:with-param>
    <xsl:with-param name="maxOccurs">1</xsl:with-param>
  </xsl:call-template>
</xsl:template>
```

Meta-Models

You have now seen four different ways to validate microformats:

- Raw Schematron, which is verbose and tough to read.
- Transforming instance documents.
- Generating the schema.
- Doing the validation in XSLT.

All these solutions remain pretty much low level. They look like implementation techniques rather than models. Norm Walsh had the good idea to propose using a RELAX NG schema as a meta-model for transforming instance documents (you can read more on his blog at http://norman.walsh.name/2006/04/13/validatingMicroformats). This meta-model is describing the logical structure of the microformat and is as simple as:

```
start = hreview.reviews
hreview.reviews = element reviews { hreview.hreview+ }
hreview.hreview =
  element hreview {
    text
    &hreview.version?
    &hreview.summary?
    &hreview.type?
    &hreview.item
    &hreview.reviewer?
    &hreview.dtreviewed?
    &hreview.rating?
    &hreview.description?
  }
hreview.version = element version { text }
hreview.summary = element summary { text }
hreview.type = element type { text }
hreview.item =
  element item { text & hreview.fn* & hreview.url* & hreview.photo* }
```

```
hreview.fn = element fn { text }
hreview.url = element url { text }
hreview.photo = element photo { text }
hreview.reviewer = element reviewer { text }
hreview.dtreviewed =
  element dtreviewed {
    attribute title { text }?,
    text
  }
hreview.rating = element rating { text }
hreview.description = element description { text }
```

From that, or rather from its XML version, Walsh suggests to generate the transformation that would transform instance documents into instances that can be validated by this schema. He has written a reference implementation to prove his point. See Figure 2.18.

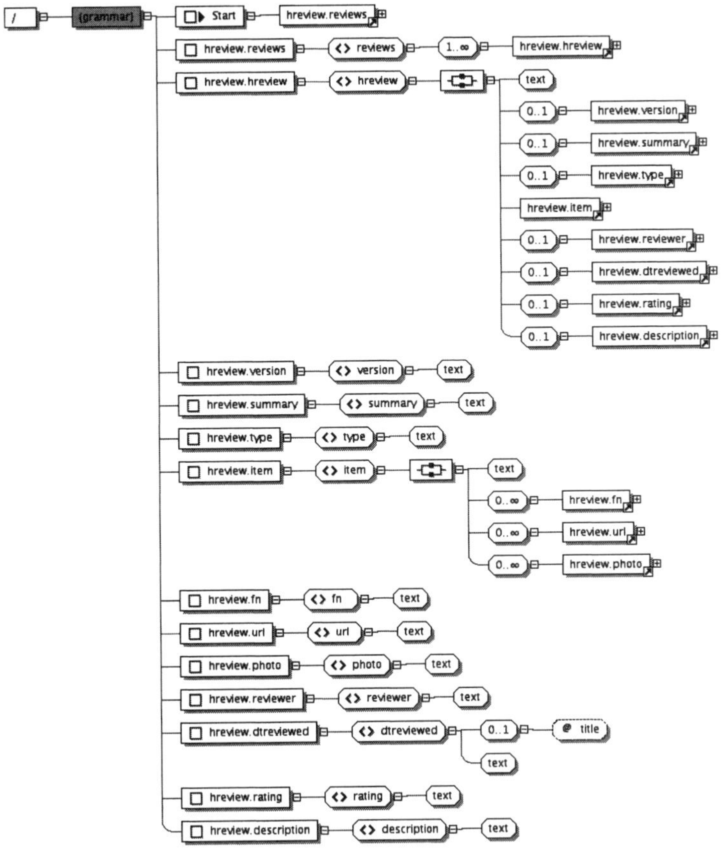

Figure 2.18
*The schema proposed by Norm Walsh to define the meta-model of the **hReview** microformat.*

The idea of using a RELAX NG schema as a meta-model is excellent, but don't forget that transforming instances is only one of the three implementation alternatives you have.

I would personally be in favor of using this same meta-model to generate the corresponding Schematron schema and have also written a reference implementation to show that this is feasible. This gives you error messages whereby the context is the original document instead and so are much easier to read.

And of course, it is also possible to generate from this meta-model a XSLT transformation that would do the validation.

The meta-model appears here to be the ideal based on which all the three implementations techniques can be built. And what is still more interesting is that the same model can be used for each of these techniques: you can start the modeling and postpone your choice of the implementation!

Wrapping Up

You have seen three different examples of use cases that cause problems to schema languages. Here are some guidelines that you've perhaps learned from these examples.

Confirm That You've Really Hit a Limitation

In this chapter, I have only shown cases that hit real limitations. If you find a problem in real life, the first thing to check is whether this is a real limitation or whether your schema couldn't be rewritten differently to express what you want to express.

The latter is often the case with "non-deterministic" models.

Let's go back to the **person** element and add references to the person's mother and father.

If you want to impose that at least one of the **mother** and **father** element is included, it might seem natural to say that you want either **mother, father** or **mother** and **father,** which in W3C XML Schema would give something such as:

```
<xs:element name="person">
  <xs:complexType>
    <xs:sequence>
      <xs:element name="firstName" type="xs:token"/>
      <xs:element name="lastName" type="xs:token"/>
      <xs:element name="givenName" type="xs:token" minOccurs="0"/>
      <xs:element name="gender" type="xs:token"/>
      <xs:choice>
        <xs:element name="mother" type="xs:token"/>
        <xs:element name="father" type="xs:token"/>
        <xs:sequence>
```

```
      <xs:element name="mother" type="xs:token"/>
      <xs:element name="father" type="xs:token"/>
     </xs:sequence>
    </xs:choice>
   </xs:sequence>
  </xs:complexType>
</xs:element>
```

Note: the preceding schema is invalid, don't use it!

Unfortunately, this schema is invalid and would give an error message such as: **E cos-nonambig: mother and mother (or elements from their substitution group) violate "Unique Particle Attribution". During validation against this schema, ambiguity would be created for those two particles."** See Figure 2.19.

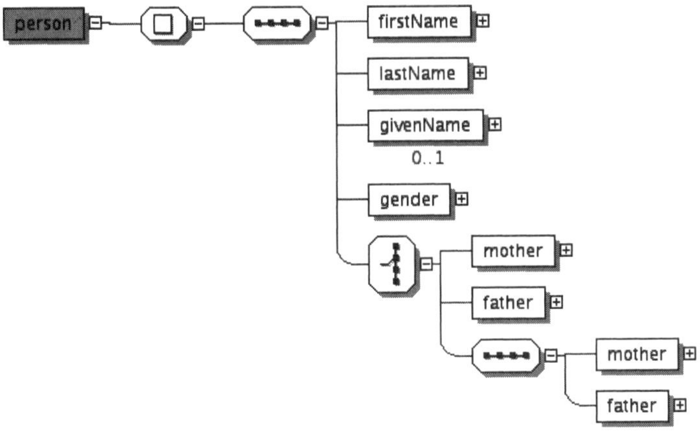

Figure 2.19
Incorrect schema allowing either ***mother*** *or* ***father*** *or both* ***mother*** *and* ***father****.*

This error is easy to work around: you just need to think of this content model as **father** alone or **mother** optionally followed by **father**:

```
<xs:element name="person">
  <xs:complexType>
   <xs:sequence>
    <xs:element name="firstName" type="xs:token"/>
    <xs:element name="lastName" type="xs:token"/>
    <xs:element name="givenName" type="xs:token" minOccurs="0"/>
    <xs:element name="gender" type="xs:token"/>
    <xs:choice>
```

```
        <xs:element name="father" type="xs:token"/>
        <xs:sequence>
          <xs:element name="mother" type="xs:token"/>
          <xs:element name="father" type="xs:token" minOccurs="0"/>
        </xs:sequence>
      </xs:choice>
    </xs:sequence>
  </xs:complexType>
</xs:element>
```

This describes the exact same set of instance documents and this is now perfectly valid, as illustrated in Figure 2.20.

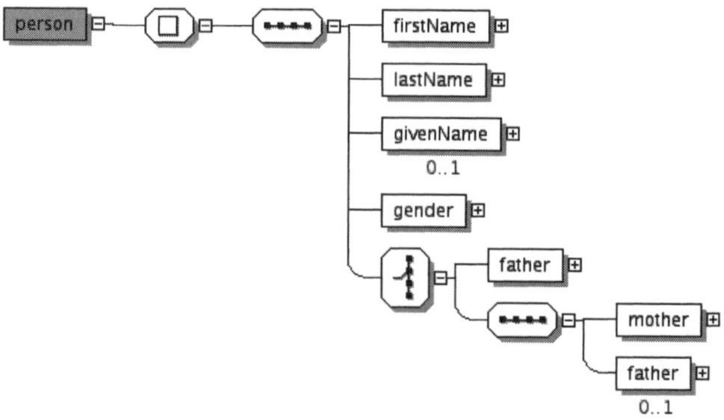

Figure 2.20
*Correct schema allowing either **mother** or **father** or both **mother** and **father**.*

In fact, very few content models are inherently non-deterministic and most of the non-deterministic models can be written in a similar way.

Detecting real limitations requires some practice. You may want to ask colleagues, either in-house or via mailing lists, to double-check if you truly have found a limitation.

Consider Using a Workaround

If you've hit a limitation, a first thing to consider is whether you can and want to use a workaround that involves changing the structure of the instance documents. If you are describing an existing vocabulary, this will be clearly unacceptable. In most other cases, things are much more open and the decision more difficult to be made.

As many decisions, this one is often a tradeoff.

If you have been careful to design a vocabulary optimized for a specific application, modifying the vocabulary so that it can be validated by W3C XML Schema will most probably be seen as a degradation of this vocabulary.

In that case, you will have to choose between this degradation and the ability to validate the vocabulary with W3C XML Schema.

Look at Other Schema Languages

If the workarounds are not an option, you can consider using other schema languages. The different scenarios are:

- Replacing W3C XML Schema by RELAX NG alone.
- Adding Schematron validation to W3C XML Schema.
- Adding Schematron validation to RELAX NG.

If you're coming from W3C XML Schema, you will probably not find the third option very attractive.

The first option is more radical because you're leaving W3C XML Schema alone. It is interesting if the tools that you'll be using support RELAX NG because in that case it is often easier to work with a single schema than with two schemas.

For instance, if your XML editor supports RELAX NG, it will be able to do context editing taking into account all the constrains expressed in your schema.

This option does still allow you to use a degraded W3C XML Schema that expresses a subset of the constrains, but this means more work because you'd have to duplicate this subset in both schemas. A tool such as *trang* can help you to generate the W3C XML Schema from the RELAX NG schema, but it will frequently be in trouble when asked to translate things that cannot be translated.

The second option degrades more gracefully: the W3C XML Schema does its best and tries to validate everything that can be validated with W3C XML Schema, whereas the Schematron schema does the final polishing.

Applications that do not support Schematron can thus still rely on W3C XML Schema for a basic validation.

Think Differently

If none of these options work for you, you should definitely think differently.

In XML this often involves XSLT and you can consider:

- Transforming documents before validation.
- Doing the validation itself in XSLT or using a programming language.
- Generating your schemas if they are verbose with a repetitive structure.

And of course, if another language is better adapted to the task than XSLT in your context, this language can be used too.

Summary

In this chapter, you have seen that XML schema languages are not magic tools that can solve all your needs and perform any kind of validation. On the contrary, like in many other domains, you have to chose between a number of tools with different approaches and features.

A general-purpose validation language such as W3C XML Schema has a wide scope but is necessarily more limited than more specialized languages such as RELAX NG and Schematron. When you find a limitation using W3C XML Schema, chances are that it can be fixed by using one of these specialized languages, either alone or together with W3C XML Schema.

And when none of these solutions works for you, you need to think differently to push the frontiers of what can be done. Thinking differently includes accepting these restrictions, changing your content model to meet the limitations of the schema languages that you are using, transforming instance documents or schemas (or both) to facilitate the validation process, or using other tools (such as XSLT or programming languages) to perform the validation.

3 XSLT

by Zarella Rendon

with contributions from Nikita Ogievetsky, Evan Lenz, and Jeni Tennison

XSLT is a language for transforming XML. You could say it is the work horse of XML because, without XSLT, XML is just a markup language. XSLT adds many dimensions to XML by giving you the ability to change it, manipulate it, transform it, and style it. Of course, you may argue that XSLT is just another XML based tool, but when you add an XSLT processor, you get power.

XSLT 1.0 became a W3C Recommendation on November 16, 1999. XSLT 2.0 is currently a Candidate Recommendation (since June of 2006), and is scheduled to move to full Recommendation status before the end of 2006.

This chapter is split into two sections, one for XSLT 1.0 and the other for XSLT 2.0. The technology is similar from one version to the next, but the differences are surprising, enough that some experts claim that they should be separate languages altogether.

XPath

XPath 1.0 is a W3C Recommendation that is used by XSLT for its addressing mechanism in order to access the information in an XML document. XPath defines expressions, and these expressions are used in XSLT attributes to identify nodes (and other XML constructs) for further processing. It is impossible to use XSLT without XPath, and this applies to both XSLT 1.0 and XSLT 2.0. You will see many examples of XPath expressions used in the XSLT samples.

Running XSLT

As a new user way back in the first days of XSLT, I was very confused and frustrated because I did not know Java and had no clue what a jar file was (besides a repository for jam). Getting an

XSLT processor to run without applying magic or enlisting the aid of a Java expert was difficult, so I turned to the simplest tools available, XP and Saxon. XP, James Clark's original XSLT processor, is no longer being supported (and hasn't been updated in a few years). Saxon, on the other hand, was updated and maintained, and had a nice "easy" process for getting started with Instant Saxon. However, since Instant Saxon was tied to the Microsoft Java Engine, which is no longer shipped with new systems, I no longer use it or recommend it. Once I finally started using Java and understanding it a bit more, I was able to use the most prominent free XSLT engines: Saxon and Xalan.

So, to start out, download Java from Sun, and then download an XSLT processor. Use the following command line to run XSLT.

For Saxon:

```
java -jar c:\saxon\saxon.jar -o outputfile xmlSource stylesheet
```

For Xalan:

```
java -jar c:\xalan\bin\xalan.jar -in xmlSource
     -xsl stylesheet -out outputfile
```

Both processors suggest you set a classpath to point to the jar files, but you don't need to if you explicitly declare the path to the jar file on your command line.

XSLT 1.0

This section provides a brief overview of XSLT 1.0 basics. If you are already familiar with XSLT 1.0, please feel free to skip to the "Tips and Tricks for XSLT 1.0" section.

XSLT is the extensible stylesheet language for transformations, and along with another related standard, XPath (the XML Path language), it provides a mechanism to transform and manipulate XML data. XSLT is cross-platform, like XML, because it is written using XML.

XSLT is a template-based language, using **<xsl:template>** as the primary structure for processing XML elements. **<xsl:template>** is used to match elements in the XML documents using a *match* attribute, and processing occurs according to the rules contained within the template structure.

XSLT relies heavily on XPath, which defines the structure of expressions that are used in the content of the *match* attribute of **<xsl:template>** and other elements' attributes. These expressions are the key to accessing text, nodes, and other information in an XML document.

The most common use for an XSLT template is to match an XML element and transform it into another element, typically in HTML or another XML structure. For example, if you have titles in XML, you might want to transform them into HTML heading structures, such as **<h1>** or **<h2>**. To do this, you create a template matching the **<title>** element of the source document, and then generate the required output tags directly:

```
<xsl:template match="title">
   <h1>
       <xsl:apply-templates/>
   </h1>
</xsl:template>
```

The **<xsl:apply-templates/>** rule simply processes the content of the title according to any additional templates that you might have, or the default template that outputs the content of the title.

Title processing gets more complicated as you add layers or structure to your XML, for example, if you have chapter titles, section titles, table titles, and so on. In these cases, you qualify the match in your template to indicate which title you are matching; for example, matching on the chapter title as follows:

```
<xsl:template match="chapter/title">
   <h1>
      <xsl:apply-templates/>
   </h1>
</xsl:template>
```

For a section title you have a similar structure. You change the qualifier to match a section title, and the resulting HTML structure to **<h2>** as follows:

```
<xsl:template match="section/title">
   <h2>
      <xsl:apply-templates/>
   </h2>
</xsl:template>
```

XSLT 1.0 Elements

Elements in XSLT 1.0 are divided into three categories: document elements, top-level elements, and instruction elements. Document elements can only be at root level of the document, top-level elements are the direct children of the document elements, and instruction elements are children of the **<xsl:template>** element.

Document Elements

Document elements can consist of **<xsl:stylesheet>**, **<xsl:transform>**, or any Literal Result Element (LRE). The document element must contain the XSLT version and XSL namespace declaration. A Literal Result Element can be any XML element that does not belong to the XSL namespace, and will be copied to the output. If an LRE is the first element in a stylesheet, it must use the same required attributes as **<xsl:stylesheet>**. For instance, if the document element is **<html>** using

XSLT 1.0, it must contain the XSL namespace declaration and the version attribute for XSLT as follows:

```
<html xmlns:xsl="http://www.w3.org/1999/XSL/Transform" version="1.0">
```

Top-Level Elements

Top-level elements are elements that can live directly inside the document element, and are used for declaring variables and keys, setting output parameters, setting up document defaults, and for declaring template rules. These elements include the following:

- **<xsl:include>** enables an XSLT stylesheet to include templates and instructions from more than one stylesheet. The **<xsl:include>** element is the only top-level element with a specific syntactic place in the document order, and must always be the first child of the XSLT stylesheet document element.
- **<xsl:import>** enables an XSLT stylesheet to import templates and instructions from external stylesheets.
- **<xsl:strip-space>** removes any text nodes that contain only whitespace from the source tree prior to any further processing.
- **<xsl:preserve-space>** does not remove text nodes that contain only whitespace from the source tree.
- **<xsl:output>** serves to specify the kind of output from the XSLT stylesheet, other than XML. XSLT stylesheets can generate XML, as well as text or HTML.
- **<xsl:key>** declares a set of keys for each document and works with the **key()** function for indexing elements.
- **<xsl:decimal-format>** declares a specific format for decimal numbers and works with the **format-number()** function by controlling the interpretation of a pattern.
- **<xsl:namespace-alias>** provides functionality to declare one namespace URI as a replacement for another, which allows the use of different namespaces in the output.
- **<xsl:attribute-set>** defines a named set of attributes that can be used as a group to define attributes for an output element.
- **<xsl:variable>** defines a value that can be used in other XSLT elements in the stylesheet. Note that this element is allowed both as an instruction element and a top-level element.
- **<xsl:param>** defines a variable that can be modified by the XSLT element using it. Note that this element is allowed both as an instruction element and a top-level element.
- **<xsl:template>** is the pattern matching construct used to select elements in the source XML that are to be processed by the instructions contained in the template.

Instruction Elements

Instruction elements are elements that can only live directly inside a template, as a child of **<xsl:template>**, and are used for processing the nodes that are matched by the template. These elements include the following:

- **<xsl:apply-templates>** processes the contents of a matched element, whether it contains text or another element.
- **<xsl:call-template>** invokes a named template that is processed as if it is contained directly in the calling template.
- **<xsl:apply-imports>** invokes templates that exist in a separate stylesheet that is called using an **<xsl:import>** rule.
- **<xsl:for-each>** iterates over a sequence of elements identified by the select attribute.
- **<xsl:value-of>** extracts the text value, or contents, of an element identified in its select attribute.
- **<xsl:copy-of>** creates a copy of an element in the output.
- **<xsl:number>** creates a sequential numbering of element in the output.
- **<xsl:choose>** allows several conditions to be tested for the selective processing of elements. Using two child elements, **<xsl:when>** and **<xsl:otherwise>**, it provides alternatives to be used for testing and one default if no condition is met.
- **<xsl:if>** performs a Boolean test, evaluating an expression defined in the test attribute to return true or false.
- **<xsl:text>** adds text directly to the output.
- **<xsl:copy>** copies an element's tag to the output. Note that this does not copy the children or the attributes of the element.
- **<xsl:variable>** defines a value that can be used in other XSLT elements in the stylesheet. Note that this element is allowed both as an instruction element and a top-level element.
- **<xsl:param>** defines a variable that can be modified by the XSLT element using it. Note that this element is allowed both as an instruction element and a top-level element.
- **<xsl:message>** generates system messages that will be sent to a standard output defined by the processor.
- **<xsl:fallback>** provides an alternative process when a function is not available.
- **<xsl:processing-instruction>** generates XML processing instructions in the output.
- **<xsl:comment>** generates XML comments in the output.

- **<xsl:element>** is an alternative way to generate new elements in the output. The other option is to use LREs.
- **<xsl:attribute>** generates XML attributes for new elements in the output.

Push versus Pull

There are two ways to access information from an XML document with XSLT, usually referred to as push and pull methods. The push method uses the structure of the XML document to "push" content to the output, and the pull method uses a predefined output structure and specific XSLT elements to "pull" information from the XML document. Both methods are equally valid, but one might be more appropriate based on the situation.

When using the push method, template rules in XSLT match on the elements in the XML input file, usually starting with a match on the root, and following the element structure down to the actual text.

The pull method does not have any template rules, but only uses elements like **<xsl:value-of>** and **<xsl:for-each>** to extract information from specific locations.

For examples of both methods, see the following section on converting XML to HTML.

Using XSLT to Convert XML to HTML

One of the most common uses of XSLT is to convert XML to HTML for viewing on the Internet. The following examples, using a DOCBOOK article with nested sections structure as the input, show the two methods of processing XML information, push and pull.

The "Pull" Method

The easiest way to create HTML from XML is to create a template of the HTML as you would like it to appear, and then fill in the values you want from the XML document. This is called the "pull" method of writing XSLT.

```
<html version="4.0" xsl:version="1.0"
xmlns:xsl="http://www.w3.org/1999/XSL/Transform">
   <head>
      <title>My Doc TOC</title>
   </head>
   <body>
      <h1>Document Table of Contents</h1>
      <xsl:for-each select="article">
         <xsl:for-each select="section">
            <h2>
```

```
            <xsl:number format="1.1 "/>
            <xsl:value-of select="title"/>
          </h2>
          <xsl:for-each select="section">
            <h3>
              <xsl:number format="1.1 " level="multiple"/>
              <xsl:value-of select="title"/>
            </h3>
            <xsl:for-each select="section">
              <h4>
                <xsl:number format="1.1 " level="multiple"/>
                <xsl:value-of select="title"/>
              </h4>
              <xsl:for-each select="section">
                <h5>
                  <xsl:number format="1.1 " level="multiple"/>
                  <xsl:value-of select="title"/>
                </h5>
              </xsl:for-each>
            </xsl:for-each>
          </xsl:for-each>
        </xsl:for-each>
      </xsl:for-each>
  </body>
</html>
```

Notice that in this example, the XSL namespace is on the **<html>** element because this is the document element. The XSL version is also on this element, but it is prefixed by the XSL namespace to distinguish it from the HTML version. All the HTML elements are copied to the output directly, whereas the XSL elements are first processed and the results are then sent to the output.

The "Push" Method

Pushing information from an XML document to the output involves writing template rules using **<xsl:template>** to match each element type in the document. The structure of the input XML is matched from the root level down, as shown in the following example:

```
<xsl:stylesheet version="1.0"
xmlns:xsl="http://www.w3.org/1999/XSL/Transform">
  <xsl:output method="html"/>
```

```
    <xsl:template match="/">
       <xsl:apply-templates/>
    </xsl:template>
    <xsl:template match="chapter">
       <xsl:apply-templates/>
    </xsl:template>
    <xsl:template match="section">
       <xsl:apply-templates/>
    </xsl:template>
    <xsl:template match="chapter/title">
       <h1>
          <xsl:apply-templates/>
       </h1>
    </xsl:template>
    <xsl:template match="section/title">
       <h1>
          <xsl:apply-templates/>
       </h1>
    </xsl:template>
    <xsl:template match="para">
       <para>
          <xsl:apply-templates/>
       </para>
    </xsl:template>
</xsl:stylesheet>
```

Notice that you do not actually have to match on the text of the title or paragraph, because there is a built-in rule that sends the text to the output. If you want to disable the built-in rule, or change its behavior, you simply write a specific rule to overwrite it.

```
<xsl:template match="text()">
   <!-- hide the contents -->
</xsl:template>
or
<xsl:template match="text()"/>
```

Another built-in rule handles any elements that are not specifically matched , using **<xsl:apply-templates/>** to process the content of each unmatched element. So in this case, it is not really

necessary to match the root, the chapter, or the section. The same functionality can be accomplished with a smaller stylesheet:

```
<xsl:stylesheet version="1.0"
xmlns:xsl="http://www.w3.org/1999/XSL/Transform">
   <xsl:output method="html"/>
   <xsl:template match="chapter/title">
      <h1>
         <xsl:apply-templates/>
      </h1>
   </xsl:template>
   <xsl:template match="section/title">
      <h1>
         <xsl:apply-templates/>
      </h1>
   </xsl:template>
   <xsl:template match="para">
      <para>
         <xsl:apply-templates/>
      </para>
   </xsl:template>
</xsl:stylesheet>
```

Tips and Tricks for XSLT 1.0

The following sections provide sample XSLT constructs that are commonly used by members of the XML Guild.

Dynamic XML Transformation Using XSLT

Dynamic transformations of XML to HTML are the ideal way to display XML on the Web. However, not all browsers support XSLT references or embedding of stylesheets, although most of them now provide a default view for XML.

There are two ways to dynamically display XML with an XSLT stylesheet in a browser. One is to embed the stylesheet directly in the XML document, and the other is to insert a processing instruction that calls the stylesheet.

Embedded Stylesheets

Embedding an XSLT stylesheet directly in an XML document is an option described by the XSLT 1.0 specification. Unfortunately, most browsers don't support this, so it's not really useful.

However, if browsers eventually do support it, be sure to include the xml-stylesheet processing instruction as shown here, and to add a corresponding ID to the **<xsl:stylesheet>** element.

```
<?xml-stylesheet type="text/xsl" href="#mystyle"?>
```

Referenced Stylesheets

To reference an external stylesheet from an XML document, all you need to do is insert the xml-stylesheet processing instruction with the reference to the file. Browsers that support referenced stylesheets will read the external file and apply the styles to the document directly. Here is an example of a processing instruction for an external stylesheet.

```
<?xml-stylesheet type="text/xsl" href="../../book/preview-html.xsl"?>
```

xml-to-string.xsl

One stylesheet that I have used at one time or another for most of my clients has been xml-to-string.xsl, which simply serializes an XPath node-set (element) into an XPath string containing a well-formed XML representation. This is useful in contexts where XML has to be submitted to a server from the browser or displayed as code in a Web page.

The stylesheet contains a named template called **xml-to-string**. The template takes a **node-set** parameter that defaults to the current node. There are a number of other global parameters that can be overridden in an importing stylesheet.

The full set of stylesheets and samples can be found at **http://www.xmlportfolio.com/xml-to-string/**.

- xml-to-string.xsl: Serializes an XPath node-set (element) into an XPath string
- xml-to-string.txt: The result of xml-to-string.xsl applied to itself
- display-document.xsl: A simple use of xml-to-string.xsl
- display-document.html: The result of display-document.xsl applied to itself
- xml-to-string.html: The result of display-document.xsl applied to xml-to-string.xsl
- javascript-literals.xsl: A more sophisticated use of xml-to-string.xsl
- javascript-literals.html: The result of display-document.xsl applied to javascript-literals.xsl
- xml-to-string2.html: The result of javascript-literals.xsl applied to xml-to-string.xsl
- javascript-literals-result.html: The result of display-document.xsl applied to xml-to-string2.html

Namespace Declaration Normalizer

It has been asserted that a "best practice" for XML namespaces is to define all namespace prefix bindings at the document (root) element context. A program that forces all documents to follow this practice, that is, a "namespace normalizer", might be a useful thing to have around.

The normalize-namespaces.xsl stylesheet uses the **exsl:node-set()** extension function (which we shouldn't need in a future version of XSLT). This works fine with Saxon and should work with any other conformant XSLT processor that also implements the **node-set()** function in the EXSLT "common" module. To make it work with Xalan or other processors that support their own **node-set()** function, simply change the namespace URI of the function (and possibly its local name, for example, Xalan's is **nodeset()**).

The stylesheet itself is heavily commented throughout, providing a walk-through of the algorithm employed. For additional context, see Jonathan Borden's prose description of the same basic algorithm.

With respect to the XPath data model, this transformation does not simply produce an alternative serialization; that is, it is indeed a transformation. In the XPath data model, prefixes are significant and exactly where namespace bindings are, in scope, is significant. Those and only those two things are precisely what this transformation (possibly) changes. In other words, if your data model is not quite as low-level as XPath's model, this transformation indeed provides you an alternate serialization that perhaps is more human-readable, and, in any case, follows the "best practice" described previously.

Conversely, it must be used with care on XSLT stylesheets, XSDL schemas, and any other grammar that uses in-scope namespace bindings to expand QNames in attribute values or element content. It will not necessarily break them, but it could. In general, use of this stylesheet on any source document that uses QNames in attribute values is discouraged.

The following is an example of what this transformation does. Note that prefixes can be removed (**abc**) and created (**d0e7**).

Before:

```
<foo xmlns="default1">
   <abc:bar xmlns="default2andfoo" xmlns:abc="default1">
      <bat xmlns:foo="default2andfoo" foo:bar="value">
         <bang xmlns="default3">
            <abc:hi xmlns:xyz="unused-uri"/>
         </bang>
      </bat>
   </abc:bar>
</foo>
```

After (serialized by Saxon):

```
<foo xmlns="default1" xmlns:bar="default2andfoo" xmlns:d0e7="default3"
xmlns:xyz="unused-uri">
```

```
    <bar>
        <bat bar:bar="value">
            <d0e7:bang>
                <hi />
            </d0e7:bang>
        </bat>
    </bar>
</foo>
```

See http://www.xmlportfolio.com/namespaces/ for updates.

Excel Spreadsheet Cleanup

Microsoft's "Save as XML Spreadsheet" option is a great improvement over previous forms of output from its spreadsheets, but it still contains many formatting codes and information that is not really necessary in processing the data. This stylesheet that takes the raw output from MS Excel's XML output and turns it into something that applications can make sense of, creating rows and columns, and using the first row of the spreadsheet to generate the names of the cells. It is much easier to generate a simple row-cell format with generic cells, but this example shows the use of keys to accomplish more difficult tasks.

Given the input of a simple Excel spreadsheet:

Month	**Jan**	**Feb**	**Mar**	**Apr**	**May**
Income	10	50	39	87	92
Expense	30	58	22	87	99

The following stylesheet processes each row and column and creates a table with rows and cells:

```
<?xml version="1.0" encoding="iso-8859-1"?>
<xsl:stylesheet xmlns:xsl="http://www.w3.org/1999/XSL/Transform"
                xmlns:s="urn:schemas-microsoft-com:office:spreadsheet"
                xmlns:o="urn:schemas-microsoft-com:office:office"
                xmlns:x="urn:schemas-microsoft-com:office:excel"
                xmlns:ss="urn:schemas-microsoft-com:office:spreadsheet"
                xmlns:html="http://www.w3.org/TR/REC-html40"
                exclude-result-prefixes="s o x ss html"
                version="1.0">
<xsl:key name="names" use="count(../preceding-sibling::s:Cell) + 1"
  match="/s:Workbook/s:Worksheet[1]/s:Table[1]/s:Row[1]/s:Cell/s:Data"/>
```

```
<xsl:template match="/">
  <workbook>
    <xsl:for-each select="/s:Workbook/s:Worksheet">
      <worksheet>
        <xsl:for-each select="s:Table">
          <table>
            <xsl:for-each select="s:Row[position()>1]">
              <row>
                <xsl:for-each select="s:Cell">
                 <xsl:element name="{translate(key('names',position()),
                    '/&#010;', '-')}">
                    <xsl:value-of select="s:Data"/>
                  </xsl:element>
                </xsl:for-each>
              </row>
            </xsl:for-each>
          </table>
        </xsl:for-each>
      </worksheet>
    </xsl:for-each>
  </workbook>
</xsl:template>
</xsl:stylesheet>
```

The resulting format is a simple table, with rows containing cells explicitly named according to the first row of the spreadsheet:

```
<?xml version="1.0" encoding="utf-8"?>
<workbook>
   <worksheet>
      <table>
         <row>
            <Month>Income</Month>
            <Jan>10</Jan>
            <Feb>50</Feb>
            <Mar>39</Mar>
            <Apr>87</Apr>
            <May>92</May>
```

```
            </row>
            <row>
                <Month>Expense</Month>
                <Jan>30</Jan>
                <Feb>58</Feb>
                <Mar>22</Mar>
                <Apr>87</Apr>
                <May>99</May>
            </row>
        </table>
    </worksheet>
</workbook>
```

Reversing a Table

Have you ever had the problem where you have a table with rows and columns, but you really need them reversed? For example, what if your table is in the following format:

Income	10	50	39	87	92
Expense	30	58	22	87	99

But you really need it to be in the reverse orientation of row-column order:

Income	Expense
10	30
50	58
39	22
87	87
92	99

You start with the XML for the first example:

```
        <table>
            <row>
                <entry>Income</entry>
                <entry>10</entry>
                <entry>50</entry>
                <entry>39</entry>
```

```
        <entry>87</entry>
        <entry>92</entry>
     </row>
     <row>
        <entry>Expense</entry>
        <entry>30</entry>
        <entry>58</entry>
        <entry>22</entry>
        <entry>87</entry>
        <entry>99</entry>
     </row>
  </table>
```

Process it with the following XSLT code:

```
<xsl:stylesheet xmlns:xsl="http://www.w3.org/1999/XSL/Transform" version="1.0">
<xsl:output method="xml" indent="yes"/>
<xsl:template match="*">
   <xsl:copy>
      <xsl:copy-of select="@*"/>
      <xsl:apply-templates/>
   </xsl:copy>
</xsl:template>
<xsl:template match="table">
   <table>
      <xsl:for-each select="row[1]/*">
         <xsl:variable name="item"><xsl:value-of select="count(preceding-
            sibling::*) + 1"/></xsl:variable>
         <row>
            <xsl:apply-templates select="../../row/*[position() = $item]"/>
         </row>
      </xsl:for-each>
   </table>
</xsl:template>
</xsl:stylesheet>
```

This code creates a new row for each child of the first row, and populates it with the contents of each entry from all the following rows.

The result is a reversed table:

```
<table>
   <row>
      <entry>Income</entry>
      <entry>Expense</entry>
   </row>
   <row>
      <entry>10</entry>
      <entry>30</entry>
   </row>
   <row>
      <entry>50</entry>
      <entry>58</entry>
   </row>
   <row>
      <entry>39</entry>
      <entry>22</entry>
   </row>
   <row>
      <entry>87</entry>
      <entry>87</entry>
   </row>
   <row>
      <entry>92</entry>
      <entry>99</entry>
   </row>
</table>
```

Generating XSLT with XSLT

There are two common scenarios when you might want to generate XSLT stylesheets dynamically:

- To build a data mapping or localization stylesheet from a mapping expressed in XML.
- To create a validation stylesheet from a set of business constraints expressed in XML.

XSLT allows you to express transformation rules in a proprietary XML format, and then translate proprietary transformation rules into XSLT. To achieve this, you segregate XSLT into two layers: a business rules layer and an XSLT-related API layer. Note that for the same business rules expressed in XML, you could alternatively generate C#, Java, PHP, and other types of code to process the data. You will read about some of these examples later in this chapter.

So the use case is clear, but how can you use XSLT expressions to generate XSLT expressions so that the processor does not confuse the XSLT expressions that it needs to process with the XSLT expressions that it needs to generate? For example, somebody might erroneously expect the following snippet to output an XSLT template for each **<Hello>** element in the input document:

```
<xsl:template match="Hello">
   <!--XSLT instruction-->
  <xsl:template match="World">
     <!--Generate XSLT template for Hello element-->
    <Hello>World</Hello>
  </xsl:template>
</xsl:template>
```

Obviously, this will never work; first because **<xsl:template>** cannot contain another **<xsl:template>**, and second because the snippet is ambiguous—the processor will always interpret elements in the XSLT namespace as instructions. The only way around this is to create XSLT elements in another intermediate namespace and then, after the transformation is complete, swap the intermediate temporary namespace for real XSLT namespace. XSLT gives you the special **<namespace-alias>** instruction to accomplish exactly that:

```
<xsl:namespace-alias stylesheet-prefix = prefix | "#default" result-prefix =
   prefix | "#default" />
```

Here, ***stylesheet-prefix*** is the prefix of the intermediate namespace used in the stylesheet, and ***result-prefix*** is the prefix of the desired namespace. Consider two examples that represent simplified versions of what you might actually encounter in real life. We hope that after reading this section you will be able to quickly adopt the code to your particular needs.

Building a Data Mapping Stylesheet from a Mapping Expressed in XML

Suppose that you are building a financial application that analyzes an investment portfolio aggregated by asset classes X and Y. However, your incoming data is aggregated into a different asset structure: classes A, B, and C:

```
<ABCInvestments>
  <Assets class="A">1000000</Assets>
  <Assets class="B">2000000</Assets>
  <Assets class="C">4000000</Assets>
</ABCInvestments>
```

In order to avoid this problem, business analysts came up with an asset class mapping that allows you to translate portfolio information expressed in A, B, and C classes into portfolio information expressed in X and Y classes.

They asserted that all assets categorized as class A belong to class X; on average 60% of assets categorized as class B should be re-categorized as class X, the remaining 40% will become categorized as class Y; and lastly, 20% of class C assets will be remapped to class X, 80% of class C will be remapped to class Y. A modeler expressed this mapping in the following way:

```
<Map>
  <From class="A">
     <To class="X">1</To>
  </From>
  <From class="B">
     <To class="X">0.6</To>
     <To class="Y">0.4</To>
  </From>
  <From class="C">
     <To class="X">0.2</To>
     <To class="Y">0.8</To>
  </From>
<Map>
```

Now your task can be formulated in the following way: create an XSLT template that matches **<ABCInvestments>** with assets categorized in the A, B, C scheme and outputs **<XYInvestments>** categorized in the X and Y scheme. In the real world, **<XYInvestments>** might belong to a different namespace, but we will ignore these subtleties for now. Here is the XSLT that takes the previous XML asset mapping and translates it into a set of XSLT instructions that will reshuffle assets according to the new scheme:

```
<xsl:stylesheet version="1.0"
   xmlns:xsl="http://www.w3.org/1999/XSL/Transform" xmlns:a="a">
<xsl:output method="xml" version="1.0" encoding="UTF-8" indent="yes"/>
<xsl:namespace-alias stylesheet-prefix="a" result-prefix="xsl"/>
<xsl:templatc match="Map">
   <a:stylesheet version="1.0">
      <a:template match="ABCInvestments">
         <XYInvestments>
            <xsl:apply-templates select="Target"/>
         </XYInvestments>
```

```
10          </a:template>
11       </a:stylesheet>
12    </xsl:template>
13    <xsl:template match="Target">
14       <a:variable name="{@class}">
15          <xsl:attribute name="select">
16             <xsl:for-each select="Source">
17                <xsl:text>Assets[@class='</xsl:text>
18                <xsl:value-of select="@class"/>']*<xsl:value-of
                        select="."/>
19                <xsl:if test="position() != last()"> + </xsl:if>
20             </xsl:for-each>
21          </xsl:attribute>
22       </a:variable>
23       <a:if test="${@class} > 0">
24         <Assets class="{@class}"><a:value-of select="${@class}"/></Assets>
25       </a:if>
26    </xsl:template>
27    </xsl:stylesheet>
```

The template on line 8 matches the root **<Map>** element of the mapping file and generates the **<a:stylesheet>** element. Prefix "a" points to an intermediate namespace and, according to the **<xsl:namespace-alias>** instruction, will be replaced with the "xsl" namespace prefix pointing to the "http://www.w3.org/1999/XSL/Transform" namespace after the transformation is done.

Let's go further. The code on line 6 generates a template that will latter match the **<ABCInvestments>** element of the source A,B,C document and output required **<XYInvestments>** element that the application understands. Following the XSLT flow, line 14 generates XSLT expressions to get the **<XYInvestments>** content. Here is the intermediate stylesheet generated from the mapping file:

```
<xsl:stylesheet version="1.0"
    xmlns:xsl="http://www.w3.org/1999/XSL/Transform">
<xsl:template match="ABCInvestments">
   <XYInvestments>
      <xsl:variable name="X" select="Assets[@class='A']*1 +
         Assets[@class='B']*0.7"/>
      <xsl:if test="$X &gt; 0">
         <Assets class="X">
```

```
                <xsl:value-of select="$X"/>
            </Assets>
        </xsl:if>
        <xsl:variable name="Y" select="Assets[@class='B']*0.3 +
            Assets[@class='C']*1"/>
        <xsl:if test="$Y &gt; 0">
            <Assets class="Y">
                <xsl:value-of select="$Y"/>
            </Assets>
        </xsl:if>
    </XYInvestments>
</xsl:template>
</xsl:stylesheet>
```

Notice how the example generated an **<xsl:variable>** element for each class X and Y. The variables' names are the same as corresponding class names, and their values are equal to the summary values of assets of the corresponding classes. Each variable is tested against zero. If the test is successful, a corresponding **<Asset>** element is inserted in the remapped **<XYInvestments>** portfolio summary. Here is the final outcome of the transformation pipe:

```
<XYInvestments>
    <Assets class="X">2400000</Assets>
    <Assets class="Y">4600000</Assets>
</XYInvestments>
```

Parsing Strings with XSLT

You have seen that XSLT works well if you want to manipulate XML elements to translate XML nodes from one XML representation to another. However, XSLT can also be used on a lower level to manipulate string values inside the text nodes of an XML document. Consider the following example.

Really Simple Syndication (RSS) is an XML format for syndicating digests of Web resources. Simply speaking, an RSS feed can represent a response to a Web query. For example, RSS responses to queries like: "What's new on your website?", "What is the latest news about global warming?", and "What is the latest sport news?" will result in a channel containing a series of information items representing Web resources. You can subscribe to a Web feed from your favorite website and receive updates using one of the freely available RSS readers. Here is an example of an RSS feed:

```
<rss version="2.0">
    <channel>
```

```
3          <title>Cogitative News</title>
4          <link>http://news.cogx.com</link>
5          <description>Cogitech Inc's news.</description>
6          <language>en-gb</language>
7          <item>
8             <title>XML Guild Advanced XML</title>
9              <author>XML Guild</author>
10             <description>XML Guild delivers the Advanced XML book - a great
                  reference for managers and developers.</description>
11              <link>http://www.xmlguild.org/AdvancedXML</link>
12              <pubDate>Dec-03-2006</pubDate>
13              <category>XML</category>
14              <category>XSLT</category>
15          </item>
16          <item>
17         ...
18          </item>
19         ...
20        </channel>
21    </rss>
```

An RSS feed contains a channel that has a title, a link to the channel's home, a description, and a list of items. For each linked resource, RSS publishers supply metadata such as resource title, author, pub date, a set of subject categories, and so on. Only the first item is shown here; the rest are omitted for brevity. Note how one item can be associated with more than one category (lines 13 and 14).

Media RSS extends the RSS standard to support syndication of video and audio media assets. For more information on the RSS and Media RSS standards, see http://blogs.law.harvard.edu/tech/rss and http://search.yahoo.com/mrss. The following is a sample Media RSS fragment from a YouTube feed:

```
<rss version="2.0" xmlns:media="http://search.yahoo.com/mrss">
   <channel>
      <title>YouTube :: Tag // little britain</title>
      <link>http://youtube.com/rss/tag/little+britain.rss</link>
      <description>Videos tagged with little britain</description>
      <item>
         <author>ilovetomc</author>
```

```
8           <title>little britain</title>
9           <link>http://youtube.com/?v=lPkxhuUFPio</link>
10           <description>...</description>
11           <guid isPermaLink="true">http://youtube.com/?v=lPkxhuUFPio
               </guid>
12           <pubDate>Sun, 13 Aug 2006 02:38:12 -0700</pubDate>
13           <media:player url="http://youtube.com/?v=lPkxhuUFPio" />
14           <media:thumbnail url="http://sjl-
                static12.sjl.youtube.com/vi/lPkxhuUFPio/
                2.jpg" width="120" height="90" />
15            <media:title>little britain</media:title>
16            <media:category label="Tags">britain, funny,
                 hilarious</media:category>
17            <media:credit>ilovetomc</media:credit>
18            <enclosure url="http://youtube.com/v/lPkxhuUFPio.swf"
                 length="95" type="application/x-shockwave-flash" />
19         </item>
20  ...
21      </channel>
22  </rss>
```

Media RSS adds metadata properties from the http://search.yahoo.com/mrss namespace to RSS items. Note that the channel link is a **REST** query definition of the returned channel: *find all videos containing "little" and "britain"*. Again, only the first item is shown here; the rest are omitted for brevity. For each item YouTube supplies, it returns a title (line 8), a link to the media item location (line 9), a thumbnail image of the video (line 14), and a space-delimited list of categories/tags (line 16), among other things. Discussion of RSS and Media RSS elements and the use of XML namespaces is outside of the scope of this chapter and we invite you look it up on your own. It is worth cautioning that the semantics of the **<pubDate>** and **<author>** elements here are ambiguous—they refer to a user who added the resource to YouTube, not the people who actually created it.

Now let's state the problem. In the classic RSS, as you saw in the previous RSS example, each category/tag deserves a separate **<category>** element, and in Media RSS, a single **<media:category>** element contains a space-delimited list of all applicable tags/categories (line 16 in the previous Media RSS fragment). Suppose that you want to convert **<media:category>** in the you tube's Media RSS to a classic RSS format where all tags are listed as separate **<category>** elements, leaving the rest of XML elements as they are.

In other words, you want to translate the YouTube Media RSS fragment to this:

```
1  <rss version="2.0" xmlns:media="http://search.yahoo.com/mrss">
2     <channel>
3        <title>YouTube :: Tag // little britain</title>
4        <link>http://youtube.com/rss/tag/little+britain.rss</link>
5        <description>Videos tagged with little britain</description>
6        <item>
7           <author>ilovetomc</author>
8           <title>little britain</title>
9           <link>http://youtube.com/?v=lPkxhuUFPio</link>
10           <description>...</description>
11          <guid isPermaLink="true">http://youtube.com/?v=lPkxhuUFPio</guid>
12           <pubDate>Sun, 13 Aug 2006 02:38:12 -0700</pubDate>
13           <media:player url="http://youtube.com/?v=lPkxhuUFPio" />
14           <media:thumbnail url="http://sjl-static12.
              sjl.youtube.com/vi/lPkxhuUFPio/
              2.jpg" width="120" height="90" />
15           <media:title>little britain</media:title>
16           <category>britain</category>
17           <category>funny</category>
18           <category>hilarious</category>
19           <media:credit>ilovetomc</media:credit>
20           <enclosure url="http://youtube.com/v/lPkxhuUFPio.swf"
                length="95" type="application/x-shockwave-flash" />
21        </item>
22      ...
23      </channel>
24  </rss>
```

Note how each subject procures its own category/tag element (lines 16–18). The following XSLT stylesheet does the job:

```
<xsl:stylesheet version="1.0"
   xmlns:xsl="http://www.w3.org/1999/XSL/Transform"
   xmlns:media="http://search.yahoo.com/mrss">
   <xsl:output method="xml" version="1.0" encoding="UTF-8" indent="yes"/>
   <xsl:template match="*|@*|text()">
      <xsl:copy>
```

```
5            <xsl:apply-templates select="@*|text()|*"/>
6         </xsl:copy>
7      </xsl:template>
8      <xsl:template match="media:category">
9         <xsl:call-template name="split-tags">
10          <xsl:with-param name="tags" select="normalize-space(.)"/>
11       </xsl:call-template>
12      </xsl:template>
13      <xsl:template name="split-tags">
14         <xsl:param name="tags"/>
15         <xsl:if test="string-length($tags)>0">
16            <category>
17            <xsl:value-of select="substring-before(concat($tags,' '),' ')"/>
18            </category>
19            <xsl:call-template name="split-tags">
20               <xsl:with-param name="tags" select="substring-after
                  ($tags,'')"/>
21            </xsl:call-template>
22         </xsl:if>
23      </xsl:template>
24   </xsl:stylesheet>
```

Let's see how this stylesheet works. The default template on lines 3–7 matches all elements, attributes, and text nodes and instructs the processor to insert identically named elements or attributes in the resulting document tree, and then to recursively apply templates for each child element, attribute, or text node. Text elements are simply copied. However, not all elements will match the default template: the XSLT processor will match the **<media:category>** element with the template on line 8. Here, you split Media RSS **<media:category>** elements into separate RSS **<category>** elements. This is a more specific match condition and the XSLT processor will assign it a higher priority and hence apply this template instead of the default one.

Inside this template, you substitute the **<media:category>** element with the results of calling the named **split-tags** template. The parameter **$tags** of the **split-tags** template is initialized with a trimmed value of the **<media:category>** (see line 10). Inside the **split-tags** template, the program checks that **$tags** parameter is not empty (line 15), and otherwise does nothing. If the **$tags** parameter is not empty, the program creates a **<category>** element in the resulting document tree with a value of the first tag-text string before the first occurrence of a space character (see line 17). On lines 19–21 the **split-tags** template calls itself, but the **$tags** parameter is now shorter; the first tag is removed from it. This recursive loop ends when there aren't any tags left in the **$tags** string. Try it on your own.

Using XSLT to Convert XML to Java/C# Code

There are many tools that can generate Java or C# classes from a schema. Suppose that you want a tool that will generate not only class definitons, but will also beef-up generated classes with code. In order not to overwhelm you further with complicated examples, this section reuses XML asset mapping excesise from the previous section, but this time it generates programming code in Java and C#. This class will similarly translate ABC portfolio into XY scheme. The following XSLT generates the Java class:

```
<xsl:stylesheet version="1.0"
     xmlns:xsl="http://www.w3.org/1999/XSL/Transform">
  <xsl:output method="text" version="1.0"/>
  <xsl:template match="Map">
class Mapper{
  class XY{
    double X;
    double Y;
  }
  class ABC{
    double A;
    double B;
    double C;
  }
  public XY MapABC2XY(ABC abc){
    XY xy = new XY();
      <xsl:apply-templates select="Target"/>
    return xy;
  }
  public void Test(){
    ABC abc = new ABC();
    abc.A=100;
    abc.B=100;
    abc.C=100;
    XY xy = MapABC2XY(abc);
    System.out.println(xy.X +" : " + xy.Y);
  }
```

```
27      public static void main(String[] args) {
28        Mapper mapper = new Mapper();
29        mapper.Test();
30      }
31  }
32    </xsl:template>
33    <xsl:template match="Target">
34      xy.<xsl:value-of select="@class"/>
          =<xsl:apply-templates select="Source"/>;
35    </xsl:template>
36    <xsl:template match="Source">
37      <xsl:text/>abc.<xsl:value-of select="@class"/>
38      <xsl:if test=". != 1"> * <xsl:value-of select="."/></xsl:if>
39      <xsl:if test="position() != last()"> + </xsl:if>
40    </xsl:template>
41  </xsl:stylesheet>
```

Note how line 2 specifies that the output method is text, unlike XML, as is in most other examples in this chapter. Line 16 creates programming instructions for converting between schemes. Line 34 iterates over all **<Source>** elements by matching template on line 36. Instruction **<xsl:text/>** on line 37 is used to avoid empty space and line breaks in front of summands. Remember that the output is text (not XML) and whitespace may be important. Line 38 multiplies the amount of the source portfolio by the corresponding weight if it is different from 1. Line 39 requests a plus sign between summands if it is not the last **<Source>** element.

In lines 32-40, notice the resemblance with the stylesheet from the previous section. In fact, the purpose of these stylesheets is similar: to generate code for translation between portfolios. Here is the generated code:

```
class Mapper{
  public class XY{
    public double X;
    public double Y;
  }
  public class ABC{
    public double A;
    public double B;
    public double C;
  }
```

```
11    public XY MapABC2XY(ABC abc){
12      XY xy = new XY();
13      xy.X=abc.A + abc.B * 0.7;
14      xy.Y=abc.B * 0.3 + abc.C;
15      return xy;
16    }
17    public void Test(){
18      ABC abc = new ABC();
19      abc.A=100;
20      abc.B=100;
21      abc.C=100;
22      XY xy = MapABC2XY(abc);
23      System.out.println(xy.X +" : " + xy.Y);
24    }
25    public static void main(String[] args) {
26      Mapper mapper = new Mapper();
27      mapper.Test();
28    }
29  }
```

Lines 13 and 14 contains the output of the target template on line 33 of the stylesheet. The example skiped generation of XY and ABC classes definitions on lines 2-9 in order to keep this simple. Currious readers might try doing it themselves. XML Web Applications Template Library at http://www.cogx.com/?si=urn:cogx:ps:xwatl gives some insight into other ideas related to programming code generation with XSLT, such as SQL, DDL, JavaScript, Python, and so on. Here is the output from running the previous console application:

```
C:>java Mapper
170.0 : 130.0
```

This code works in C# with a few minor tweaks. For readers more fluent in .NET, here is the XSLT stylesheet that generates C# code:

```
<xsl:stylesheet version="1.0"
  xmlns:xsl="http://www.w3.org/1999/XSL/Transform" xmlns:a="a">
  <xsl:output method="text" version="1.0"/>
  <xsl:template match="Map">
using System;
class Mapper{
  public struct XY{
```

```
      public double X;
      public double Y;
    }
    public struct ABC{
      public double A;
      public double B;
      public double C;
    }
    public XY MapABC2XY(ABC abc){
      XY xy = new XY();
        <xsl:apply-templates select="Target"/>
      return xy;
    }
    public void Test(){
      ABC abc = new ABC();
      abc.A=100;
      abc.B=100;
      abc.C=100;
      XY xy = MapABC2XY(abc);
      Console.Out.WriteLine(xy.X +" : " + xy.Y);
    }
    public static void Main(String[] args){
      Mapper mapper = new Mapper();
      mapper.Test();
    }
  }
    </xsl:template>
    <xsl:template match="Target">
      xy.<xsl:value-of select="@class"/>
          =<xsl:apply-templates select="Source"/>;
    </xsl:template>
    <xsl:template match="Source">
      <xsl:text/>abc.<xsl:value-of select="@class"/>
      <xsl:if test=". != 1"> * <xsl:value-of select="."/></xsl:if>
      <xsl:if test="position() != last()"> + </xsl:if>
    </xsl:template>
  </xsl:stylesheet>
```

XSLT Example of "for i=1 to n do"

A very common programming construct that does not have an intuitive rule in XSLT is **for i=1 to n**, where a process is repeated as many times as necessary, based on the input start and end values, *i* and *n*. This can be accomplished using a recursive template in XSLT that continuously calls itself until the condition is exhausted. Using parameters, you pass the initial values from the calling template, which are then updated by the process template on each iteration. The template uses an **<xsl:choose>** element to check for the updated values on each pass.

```
<xsl:template match="/">
   <xsl:call-template name="counter">
      <xsl:with-param name="start-value">1</xsl:with-param>
      <xsl:with-param name="end-value">10</xsl:with-param>
   </xsl:call-template>
</xsl:template>
<xsl:template name="counter">
   <xsl:param name="start-value"/>
   <xsl:param name="end-value"/>
   <xsl:choose>
      <xsl:when test="$start-value &lt; $end-value + 1">
     <!-- Insert the rules that should be applied on each pass of the template
         here. -->
         <xsl:call-template name="counter">
            <xsl:with-param name="start-value" select="$start-value + 1"/>
            <xsl:with-param name="end-value" select="$end-value"/>
         </xsl:call-template>
      </xsl:when>
      <xsl:otherwise>
         <xsl:message>END</xsl:message>
      </xsl:otherwise>
   </xsl:choose>
</xsl:template>
```

Muenchian Method for Grouping

Grouping is a common problem in XSLT 1.0 stylesheets. How do you take a list of elements and arrange them into groups? One of the most common situations in which it occurs is when you are getting XML output from a database. The database usually gives you results that are structured according to the records in the database. If it's an address book, for example, it might give you something like this:

```
<records>
   <contact
id="0001"><title>Mr</title><forename>John</forename><surname>Smith</surname>
</contact>
   <contact
id="0002"><title>Dr</title><forename>Amy</forename><surname>Jones</surname>
</contact>
   . . .
</records>
```

The problem is how to turn this flat input into a number of lists, grouped by surname, to give something like this:

```
Jones,
   Amy (Dr)
   Brian (Mr)
Smith,
   Fiona (Ms)
   John (Mr)
```

There are two steps in getting to a solution:

- Identifying what the surnames are
- Getting all the contacts that have the same surname

Identifying what the surnames are involves identifying one contact with each surname within the XML, which may as well be the first one that appears in it. One way to find these is to get those contacts that do not have a surname that is the same as a surname of any previous contact:

```
contact[not(surname = preceding-sibling::contact/surname)]
```

Once these contacts have been identified, it's easy to find out their surnames and to gather together all the contacts that have the same surname:

```
<xsl:apply-templates select="/records/contact[surname = current()/surname]" />
```

The trouble with this method is that it involves two XPaths that take a lot of processing for big XML sources (such as those from big databases). Searching through all the preceding siblings with the preceding-siblings axis takes a long time if you're near the end of the records. Similarly, getting all the contacts with a certain surname involves looking at every single contact each time. This makes it very inefficient.

The Muenchian method is a method developed by Steve Muench for performing these functions in a more efficient way, using *keys*. Keys work by assigning a key value to a node and giving you easy access to that node through the key value. If there are lots of nodes that have the same key value, all those nodes are retrieved when you use that key value. Effectively, this means that if you want to group a set of nodes according to a particular property of the node, you can use keys to group them together.

Let's take the address book example. You want to group the contacts according to their surname, so you create a key that assigns each contact a key value that is the surname given in the record. The nodes that you want to group should be matched by the pattern in the match attribute. The key value that you want to use is the one that's given by the **use** attribute:

```
<xsl:key name="contacts-by-surname" match="contact" use="surname" />
```

Once this key is defined, if you know a surname, you can quickly access all the contacts that have that surname. For example,

```
Key('contacts-by-surname', 'Smith')
```

will give all the records that have the surname 'Smith'. So it's easy to satisfy the second thing you needed to do (to get all the contacts with the same surname):

```
<xsl:apply-templates select="key('contacts-by-surname', surname)" />
```

The first thing that you needed to do, though, was identify what the surnames were, which involved identifying the first contact within the XML that had a particular surname. You can use keys again here. You know that a contact will be part of a list of nodes that is given when you use the key on its surname: the question is whether it will be the first in that list (which is arranged in document order) or further down. You're only interested in the records that are first in the list.

Finding out whether a contact is first in the list returned by the key involves comparing the contact node with the node that is first in the list returned by the key. There are a couple of generic methods for testing whether two nodes are identical:

1. Compare the unique identifiers generated for the two nodes using **generate-id()**:

   ```
   contact[generate-id() generate-id(key('contacts-by-surname', surname)[1])]
   ```

2. See whether a node-set made up of the two nodes has one or two nodes in it. Nodes can't be repeated in a node-set, so if there's only one node in it, they must be the same node:

   ```
   contact[count(. | key('contacts-by-surname', surname)[1]) = 1]
   ```

Once you've identified the groups, you can sort them in whatever order you like. Similarly, you can sort the nodes within the group however you want. Here is a template, then, that creates the output that you specified from the XML you were given from the database:

```
<xsl:key name="contacts-by-surname" match="contact" use="surname" />
<xsl:template match="records">
```

```
    <xsl:for-each select="contact[count(. | key('contacts-by-surname',
       surname)[1]) = 1]">
       <xsl:sort select="surname" />
       <xsl:value-of select="surname" />,<br />
       <xsl:for-each select="key('contacts-by-surname', surname)">
          <xsl:sort select="forename" />
          <xsl:value-of select="forename"/>(<xsl:value-of select="title" />)<br />
       </xsl:for-each>
    </xsl:for-each>
</xsl:template>
```

The Muenchian method is usually the best XSLT 1.0 method to use for grouping nodes together from the XML source to your output because it doesn't involve trawling through large numbers of nodes, and it's therefore more efficient. It's especially beneficial when you have a flat output from a database, for example, that you need to structure into some kind of hierarchy. It can be applied in any situation where you are grouping nodes according to a property of the node that is retrievable through an XPath.

The downside is that using keys can be quite memory-intensive, because all the nodes and their key values have to be kept in memory. It can also be quite complicated to use keys where the nodes that you want to group are spread across different source documents.

XSLT 2.0 adds facilities that solve the problem of grouping in a neat simple way. See the section on XSLT 2.0 for more information.

Handling Character Entities in XSLT 1.0

HTML users are used to having a lot of named character entities available. They can use ** ** to insert a non-breaking space, **©** to insert a copyright symbol, and **€** to insert the symbol for the new European currency, the Euro. Almost all of these symbols are *not* automatically defined in XML. To make them available, you have to use a DTD that defines them, or you have to define them in the internal DTD subset of your document. Either way, you need to have a DOCTYPE declaration in your XML documents, which is not appropriate for documents that only need to be well-formed, and for which a DTD would only add more work without creating more value.

In particular, XML validation tools often use the presence of a DOCTYPE declaration as an indication that DTD validation should be used. This is a problem if you are using W3C XML schemas for your validation, and only have a DOCTYPE for the purposes of enabling named characters in your XML documents. It means that you will not get the validation results that you expect. This is the kind of problem that can lead to a lot of wasted time for newer XML users.

The right way to give human-readable names to special characters is to define XML elements for them. You can then process these elements out at the last moment and replace them with the appropriate numeric character entities. The disadvantage to this approach is that it only works with element content, not with attribute values. However, it does allow you to work with purely well-formed XML, without any DTD or DOCTYPE required.

If you have a more traditional XML implementation where your characters are already defined, you can actually redefine the character entities in a separate entity file similar to the definitions in the ISO character set, and just change the reference in your DTD to point to this new file. Here is an example of a character entity redefinition, using **charent** as the element name:

```
<!ENTITY euro "<charent name="euro"/>" >
```

This would replace the ISO definition:

```
<!ENTITY euro   CDATA "&#8364;">
```

xmlchar: A Special Character Library

In 2002, Anthony Coates and Zarella Rendon wrote an XSLT library of special character elements called **xmlchar** that could be freely used by anyone by simply importing into a stylesheet. Available at http://xmlchar.sourceforge.net/, the **xmlchar** set provides XML elements for all of the special characters defined in HTML 4, and shows by example how to extend the set to other special characters.

The **xmlchar** special character element set uses a namespace prefix **ch** (namespace **xmlns:ch="http://xmlchar.sf.net/ns#)** to separate the special character elements from other content in a user's document.

For example, the following XML sample contains the **xmlchar** elements for the currency symbols for the British Pound (£) and the European Euro (€). It also includes some non-breaking spaces to provide double-spacing between sentences:

```
<html xmlns:ch="http://xmlchar.sf.net/ns#">
   <body>
      <p>My sandwich cost <ch:pound/>2.</p>
      <p>Really?<ch:nbsp/>You were cheated.<ch:nbsp/>My sandwich only cost
<ch:euro/>2.</p>
   </body>
</html>
```

When you apply the **xmlchar** stylesheets to this, you get this HTML result, which has the correct HTML **£**, **€**, and ** ** entities.

```
<html>
   <body>
      <p>My sandwich cost &pound;2.</p>
      <p>Really?  You were cheated.  My sandwich only cost
&euro;2.</p>
   </body>
</html>
```

The **xmlchar** stylesheets are designed to be used in combination with your existing XSLT stylesheets. Simply use **<xsl:import>** to call in the html4-all.xsl stylesheet from the xmlchar-1.1 directory. Any character elements you've added to your document will be converted to the appropriate character entity in the output. The stylesheet that was used for this example is as follows:

```
<xsl:transform version="1.0" xmlns:xsl="http://www.w3.org/1999/XSL/Transform">
   <xsl:import href="xmlchar-1.1/html4-all.xsl"/>
   <xsl:param name="xmlcharNsUri" select="'http://xmlchar.sf.net/ns#'"/>
   <xsl:output method="html"/>
   <!-- You need to explicitly call the imported xmlchar -->
   <!-- templates if they would be overridden by the -->
   <!-- templates in the importing file, -->
   <!-- as is the case here. -->
   <!-- This can always be avoided, though. -->
   <xsl:template match="*[namespace-uri() = $xmlcharNsUri]">
      <xsl:apply-imports/>
   </xsl:template>
   <!-- Everything from here copies the non-xmlchar -->
   <!-- content unchanged from the input to the output. -->
   <xsl:template match="text()|comment()|processing-instruction()">
      <xsl:copy/>
   </xsl:template>
   <xsl:template match="*">
      <xsl:text/>
      <xsl:element name="{name()}" namespace="{namespace-uri()}">
         <xsl:for-each select="@*">
            <xsl:copy/>
         </xsl:for-each>
         <xsl:apply-templates/>
```

```
      </xsl:element>
   </xsl:template>
</xsl:transform>
```

Preserving xmlchar Elements

When an XML document passes through a series of processing stages, the **xmlchar** elements will normally be preserved until the final stage. If your XSLT stylesheets have been designed to copy elements by default, the **xmlchar** elements will be preserved as required.

Otherwise, you can import the **xmlchar copy** stylesheets to make sure that **xmlchar** elements are copied from input to output. Consider the following example. The input document is

```
<html xmlns:ch="http://xmlchar.sf.net/ns#">
   <head>
      <title>XML Char 1.0 - Test</title>
   </head>
   <body>
      <h1>XML Char 1.0 Test</h1>
      <p>My sandwich cost <ch:pound/>2.</p>
      <p>Really?<ch:nbsp/>You were cheated.<ch:nbsp/>My sandwich only cost
<ch:euro/>2.</p>
   </body>
</html>
```

This is to translate from XHTML+xmlchar into DocBook+xmlchar. Because DOCBOOK and XHTML do not use the same elements, the stylesheet cannot be set to copy content by default. Instead, the **xmlchar copy** stylesheet html4-all-copy.xsl is imported into the stylesheet.

```
<xsl:transform version="1.0" xmlns:xsl="http://www.w3.org/1999/XSL/Transform">
   <xsl:import href="xmlchar-1.1/html4-all-copy.xsl"/>
   <xsl:output method="xml"/>
   <xsl:template match="/html">
      <xsl:text/>
      <article xmlns:ch="http://xmlchar.sf.net/ns#">
         <title>
            <xsl:apply-templates select="/html/head/title/node()"/>
         </title>
         <xsl:for-each select="/html/body/h1">
            <section>
               <title>
                  <xsl:apply-templates select="current()/node()"/>
```

```
                </title>
                <xsl:variable name="theTitle" select="."/>
                <xsl:apply-templates select = "/html/body/*[preceding-
                   sibling::h1[text() = $theTitle]]"/>
             </section>
          </xsl:for-each>
       </article>
    </xsl:template>
    <xsl:template match="p">
       <para>
          <xsl:apply-templates/>
       </para>
    </xsl:template>
</xsl:transform>
```

The result is as follows:

```
<article xmlns:ch="http://xmlchar.sf.net/ns#">
   <title>XML Char 1.0 - Test</title>
   <section>
      <title>XML Char 1.0 Test</title>
      <para>My sandwich cost <ch:pound/>2.</para>
      <para>Really?<ch:nbsp/>You were cheated.<ch:nbsp/>My sandwich only cost
<ch:euro/>2.</para>
   </section>
</article>
```

The **xmlchar** elements have been preserved in the output as required. In a later part of the document process, the **xmlchar** elements would be transformed into character entities to produce standard DOCBOOK.

Converting Legacy Documents with Character Entities

If you want to convert legacy XML documents containing named HTML 4 character entities to use the **xmlchar** elements instead, you can use the **xmlchar** entity definitions. These definitions expand the entities into their matching **xmlchar** elements.

> **Warning**
> The xmlchar entity definitions must not be used on XML documents that contain character entities in attribute values. Doing so will produce badly formed XML.

Consider the following legacy document, which contains named character entities. The document is modified to import the xmlchar entities.

```
<!DOCTYPE html [
<!ENTITY % html.4.entities SYSTEM "xmlchar-1.1/html4-all.ent"> %html.4.
   entities; ]>
<html xmlns:ch="http://xmlchar.sf.net/ns#">
   <head>
      <title>XML Char 1.1 - Test</title>
   </head>
   <body>
      <h1>XML Char 1.1 Test</h1>
      <p>My sandwich cost &pound;2.</p>
     <p>Really? You were cheated. My sandwich only cost &euro;2.</p>
   </body>
</html>
```

The entities will now be expanded into xmlchar elements when this file is parsed. To show that it works, consider this file, which is transformed by the following "copy-through" XSLT stylesheet

```
<xsl:transform version="1.0" xmlns:xsl="http://www.w3.org/1999/XSL/Transform">
   <xsl:output method="xml" encoding="ISO-8859-1"/>
   <xsl:template match="/html">
      <xsl:text/>
      <html xmlns:ch="http://xmlchar.sf.net/ns#">
         <xsl:apply-templates/>
      </html>
   </xsl:template>
   <xsl:template match="text()|comment()|processing-instruction()">
      <xsl:copy/>
   </xsl:template>
   <xsl:template match="*">
      <xsl:text/>
      <xsl:element name="{name()}" namespace="{namespace-uri()}">
         <xsl:for-each select="@*">
            <xsl:copy/>
         </xsl:for-each>
         <xsl:apply-templates/>
      </xsl:element>
```

```
    </xsl:template>
</xsl:transform>
```

In the resulting file, the character entities have been converted to **xmlchar** elements as required:

```
<html xmlns:ch="http://xmlchar.sf.net/ns#">
   <head>
      <title>XML Char 1.1 - Test</title>
   </head>
   <body>
      <h1>XML Char 1.1 Test</h1>
      <p>My sandwich cost <ch:pound/>2.</p>
      <p>Really?<ch:nbsp/>You were cheated.<ch:nbsp/>My sandwich only cost
<ch:euro/>2.</p>
   </body>
</html>
```

XPath 1.0 Subtleties

XPath is a pivotal part of using XSLT because all of the contents of XSLT attributes are XPath expressions. However, the use of XPath is not always straightforward.

Using position() Properly

Many people new to XPath mistakenly assume that **position()** can be used anywhere in an XPath expression to get an accurate sequential number. It is true that **position()** returns the numeric position of a node in a specific node-set, but when you use it on the entire input document tree, some unexpected things are counted.

Given the following example and XSLT template:

```
<section>
  <para>paragraph content</para>
  <para>paragraph content</para>
  <para>paragraph content</para>
</section>

<xsl:template match="para">
<xsl:value-of select="position()"/><xsl:text>, </xsl:text>
</xsl:template>
```

The result of using **position()** directly on part of the input document is as follows:

```
2, 4, 6,
```

What's going on? You would expect the numbers to be sequential, but because of the whitespace nodes between the **<para>** elements in the tree, extra nodes are counted. If the line breaks and tabs were removed (or if you used **<xsl:strip-space elements="*"/>**) you would get what you expected:

```
1, 2, 3,
```

However, if the node set in the input document has different elements, for example, when adding a list after the second paragraph, your counting would again break:

```
<section><para>paragraph content</para><para>paragraph content</para>
   <list>list content</list><para>paragraph content</para></section>
```

This returns:

```
1, 2, 4,
```

You don't always have control over your input document to remove whitespace, and in any case, modifying the input is never a good solution. The best approach is to avoid using **position()** and use **count()** or **<xsl:number>** to get an accurate view of your numbering:

```
<xsl:template match="para">
<xsl:number/><xsl:text>, </xsl:text>
</xsl:template>
```

This returns:

```
1, 2, 3,
```

However, if you don't actually want to use the number in the output, getting the accurate position of a node is best done with **count()**:

```
<xsl:value-of select="count(preceding-sibling::para) + 1"/>
```

This returns:

```
1, 2, 3,
```

Because **count()** is confined to the XPath expression, the result can then be used for other calculations or further processing, as is shown in the following **<xsl:if>**:

```
<xsl:if test="count(preceding-sibling::para) + 1 = 20"> . . . </xsl:if>
```

Using Variables to Store Literal or Numeric Values

There is some general confusion about how to set the value of a variable to a literal or numeric value without accidentally creating a result tree fragment. It is important to remember that the contents of a variable will always create a result tree fragment, and will be treated as such in expressions referencing the variable. However, the **select** attribute of **<xsl:variable>** contains an expression, which can be a number or a string, among other things.

For example, when setting a variable to the number 2, use the **select** attribute instead of the contents of the variable:

```
<xsl:variable name="myvar" select="2"/>
```

Do not use the contents of the variable to set the value to 2:

```
<xsl:variable name="myvar">2</xsl:variable>
```

If you need to specify an empty node-set as the default value of a parameter, use the **select** attribute as follows:

```
<xsl:param name="x" select="/.."/>
```

XSLT 2.0

XSLT 1.0 and XSLT 2.0 are very different, and users who are used to using XSLT 1.0 may be a bit surprised by the size and functionality changes. The most obvious change is the addition of XML Schema datatypes to XPath 2.0, which is very closely interconnected with XSLT 2.0. Some of the major new features include:

- **Temporary trees**—The content of a variable is now directly accessible as a temporary tree, similar to the functionality of **node-set()** extension functions.
- **Grouping facilities**—Built-in functionality for grouping has been introduced with **<xsl:for-each-group>**.
- **Regular expressions**—A new instruction **<xsl:analyze-string>** is provided to process text by matching it against a regular expression.
- **Sequences**—The list of nodes returned by an expression or sequence constructor is now a sequence of nodes.
- **Multiple output files**—A transformation is now able to produce multiple output files without using extension elements.
- **Stylesheet functions**—It is now possible to define custom functions within the stylesheet, and to use those functions in XPath expressions.
- **Schema awareness and type checking**—Schema awareness adds the ability to access schema components such as type definitions, element declarations, and attribute declarations.

There are also some built-in datatypes that are available even without adding a schema declaration.
It is possible to declare the types of variables and parameters, and the result types of templates and functions. The types can either be built-in types, or user-defined types imported from a schema using a new **xsl:import-schema** declaration.

- **Special character handling**—XSLT 2.0 adds functionality for handling special characters through the use of character maps.
- **Tunnel parameters**—Provides the ability to pass parameter values through a series of templates without actually declaring them and explicitly passing them through each template.
- **Next match**—Multiple template rules can now be applied to the same source node.
  A transformation can now be invoked by calling a named template. This creates the potential for a transformation to process large collections of input documents. The input to such a transformation may be obtained using the **collection** function defined in functions and operators, or it can be supplied as a stylesheet parameter.

Additional new features include:

- A new instruction **<xsl:namespace>** is available, for creating namespace nodes.
- A new instruction **<xsl:perform-sort>** is available, for returning a sorted sequence.
- A new **[xsl:]xpath-default-namespace** attribute is available for defining the default namespace for unqualified names in an XPath expression or XSLT pattern.
- The attributes **[xsl:]version, [xsl:]exclude-result-prefixes**, and **[xsl:]extension-element-prefixes,** as well as the new **[xsl:]xpath-default-namespace** and **[xsl:]default-collation** attributes, can be used on any XSLT element, not only on **<xsl:stylesheet>** and on literal result elements as before. In particular, they can now be used on the **<xsl:template>** element.
- A new **unparsed-text** function is introduced. It allows the contents of an external text file to be read as a string.
- Restrictions on the use of variables within patterns and key definitions have been removed; in their place a more general statement of the restrictions preventing circularity has been formulated. The **current** function may also now be used within patterns.
- The built-in templates for element and document nodes now pass any supplied parameter values on to the templates that they call.
- A detailed specification of the **format-number** function is now provided, thus removing the reliance on specifications in Java JDK 1.1.

In order for an XSLT processor to know which version of XSLT you are using, you must change the version attribute on the **<xsl:stylesheet>** or **<xsl:transform>** elements:

```
<xsl:stylesheet
        xmlns:xsl="http://www.w3.org/1999/XSL/Transform"
        version="2.0">
```

There are quite a few incompatibilities between the two versions, so just changing the version number is not always a good idea. Check the XSLT 2.0 specification at http://www.w3.org/TR/xslt20/ for more information.

XSLT 2.0 Features Overview

XSLT 2.0 adds sequences, functionality for grouping, regular expressions, temporary trees, schema awareness, and multiple output files, in addition to the many new XPath functions that are available with XPath 2.0. This section briefly describes the functionality of some of these new features.

Temporary Trees

Temporary trees are virtual containers for the results of a process, and enable multiple phase processing by enabling the passing of information from one process module to another. In XSLT 1.0, the only way to make this same functionality work was to use separate stylesheets and save the results to a file on the file system, or to use an extension function like **node-set()** to access result tree fragments. Now multiple processes can be strung together within the same stylesheet or groups of stylesheets without the mess of creating separate intermediate files.

A temporary tree is created by storing a sequence, or XML fragment, in a variable, and then using the name of the variable followed by the path to the nodes that you want to access. The variable can contain a static XML fragment or a set of XSLT instructions to build the XML on the fly.

Here is an example of a temporary tree with XSLT instructions:

```
<xsl:variable name="mytree">
   <xsl:element name="address-book">
      <xsl:apply-templates select="//contact">
   </xsl:element>
</xsl:variable>
```

In this example, you are building an address book with contacts pulled from the source tree. The temporary tree has a root node, which is a document node, and you can access that node by using the variable reference **$mytree** followed by a slash for the root node, followed by any path within the temporary tree.

```
<xsl:value-of select="$mytree//address[contains(city, 'Austin')]"/>
```

By using temporary trees with nodes, you can keep the phases of the transformation separate.

Grouping

In XSLT 1.0, grouping was an almost impossible task. It was solved to a point by using complex manipulations, and often required at least one pre-processing phase. See the Muenchian method for grouping in the XSLT 1.0 section for an example. For XSLT 2.0, grouping is built-in, using the **<xsl:for-each-group>** element, along with its attributes **select**, **group-by**, **group-adjacent**, **group-starting-with**, **group-ending-with**, and **collation**.

The **select** attribute on **<xsl:for-each-group>** selects which nodes to iterate over, and the other attributes are used to specify what criteria to use for grouping the nodes. The content of the **<xsl:for-each-group>** element is then applied to each group.

Once the groups are selected, the **current-grouping-key()** and **current-group()** functions can be applied to access them individually.

Given the following sample data, you can group the addresses by city:

```
<address-book>

<contact><name>Zoila</name><address><city>Dallas</city><state>Texas</state>
</address></contact>

<contact><name>Mark</name><address><city>Belton</city><state>Texas</state>
</address></contact>

<contact><name>Zarella</name><address><city>Austin</city><state>Texas</state>
</address></contact>

<contact><name>Zellia</name><address><city>Dallas</city><state>Texas</state>
</address></contact>

<contact><name>Zusann</name><address><city>Homestead</city><state>Florida
</state></address></contact>

<contact><name>Zinida</name><address><city>Homestead</city><state>Florida
</state></address></contact>
```

```
<contact><name>Michael</name><address><city>Dallas</city><state>Texas</state>
</address></contact>

<contact><name>Maurice</name><address><city>Cleveland</city><state>Ohio
</state></address></contact>

<contact><name>Zophia</name><address><city>Raleigh</city><state>North
Carolina</state></address></contact>

</address-book>
```

The XSLT 2.0 stylesheet would contain template rules to group the children of the **contact** element:

```
<xsl:template match="contact">
   <xsl:for-each-group select="." group-by="address/city">
      <xsl:text>===</xsl:text>
      <xsl:value-of select="current-grouping-key()"/>
      <xsl:text>===
</xsl:text>
      <xsl:for-each select="current-group()">
         <xsl:value-of select="name"/><xsl:text>
</xsl:text>
      </xsl:for-each>
   </xsl:for-each-group>
</xsl:template>
```

This code will result in the following text file:

```
===Dallas===
Zoila
Zellia
Michael
===Belton===
Mark
===Austin===
Zarella
===Homestead===
Zusann
Zinida
```

```
===Cleveland===
Maurice
===Raleigh===
Zophia
```

Notice that the order of the results is the same as the order of the input, according to first occurrence. If you wanted the output sorted, you could add an **<xsl:sort>** element to the content of the **<xsl:for-each-group>**.

If you needed to add a grouping by state, followed by the city grouping, you could use two sets of nested **<xsl:for-each-group>** elements:

```
<xsl:template match="contact">
   <xsl:for-each-group select="." group-by="address/state">
      <xsl:text>***</xsl:text>
      <xsl:value-of select="current-grouping-key()"/><xsl:text>***
</xsl:text>
      <xsl:for-each-group select="current-group()" group-by="address/city">
         <xsl:text>===</xsl:text>
         <xsl:value-of select="current-grouping-key()"/><xsl:text>===
</xsl:text>
         <xsl:for-each select="current-group()">
            <xsl:value-of select="name"/><xsl:text>
</xsl:text>
         </xsl:for-each>
      </xsl:for-each-group>
   </xsl:for-each-group>
</xsl:template>
```

This code will result in the following:

```
***Texas***
===Dallas===
Zoila
Zellia
Michael
===Belton===
Mark
===Austin===
Zarella
```

```
***Florida***
===Homestead===
Zusann
Zinida
***Ohio***
===Cleveland===
Maurice
***North Carolina***
===Raleigh===
Zophia
```

To group items only if they happen to be adjacent to each other, you use the **group-adjacent** attribute instead of **group-by**. The result of this would only group the two "Homestead" contacts because they are the only ones that are adjacent:

```
<xsl:template match="contact">
   <xsl:for-each-group select="." group-adjacent="address/city">
      <xsl:text>===</xsl:text>
      <xsl:value-of select="current-grouping-key()"/>
      <xsl:text>===
</xsl:text>
      <xsl:for-each select="current-group()">
         <xsl:value-of select="name"/><xsl:text>
</xsl:text>
      </xsl:for-each>
   </xsl:for-each-group>
</xsl:template>
```

This code results in the following:

```
===Dallas===
Zoila
===Belton===
Mark
===Austin===
Zarella
===Dallas===
Zellia
===Homestead===
```

```
Zusann
Zinida
===Dallas===
Michael
===Cleveland===
Maurice
===Raleigh===
Zophia
```

The **group-starting-with** and **group-ending-with** attributes facilitate creating structure for relatively flat structures or for XML files that have many siblings that are different types. For example, what if you have a flat XML structure without the necessary containers, such as:

```
<addresses>
<name>Zoila</name><city>Dallas</city><state>Texas</state>
<name>Mark</name><city>Belton</city><state>Texas</state>
<name>Zarella</name><city>Austin</city><state>Texas</state>
<name>Zellia</name><city>Dallas</city><state>Texas</state>
<name>Zusann</name><city>Homestead</city><state>Florida</state>
<name>Zinida</name><city>Homestead</city><state>Florida</state>
<name>Michael</name><city>Dallas</city><state>Texas</state>
<name>Maurice</name><city>Cleveland</city><state>Ohio</state>
<name>Zophia</name><city>Raleigh</city><state>North Carolina</state>
</addresses>
```

You can add containers by selecting the element to start grouping by:

```
<xsl:template match="addresses">
   <address-book>
      <xsl:for-each-group select="*" group-starting-with="name">
         <contact>
            <xsl:for-each select="current-group()">
               <xsl:apply-templates/>
            </xsl:for-each>
         </contact>
      </xsl:for-each-group>
   </address-book>
</xsl:template>
<xsl:template match="city">
```

```
   <xsl:for-each-group select="current-group() except name" group-starting-
      with="city">
      <address>
         <xsl:for-each select="current-group()">
            <xsl:copy>
               <xsl:apply-templates/>
            </xsl:copy>
         </xsl:for-each>
      </address>
   </xsl:for-each-group>
</xsl:template>
```

The result is a rebuilding of our **address-book** structure:

```
<address-book>

<contact><name>Zoila</name><address><city>Dallas</city><state>Texas</state>
</address></contact>
  ...
<contact><name>Zophia</name><address><city>Raleigh</city><state>North
Carolina</state></address></contact>
</address-book>
```

Regular Expressions

Regular expressions are now available in XSLT 2.0 with the syntax described by XPath 2.0, and are allowed in the **tokenize()**, **matches()**, and **replace()** functions, and in the content of the **regex** attribute on **<xsl:analyze-string>**.

A partial list of tokens is shown here:

- **\n** A newline character.
- **.** Any single character except **\n**.
- **[a-z]** The lowercase letters a, z, or anything in that range.
- **[0-9]** Any numeric digit, anything in that range.
- **\d** Any numeric digit. The same as [0-9].
- **\s** Any single whitespace character space, tab, carriage return, or linefeed.
- ***** Zero or more characters.
- **+** One or more characters.

- ? Zero or one character.
- \ The character used to escape special characters such as *, +, ?, ., $, and so on.
- {} Used to specify a number to be applied to the preceding expression: **\d{2}** indicates exactly two digits.

The **<xsl:analyze-string>** instruction is used with a **select** attribute to select a string and the **regex** attribute to select a subset of the matched string based on the regular expression provided. The result of the **regex** match is passed to the contents of the **<xsl:analyze-string>** instruction element and processed according to the rules it finds.

The **<xsl:analyze-string>** instruction element can contain **<xsl:matching-substring>** and **<xsl:non-matching-substring>** elements, each of which contains template rules to process the matched string, or any part of the string that is not matched by the **regex** expression. Use one or the other, or both, but the **<xsl:matching-substring>** must be first if you use both. The following example searches for the text "Figure 1-9" in a caption and removes it, passing the rest of the caption text back out:

```
<xsl:template match="caption">
   <p>
      <xsl:analyze-string select="." regex="Figure [1-9]\.[1-9]\s">
         <xsl:non-matching-substring>
            <xsl:value-of select="."/>
         </xsl:non-matching-substring>
      </xsl:analyze-string>
   </p>
</xsl:template>
```

Sequences

A *sequence* is an ordered list of zero or more items, which can be nodes, atomic values, or simple XML schema datatypes. In XSLT 1.0, the result of an expression was a list of nodes. In XSLT 2.0, the result of an expression is a sequence.

The **<xsl:sequence>** instruction is used within a template (now called *sequence constructors*) to generate a sequence of values that can be either nodes, similar to the result of **<xsl:copy-of>**, or atomic values. This is useful when you really need an atomic value instead of a text node, because using **<xsl:value-of>** would return a text node that would then need to be converted to the atomic value.

For example, the following code constructs a sequence of integers, as specified by the **as** attribute on the **<xsl:variable>** element:

```
<xsl:variable name="values" as="xs:integer*">
```

```
    <xsl:sequence select="(1,2,3,4)"/>
    <xsl:sequence select="(8,9,10)"/>
</xsl:variable>
<xsl:value-of select="sum($values)"/>
```

The result of the sum of **$values** would be the integer **37**. Recall that the **sum()** function only works on a sequence of nodes, so now it is possible to declare the nodes using **<xsl:sequence>**, and then add them together.

The result of using **<xsl:value-of>** on **$values** is a text string of space-separated values:

```
1 2 3 4 8 9 10
```

Multiple Output Files

Generating multiple documents from one process in XSLT 1.0 was only possible by using extension functions like Saxon's **<xsl:document>** or Xalan's **<redirect:write>**. For example, generating separate HTML chapter or section files for one XML input document has always been a requirement for Web publishing. Now in XSLT 2.0, the functionality exists by using **<xsl:result-document>**.

For example, given the following data, you can create separate HTML pages for each contact:

```
<address-book>

<contact><name>Zoila</name><address><city>Dallas</city><state>Texas</state>
</address></contact>

<contact><name>Mark</name><address><city>Belton</city><state>Texas</state>
</address></contact>

<contact><name>Zarella</name><address><city>Austin</city><state>Texas
</state></address></contact>

<contact><name>Zellia</name><address><city>Dallas</city><state>Texas
</state></address></contact>

<contact><name>Zusann</name><address><city>Homestead</city><state>Florida
</state></address></contact>

<contact><name>Zinida</name><address><city>Homestead</city><state>Florida
</state></address></contact>
```

```
<contact><name>Michael</name><address><city>Dallas</city><state>Texas
</state></address></contact>

<contact><name>Maurice</name><address><city>Cleveland</city><state>Ohio
</state></address></contact>

<contact><name>Zophia</name><address><city>Raleigh</city><state>North
Carolina</state></address></contact>

</address-book>
```

The XSLT needed to generate separate output documents for each contact is as follows:

```
<xsl:template match="contact">
      <xsl:result-document href="{name}.html">
         <html xmlns="http://www.w3.org/1999/xhtml">
            <head><title><xsl:value-of select="name"/></title></head>
            <body>
               <xsl:apply-templates/>
            </body>
         </html>
      </xsl:result-document>
</xsl:template>
```

The result is a set of html files for each contact, named using the **name** element as the filename with an .html extension.

Stylesheet Functions

User-defined functions are now available directly in XSLT 2.0 by using the **<xsl:function>** declaration. Once a function is declared, it can be called and used by any XPath expression used in the stylesheet. Similar to named templates in XSLT 1.0, the content of the **<xsl:function>** element contains instructions that are applied at the point of the calling of the function. The difference is that now the function is available inside an XPath expression instead of just inside another template. You can even override existing functions by using the **override="yes"** attribute.

Declaring a function is much like creating a named template, except you must have a namespace prefix:

```
<xsl:function name="myfunc:lower-to-upper">
   <xsl:param name="in-string"/>
   <xsl:value-of select="translate($in-string,
```

```
    'abcdefghijklmnopqrstuvwxyz',
    'ABCDEFGHIJKLMNOPQRSTUVWXYZ')"/>
</xsl:function>
```

You then call the function directly in an XPath expression:

```
<xsl:template match="contact">
    <xsl:value-of select="myfunc:lower-to-upper(name)"/>
</xsl:template>
```

The result of this function would generate an uppercase list of names from the **contact elements.**

Schema Awareness and Type Checking

XPath 2.0 provides access to the XML Schema datatypes as defined by the W3C Schema. To take advantage of this capability in XSLT, you use the **<xsl:import-schema>** element:

```
<xsl:import-schema
    namespace="http://www.w3.org/2001/XMLSchema-instance"
    schema-location="myschema.xsd" />
```

This gives you access to the datatype model provided in XML Schema. You'll need it if you want to do any explicit type casting, which is beyond the scope of this article but allows you to specify how you want data results returned to you (as decimal types, date types, date-time types, and so on).

A basic XSLT 2.0 processor has the following built-in datatypes:

- All the primitive atomic types defined in XML Schema Part 2, with the exception of **xs:NOTATION**. That is: **xs:string, xs:boolean, xs:decimal, xs:double, xs:float, xs:date, xs:time, xs:dateTime, xs:duration, xs:QName, xs:anyURI, xs:gDay, xs:gMonthDay, xs:gMonth, xs:gYearMonth, xs:gYear, xs:base64Binary**, and **xs:hexBinary**.
- The derived atomic type **xs:integer** defined in XML Schema Part 2.
- The types **xs:anyType** and **xs:anySimpleType**.
- The following types defined in XPath 2.0: **xs:yearMonthDuration, xs:dayTimeDuration, xs:anyAtomicType, xs:untyped**, and **xs:untypedAtomic**.

Handling Special Characters

XSLT 2.0 adds a new feature for handing special characters, without having to preprocess them into another format as you have to in XSLT 1.0. The **<xsl:character-map>** element is a declaration element that must be a child of the **<xsl:stylesheet>**, and it contains output definitions (**<xsl:output-character>**) for each character that you want to remap to some other format. For example, here is a partial character map for the ISO Latin 1 character set:

```
<xsl:character-map name="ISO-lat1">
   <xsl:output-character character=" " string="&amp;nbsp;" />
   <xsl:output-character character="&#161;" string="&amp;iexcl;" />
   <xsl:output-character character="&#163;" string="&amp;pound;" />
...
   <xsl:output-character character="&#8364;" string="&amp;euro;" />
</xsl:character-map>
```

You can define many character maps, but to use them, you have to call them from the **<xsl:output>** element:

```
<xsl:output use-character-maps="ISO-lat1" />
```

You can also reference other character maps inside a character map to build a complete list of character sets from modular sets:

```
<xsl:character-map name="ISO-set"
  use-character-maps="ISO-lat1 ISO-lat2 ISO-pub" />
```

Using the previous example from the **xmlchar** section, you start with an input document that contains character entities:

```
<body>
   <p>My sandwich cost &pound;2.</p>
   <p>Really? You were cheated. My sandwich only cost &euro;2.</p>
</body>
```

During the XML parsing stage, the characters are converted to their final value as defined in a character entity set:

```
<body>
   <p>My sandwich cost &#163;2.</p>
   <p>Really? You were cheated. My sandwich only cost &#8364;2.</p>
</body>
```

When you apply the character map defined previously, the characters in the resulting output will be returned to their original state:

```
<body>
   <p>My sandwich cost &pound;2.</p>
   <p>Really? You were cheated. My sandwich only cost &euro;2.</p>
</body>
```

Tunnel Parameters

One of the most annoying (in our opinion) things about XSLT 1.0 is the template parameter barrier. Basically, a parameter value can only be passed from one template to the next if it is explicitly declared and sent to the next template using **<xsl:with-param>**, and this must be done for each level of called templates. In XSLT 2.0, the barrier is lifted. Tunnel parameters are automatically passed on by the template to any templates that it calls, recursively, without having to re-declare them explicitly. Once you reach a level where the parameter is to be used, however, you do have to re-declare it at that point.

You declare an initial tunnel parameter at a high level in a stylesheet, say at the chapter level:

```
<xsl:template match="chapter">
   <xsl:apply-templates>
      <xsl:with-param name="prefix" select="'Figure'" tunnel="yes"/>
   </xsl:apply-templates>
</xsl:template>
```

Note that you don't have to declare the **<xsl:param>** on this element, only on the element that uses the **param**:

```
<xsl:template match="figure">
   <xsl:param name="prefix" tunnel="yes"/>
   <xsl:value-of select="$prefix"/>
   <xsl:apply-templates/>
</xsl:template>
```

You can declare a different initial value for the tunnel parameter at a sibling of chapter:

```
<xsl:template match="appendix">
   <xsl:apply-templates>
      <xsl:with-param name="prefix" select="'Example'" tunnel="yes"/>
   </xsl:apply-templates>
</xsl:template>
```

The result is that all figures in a chapter would be prefixed with "Figure" while all figures in an appendix would be prefixed with the word "Example". The example shows that, no matter what level within a chapter or appendix, the value of the prefix parameter is available to the **figure** element.

Next Match

With XSLT 1.0, a template matched a set of nodes in a source document, and the contents of the template were applied to each node in the set. With XSLT 2.0, functionality has been added to allow multiple templates to be applied to one set of matched nodes. Similar to **<xsl:apply-imports>**, the **<xsl:next-match>** instruction looks for and applies template rules defined for the same matched set of nodes, whether they are declared within the same stylesheet or in imported stylesheets.

For example, if you declare two templates matching on the same element:

```
<xsl:template match="para">
   <bold><xsl:apply-templates/></bold>
</xsl:template>
<xsl:template match="para">
   <p>
       <xsl:next-match/>
   </p>
</xsl:template>
```

The result is all paragraphs wrapped with both **<p>** and **<bold>** tags:

```
<p><bold>para content</bold></p>
```

Note that all rules of precedence and order of template declaration still apply, so that if you accidentally reversed the order of these two templates in the stylesheet, the second one would apply and the first one would be ignored.

Summary

XSLT is a powerful tool in the XML world, because it allows you to process XML into other formats. XSLT 1.0 has been very well-received since it became a recommendation in 1999, and now XSLT 2.0 adds new features and functionality that many XSLT 1.0 users have expressed a need for.

XSLT 1.0 provided the basic tools for manipulating XML elements and attributes, and XSLT 2.0 added functionality for schema aware processing, grouping, regular expressions, temporary trees, multiple output files, special character handling, and tunnel parameters, among others.

The members of the XML Guild hope that the tips, tricks, and examples in this chapter will help you understand and use XSLT, whether you choose version 1.0 or 2.0.

4 Web Services

by Benoît Marchal and Zarella Rendon

Web Services is one of those concepts that is both deceptively simple from a technical standpoint and incredibly powerful from a user standpoint. Unfortunately, the contrast between the technical simplicity and the functional power makes it somewhat confusing. As you will see, Web Services is a very logical evolution for websites but it is revolutionary in terms of what it offers to end users.

This section introduces Web Services as a concept. It seems fitting to approach this concept both from a functional angle and from a technical one. The functional view, however, is more fun so let's start with it.

Functional Overview

To understand Web Services, it helps to start from the most basic tool for information sharing on a computer: the Clipboard. By Clipboard, I refer to the service that lives within the Edit menu of most applications, and allows you to cut or copy data from one application and paste it into another. See Figure 4.1.

Nowadays we take the Clipboard for granted but it was not always the case. There was a time when exchanging data between applications from different manufacturers required some very geeky operations. Heck, even sharing data between two different applications from the same manufacturer used to be an accomplishment. The Clipboard was the first practical solution to share data that did not require a PhD in computer science.

It is even more remarkable when you consider that you can copy and paste information between the latest gizmo and a 10-year-old application. The programmers never met and they probably used languages that are as alien to each other as possible to write their software, yet still it just works.

How is that possible? Because the Clipboard is based on a rock-solid foundation that includes both stable APIs and open formats.

Figure 4.1
The humble Clipboard

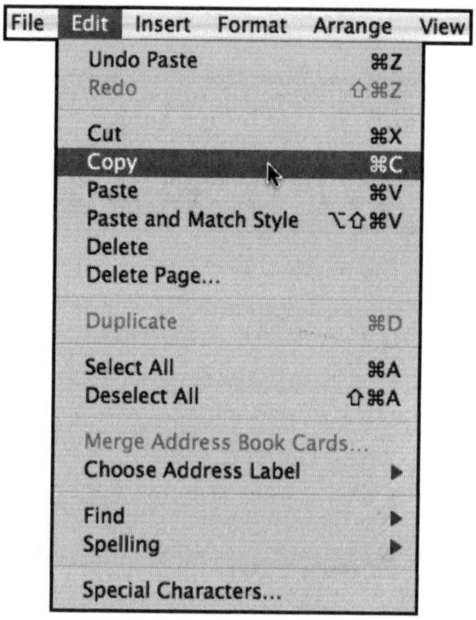

Ultimately the concept of the Clipboard goes beyond the mechanics of sharing information. What makes it valuable is the additional power that it offers to computer users. Indeed the Clipboard allows users to overcome the limitations of one software by calling into another one for specific tasks.

For example, it is simple to create composite documents that integrate text, images, tables, and charts by copying and pasting data from specialized applications into a word processor, as shown in Figure 4.2.

Again, in this day and age, this is nothing extraordinary from a technical standpoint. From a practical standpoint, though, it means that to address a task, you can use any software on your computer. Your entire computer acts as one tool, instead of piecemeal softwares. The Clipboard greatly expands the usefulness of any application by allowing it to expand or be expanded by every other application on your computer.

As it turns out, the Clipboard was the tip of the iceberg. The basic concept rapidly evolved into drag and drop (one less trip to the menu, one less key combination to remember). It also led to OLE and other component based systems, where you're not pasting data from the application but retaining a live link to the originating application—allowing you to edit that Excel spreadsheet directly in Word.

By now you are probably asking yourself why go on and on over the Clipboard in a chapter on Web Services? The answer is that, from a functional view, Web Services is an evolution of that basic concept. It's another tool to combine different applications to offer better services to the user.

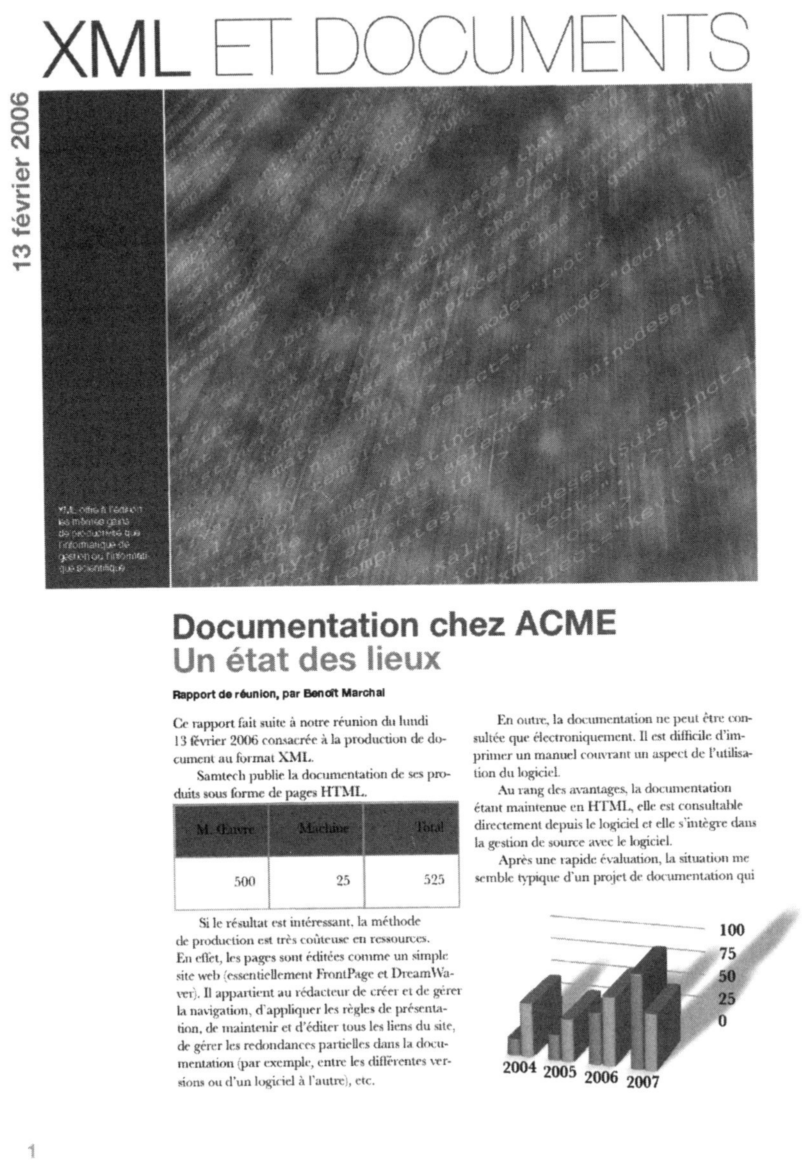

XML ET DOCUMENTS

13 février 2006

Documentation chez ACME
Un état des lieux

Rapport de réunion, par Benoît Marchal

Ce rapport fait suite à notre réunion du lundi 13 février 2006 consacrée à la production de document au format XML.

Samtech publie la documentation de ses produits sous forme de pages HTML.

M. Œuvre	Machine	Total
500	25	525

Si le résultat est intéressant, la méthode de production est très coûteuse en ressources. En effet, les pages sont éditées comme un simple site web (essentiellement FrontPage et DreamWaver). Il appartient au rédacteur de créer et de gérer la navigation, d'appliquer les règles de présentation, de maintenir et d'éditer tous les liens du site, de gérer les redondances partielles dans la documentation (par exemple, entre les différentes versions ou d'un logiciel à l'autre), etc.

En outre, la documentation ne peut être consultée que électroniquement. Il est difficile d'imprimer un manuel couvrant un aspect de l'utilisation du logiciel.

Au rang des avantages, la documentation étant maintenue en HTML, elle est consultable directement depuis le logiciel et elle s'intègre dans la gestion de source avec le logiciel.

Après une rapide évaluation, la situation me semble typique d'un projet de documentation qui

1

Figure 4.2
Composite document

Those things I said about a rock-solid foundation of stable APIs and open formats: they remain largely true but you need to substitute protocol for API.

In terms of functionality, if you remember how incredibly useful it is to combine all the software on your machine, imagine how useful combining all the software on the Internet could be! That is the promise behind Web Services.

Any information that is published on a website can be turned into a Web Service. The difference? A regular website is geared towards browsers so, although it provides useful information, it requires somebody to browse and click.

A Web Service, on the other hand, is designed to be accessed through other software. The Web Service acts as a data provider for the application. The benefits? There are many but they mostly revolve around the ability to share information between websites and between websites and desktop applications. This is not unlike how composite documents are assembled by pasting data from different applications.

Web Services Technology Overview

This section is about how middleware, EDI, and our trusty Web have grown into Web Services.

Examples of Web Services

There are already many great applications based on Web Services. I'll use Delicious Library as an example because I believe it is an example that will speak to most software engineers.

I don't know a software engineer who has not, at one time or another, attempted to create a database to record his or her collection: records, movies, recipes, and the like. In my case, that would be books (and photo gear but that's an entirely different issue).

Typically a variation of the following scenario unfolds: a database schema is drawn enthusiastically, development unfolds, and a mostly functional version of the database is soon ready.

It is only then that the actual size of the effort becomes clear: now is the time to populate this cleverly designed database. For most collections, that's a lot of typing to do.

Ironically, the larger the collection, and therefore the more necessary a database is, the more work it takes to type in all the entries. Likewise, the better designed databases have more fields, which again requires more work. Most people (including myself) simply plug along for a couple of hours, take a break, and never come back.

Introducing Web Services. It turns out that the information you're painfully typing is already available somewhere on the Internet. For example, Amazon.com has a rich database of book descriptions, including covers, comments, recommendations, relationships to other books, and more.

Imagine if you could just paste Amazon.com into your own database—turns out you can thanks to Amazon Web Services, which allow your application to query the Amazon.com database almost as if it was local.

That's the promise behind Delicious Library. The software essentially is a fancy-looking books/records/movies database but with a twist—it relies on the Amazon Web Service to fill in its database. To record a book, you only need to fill in one field: the barcode (and Delicious Library can even read it for you, if you have a webcam). Delicious Library will retrieve the title, cover, author name, description, page count, publishing date, and more (including other book recommendations through Amazon affiliates program) from the Amazon Web Service.

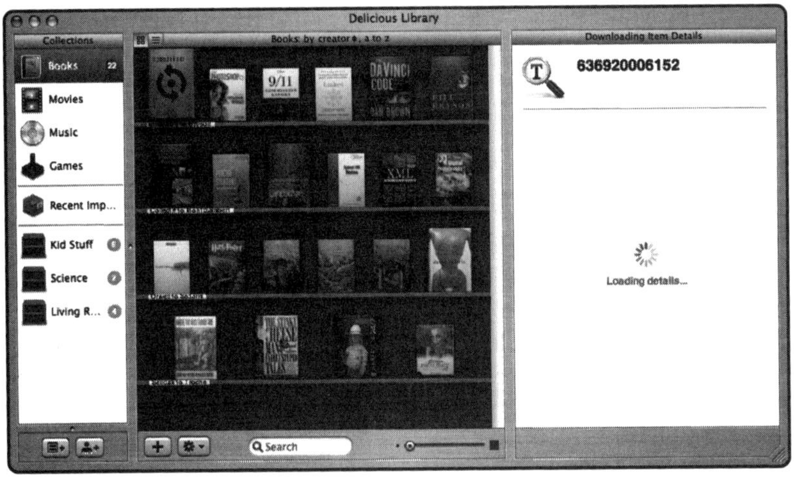

Figure 4.3
Delicious Library "pasting" a book description from Amazon

Under the hood, when you create a new book Delicious Library calls the Amazon website, passing the barcode as a parameter and retrieves the description as an XML document. Again, I find it helpful to make a comparison with the Clipboard, but this time pasting over the Internet.

If you're curious to try this out for yourself, visit www.delicious-monster.com and the Amazon Web Services site at aws.amazon.com. The later includes developer's tutorials and lots of other useful material.

Other examples of Web Services include:

- Google Web API, which lives at www.google.com/apis and allows you to search Google from any application.
  As I write this, I look up references through Google and indeed it would be convenient if my editor of choice had Google search built-in. Note however that, at the time of writing, the Google licence does not allow commercial developments.
- Flick API is documented at www.flickr.com/services/api. Through the API, applications can post, retrieve, tag, and otherwise manipulate photos on the popular photo-sharing site.
- BBC Web API is available through www.rdthdo.bbc.co.uk/services/. At the time of writing, it is still in the experimental phase. This service allows you to search BBC programs and channels to create your own TV and radio guides.

SOAP

SOAP is an XML protocol used to send XML messages over a network. It is a convergence of two fields that were previously unrelated: Application Middleware and Web Publishing. SOAP 1.2 is a Recommended Specification published by the W3C XML Protocol Working Group, available at http://www.w3.org/TR/2003/REC-soap12-part1-20030624/.

At the time of the creation of the standard, SOAP was an acronym for Simple Object Access Protocol. SOAP is the cornerstone of many Web Services architectures. This section discusses why you should consider it, and why you might want to ignore it.

SOAP Messaging and HTTP Binding

SMTP and HTTP are commonly used for SOAP, and there is even an implementation using FTP, but HTTP is more widely used because it fits in nicely with the infrastructure of the Internet.

A SOAP request is sent with an HTTP request, most often sent using the POST verb (the GET verb is supported only since SOAP 1.2), and the SOAP response is transmitted with the HTTP response. HTTP requests and responses contain one or more headers and one payload. SOAP uses the **Content-Type** header to identify SOAP requests.

Content-Type

The **Content-Type** header must be set to **application/soap+xml**, which is expected because it is the regular type for XML documents.

SOAPAction

SOAP 1.0 and SOAP 1.2 used an additional header field, **SOAPAction**, to let proxies and firewalls know that a SOAP request is coming. Proxies and firewalls read only the headers for increased efficiency. Also with those implementations, the **Content-Type** was set to **text/xml**.

The **SOAPAction** content is a URI that identifies the intent of the call. However, most SOAP implementations ignore **SOAPAction**.

SMTP Bindings

The SOAP 1.2 recommendation defines generic binding rules that enable binding SOAP requests to any protocol. Consequently, the framework describes the process to bind SOAP to non-HTTP protocols such as SMTP. However, many SOAP implementations already include some form of SMTP binding, based on the ebXML Transport, Routing, and Packaging specification (see http://www.ebxml.org).

Because HTTP and SMTP headers are similar, an SMTP binding is easily derived from the HTTP binding. Although the SOAP message header includes the **Content-Type** of text/xml, the **To** and **From** are set according to the SMTP rules.

SMTP works in asynchronous mode, where the client sends a request and does not wait for a response. If the server sends a response, it comes in a different message and is processed separately.

Example SOAP Messages

Here is an example of a SOAP message:

```
POST /soap/servlet/rpcrouter HTTP/1.1
Host: joker.psol.com
Content-Type: application/soap+xml; charset=utf-8
Content-Length: 530
<?xml version='1.0'?>
<env:Envelope xmlns:xsd="http://www.w3.org/1999/XMLSchema"
             xmlns:env="http://www.w3.org/2003/05/soap-envelope"
             xmlns:xsi="http://www.w3.org/1999/XMLSchema-instance">
  <env:Body>
    <rs:getFreeResourcesOn xmlns:rs="http://psol.com/2001/resourceful"
     env:encodingStyle="http://www.w3.org/2003/05/soap-encoding">
    <start xsi:type="xsd:timeInstant">2001-01-15T00:00:00Z</start>
    <end xsi:type="xsd:timeInstant">2001-01-17T00:00:00Z</end>
    </rs:getFreeResourcesOn>
  </env:Body>
</env:Envelope>
```

The server response is as follows:

```
HTTP/1.0 200 OK
Server: Jetty/3.1.4 (MacOS)
Servlet-Engine: Jetty/3.1 (JSP 1.1; Servlet 2.2; java 1.3.0)
Content-Type: application/soap+xml; charset=utf-8
Content-Length: 657

<?xml version='1.0' encoding='UTF-8'?>
<env:Envelope xmlns:xsd="http://www.w3.org/1999/XMLSchema"
        xmlns:env="http://www.w3.org/2003/05/soap-envelope"
        xmlns:enc="http://www.w3.org/2003/05/soap-encoding"
        xmlns:xsi="http://www.w3.org/1999/XMLSchema-instance">
<env:Body>
```

```
<ns1:getFreeResourcesOnResponse
   xmlns:ns1="http://psol.com/2001/resourceful"
   env:encodingStyle="http://www.w3.org/2003/05/soap-encoding">
<return enc:arraySize="3" enc:nodeType="xsd:string">
<item>Meeting room 1</item>
<item>Meeting room 2</item>
<item>Board room</item></return>
</ns1:getFreeResourcesOnResponse>
</env:Body>
</env:Envelope>
```

Soap and RPCs

SOAP was originally designed to enable Remote Procedure Calls (RPC) over HTTP. In an RPC call, the client invokes a procedure (running some process) from a server. For example, in the example in the previous section, the client was asking the server to look up the availability of meeting rooms.

To enable RPC, SOAP defines a sophisticated set of encoding rules that enable programmers to map any data structure from their programming language into SOAP. It is therefore possible to pass sophisticated arguments to the server and return complex data structures.

In practice, however, the use of SOAP for RPC, although still common, is being replaced with direct exchange of XML messages over a SOAP request. This gives the programmers access to an even richer data structure (the entire XML syntax) at the cost of a slight increase in complexity.

WSDL and SOAP

The Web Services Description Language (WSDL) is an XML language for describing Web Services. Version 2.0, which provides a model and an XML format, is a W3C Candidate Recommendation as of March 27, 2006, and is expected to become a full recommendation by the end of 2006.

WSDL describes a platform-independent Web Service message in XML, and separates the message from the binding protocol.

Web Services resources are accessed through a WSDL service description, which lists the available services and describes how the client can interact with each service. SOAP can then be used to call and interact with one of the services listed in the WSDL.

XML Schema can be used directly in the WSDL file to describe any special datatypes that might be required. The WSDL specification describes the following specific parts to a Web Service:

- Message: A one-way message (request or response).
- Binding: Specific instructions for implementing a Web Service.
- Service: The location (URL) of a Web Service.

In addition, the WSDL specification defines the structure of the XML message, including the **<definitions>** top-level element, the **<types>** element describing the datatypes used by a Web Service, and the **<portType>** wrapper to combine request and response messages.

WSDL describes a platform-independent Web Service message in XML, and separates the message from the binding protocol. Why is it important? Remember the Clipboard example used at the beginning of this chapter? Its usefulness derives from its ability to connect applications that do not know about each other beforehand. It defines loose couplings that can be arranged dynamically by the end user to fit the needs of a given task.

Likewise, Web Services must offer this loose coupling, making it possible to create new clients rapidly and efficiently. Therefore it is essential that a Web Service be able to describe itself formerly to clients. The WSDL description allows client to learn the specifics of a Web Service (what services it provides and how to call them) at runtime and therefore to bind themselves to the service in a fluid, dynamic fashion.

WSDL Message

The WSDL **<message>** element contains the instructions and datatypes that are expected by the Web Service for the request, and the response and returned datatypes expected by the client.

Request message definition:

```
<wsdl:message name="getAllResourcesRequest"></wsdl:message>
```

Response message definition:

```
<wsdl:message name="getAllResourcesResponse">
   <wsdl:part name="getAllResourcesResult"
        type="intf:ArrayOf_tns1_Resource"/>
</wsdl:message>
```

WSDL Binding

The binding of a Web Services message is separate from the message itself. This allows for more options on the types of interfaces that can interact with the message. The WSDL **<binding>** element specifies the operation, transport, and wire format details, in most cases a SOAP binding:

```
<description>
<binding name="BookingServiceSoapBinding"
              type="intf:BookingServicePortType">
      <operation name="getAllResources">
```

```
. . .
            </operation>
      </binding>
</description>
```

WSDL Service

The WSDL **<service>** element provides the address or URL for accessing a Web Service.

A network address is directly associated with a binding using a name and binding combination; the **name** attribute on the binding and the **binding** attribute on the **<port>** element in the service must be equal.

```
   <wsdl:binding name="BookingServiceSoapBinding"
                  type="intf:BookingServicePortType">
...
   <wsdl:service name="BookingService">
      <wsdl:port binding="intf:BookingServiceSoapBinding"
                  name="BookingServicePort">
         <soap:address location=
               "http://joker.psol.com/soap/servlet/rpcrouter"/>
      </wsdl:port>
   </wsdl:service>
```

Example WSDL Message

Here is an example of a WSDL message:

```
<?xml version="1.0" encoding="UTF-8"?>
<wsdl:definitions xmlns=http://schemas.xmlsoap.org/wsdl/
   targetNamespace=http://psol.com/2001/resourceful
   xmlns:impl=http://psol.com/2001/resourceful-impl
   xmlns:intf=http://www.psol.com/2001/resourceful
   xmlns:soap=http://schemas.xmlsoap.org/wsdl/soap/
   xmlns:soapenc=http://schemas.xmlsoap.org/soap/encoding/
   xmlns:tns1=http://psol.com/2001/resourceful
   xmlns:wsdl=http://schemas.xmlsoap.org/wsdl/
   xmlns:xsd="http://www.w3.org/2001/XMLSchema">
   <types>
      <schema targetNamespace=
         http://psol.com/2001/resourceful
         xmlns="http://www.w3.org/2001/XMLSchema">
         <complexType name="Resource">
```

```
        <sequence>
          <element name="name" nillable="true"
                                type="xsd:string"/>
          <element name="description" nillable="true"
                                type="xsd:string"/>
        </sequence>
      </complexType>
    </schema>
    <schema targetNamespace=http://psol.com/2001/resourceful
                        xmlns="http://www.w3.org/2001/XMLSchema">
      <complexType name="ArrayOf_tns1_Resource">
        <complexContent>
          <restriction base="soap:Array">
            <attribute ref="soapenc:arrayType"
                      wsdl:arrayType="tns1:Resource[]"/>
          </restriction>
        </complexContent>
      </complexType>
      <element name="el0" nillable="true" type=
                                "intf:ArrayOf_tns1_Resource"/>
      <element name="el1" nillable="true" type=
                                "intf:ArrayOf_tns1_Resource"/>
    </schema>
    <schema targetNamespace=http://www.w3.org/2001/XMLSchema
                        xmlns="http://www.w3.org/2001/XMLSchema">
      <element name="el0" nillable="true" type="xsd:dateTime"/>
      <element name="el1" nillable="true" type="xsd:dateTime"/>
    </schema>
  </types>
  <wsdl:message name="getFreeResourcesOnRequest">
    <wsdl:part name="arg0" type="xsd:dateTime"/>
    <wsdl:part name="arg1" type="xsd:dateTime"/>
  </wsdl:message>
  <wsdl:message name="getFreeResourcesOnResponse">
    <wsdl:part name="getFreeResourcesOnResult"
                type="intf:ArrayOf_tns1_Resource"/>
  </wsdl:message>
  <wsdl:message name="getAllResourcesRequest"></wsdl:message>
  <wsdl:message name="getAllResourcesResponse">
```

```
    <wsdl:part name="getAllResourcesResult"
                    type="intf:ArrayOf_tns1_Resource"/>
  </wsdl:message>
  <wsdl:portType name="BookingServicePortType">

    <wsdl:operation name="getAllResources">
      <wsdl:input message="intf:getAllResourcesRequest"/>
      <wsdl:output message="intf:getAllResourcesResponse"/>
    </wsdl:operation>
    <wsdl:operation name="getFreeResourcesOn">
      <wsdl:input message="intf:getFreeResourcesOnRequest"/>
      <wsdl:output/>
    </wsdl:operation>
  </wsdl:portType>
  <wsdl:binding name="BookingServiceSoapBinding"
                    type="intf:BookingServicePortType">
    <soap:binding style="rpc"
              transport="http://schemas.xmlsoap.org/soap/http"/>
    <wsdl:operation name="getAllResources">
      <soap:operation soapAction="" style="rpc"/>
      <wsdl:input>
        <soap:body encodingStyle=
          http://schemas.xmlsoap.org/soap/encoding/
          namespace=http://psol.com/2001/resourceful
          use="encoded"/>
      </wsdl:input>
      <wsdl:output>
        <soap:body encodingStyle=
            http://schemas.xmlsoap.org/soap/encoding/
            namespace=http://psol.com/2001/resourceful
            use="encoded"/>
      </wsdl:output>
    </wsdl:operation>
    <wsdl:operation name="getFreeResourcesOn">
      <soap:operation soapAction="" style="rpc"/>
      <wsdl:input>
        <soap:body encodingStyle=
           http://schemas.xmlsoap.org/soap/encoding/
           namespace=http://psol.com/2001/resourceful
           use="encoded"/>
```

```
        </wsdl:input>
        <wsdl:output>
           <soap:body encodingStyle=
               http://schemas.xmlsoap.org/soap/encoding/
               namespace=http://psol.com/2001/resourceful
               use="encoded"/>
        </wsdl:output>
     </wsdl:operation>
  </wsdl:binding>
  <wsdl:service name="BookingService">
     <wsdl:port binding="intf:BookingServiceSoapBinding"
                 name="BookingServicePort">
        <soap:address location=
               "http://joker.psol.com/soap/servlet/rpcrouter"/>
     </wsdl:port>
  </wsdl:service>
</wsdl:definitions>
```

UDDI

Universal Description Discovery and Integration (UDDI) is an OASIS specification that defines a standard method for building and publishing a directory (or registry) of Web Services and the organizations that provide the Web Services. In addition to defining a Web Services registry, UDDI defines how the Web Services interact, and implements controls for access and dissemination of records. UDDI v3 became an OASIS standard on February 3, 2005.

UDDI is based on industry standards like HTTP, XML, XML Schema, and SOAP, and was designed to be used with SOAP and WSDL, as well as other service interfaces. Like a Yahoo for Web Services, it allows potential users to search and find information on Web Services and gives them the information required to interface with a service.

UDDI v3 adds many features, including multi-registry topologies, increased security features, improved WSDL support, a new subscription API, and core information model advances.

UDDI gives organizations the ability to represent information about their Web Services in a standard way to address the following scenarios:

- Find Web Services implementations that are based on a common abstract interface definition.
- Find Web Services providers that are classified according to a known classification scheme or identifier system. Industrial categorizations are based on standard taxonomies, including

the North American Industry Classification System (NAICS), the Universal Standard Products and Services Classification (UNSPSC), and ISO 3166.

- Determine the security and transport protocols supported by a given Web Service.
- Issue a search for services based on a general keyword.
- Cache the technical information about a Web Service and then update that information at runtime.

The External Web Services UDDI model is shown in Figure 4.4.

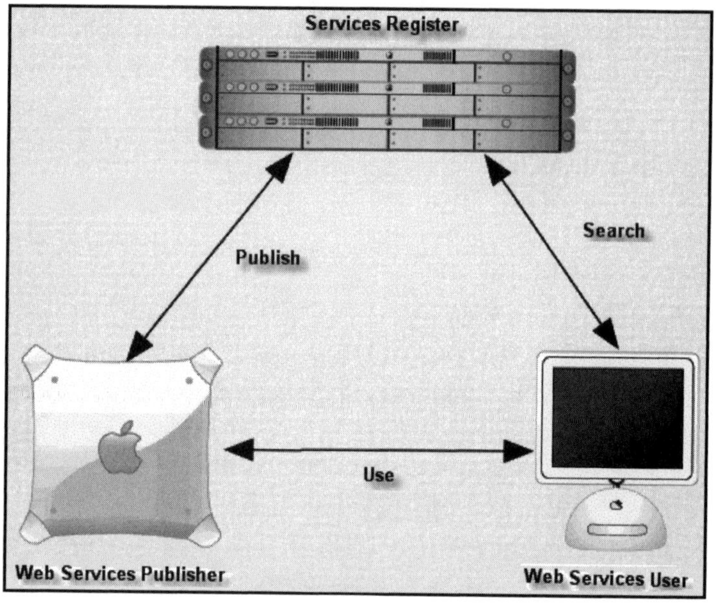

Figure 4.4
The External Web Services UDDI model.

A UDDI information model is composed of instances of the following entity types:

- **businessEntity**: A business or other organization that provides Web Services.
- **businessService**: A collection of related Web Services offered by an organization.
- **bindingTemplate**: The technical information necessary to use a particular Web service.
- **tModel**: A "technical model" representing a reusable concept, such as a Web Service type, a protocol used by Web Services, or a category system.
- **publisherAssertion**: The relationship of a **businessEntity** with another **businessEntity**.
- **subscription**: A standing request to keep track of changes to the entities described by the subscription.

Here's a sample businessEntity from the UDDI v3 specification:

```
<businessDetail generic="2.0" operator="Microsoft UDDI Services"
       truncated="false" xmlns="urn:uddi-org:api_v2">
   <businessEntity businessKey="176a3131-0c20-45d1-b31d-efb4f61b8b14"
       operator="sample" authorizedName="sample">
       <discoveryURLs>
          <discoveryURL useType="businessEntity">
              http://sample/uddipublic/
                     discovery.ashx businessKey=176a3131...
          </discoveryURL>
       </discoveryURLs>
       <name>sample</name>
   </businessEntity>
</businessDetail>
```

Here's a sample tModel using the General Keywords Category System from the UDDI v3 specification:

```
<businessServices>
  <businessService>
    <name>Island Trading Tame Animal Catalog Service</name>
    <description xml:lang="en">
       Search our Tame animals catalog on line
    </description>
    <bindingTemplates>
      <bindingTemplate>
        <accessPoint useType="endpoint">
           https://islandtrading.example/tame/catalog.html
        </accessPoint>
        <tModelInstanceDetails>
          <tModelInstanceInfo
            tModelKey="uddi:uddi.org:ubr:transport:http">
          </tModelInstanceInfo>
        </tModelInstanceDetails>
      </bindingTemplate>
    </bindingTemplates>
    <categoryBag>
      <keyedReference
```

```
        tModelKey="uddi:uddi.org:categorization:general_keywords"
        keyName="islandtrading.example:categorization:animals"
        keyValue="c"/>
      <keyedReference
        tModelKey="uddi:uddi.org:ubr:categorization:unspsc"
        keyName="UNSPSC: Livestock" keyValue="101015"/>
    </categoryBag>
  </businessService>
  <businessService>
    <name>
      Celestial Animals Fabulous Animal Books Catalog Service
    </name>
    <description xml:lang="en">
      Search our tame animals catalog on line
    </description>
    <bindingTemplates>
      <bindingTemplate>
        <accessPoint content="endpoint">
          https://islandtrading.example/fabulous/catalog.html
        </accessPoint>
        <tModelInstanceDetails>
          <tModelInstanceInfo
            tModelKey="uddi:uddi.org:ubr:transport:http">
          </tModelInstanceInfo>
        </tModelInstanceDetails>
      </bindingTemplate>
    </bindingTemplates>
    <categoryBag>
      <keyedReference
        tModelKey="uddi:uddi.org:categorization:general_keywords"
        keyName="islandtrading.example:categorization:animals"
        keyValue="f"/>
      <keyedReference
        tModelKey="uddi:uddi.org:ubr:categorization:unspsc"
        keyName="unspsc-org:UNSPSC: Picture or drawing or
            coloring books for children"
        keyValue="55-10-15-07"/>
```

```
    </categoryBag>
  </businessService>
</businessServices>
```

Here's a sample **publisherAssertion** from the UDDI v3 specification:

```
<publisherAssertion>
  <!-- Specify ws-o-rama-cars.com:be47 businessKey as fromKey-->
  <fromKey>
    uddi:ws-o-rama-cars.com:be47
  </fromKey>
  <!-- Specify ws-o-rama-cars.com:mattsgarage:be3's businessKey as toKey-->
  <toKey>
    uddi:ws-o-rama-cars.com:mattsgarage:be3
  </toKey>
  <!--Specify a subsidiary relationship using uddi-org:relationships -->
  <keyedReference keyName="Subsidiary"
    keyValue="parent-child"
    tModelKey="uddi:uddi.org:relationships"/>
</publisherAssertion>
```

WS-I

The Web Services Interoperability Organization (WS-I) is an open industry consortium chartered to promote interoperability between the many Web Services specifications across platforms, operating systems, and programming languages (see http://www.ws-i.org/).

The founding members of WS-I include IBM, Microsoft, BEA Systems, SAP, Oracle, Fujitsu, Hewlett-Packard, and Intel. The Board of Directors consisting of the founding companies and two elected members (currently, Sun Microsystems and webMethods) govern the consortium.

WS-I promotes interoperability by publishing profiles, sample applications, and testing tools for Web Services:

- **Profiles:** Guidelines for implementing related Web Services specifications for best interoperability. These currently include:
  - Basic Profile
  - Attachments Profile
  - Simple SOAP Binding Profile

- **Sample Applications:** Working examples of Web Services applications that are compliant with WS-I guidelines. WS-I has published 11 Sample Applications for the Basic Profile.
- **Testing Tools:** Test suites that help determine WS-I conformance by a Web Service message.

WS-I Profiles

Updates to this list are available at: http://www.ws-i.org/:

- The WS-I Basic Profile 1.0 provides interoperability guidance for the following Web Services specifications: SOAP 1.1, WSDL 1.1, UDDI 2.0, XML 1.0, XML Schema, and HTTP 1.1.
- The Basic Security Profile, once published, will provide interoperability guidance transport security, including SOAP messaging security and other Web Services security considerations.

WS-I Sample Applications

Updates to this list are available at http://www.ws-i.org/deliverables/workinggroup.aspx?wg=sampleapps:

- Sample Application Implementations for BSP Implementation (Working Group Draft 25 May 2006). Basic Security Profile 1.0 samples.
- Sample Applications Security Architecture Document Specification (Working Group Draft 10 April 2006).
- Sample Application Implementations (Implementation Final 9 December 2003). Supply chain management application use cases conformant to the Basic Profile 1.0. Sample Applications have been submitted for BEA, Bowstreet, Corillian, IBM, Microsoft, Nokia, Novell, Oracle, Quovadx, SAP, and Sun Microsystems.
- Sample Architecture Usage Scenarios (Specification Final 9 December 2003). Usage Scenarios for Web Services in structured interactions.
- Supply Chain Management Sample Architecture (Specification Final 9 December 2003).
- Supply Chain Management use cases.

WS-I Testing Tools

Updates to this list are available at http://www.ws-i.org/deliverables/workinggroup.aspx?wg=testingtools:

- BSP 1.0 Test Assertion Document (TAD) (Working Group Draft 17 October 2006). The formal specification of the tests performed by the WS-I tools as specified in the interoperability profiles.
- BSP 1.0 Enhanced Logging Specification (Working Group Draft 13 July 2006). Defines enhanced logging facilities used by the WS-I test tools to support the Basic Security Profile.

- Analyzer Tool Functional Specification (Specification Final Material 13 June 2005). This is the final functional specification for version 1.1 of the Analyzer tool.
- AP 1.0 SSBP 1.0 TAD Version 1.0 (Final Material 13 June 2005). Supports testing of the Basic Profile 1.1, Attachments Profile 1.0, and the Simple SOAP Binding Profile 1.0.
- Interoperability Testing Tools 1.1 (Final 13 June 2005). Helps determine whether Web Services tools are conformant with WS-I profile guidelines Basic Profile 1.1 and SSBP 1.0.
- Monitor Tool Functional Specification (Final Material 13 June 2005).
- Basic Profile 1.0 TAD Version 1.1 (Final Material 12 January 2005). The formal specification of the tests performed by the WS-I tools as specified in the interoperability profiles.
- Basic Profile 1.1 TAD Version 1.1 (Final Material 12 January 2005). The formal specification of the tests performed by the WS-I tools as specified in the interoperability profiles.
- SSBP 1.0 BP 1.1 TAD Version 1.0 (Final Material 12 January 2005). The formal specification of the tests performed by the WS-I tools as specified in the interoperability profiles.
- Interoperability Testing Tools 1.1 (SSBP) (Board Approval Draft 14 December 2004). The WS-I testing tools are designed to help developers determine whether their Web Services are conformant with WS-I profile guidelines. This updated version is designed to test the Basic Profile 1.1 and the Simple SOAP Binding Profile 1.0.
- Test Tool Test Assertion Document (Specification Final 1 January 2004). Formal specification of the tests performed by the WS-I tools as specified in the interoperability profiles.

Alternatives: REST and ebXML

Although SOAP is the most talked about standard for Web Services, it is not the only one. At least two other major initiatives exist: REST and ebXML.

REST

REST is a standard for REpresentational State Transfer. In a nutshell, REST states that to implement Web Services one does not need an additional layer of abstraction, such as the one provided by SOAP and that it is more sensible to implement Web Services directly over XML and HTTP.

Generally speaking, many developers feel like SOAP is too complex for their needs. They prefer a simple approach based on the exchange of XML documents, following a pre-defined vocabulary.

An argument against the first versions of SOAP was that is was not very efficient. One of the reasons for the inefficiency was the reliance on POST exclusively. The semantic of POST in HTTP is such that it is impossible to cache requests and responses that therefore defeat the purpose of many network optimizations such as proxies and caches. SOAP 1.2 has RESTified by adding support for more HTTP verbs, most importantly GET. The GET verb is more efficient because it can be cached and optimized by application servers, proxies, and other network devices.

Although the difference appears small, it can result in a very significant performance boost so it's a worthwhile improvement. Unfortunately, at the time of writing, few libraries encourage the use of the more efficient GET form.

ebXML

ebXML is a global initiative founded by the UN/CEFACT and OASIS to standardize Web Services in the context of electronic business. ebXML places a very strong emphasis on semantic definitions. Ultimately it aims to build a catalogue of standard Web Services such as supply chain order, holiday booking, archiving accounting entries, and the like.

The emphasis on defining complete business interactions makes ebXML unique. You may think REST is an oversimplification but think again: HTTP is a solid protocol that defines a rich set of verbs to manipulate resources—GET to query a resource (think GET in SQL), POST to modify (think UPDATE in SQL), DELETE to remove one (think REMOVE in SQL), and PUT to create a new resource (think INSERT in SQL).

Combined with the rich syntax of XML, it is not difficult to build sophisticated services. Indeed Amazon Web Service is one of the most popular Web Service in the world and it is mostly accessed through a REST interface.

Summary

The promise behind Web Services is to treat the Web as a gigantic computer, accessible from any application that needs information or services it cannot render locally. One can tap into the Amazon.com database, perform extensive computing, validate address, track parcels, and more. All of these services can be integrated into applications.

In practice, it turns websites into software components that can be accessed and combined to serve the needs of a given user. However, because the components are loosely coupled instead of being hard-wired with each other, it's possible to recombine them in different fashions.

Whether you design desktop applications or websites, consider pasting some of the Web Service magic into your next development.

5 XML APIs

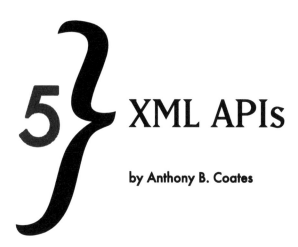

by Anthony B. Coates

XML is now the preferred format, the *lingua franca*, for sending data between computers in a platform-agnostic manner. Few major applications are now written without support for XML input and/or output. This chapter looks at the choices that developers have for APIs (libraries) that read/write/manipulate XML. It is important to realize that there are different varieties of XML API, and each is suited to a different set of application requirements. There is no single XML API that is the best choice for all cases. After reviewing a number of popular types of XML APIs (and related tools), the chapter finishes with a discussion of things to consider when choosing an XML API.

These different types of XML API have been designed to suit different application needs:

- Working with large files versus working with small files.
- Relying on user-written code versus relying on tool-generated code.
- Representing in-memory data as XML versus representing XML as in-memory data.
- Reading the information in an XML document versus transforming the document into a different XML format.

A common mistake that some developers make when first tasked with adding XML support to an application is that they find the most computationally efficient XML API and just use that, regardless of the actual application requirements. This will be one of the streaming APIs, and although these APIs are certainly computationally efficient, they generally require a lot more hand-written supporting code to use them. This means that the streaming APIs generally are not resource efficient in the project-management sense of you and I being project resources. It isn't only computational efficiency that matters when you have to get a project finished on time, in budget, and to a particular quality standard.

Comparison of XML APIs

Table 5.1 summarizes the different types of XML APIs and their features. Each API type is then discussed in the following sections.

Table 5.1 Summary of XML API Types

XML API Type	Comment
Streaming API	Computationally efficient, low memory consumption, start-to-finish only (no random access), usually requires more user-written code than other APIs.
Random-access API	Less computationally efficient, higher memory consumption, allows random access to any part of the document, usually requires less user-written code than for a streaming API. This category includes XPath-based APIs.
Schema compiler	Processes a schema to produce classes that represent XML content for the schema, as well as binding classes that can serialize Java objects to XML and deserialize XML to Java objects. Can cause unwanted tight coupling between applications and messages if used inappropriately.
XML-object mapper	Maps between XML structures and Java structures without requiring that the Java and XML have the same structure. Less likely to cause tight coupling than a schema compiler, but more work initially to set up the mapping.
Object serializer	Serializes Java objects to XML and deserializes that same XML to Java objects without using a schema. Can be useful for short-term storage; can cause problems for long-term storage. Difficult to hand-write XML correctly for system initialization and testing.
Transformer	Transforms the structure and content of an XML document using an XML transformation language (XSLT or XQuery). Less computationally efficient, higher memory consumption, but can be easier to code and maintain if your team has XSLT or XQuery skills.

Streaming APIs

Streaming XML APIs are used to read an XML document from beginning to end. They do not allow you to move back and forth to arbitrary locations in XML document in the way that

random-access XML do. This is because they do not build an in-memory model of the XML document as random-access APIs do.

Reading the XML document from start to finish, a streaming API can tell you:

- When it finds the start tag for an element.
- When it finds one or more attributes of an element.
- When it finds some or all of the text content of an element.
- When it finds the end tag for an element.
- When it finds a comment.
- When it finds a processing instruction (these are not widely used).

Streaming APIs give you *just* enough information to know what is in an XML document, but they don't give you any extra help. A streaming API is likely to work well if you can process your XML documents by examining the contents of one XML element at a time:

- Without knowing what the parent and ancestor elements are
- Without knowing what is contained in preceding or following elements

On the other hand, if your processing requires you to know exactly where in the document an element occurs, or if your processing requires you to examine values from multiple locations in the document together (not one at a time), you have to build your own application code on top of the streaming API. It is important to factor this in to your project plans.

The random-access APIs themselves are built on top of streaming APIs, and provide generic added-value to the limited information (albeit technically complete) that is provided by the streaming APIs. If you find that your processing requires you to build some kind of added-value layer of your own on top of a streaming API, such as to:

- Track where you are in a document during processing
- Store the information that has already been read, especially if in memory
- Examine values from different parts of the document

you should ask yourself whether you might be re-inventing the wheel, and whether one of the other XML APIs would give you much the same result for less effort (and less ongoing maintenance).

SAX

The first standardized XML parser API was *SAX*, the Simple API for XML. SAX is a Java API. Historically, a lot of XML software has been implemented in Java first, due to Java's native support of Unicode, which is also used for XML. However, there are non-Java implementations of SAX; see the "other languages" page on the SAX website for details (www.saxproject.org).

SAX is a streaming XML API, and it is also a callback API. This means that a SAX implementation is a parsing framework; when you are parsing an XML document, the SAX parser functions as the main program, and your code is only called when the SAX parser wants to register an *event*, for example, a start tag event or an end tag event. This differs from the other streaming APIs in the following subsections, where your main program directs the parsing.

The latest version of SAX is 2.0. The most common way to program for SAX is to extend one of the helper classes:

- **org.xml.sax.helpers.DefaultHandler**
- **org.xml.sax.helpers.DefaultHandler2**

You then add implementations for the callback methods that you are interested in. For example, you will want to override the default **startElement** and **endElement** methods.

```
public void startElement(java.lang.String uri,
 java.lang.String localName,
 java.lang.String qName,
 Attributes atts) throws SAXException;

public void endElement(java.lang.String uri,
 java.lang.String localName,
 java.lang.String qName) throws SAXException;
```

- **uri** – The namespace URI or the empty string if the element has no namespace URI or if namespace processing is not being performed.
- **localName** – The local name (without prefix), or the empty string if namespace processing is not being performed.
- **qName** – The qualified XML name (with prefix), or the empty string if qualified names are not available.
- **SAXException** – Any SAX exception, possibly wrapping another exception.

What is important to note here is that when the SAX parser calls your code using **startElement** or **endElement**, it provides you with the element name. Where appropriate, it also provides you with the namespace URI and the prefixed element name (QName). For **startElement**, it provides you with the element's attributes. Your code is not provided with information about where in the XML document tree the element is located. The SAX API does not provide you with *context* about the events (callbacks); that is something that you have to manage in your own code.

For example, you might need to track the ancestors of elements, perhaps because you have **Address** elements for both persons and companies, but you only want to process the company addresses:

- **Person/Address**
- **Company/Address**

You can do this using a stack to track the elements, for example:

```
// This is sample code, not production code. Written for Java 5.

import java.io.File;
import java.util.Stack;
import javax.xml.parsers.SAXParser;
import javax.xml.parsers.SAXParserFactory;
import org.xml.sax.Attributes;
import org.xml.sax.InputSource;
import org.xml.sax.SAXException;
import org.xml.sax.helpers.DefaultHandler;

/**
* This is an all-in-one class than implements
* SAX callback methods, and runs a SAX parser
* (using JAXP) from its main method.
*/
public class SaxSample extends DefaultHandler
{
 // The element XPath of interest.
 private static final String COMPANY_ADDRESS_XPATH = "Company/Address";

 // Counter for company addresses.
 private int numCompanyAddresses = 0;

 // This stack is used to track the context.
 private Stack<String> elementStack = new Stack<String>();

 public void startElement(String uri, String localName, String qName, Attributes
attributes)
 {
  // Just some logging to see what is happening.
  System.out.println("\nstartElement:");
  System.out.println(" qName = " + qName);
  System.out.flush();
```

```
    // Namespaces are ignored for this
    // simple example, but they are usually important.
    elementStack.push(qName);

    // Some more logging.
    System.out.println(" XPath = " + getXPath());
    System.out.flush();

    // Check if this element matches the XPath of interest.
    if (getXPath().endsWith(COMPANY_ADDRESS_XPATH))
    {
     numCompanyAddresses++;
    }
   }

   /**
   * Returns the XPath matching the current element stack contents.
   */
   public String getXPath()
   {
    // The result buffer.
    StringBuilder buffer = new StringBuilder();

    // Concatenate element names to produce XPath.
    for (String element : elementStack)
    {
     buffer.append('/');
     buffer.append(element);
    }

    // Return XPath.
    return buffer.toString();
   }

   public void endElement(String uri, String localName, String qName) throws
     SAXException
   {
```

```
 // Just some logging to see what is happening.
 System.out.println("\nendElement:");
 System.out.println(" qName = " + qName);
 System.out.flush();

 // Check which element is on the top of the stack
 String matchElement = elementStack.peek();

 // Make sure it matches the end element.
 if ((matchElement == null) || !matchElement.equals(qName))
 {
  throw new SAXException("unable to match end element for: " + qName +
     "(found: " + matchElement + ")");
 }

 // Match was OK, so pop end element from stack.
 elementStack.pop();
}

/**
* The main method. Expects an XML file
* name as a parameter.
* @param args command line arguments.
*/
public static void main(String[] args) throws Exception
{
 // Check for a single command line argument.
 if (args.length != 1)
 {
  printUsage();
  return;
 }

 // Create a SAX parser using JAXP.
 SAXParserFactory factory = SAXParserFactory.newInstance();
 SAXParser parser = factory.newSAXParser();
```

```
   // Create the SAX handler.
   SaxSample handler = new SaxSample();

   // Reset the address count and element stack.
   handler.resetNumCompanyAddresses();
   handler.resetElementStack();

   // Parse the XML file.
   System.out.println("Parsing ...");
   System.out.flush();
   parser.parse(new InputSource(args[0]), handler);

   // Check that element stack is empty.
   if (handler.getElementStackSize() > 0)
   {
    throw new Exception("Element stack not empty at end of parse: size = " +
        handler.getElementStackSize());
   }

   // Print out the results.
   System.out.println("\nCounted " + handler.getNumCompanyAddresses() +
       " company addresses.");
   System.out.flush();
  }

  /** Prints a simple usage message to the error stream. */
  public static void printUsage()
  {
   System.err.println("Usage is: java SaxSample <xml-file-name>");
   System.err.flush();
  }

  /**
  * @return the number of company addresses that were found.
  */
  public int getNumCompanyAddresses()
  {
```

```
  return numCompanyAddresses;
 }

 /**
 * Resets the number of company addresses to zero.
 */
 public void resetNumCompanyAddresses()
 {
  numCompanyAddresses = 0;
 }

 /**
 * @return the element stack size.
 */
 public int getElementStackSize()
 {
  return elementStack.size();
 }

 /**
 * Resets the element stack to empty.
 */
 public void resetElementStack()
 {
  elementStack.removeAllElements();
 }
}
```

Now, if you run the previous code using the following XML file, which contains two personal addresses and two company addresses:

```
<?xml version="1.0" encoding="UTF-8"?>
<AddressList>
 <Person>
  <Name>Anthony B. Coates</Name>
  <Address>London, UK</Address>
 </Person>
 <Person>
```

```
  <Name>William H. Gates</Name>
  <Address>Lake Washington, USA</Address>
 </Person>
 <Company>
  <Name>Miley Watts LLP</Name>
  <Address>Northampton, UK</Address>
 </Company>
 <Company>
  <Name>Sun Microsystems</Name>
  <Address>Menlo Park, USA</Address>
 </Company>
</AddressList>
```

The output is as follows:

```
Parsing ...

startElement:
qName = AddressList
XPath = /AddressList

startElement:
qName = Person
XPath = /AddressList/Person

startElement:
qName = Name
XPath = /AddressList/Person/Name

endElement:
qName = Name

startElement:
qName = Address
XPath = /AddressList/Person/Address

endElement:
qName = Address
```

```
endElement:
qName = Person

startElement:
qName = Person
XPath = /AddressList/Person

startElement:
qName = Name
XPath = /AddressList/Person/Name

endElement:
qName = Name

startElement:
qName = Address
XPath = /AddressList/Person/Address

endElement:
qName = Address

endElement:
qName = Person

startElement:
qName = Company
XPath = /AddressList/Company

startElement:
qName = Name
XPath = /AddressList/Company/Name

endElement:
qName = Name

startElement:
qName = Address
```

```
XPath = /AddressList/Company/Address

endElement:
qName = Address

endElement:
qName = Company

startElement:
qName = Company
XPath = /AddressList/Company

startElement:
qName = Name
XPath = /AddressList/Company/Name

endElement:
qName = Name

startElement:
qName = Address
XPath = /AddressList/Company/Address

endElement:
qName = Address

endElement:
qName = Company

endElement:
qName = AddressList

Counted 2 company addresses.
```

Note that the number of company addresses is correctly counted. This example gives you some idea of what is involved in handling the document context in your own code when using SAX. It also shows how element occurrences can be counted (this is the kind of thing you might need to do in some of your own callback methods). More complex processing might require you to store information from some or all of the preceding elements in the document. If you find that you need to store information for all of the elements in the document, you would probably be better off using a random-access API.

SAX is included in the JAXP API for Java (see java.sun.com/webservices/jaxp).

XMLReader

The XMLReader API takes a different approach to SAX. The application controls the processing, rather than waiting for callbacks from the parser. The API is implemented in .NET and Mono. Let's see how the SAX example is coded in C# using the XMLReader API.

When using an XMLReader, your code has to call the **Read** method to advance to the next node (for example, start element node, text node, and end element node). The XMLReader provides the methods needed to give you the details of the current node, so you can tell whether you have reached what you are after.

```
// This is sample code, not production code.
// Written for Mono 1.1.8.3 & .NET 1.1.

using Console = System.Console;
using XmlReader = System.Xml.XmlReader;
using XmlTextReader = System.Xml.XmlTextReader;

class XMLReaderSample
{
 /// <summary>The main method. Expects an XML file
 /// name as a parameter.</summary>
 /// <param name="args">command line arguments.</param>
 public static void Main(string[] args)
 {
  // Check for a single command line argument.
  if (args.Length != 1)
  {
   printUsage();
   return;
  }

  // The "Company" element.
  string COMPANY_ELEMENT = "Company";
```

```
// The "Address" element.
string ADDRESS_ELEMENT = "Address";

// Counter for company addresses.
int numCompanyAddresses = 0;

// Create an XMLReader, specifically an non-validating XMLTextReader.
XmlReader reader = new XmlTextReader(args[0]);

// Loop through the XML nodes, looking for "Company" elements.
while (!reader.EOF)
{
 reader.Read();
 if (!reader.IsStartElement(COMPANY_ELEMENT))
  continue;

 // Continue if this "Company" element is empty.
 if (reader.IsEmptyElement)
  continue;

 // Log that we found a "Company" element.
 Console.Out.WriteLine("Found element: " + COMPANY_ELEMENT);
 Console.Out.Flush();

 // Calculate depth of child elements in the XML tree.
 int childDepth = reader.Depth + 1;

 // Move to first child node.
 while (!reader.EOF && (reader.Depth < childDepth))
  reader.Read();

 // Loop through the child XML nodes, looking for "Address" elements.
 while (!reader.EOF && (reader.Depth == childDepth))
 {
  reader.Read();
  if (!reader.IsStartElement())
   continue;
```

```
      // Look for child "Address" elements.
      if (!reader.IsStartElement(ADDRESS_ELEMENT))
      {
       // Jump over the rest of this element's content, then continue.
       reader.Skip();
       continue;
      }

      // Found a Company/Address element, so incremement the count.
      numCompanyAddresses++;

      // Log that we found a "Company/Address" element.
      Console.Out.WriteLine("Found element: " + COMPANY_ELEMENT + "/" +
         ADDRESS_ELEMENT);
      Console.Out.Flush();
     }
    }

    // Print out the results.
    Console.Out.WriteLine("\nCounted " + numCompanyAddresses +
       " company addresses.");
    Console.Out.Flush();
   }

   /// <summary>Prints a simple usage message to the error stream.</summary>
   public static void printUsage()
   {
    Console.Error.WriteLine("Usage is: [mono] XMLReaderSample.exe <xml-file-
       name>");
    Console.Error.Flush();
   }
  }
```

Note that we didn't have to use a stack in the C#/XMLReader version to track where we were in the XML tree. That is a positive aspect of using the XMLReader API. A negative aspect is that your code has to explicitly read one node at a time to find the element that you want. With SAX, you can just wait for a **startElement** callback and ignore the other callbacks. That said, a lot of developers find it easier to write code where the application is in direct control of the XML parsing.

StAX

The Java world didn't stand still after the .NET XMLReader API appeared. Many Java developers felt that Java would benefit from a similar directed streaming API. As part of the Java community process, JSR 173(Streaming API for XML, also known as StAX) was developed. An implementation is available in the Java Web Services Developer Pack. The StAX implementation of the SAX example is very similar to the XMLReader implementation.

```
// This is sample code, not production code. Written for Java 5 & JWSDP 2.0.

import javax.xml.stream.XMLInputFactory;
import javax.xml.stream.XMLStreamReader;
import javax.xml.transform.stream.StreamSource;

public class StAXSample
{
 /**
 * The main method. Expects an XML file
 * name as a parameter.
 * @param args command line arguments.
 */
 public static void main(String[] args) throws Exception
 {
  // Check for a single command line argument.
  if (args.length != 1)
  {
   printUsage();
   return;
  }

  // The "Company" element.
  String COMPANY_ELEMENT = "Company";

  // The "Address" element.
  String ADDRESS_ELEMENT = "Address";

  // Counter for company addresses.
  int numCompanyAddresses = 0;
```

```
// Create an XML reader factory
XMLInputFactory factory = XMLInputFactory.newInstance();

// Create an XML reader.
XMLStreamReader reader = factory.createXMLStreamReader(
 new StreamSource(args[0])
);

// Loop through the XML nodes, looking for "Company" elements.
while (reader.hasNext())
{
 reader.next();
 if (reader.isStartElement()
     &&COMPANY_ELEMENT.equals(reader.getName().toString()))
 {
  // Log that we found a "Company" element.
  System.out.println("Found element: " + COMPANY_ELEMENT);
  System.out.flush();

  // Variable used to track the depth relative to the "Company" element.
  int depth = 0;

  // Loop through the child XML nodes, looking for "Company" elements.
  while (reader.hasNext())
  {
   reader.next();
   if (reader.isStartElement())
   {
    // Start element. Increase the depth.
    depth++;

    // If this is a descendent, not a child, continue.
    if (depth > 1)
     continue;

    // Look for child "Address" elements.
    if (!ADDRESS_ELEMENT.equals(reader.getName().toString()))
```

```
        continue;

      // Found a Company/Address element, so incremement the count.
      numCompanyAddresses++;

      // Log that we found a "Company/Address" element.
      System.out.println("Found element: " + COMPANY_ELEMENT + "/" +
         ADDRESS_ELEMENT);
      System.out.flush();
     }
     else if (reader.isEndElement())
     {
      // End element. Decrease the depth.
      depth--;

      // Check that it is a descendent element.
      if (depth < 0)
       break;
     }
    }
   }
  }

  // Tidy up.
  reader.close();

  // Print out the results.
  System.out.println("\nCounted " + numCompanyAddresses +
     " company addresses.");
  System.out.flush();
 }

 /** Prints a simple usage message to the error stream. */
 public static void printUsage()
 {
```

```
    System.err.println("Usage is: java StAXSample <xml-file-name>");
    System.err.flush();
  }
}
```

Compared to the XMLReader API, StAX doesn't give you a method to track the depth of the current node in the document. However, it is straightforward to do this by tracking start element and end element events. A start element event increases the depth by one and an end element event decreases the depth by one. The StAX API also doesn't provide a **skip** method to skip the content of the current element, but the equivalent effect is achieved by ignoring elements that are too deep to be direct child elements.

Random-Access APIs

Random-access XML APIs allow an XML document to be processed in something other than a simple start-to-finish order. A random-access API does this by parsing the XML document (from start-to-finish, using a streaming API) and building a representation of the document, in-memory or in-database. Once a random-access API has built a representation of an XML document, you can typically edit that representation and then write it out as a new XML document, or you can apply further processing to the same representation.

Not all random-access APIs allow you to edit a document. XPath-based APIs are random-access APIs in the sense that they allow you to use an XPath expression to select content from arbitrary locations in an XML document. However, they don't allow you to edit the document as you can with other random-access APIs.

The common objection to random-access APIs is that they use too much memory. The amount of memory required to build a complete representation of an XML document is larger than the size of the original XML document. How much larger depends on the particular API, but the amount of memory required to build the representation can be in the range of 1.5 to 10 times the size of the XML document (yes, that was *10*; you read it correctly). For single documents that are no more than 100KB in size, this memory usage usually isn't an issue. When you have many documents to process in memory simultaneously, or when the documents are more than 1MB in size, the memory usage can be a showstopper, and needs to be managed carefully.

However, the upside to random-access APIs that they provide more functionality than do the streaming APIs. You can edit your document programmatically. You can filter, sort, or pre-process the contents of your document before your core processing. You can move seamlessly from one part of the document to another during processing, which can save you from having to design, program, and maintain your own alternative representation of what content is in your document. Typically, you will have less code to write when working with a random-access API than you will when working with a streaming API, and that means less time to get your application running and more time available to test and debug it. The potential improvement in the quality of your final application shouldn't be ignored if you are working on an application where the memory usage of the random-access API does not cause any problems.

DOM

The DOM (Document Object Model) is the XML and HTML API from the W3C (World Wide Web Consortium). It was designed from the outset to be a programming language-independent API. The DOM API is only formally defined for Java and ECMAScript (JavaScript/VBScript), but there are numerous other implementations. A number of languages implement a DOM API by calling out to a C/C++ implementation.

One negative aspect of the language independence is that the DOM API doesn't feel like a *natural* API in any programming language (it probably works most naturally in ECMAScript). Because most developers only need to work with the DOM using a single programming language, there is not usually a strong advantage to having the same API across different languages.

However, a strong advantage for the DOM API is that it is widely implemented. Many programming languages now come with a DOM implementation, which means not having to find and install a third-party API. In many enterprise development setups, the DOM API may be one of the few choices of XML API available in the approved development software set.

The DOM often comes under criticism for the amount of memory it uses to represent an XML document, but there are a lot of XML documents that are small enough, so this is not necessarily an issue. The convenience of using the DOM should not be overlooked. For example, here is a C# DOM implementation (.NET/Mono) of the SAX example.

```
// This is sample code, not production code.
// Written for Mono 1.1.8.3 & .NET 1.1.

using Console = System.Console;
using XmlDocument = System.Xml.XmlDocument;
using XmlElement = System.Xml.XmlElement;
using XmlNode = System.Xml.XmlNode;
using XmlNodeList = System.Xml.XmlNodeList;
using XmlNodeType = System.Xml.XmlNodeType;

class DomSample
{
 /// <summary>The main method. Expects an XML file
 /// name as a parameter.</summary>
 /// <param name="args">command line arguments.</param>
```

```
static void Main(string[] args)
{
 // Check for a single command line argument.
 if (args.Length != 1)
 {
  printUsage();
  return;
 }

 // The "Company" element.
 string COMPANY_ELEMENT = "Company";

 // The "Address" element.
 string ADDRESS_ELEMENT = "Address";

 // Counter for company addresses.
 int numCompanyAddresses = 0;

 // XmlDocument is the .NET/Mono DOM implementation.
 XmlDocument document = new XmlDocument();

 // Load the file.
 document.Load(args[0]);

 // Iterate through the "Company" elements.
 XmlNodeList companyNodes = document.GetElementsByTagName(COMPANY_ELEMENT);
 foreach (XmlNode companyNode in companyNodes)
 {
  // This is a "Company" element.
  XmlElement company = (XmlElement) companyNode;

  // Log that we found a "Company" element.
  Console.Out.WriteLine("Found element: " + COMPANY_ELEMENT);
  Console.Out.Flush();

  // Now search the direct children for an "Address" element.
  XmlNodeList childNodes = company.ChildNodes;
```

```
    foreach (XmlNode childNode in childNodes)
    {
     // Look for element nodes with the name "Address".
     if (childNode.NodeType == XmlNodeType.Element)
     {
      XmlElement child = (XmlElement) childNode;
      if (ADDRESS_ELEMENT.Equals(child.Name))
      {
       // Found a Company/Address element, so incremement the count.
       numCompanyAddresses++;

       // Log that we found a "Company/Address" element.
       Console.Out.WriteLine("Found element: " + COMPANY_ELEMENT + "/" +
          ADDRESS_ELEMENT);
       Console.Out.Flush();
      }
     }
    }
   }

   // Print out the results.
   Console.Out.WriteLine("\nCounted " + numCompanyAddresses +
      " company addresses.");
   Console.Out.Flush();
  }

  /// <summary>Prints a simple usage message to the error stream.</summary>
  public static void printUsage()
  {
   Console.Error.WriteLine("Usage is: [mono] DomSample.exe <xml-file-name>");
   Console.Error.Flush();
  }
 }
```

The DOM implementation is more straightforward than the streaming API equivalents. It's not that the code is so much shorter, but it is simpler to write, and there are fewer ways to get the code wrong. That's important when code quality and schedules matter at least as much as speed of execution. See www.w3.org/DOM for more details.

dom4j, JDOM, and XOM

As noted in the section on the DOM API, the DOM's cross-language design means that it lacks a natural feel in any particular programming language. There have been a number of alternative APIs developed for Java that aim to be more consistent with the style of familiar non-XML Java APIs. The main alternative APIs are dom4j, JDOM, and XOM. Of these, JDOM isn't being developed beyond the 1.0 release, whereas XOM is something of a spiritual successor to JDOM, with the aim of improving on the JDOM approach. XOM also aims to be the most technically correct of the XML APIs.

An interesting aspect of XOM is that it combines the streaming and in-memory-tree approaches. XOM streams content into an in-memory tree, and you can start processing the tree before the streaming is finished. This differs from other in-memory APIs (but you might be hard pressed to measure the performance differences in practice).

If you are using Java and an in-memory-tree API suits your requirements, you might want to check out all of these alternatives to the DOM API. In making a choice, the following criteria are useful:

- Are you able to choose and install the XML API of your choice? If not, you may have to stick to the DOM.
- Are the license terms for the XML API compatible with your project? Don't choose an XML API that your legal department will make you remove before your product can be released.
- The smaller the problem, the less of an issue the choice of API is. There is little point in introducing a separate XML API if you are only using it for tens of lines of code or fewer.

VTD-XML

If you find that the memory consumption of the DOM API is too great for a particular application, you can try VTD-XML, which claims to only require 1.5x the document size in memory, much less than the 10x required by the DOM API. Interest in DOM-style APIs with a small memory footprint is being driven by the need to support XML on mobile phones. Some experimental APIs have been reported to need no more than the document size in memory, so we are likely to see further improvements in this area. For more information, see vtd-xml.sourceforge.net.

JAXP XPath

JAXP (Java API for XML Processing) includes the **javax.xml.xpath** package, which allows you to run an XPath expression against an XML document. The document can be loaded from a file or URL, or it can already be in-memory as a DOM document. XPaths provide a compact syntax for locating and extracting information from XML documents. Using the JAXP XPath classes, the SAX example becomes:

```
// This is sample code, not production code. Written for Java 5 & JWSDP 2.0.

import java.io.FileReader;
import javax.xml.xpath.XPath;
import javax.xml.xpath.XPathConstants;
import javax.xml.xpath.XPathExpression;
import javax.xml.xpath.XPathFactory;
import org.w3c.dom.NodeList;
import org.xml.sax.InputSource;

public class JaxpXpathSample
{
 /**
 * The main method. Expects an XML file
 * name as a parameter.
 * @param args command line arguments.
 */
 public static void main(String[] args) throws Exception
 {
  // Check for a single command line argument.
  if (args.length != 1)
  {
   printUsage();
   return;
  }

  // Create the XPath expression to count the company addresses.
  XPathFactory xpfactory = XPathFactory.newInstance();
  XPath xpath = xpfactory.newXPath();

  // Count the company addresses directly using XPath.
  NodeList companyAddresses = (NodeList) xpath.evaluate(
   "//Company/Address",
   new InputSource(new FileReader(args[0])),
   XPathConstants.NODESET
  );
```

```
    // Print out the results.
    System.out.println("Counted " + companyAddresses.getLength() +
        " company addresses.");
    System.out.flush();
  }

  /** Prints a simple usage message to the error stream. */
  public static void printUsage()
  {
    System.err.println("Usage is: java DomXpathSample <xml-file-name>");
    System.err.flush();
  }
}
```

This is the simplest yet, simpler than both the streaming API and DOM examples. That is assuming that the developer understands how to write XPaths. XPath is much smaller and quicker to learn than XSLT, for example, so a developer who is not an XML specialist should still pick up the basics of XPath quickly.

Some developers don't like XPaths because they can't be validated at compile time. That is an issue, but compile time validation is all about finding errors early so that you can minimize the number of bugs in your code. The fact is that XPaths are shorter to write than the equivalent Java/C# (and so on) code, and easier to read for anyone maintaining the code. On that basis, they make a significant enough contribution to the reduction of bugs in your code that the lack of compile-time checking doesn't outweigh the advantages.

XPathDocument (.NET, Mono)

The .NET/Mono world also has an XPath API. The XPathDocument API is a read-only API designed not only to evaluate XPaths, but also to minimize the memory usage where possible. It is important to remember with XPaths that some XPath expressions require the whole document to be in memory (for example, anything using **preceding::** or **following::**), whereas others only require that a localized portion of the document is in memory (as is the case with the running SAX example). Used carefully, XPath APIs can strike a good balance between conciseness of code and memory usage. Coded using C# (.NET or Mono), the SAX example becomes:

```
// This is sample code, not production code.
// Written for Mono 1.1.8.3 & .NET 1.1.

using Console = System.Console;
using XPathDocument = System.Xml.XPath.XPathDocument;
```

```
using XPathNavigator = System.Xml.XPath.XPathNavigator;
using XPathNodeIterator = System.Xml.XPath.XPathNodeIterator;

class XPathDocumentSample
{
 /// <summary>The main method. Expects an XML file
 /// name as a parameter.</summary>
 /// <param name="args">command line arguments.</param>
 public static void Main(string[] args)
 {
  // Check for a single command line argument.
  if (args.Length != 1)
  {
   printUsage();
   return;
  }

  // Create an XPathDocument.
  XPathDocument document = new XPathDocument(args[0]);

  // Create an XPathNavigator to process the XPath.
  XPathNavigator navigator = document.CreateNavigator();

  // Evaluate the XPath.
  XPathNodeIterator companyAddresses =
   (XPathNodeIterator) navigator.Evaluate("//Company/Address");

  // Print out the results.
  Console.Out.WriteLine("Counted " + companyAddresses.Count +
     " company addresses.");
  Console.Out.Flush();
 }

 /// <summary>Prints a simple usage message to the error stream.</summary>
 public static void printUsage()
 {
```

```
  Console.Error.WriteLine("Usage is: [mono] XPathDocumentSample.exe <xml-file-
     name>");
  Console.Error.Flush();
 }
}
```

This is very similar to the JAXP XPath example.

Schema Compilers

If you use a random-access XML API to process an XML document, you are using a generic API that is not customized to your particular XML documents. This tends to make programming more tedious and more error-prone. For example, would you rather work with a generic API where you write code like

```
getElement("CustomerName").getText()
```

or would you rather write

```
getCustomerName()
```

The first style is useful if you need to configure the element name at runtime, but the second style is what most programmers want to use, because that is the style that most non-XML Java/C# (and so on) APIs are written in. The second style also allows the compiler to check that **CustomerName** has been spelled correctly.

Schema compilers (also known as *binding tools*) work by "compiling" one or more XML schemas (DTDs, W3C XML Schemas, or RELAX NG schemas) to produce the following:

- A set of object-oriented classes representing the data structure of the schema.
- Auxiliary classes that convert the data to and from XML.
- Validation code that performs, on the in-memory data, the same validations that a schema validator would perform on the equivalent XML document.

This produces an API where the classes and methods are named after the elements, attributes, and types in the schema(s). This is so attractive to programmers who aren't XML specialists that it is often the first thing that is tried. Once the schemas have been compiled, the programmers can all but ignore the fact that they are working with XML, and just work with an API in their preferred programming language.

This convenience comes at a price, however. When you compile a schema to produce code, you introduce a *tight coupling* between the code and the schema. If the schema changes, the code needs to be recompiled, and the new API might not be backwards compatible with the old API. This can lead to widespread code breakage unless you have put in place a suitable architectural mechanism to mitigate the knock-on effects of schema changes. The situation is worse if the schema is controlled by an outside development team or organization, because then the schema changes could come at any time, and might not fit in easily with your development schedule.

It is important to remember that XML messages are commonly used to decouple applications running on different systems, so that changes to one system don't necessarily impact all other systems. If you couple your application code to your XML schemas by tightly coupling the application code to code compiled from the schemas, your systems are no longer decoupled. This is not to say that you should not use schema compilers. They are extremely useful when used correctly. However, if you do compile your schemas, it is a good idea to put a façade layer between the schema-generated code and your core application code, so that core application code only uses the façade API and not the schema-generated API. The façade layer is a mapping layer, typically hand-coded, that allows you to protect your application code from schema changes that are not significant to the application. Alternatively, you could use an XML-object mapping tool to provide the decoupling, as shown in Figure 5.1.

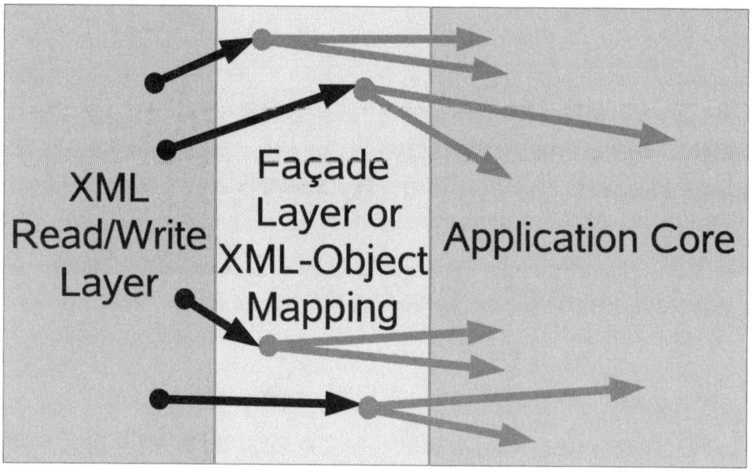

Figure 5.1
Decoupling application code from code compiled from an XML schema.

There is a special benefit that comes from using code that has been compiled from an XML schema. If you create your data classes by compiling XML schemas, you are assured of being able to serialize your data classes as XML. Serializing your hand-coded Java classes to XML can be difficult if you have a complicated graph of references connecting objects (but see the section later in this chapter called "Object Serializers" for tools that do this, albeit with limitations).

Some programmers are opposed to having "data only" classes, as produced by schema compilers, and argue that such classes break the *object-oriented programming paradigm*. However, it is important to remember that object-oriented programming is no more of a silver bullet than any other software technique. There are times when object-oriented programming works very well, for example, for an application's in-memory data. However, the well-known object-database and object-XML "impedance mismatches", combined with the failure of object databases to gain significant commercial traction for cross-application data, should be seen an indicative of the object-oriented paradigm failing to provide a good solution when it comes to serialized (stored) data, especially where the stored data is long-lived. When using XML, just as with relational databases, it can be easier to develop and manage an application if the serializable objects (as opposed to the transient, non-serializable objects) are data-only objects that reflect the underlying data structure of the persistence mechanism (XML or database).

JAXB

JAXB, the Java API for XML Binding, is a standard Java API for W3C XML Schema to Java binding tools (schema compilers). In spite of it being a standard that can be implemented by multiple schema compilers, in practice the only JAXB implementation in wide use is Sun's JAXB implementation.

To use JAXB for the SAX example, you need a W3C XML schema for the address list XML. A suitable schema is **AddressList.xsd**:

```
<?xml version="1.0" encoding="UTF-8"?>
<xs:schema xmlns:xs="http://www.w3.org/2001/XMLSchema">

 <xs:element name="AddressList" type="AddressList">
  <xs:annotation>
   <xs:documentation>
    This is the root (top-level) element of the address list document.
   </xs:documentation>
  </xs:annotation>
 </xs:element>

 <xs:complexType name="AddressList">
  <xs:annotation>
   <xs:documentation>
    Any number of personal or company address details.
    Note that the same complex type is used for both
    personal and company address details, but the
    XML element name is different.
   </xs:documentation>
  </xs:annotation>
  <xs:choice minOccurs="0" maxOccurs="unbounded">
```

```
    <xs:element name="Person" type="NameAndAddress"/>
    <xs:element name="Company" type="NameAndAddress"/>
   </xs:choice>
  </xs:complexType>

  <xs:complexType name="NameAndAddress">
   <xs:annotation>
    <xs:documentation>
     A matching name and address pair.
    </xs:documentation>
   </xs:annotation>
   <xs:sequence>
    <xs:element name="Name" type="xs:string"/>
    <xs:element name="Address" type="xs:string"/>
   </xs:sequence>
  </xs:complexType>

</xs:schema>
```

There are different ways you could have created an equivalent schema. I have chosen to use the so-called "Venetian blind" technique, which I prefer to call the "local element, global type" technique. The types in the schema are globally defined, whereas all of the elements in the schema are locally defined within types, with the exception of a single global element definition for the root element of the document. This is the most common type of schema structure for "data-oriented" XML, and it is the structure that tends to work best with schema compilers, because it maps well to object-oriented structures (types map to classes, and elements map to properties of classes).

JAXB supports many configuration options for the Java that it generates, and these options can be embedded in the schema(s) or stored in a separate external XML control file. This example examines the classes produced by JAXB using only the default settings. The command-line tool for compiling W3C XML Schemas with JAXB is **xjc**. To compile **AddressList.xsd**, the command line for Windows is

```
xjc.bat -p org.thexmlguild.sample AddressList.xsd -d src\java AddressList.xsd
```

and the command line for Linux/Unix is

```
xjc.sh -p org.thexmlguild.sample AddressList.xsd -d src/java AddressList.xsd
```

This command line compiles **AddressList.xsd** using **org.thexmlguild.sample** as the package for the generated Java classes, and the Java sources will be generated in the **src\java** (or **src/java**) directory, that is, the directory tree **org\thexmlguild\sample** will be created in **src\java**, and the Java sources files will be generated directly into the **src\java\org\thexmlguild\sample** directory. Note that **xjc** assumes (unfortunately) that you are using a directory path that does *not* contain spaces.

With the default settings, **xjc** produces three Java classes: **AddressList.java**, **NameAndAddress.java**, and **ObjectFactory.java**. Note that **AddressList** and **NameAndAddress** are the names of the two global complex types defined in the schema, so there is one class for each global complex type plus an object factory class. Using JAXB 2.0, the generated classes include Java 5 annotations.

AddressList.java (comments removed for brevity):

```
package org.thexmlguild.sample;

import java.util.ArrayList;
import java.util.List;
import javax.xml.bind.JAXBElement;
import javax.xml.bind.annotation.XmlAccessType;
import javax.xml.bind.annotation.XmlAccessorType;
import javax.xml.bind.annotation.XmlElementRef;
import javax.xml.bind.annotation.XmlElementRefs;
import javax.xml.bind.annotation.XmlType;

@XmlAccessorType(XmlAccessType.FIELD)
@XmlType(name = "AddressList", propOrder = {
 "personOrCompany"
})
public class AddressList {

 @XmlElementRefs({
  @XmlElementRef(name = "Company", type = JAXBElement.class),
  @XmlElementRef(name = "Person", type = JAXBElement.class)
 })
 protected List<JAXBElement<NameAndAddress>> personOrCompany;

 public List<JAXBElement<NameAndAddress>> getPersonOrCompany() {
  if (personOrCompany == null) {
```

```
    personOrCompany = new ArrayList<JAXBElement<NameAndAddress>>();
   }
   return this.personOrCompany;
  }

}
```

NameAndAddress.java (comments removed for brevity):

```
package org.thexmlguild.sample;

import javax.xml.bind.annotation.XmlAccessType;
import javax.xml.bind.annotation.XmlAccessorType;
import javax.xml.bind.annotation.XmlElement;
import javax.xml.bind.annotation.XmlType;

@XmlAccessorType(XmlAccessType.FIELD)
@XmlType(name = "NameAndAddress", propOrder = {
 "name",
 "address"
})
public class NameAndAddress {

 @XmlElement(name = "Name", required = true)
 protected String name;
 @XmlElement(name = "Address", required = true)
 protected String address;

 public String getName() {
  return name;
 }

 public void setName(String value) {
  this.name = value;
 }

 public String getAddress() {
  return address;
```

```
 }
 public void setAddress(String value) {
  this.address = value;
 }

}
```

ObjectFactory.java (comments removed for brevity):

```
package org.thexmlguild.sample;

import javax.xml.bind.JAXBElement;
import javax.xml.bind.annotation.XmlElementDecl;
import javax.xml.bind.annotation.XmlRegistry;
import javax.xml.namespace.QName;

@XmlRegistry
public class ObjectFactory {

 private final static QName _AddressList_QNAME = new QName("", "AddressList");
 private final static QName _AddressListCompany_QNAME = new QName("",
    "Company");
 private final static QName _AddressListPerson_QNAME = new QName("", "Person");

 public ObjectFactory() {
 }

 public AddressList createAddressList() {
  return new AddressList();
 }

 public NameAndAddress createNameAndAddress() {
  return new NameAndAddress();
 }

 @XmlElementDecl(namespace = "", name = "AddressList")
 public JAXBElement<AddressList> createAddressList(AddressList value) {
```

```
  return new JAXBElement<AddressList>(_AddressList_QNAME, AddressList.class,
    null, value);
 }

 @XmlElementDecl(namespace = "", name = "Company", scope = AddressList.class)
 public JAXBElement<NameAndAddress> createAddressListCompany(NameAndAddress
   value) {
  return new JAXBElement<NameAndAddress>(_AddressListCompany_QNAME,
NameAndAddress.class, AddressList.class, value);
 }

 @XmlElementDecl(namespace = "", name = "Person", scope = AddressList.class)
 public JAXBElement<NameAndAddress> createAddressListPerson(NameAndAddress
   value) {
  return new JAXBElement<NameAndAddress>(_AddressListPerson_QNAME,
NameAndAddress.class, AddressList.class, value);
 }

}
```

The following code counts the company addresses in the address list XML using the JAXB classes:

```
// This is sample code, not production code. Written for Java 5 & JAXB 2.1EA.

import java.io.File;
import java.util.Collection;
import java.util.Iterator;
import java.util.List;
import javax.xml.bind.JAXBContext;
import javax.xml.bind.JAXBElement;
import javax.xml.bind.Unmarshaller;
import org.thexmlguild.sample.AddressList;
import org.thexmlguild.sample.NameAndAddress;

public class JAXBSample
{
 /** The main method. Expects an XML file
 * name as a parameter.
```

```
* @param args command line arguments.
*/
public static void main(String[] args) throws Exception
{
 // Check for a single command line argument.
 if (args.length != 1)
 {
  printUsage();
  return;
 }

 // Set up a JAXB unmarshalling (deserialization) context.
 // Note how the package name is used so that the generic
 // JAXB unmarshaller can locate the JAXB classes specific
 // to "AddressList.xsd".
 JAXBContext jc = JAXBContext.newInstance("org.thexmlguild.sample");

 // Now create the unmarshaller for "AddressList.xsd" instances.
 Unmarshaller unmarshaller = jc.createUnmarshaller();

 // Now unmarshal (deserialize) the XML address list
 // and produce a top-level Java object.
 Object topObject = unmarshaller.unmarshal(new File(args[0]));

 // The top-level object should be a JAXB element with "AddressList" type.
 JAXBElement<AddressList>addressListElement = null;
 try
 {
  addressListElement = (JAXBElement<AddressList>) topObject;
 }
 catch (ClassCastException e){
  System.err.println(
   "Wrong type of top-level unmarshalled object: "
   + topObject.getClass().getName()
  );
  System.err.flush();
  System.exit(1);
```

```
  }
  AddressList addressList = addressListElement.getValue();

  // Now count the number of child "Company" objects
  // in the address list to get the number of
  // company addresses.
  List<JAXBElement<NameAndAddress>>addresses = addressList.getPersonOrCompany();
  int numCompanyAddresses = 0;
  for (JAXBElement<NameAndAddress> addressElement : addresses)
  {
   System.out.println("Found element: " + addressElement.getName());
   if ("Company".equals(addressElement.getName().toString()))
   {
    numCompanyAddresses++;
   }
  }

  // Print out the results.
  System.out.println("\nCounted " + numCompanyAddresses +
     " company addresses.");
  System.out.flush();
 }

 /** Prints a simple usage message to the error stream. */
 public static void printUsage()
 {
  System.err.println("Usage is: java JaxbSample <xml-file-name>");
  System.err.flush();
 }
}
```

The output of the program is

```
Found element: Person
Found element: Person
Found element: Company
```

```
Found element: Company

Counted 2 company addresses.
```

.NET XML Schema Definition Tool

The W3C XML Schema compiler for .NET and Mono is **xsd.exe**. To compile **AddressList.xsd** from JAXB and produce C#, the command line for Windows is

```
xsd AddressList.xsd /c /n:org.thexmlguild.sample /o:src\cs /l:CS
```

and the almost identical command line for Linux/Unix is

```
xsd AddressList.xsd /c /n:org.thexmlguild.sample /o:src/cs /l:CS
```

where in this example **org.thexmlguild.sample** is the C# namespace for the generated classes, **src\cs** (or **src/cs**) is the directory into which the generated sources are created, and CS selects C# generation (as opposed to using **VB** to generate Visual Basic). This produces the C# file **AddressList.cs** (with comments removed for brevity):

```
namespace org.thexmlguild.sample {

 public class AddressList {

  [System.Xml.Serialization.XmlIgnoreAttribute()]
  public ItemsChoiceType[] ItemsElementName;

  [System.Xml.Serialization.XmlElement("Person")]
  [System.Xml.Serialization.XmlElement("Company")]
  [System.Xml.Serialization.XmlChoiceIdentifier("ItemsElementName")]
  public NameAndAddress[] Items;
 }

 public enum ItemsChoiceType {

  Person,

  Company,
 }

 public class NameAndAddress {
```

```
  public string Name;

  public string Address;
 }

}
```

This generated file is quite short, due to its use of the built-in XML serialization functionality in .NET and Mono; the file contains two classes (AddressList and NameAndAddress) and an enumeration (ItemsChoiceType). To count the number of company addresses in AddressList.xml, the code is:

```
// This is sample code, not production code.
// Written for Mono 1.1.8.3 & .NET 1.1.

using Console = System.Console;
using XmlSerializer = System.Xml.Serialization.XmlSerializer;
using XmlTextReader = System.Xml.XmlTextReader;
using AddressList = org.thexmlguild.sample.AddressList;
using ItemsChoiceType = org.thexmlguild.sample.ItemsChoiceType;

class XsdCsSample
{
 /// <summary>The main method. Expects an XML file
 /// name as a parameter.</summary>
 /// <param name="args">command line arguments.</param>
 public static void Main(string[] args)
 {
  // Check for a single command line argument.
  if (args.Length != 1)
  {
   printUsage();
   return;
  }

  // Create an XML serializer/deserializer for address list XML.
  XmlSerializer serializer = new XmlSerializer(typeof(AddressList));

  // Deserialize the XML address list.
```

```
 AddressList addressList = (AddressList) serializer.Deserialize(
  new XmlTextReader(args[0])
 );

 // Count the company addresses.
 ItemsChoiceType[] addressElements = addressList.ItemsElementName;
 int numCompanyAddresses = 0;
 foreach (ItemsChoiceType addressElement in addressElements)
 {
  Console.Out.WriteLine("Found: " + addressElement);
  if ("Company".Equals(addressElement.ToString()))
  {
   numCompanyAddresses++;
  }
 }

 // Print out the results.
 Console.Out.WriteLine("\nCounted " + numCompanyAddresses +
    " company addresses.");
 Console.Out.Flush();
}

/// <summary>Prints a simple usage message to the error stream.</summary>
public static void printUsage()
{
 Console.Error.WriteLine("Usage is: [mono] XsdCsSample.exe <xml-file-name>");
 Console.Error.Flush();
}
}
```

The output of this program is once again

```
Found: Person
Found: Person
Found: Company
Found: Company

Counted 2 company addresses.
```

C24 IO

Integration objects from Century 24 Solutions (hereafter called C24 IO) is a Java data modeling, binding, and transformation tool that comes in both open and commercial versions. One of the numerous things that it can do is compile W3C XML schemas (as well as DTDs and RELAX NG schemas; the latter are discussed in another chapter). C24 IO is GUI-based, unlike the other software discussed in this chapter. (See www.c24.biz for more information.)

To compile a schema with C24 IO, you first import it to produce a C24 IO model as shown in Figure 5.2.

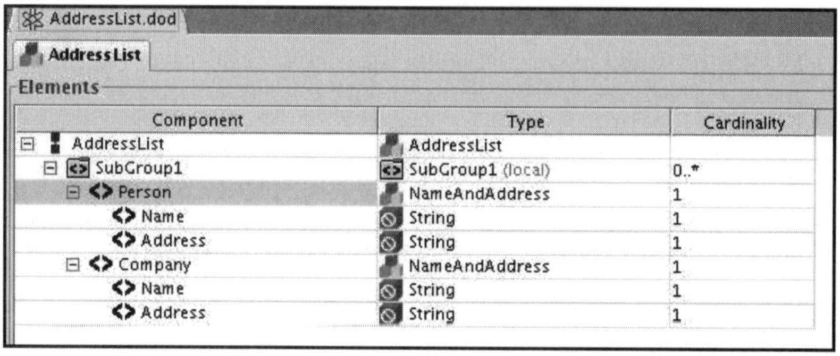

Figure 5.2
C24 IO model produced by importing ***AddressList.xsd.***

If you examine the model, you will see that the (unnamed) choice in the Schema (between **<Person>** and **<Company>**) has been given the meaningless name **SubGroup1**. This is a problem that can arise generally with schema compilers when a schema contains unnamed constructs such as sequences or choices. These are generally mapped onto a class, and that class needs a name. With C24 IO, automatically generated names can be edited (by hand). After changing the name from **SubGroup1** to **PersonOrCompany**, the model is shown in Figure 5.3.

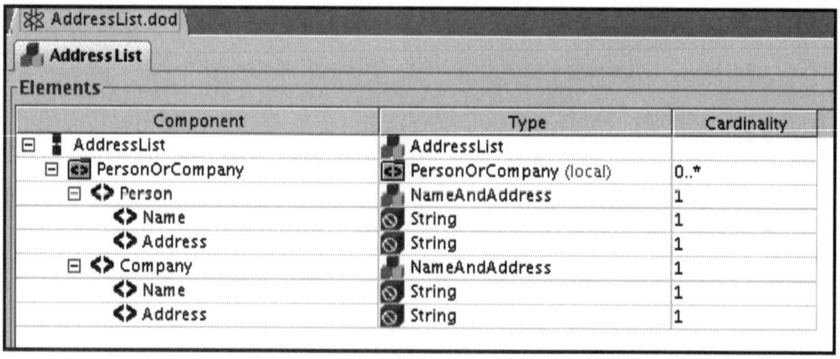

Figure 5.3
Edited C24 IO model produced after importing ***AddressList.xsd.***

Like W3C XML Schemas, C24 IO models are identified by a namespace URI, so **http://sample.thexmlguild.org/** was chosen (this is just an identifier string; it is not an active Web address). Java classes for the model can be deployed (exported) either from the GUI or from the command line (using Apache Ant). C24 IO implements Java classes based on a generic data model. This makes it possible use XPath and/or XQuery on the Java objects, but at the expense of producing more code than the other schema compilers do. The generated classes are:

- **AddressListElement** – Class that represents the document root **AddressList** element. It is also a factory class for reading and writing XML address lists.
- **AddressListClass** – Class that represents the global **AddressList** complex datatype.
- **AddressListDataModel** – Helper class that contains model information about the **AddressList** type.
- **AddressList** – Class that represents the actual address list data.
- **NameAndAddressClass** – Class that represents the global **NameAndAddress** complex datatype.
- **NameAndAddress** – Class that represents the actual name and address data.

The following Java code can be used to count the number of company addresses using the classes generated by C24 IO:

```
// This is sample code, not production code. Written for Java 5 & C24 IO 3.5.7.

import java.io.FileReader;
import org.apache.log4j.ConsoleAppender;
import org.apache.log4j.Level;
import org.apache.log4j.Logger;
import org.apache.log4j.SimpleLayout;
import org.thexmlguild.sample.AddressList;
import org.thexmlguild.sample.AddressListElement;

public class C24IOSample
{
 /** The main method. Expects an XML file
  * name as a parameter.
  * @param args command line arguments.
  */
 public static void main(String[] args) throws Exception
 {
```

```
// Check for a single command line argument.
if (args.length != 1)
{
 printUsage();
 return;
}

// Set up "log4j" error/warning logger.
ConsoleAppender rootAppender = new ConsoleAppender(new SimpleLayout());
Logger rootLogger = Logger.getRootLogger();
rootLogger.addAppender(rootAppender);
rootLogger.setLevel(Level.WARN);

// Create an "AddressListElement" class to act as deserializer.
AddressListElement rootElement = new AddressListElement();

// Read the XML file into a StringBuilder.
StringBuilder xmlBuilder = new StringBuilder();
char[] buffer = new char[4096];
FileReader input = new FileReader(args[0]);
while (true)
{
 int numChars = input.read(buffer);
 if (numChars < 0)
 {
  break;
 }
 xmlBuilder.append(buffer, 0, numChars);
}

// Read the XML address list and produce a matching Java object.
AddressList addressList = (AddressList) rootElement.parseObject(
 xmlBuilder.toString()
);

// Count the number of company addresses.
// This uses both the JavaBean API (there is also a generic API).
```

```
  // "getPersonOrCompany()" returns an array of choice objects.
  // Those choice objects have a non-null value for "getPerson()"
  // or "getCompany", but not for both.
  int numCompanyAddresses = 0;
  for (int idx = 0; idx < addressList.getPersonOrCompany().length; idx++)
  {
   if (addressList.getPersonOrCompany()[idx].getCompany() != null)
   {
    // A non-null value indicates that a company was found.
    numCompanyAddresses++;
   }
  }

  // Print out the results.
  System.out.println("Counted " + numCompanyAddresses + " company addresses.");
  System.out.flush();
 }

 /** Prints a simple usage message to the error stream. */
 public static void printUsage()
 {
  System.err.println("Usage is: java C24IOSample <xml-file-name>");
  System.err.flush();
 }
}
```

Relaxer

If you are using RELAX NG schemas (discussed in Chapter 3), the alternative to using C24 IO to compile the schemas is to use *Relaxer*, which was the first schema compiler for RELAX NG. (See www.relaxer.org for more information.)

XML-Object Mappers

XML-object mappers are related to schema compilers. However, they don't (necessarily) produce object-oriented classes to represent the data structure of the schema. Instead, they work with your own object-oriented classes, that is, with classes that reflect your core application's data model, your core application's view of the world. An XML-object mapper generates only auxiliary classes that convert the data to and from XML, but it does so based on a set of mapping rules that you create and maintain. This means that if the schema changes in future, you can protect your application from schema changes that don't affect it by changing the mapping rules and not your application. This keeps your core application code as decoupled as possible from the XML.

Some XML-object mappers can also function as schema compilers, and can generate object-oriented classes to represent the data structure of the schema, as well as producing an initial set of mapping rules. The difference from a pure schema compiler is that if the schema changes, you have two options:

- Recompiling the updated schema from scratch (as you would with a pure schema compiler).
- Keeping the data structure classes generated from the original schema, and updating the mapping rules to accommodate the differences in the new schema.

Having both options gives you significantly more flexibility in how you manage change than you have with just a pure schema compiler. Two popular XML-object mappers are Castor (www.castor.org) and JiBX (jibx.sourceforge.net). Note that both can do more than just XML-object mapping.

Object Serializers

An object serializer is the reverse of a schema compiler. It doesn't compile schemas, nor does it work with schemas. An object serializer is applied to set of in-memory data objects, and it produces an XML representation of that data that can be stored now and reloaded later. This XML representation has no schema, because it is just a representation of what objects are in memory now. To produce a schema, it would need to be able to calculate what objects from what classes can be in memory at any time in the future (and how they can be interlinked), and that is a level of code analysis that current object serializers do not implement.

XML object serializers suffer from the same issues that binary object serializers (for example, Java serialization) suffer from. If you save some objects as XML today, you might not be able to reload them from that XML in the future if the classes have changed structure. As there are no schemas, there is no straightforward way to determine how you might be able to edit today's XML so that it can be loaded to work with tomorrow's classes. Nor is there an easy way to produce test data that can be loaded reliably, because there is again no schema to validate the test data against. All you can do is to keep checking whether you can load your test data as you edit it, and see if it works or fails (and hope that the error messages tell you something useful).

Like any object serializers, XML object serializers have a place, and that is for short-term storage of information. What this means in practice is that the classes should be unlikely to change in the time between when data is stored as XML, and when it is reloaded from XML. If any of the data is more long-lived than the classes, an object serializer is probably going to be a hindrance rather than a help. Two object serializers are XStream (xstream.codehaus.org/) and TreeBind (www.nongnu.org/treebind/).

Transformers

If your task is to read in XML in one format and write it out in a different format and/or with modified content, there are two broad approaches you can take. You can

- Use an XML API to read/write the XML, and hand-written code in Java/C#/C++/Python/Perl (and so on) to implement the transformation (including sorting, filtering, or enhancing the data).
- Use an XML-specific transformation language to implement the transformation, and then call out to that from your Java/C# (and so on) code. This would probably mean calling out to XSLT 1.x or 2.0, or perhaps XQuery (described in Chapter 7).

The advantage to using an XML-specific transformation language is that you write less code. XSLT, for example, is designed from the ground up for transforming XML into XML (or HTML), and it is able to express those transformation rules very concisely, in spite of XSLT itself being written in XML. Some developers sometimes complain that XSLT is too long-winded to type because it is written in XML. Invariably, those developers are using a simple text editor to edit the XSLT, and that is the real problem. There are XSLT editors that provide pop-up selection of XSLT elements, just as there are Java/C# (and so on) editors that provide pop-up selection of class methods. When you use an XSLT-aware editor, XSLT is no harder to type than a plain text programming language.

In comparison, if you use a Java/C#/C++ (and so on) API to write your transformation code, there are a lot more lines of code to write (usually) to achieve the same result. On the other hand, if you don't have someone with sufficient XSLT experience on your team, writing XSLT code (and getting it to work correctly) could take longer than writing Java/C#/C++ (and so on). So the choice of whether to call out to a transformation language depends on what skills you have, or what skills you have available to you. If you do have XSLT experience (available), you should consider calling out to XSLT whenever the job at hand is an XML transformation task.

XML Guild members generally use Michael Kay's Saxon XSLT transformer (and this was the case even before Mike was invited to join the XML Guild). Saxon is the only XSLT 2.0 transformer that is available at the time of writing, and XSLT 2.0 adds a lot of new functionality that can make your XSLT scripts shorter and easier to understand. It also implements XQuery 1.0. There are both Java and .NET implementations of Saxon.

JAXP Transformation API (TrAX)

The JAXP API for Java includes an API for calling XSLT transformations (this was originally known as the TrAX API). This API can be used with files, URLs, in-memory DOM documents, or SAX event streams. It is important to note that XSLT transformers do not use the DOM as their in-memory representation. For performance reasons, they use their own custom in-memory representations. That means that applying an XSLT transformation to a DOM document is not as efficient as might

be expected, and uses more memory than might be expected, due to the need to convert one in-memory representation to the other.

To carry on with the SAX example, you need an XSLT stylesheet to count the <Company>/<Address> occurrences. You can use the following XSLT 1.0 stylesheet (count-company-addresses.xsl):

```
<?xml version="1.0" encoding="UTF-8"?>
<xsl:stylesheet xmlns:xsl="http://www.w3.org/1999/XSL/Transform" version="1.0">
 <xsl:template match="/">
  <document>
   <p>Counted <xsl:value-of select="//Company/Address"/> company addresses.</p>
  </document>
 </xsl:template>
</xsl:stylesheet>
```

The JAXP code to run this XSLT stylesheet (using the Java version of the Saxon XSLT engine) is

```
// This is sample code, not production code. Written for Java 5.

import java.io.File;
import javax.xml.transform.OutputKeys;
import javax.xml.transform.Transformer;
import javax.xml.transform.TransformerFactory;
import javax.xml.transform.stream.StreamResult;
import javax.xml.transform.stream.StreamSource;

public class JaxpTransformationSample
{
 /**
 * The main method. Expects an XML input file, a stylesheet file,
 * and an XML output file as parameters.
 * @param args command line arguments.
 */
 public static void main(String[] args) throws Exception
 {
  // Check for a three command line arguments.
  if (args.length != 3)
  {
   printUsage();
```

```
    return;
  }

  // Set JAXP properties to select Saxon as the XSLT transformer.
  System.setProperty(
    "javax.xml.transform.TransformerFactory",
    "net.sf.saxon.TransformerFactoryImpl"
  );

  // Create an XSLT transformer. Argument #1 is the stylesheet.
  TransformerFactory factory = TransformerFactory.newInstance();
  Transformer transformer = factory.newTransformer(
    new StreamSource(new File(args[1]))
  );

  // Set the transformation options. These lines are not actually necessary,
  // as the stylesheet sets the same options using 'xsl:output'.
  transformer.setOutputProperty(OutputKeys.METHOD, "xml");
  transformer.setOutputProperty(OutputKeys.INDENT, "yes");
  transformer.setOutputProperty(OutputKeys.ENCODING, "UTF-8");

  // Perform the transformation.
  // Argument #0 is the input, argument #2 is the output.
  transformer.transform(
    new StreamSource(new File(args[0])),
    new StreamResult(new File(args[2]))
  );
 }

 /** Prints a simple usage message to the error stream. */
 public static void printUsage()
 {
  System.err.println("Usage is: java TrAXSample <xml-input-file-name>
<stylesheet-file-name> <xml-output-file-name>");
  System.err.flush();
 }
}
```

Note how the file input/output paths are wrapped using the following construct for input XML and the stylesheet:

```
new StreamSource(new File(...))
```

And use the following construct for the output XML: `new StreamResult(new File(...))`

There are also SAX and DOM versions of the **Source** and **Result** classes.

When this program is run with the company address XML sample as the input, the output of the transformation is

```
<?xml version="1.0" encoding="UTF-8"?>
<document>
 <p>Counted 2 company addresses.</p>
</document>
```

The output message

```
Warning: Running an XSLT 1.0 stylesheet with an XSLT 2.0 processor
```

is normal and is not a problem. Occasionally, XSLT 1.0 stylesheets do not run correctly with an XSLT 2.0 stylesheet processor like Saxon (due to differences between XSLT 1.0 and 2.0), so Saxon prints a warning as a reminder. It is not usually a problem in practice; it is just something to be aware of.

System.Xml.Xsl

For XSLT stylesheets, .NET and Mono have the **System.Xml.Xsl** classes, in particular **XslTransform**. To run the same example stylesheet as for the JAXP Transformation API, the **XslTransform** code is

```
// This is sample code, not production code.
// Written for Mono 1.1.8.3 & .NET 1.1.

using Console = System.Console;
using XmlResolver = System.Xml.XmlResolver;
using XmlUrlResolver = System.Xml.XmlUrlResolver;
using XslTransform = System.Xml.Xsl.XslTransform;

class XslTransformSample
{
 /// <summary>The main method. Expects an
 /// XML input file name, a stylesheet file name,
```

```
/// and an XML output file name as parameters.</summary>
/// <param name="args">command line arguments.</param>
public static void Main(string[] args)
{
 // Check for a single command line argument.
 if (args.Length != 3)
 {
  printUsage();
  return;
 }

 // Create an XSLT transformer.
 XslTransform transformer = new XslTransform();

 // Load the stylesheet. Argument #1 is the stylesheet.
 transformer.Load(args[1]);

 // Create a resolver for loading files associated with URLs.
 XmlResolver resolver = new XmlUrlResolver();

 // Transform the input file to produce the output file.
 // Argument #0 is the input, argument #2 is the output.
 transformer.Transform(args[0], args[2], resolver);
}

/// <summary>Prints a simple usage message to the error stream.</summary>
public static void printUsage()
{
 Console.Error.WriteLine(
  "Usage is: [mono] XslTransformSample.exe "
  + "<xml-input-file-name> <xsl-stylesheet-file-name> <xml-output-file-name>"
 );
 Console.Error.Flush();
}
}
```

and the output, as expected, is

```
<?xml version="1.0" encoding="utf-8"?>
<document>
 <p>Counted 2 company addresses.</p>
</document>
```

XQJ

For some applications, an alternative to using XPath or XSLT APIs is to use XQuery (covered in Chapter 7). At the time of writing there is no common API implemented by the available XQuery processors, but a standard Java API for XQuery is currently under development—JSR 225: XQuery API for Java (XQJ).

Selecting the Right XML API for the Job

An unfortunate fad in IT development at the moment is the cult of "best practices". Being seen to implement best practices now is considered to be a safe move for your career in the way that buying IBM was a generation ago. The problem with the "best practices" approach is that there are very few genuine "best practices" that apply to all situations.

A lot of so-called "best practices" are simply good practices. They are good practices that work in a particular context or for a particular kind of problem. It is as important to understand the details of the context as it is to understand the details of the good practice, because it can be bad practice to apply a "good practice" in a context where it doesn't work. This is why there are few "best practices," and it is why you should be wary of any proposed good practice that doesn't clearly describe the context where it is appropriate.

In this chapter, I haven't tried to single out any best practices. What I have tried to emphasize instead is that you have choices, and that the best choice for you will depend on what your context is. It will depend on what the problem is, which XML APIs are available to you, what skills you have available to you, and what schedule and budget pressures you have to work within. The following are some guidelines to help you make an appropriate choice for yourself.

Choose the Right Kind of Efficiency

There is no *one size fits all* approach for XML processing. Different applications and different problems require different solutions and benefit from different XML APIs. There are different kinds of efficiency that an XML API can offer:

- Computational efficiency – The fastest results, but usually at the expense of the most hand-coding.
- Code efficiency – The shortest, most readable and maintainable code, but usually at the expense of processing speed or maximum XML file size.

- Training efficiency — The least time spent on the learning curve by your developers, the more time available for coding, debugging, optimizing.

It is important to pick the efficiency that gives you the most benefit when you choose an XML API. For example:

- For a small amount of XML processing that doesn't contribute significantly to the overall amount of time your application takes to run, there is little point in using a streaming XML API to get maximum computational efficiency. You won't be able to measure the benefit. You would be better off picking an XML API that is quick to write code for.
- XPath, XSLT, and XQuery are all quick and compact ways to write XML query and/or transformation code, but if your development team currently only has Java/C# (and so on) skills, your team may be better off using a Java/C# (and so on) XML API, to avoid the downtime required to learn the more specific XML tools. On a longer project you may have enough time to schedule training, but on a shorter project you probably won't. Similarly, you might choose to just use the same XML API that you used on your last project, even if it isn't the ideal choice, just because your team already knows how to use it and can start being productive more quickly.

Don't ignore project management efficiency in the quest for computation efficiency, nor vice-versa. There is no point in having a fast program that you can't finish writing within your schedule and budget. There is also no point in finishing on time but producing a program that is far too slow to use in practice. There is a choice that you have to make, so make sure you identify what kind of efficiency is most important to your project.

Use Multiple XML APIs When Appropriate

Often, you will want to use just a single XML API within a project. Using more than one API can just increase the learning curve for your developers, without providing any measurable benefits. In spite of that, there are times when you should consider using multiple XML APIs within a single project.

In particular, if you are processing large XML files (for example, 10MB or larger), you may find that in-memory XML APIs (DOM, XPath, XSLT, and so on) require so much memory that the application starts swapping memory to disk, and the performance drops significantly and sharply. This is the situation where people typically turn to a streaming XML API instead. The problem with streaming XML APIs is that they typically require you to write more code, and that code is harder to write correctly and to maintain correctly. So, rewriting your code to use only the streaming XML API can be an expensive change to make.

In some cases, large XML files can be processed one piece at a time, and this is where it can make sense to use multiple XML APIs. You can use a streaming API to break the large XML files up into a series of manageably small XML files. You can then use whichever XML API is most appropriate on those smaller XML files, which can make coding easier for some complex manipulations.

Don't use multiple XML APIs in a project unless you really need to, but don't force yourself to do everything with a single XML API if two XML APIs together can give you a quicker or more maintainable solution.

Robustness of XML APIs

Any XML parsing strategy can be affected by schema changes, but some mechanisms are more robust (less likely to fail) than others. XPath-based addressing is more robust than using a generated getter/setter API. For example, consider these three pieces of code:

```
return getXPath("/UserList/Person[1]/Address/City/text()");
```

and

```
return getUserList().getPerson()[0].getAddress().getCity();
```

and

```
UserList userList = document.getUserList();
Person person = userList.getPerson()[0];
Address address = person.getAddress();
return address.getCity();
```

These all should give the same result: a string containing the city from the address of the first person in the user list. However, there are subtle differences that can be important in practice:

- The first example will simply return a null value if there are no **<UserList>**, **<Person>**, or **<Address>** elements in the document. The second and third examples will throw a null pointer exception if this happens.
- The second example doesn't give you any place in the code where you can detect and catch a missing (null) **<UserList>**, **<Person>**, or **<Address>** element, whereas the third example does.
- The third example, if derived from a W3C XML schema, will be sensitive to the names (and packages/namespaces) of the complex types in the schema. So if the type of the **<Address>** element is changed from **Address** to **USAddress** (assuming **USAddress** is not a generalization of **Address**), the code will be broken until the line

```
Address address = person.getAddress();
```

is changed to

```
USAddress address = person.getAddress();
```

This issue does not affect the first and second examples.

The important thing here is that the robustness of your XML processing code depends both on your choice of XML API and on the style of your own code. You need to manage both choices appropriately.

Summary

The aim of this chapter was to give you an overview of the different XML APIs that are available, and to demonstrate how many of them are used. There are XML APIs that could not be included here, such as XML APIs for Python/Ruby/Perl, but the XML APIs that have been covered are representative of the types of XML API that are available. In addition, the chapter reviewed some guidelines that can help you to choose the most appropriate XML API for your current or next project. There will often be conflicting requirements when you need to choose an XML API, so your challenge is to choose the XML API that best balances your different needs. The good news is that there is a good XML API for most situations and needs.

6 XML and Databases

by Michael Kay

This chapter is about storing XML. It's called "XML and Databases" rather than "XML Databases", because an XML database is just one of the possible ways of storing XML.

It's important to remember that XML didn't start out as a data model for organizing databases. It started out as a way of structuring documents, both narrative documents (such as this chapter), and business documents (such as invoices and purchase orders). The structure of XML was designed for exchanging information, either between people or between software applications, and not for storing and querying information. This means that when you put XML in a database there are sometimes messy design decisions and compromises that you have to make.

Nevertheless, XML information does have to be stored, and once stored, it has to be retrieved. After applications start sending and receiving their data in XML, the messages need to be kept somewhere.

The first part of this chapter looks at three broad approaches to organizing XML for storage and retrieval: blob storage, shredded storage, and native storage, and you'll see some examples of how these three approaches are realized in actual products.

The second part of the chapter examines what part schemas play in storing XML. Schemas in XML are traditionally used for validating the structure of documents, which is subtly different from the traditional role of a database schema, and you'll see how the two things relate to each other.

The final section looks at the criteria you might use for evaluating XML database products. There's no room here for a detailed feature analysis of the products available (such information would quickly become out of date), so we'll concentrate on the questions you need to ask, rather than the answers you might get from individual vendors.

Approaches to Storing XML Data

There are a number of approaches to storing data that arrives in XML form:

- *Blob storage:* The XML document is stored as a chunk of text, complete with markup, using external mechanisms to index it so that it can subsequently be located.
- *Shredded storage:* The information is extracted from the XML document and stored in some non-XML representation, for example as rows and columns in a relational database.
- *Native storage:* The information is stored as an XML infoset, in a way that allows queries to access the information by reference to its XML structure (elements and attributes).
- *Free text storage:* This is a special case of blob storage. The XML document is stored as a chunk of text, but the text is indexed (perhaps along with structural information from the XML markup) to permit content-based retrieval using free text information retrieval techniques. Free text indexing is also often used to complement native storage.

None of these approaches is always right or always wrong; it all depends on the application requirements.

Before you can decide how it's best to store XML documents, you need to have some idea why you are storing them: in other words, you need some idea of how the information will be accessed. As a first cut, try to distinguish two kinds of queries, those that ask *Get me the documents* and those that ask *Get me the facts*.

A *Get me the documents* query is used either with narrative XML or with highly structured XML. Typical examples of such queries are *Find me the last annual appraisal for Jane Smith* or *Get me the descriptions of all three-bedroomed semi-detached houses for sale in Reading between £250K and £300K*. In XQuery this might look like this:

```
for $h in collection('houses-for-sale')
where $h/property/details/location = 'Reading'
  and $h/property/details/style = 'semi-detached'
  and $h/property/offer/asking-price ge 250000
  and $h/property/offer/asking-price le 300000
  and $h/property/details/count(room[@role='bedroom']) = 3
return $h
```

The essential characteristic of these queries is that they return a set of XML documents—typically XML documents as originally stored in the database, although one can stretch the concept to include partial documents in which some sections have been omitted, or aggregated documents assembled from multiple input document.

By contrast, a *Get me the facts* query only works with XML documents that are known to hold structured factual information. Examples of such queries are *Was Jane Smith recommended for promotion in her last annual appraisal?* or *How much has the average selling price of three-bedroomed semi-detached houses in Reading changed over the last year?* In XQuery that might be:

```
let $properties :=
  for $h in collection('houses-for-sale')
  where $h/property/details/location = 'Reading'
    and $h/property/details/style = 'semi-detached'
    and $h/property/details/count(room[@role='bedroom'] = 3
  return $h
let $this-month :=
  for $h in $properties
  where $h/property/sale/date gt
                    current-date() - xs:duration('PT1M')
  return $h/property/sale/price
```

```
let $last-year :=
  for $h in $properties
  where $h/property/sale/date gt
            current-date() - xs:yearMonthDuration('PT13M')
    and $h/property/sale/date le
            current-date() - xs:yearMonthDuration('PT12M')
  return $h/property/sale/price
return ("Price increase / decrease:",
        ($avg(this-year) div avg($last-year) - 1.0) * 100,
        "percent")
```

The first kind of query, *Get me the documents,* tends to be used where the information in the documents requires human interpretation (for example in the form of narrative text and pictures). However, the documents may also contain detailed structured data used to enable precise retrieval. These are information retrieval applications where the task of the system is to locate the data, not to interpret it. The second kind of query, *Get me the facts,* works only with structured data with well-defined syntax and semantics, so that the system can be used to analyze the data and make inferences. This is much more the domain of the typical relational database.

Of course, the great thing about XML is its breadth of coverage. Most systems contain a mixture of different kinds of information, from the highly-structured to the very unstructured, and a corresponding variety of queries. In the past, we've often segmented our applications because there's no one technology that can handle this breadth: so a holiday company might put photographs of hotels in a content-management system while holding details of room availability and customer transactions in a relational database. In fact, such segmentation is so widespread that many IT people don't find it at all strange. But it's very hard to make the system offer a seamless service to its users (your customers!) when its component parts are implemented using such disparate technologies.

Using Blob Storage

Blob stands for *binary large object*, and it essentially refers to a lump of data whose internal structure is unknown. Not unknown to everyone, of course, but unknown at a particular level of the system. Most of today's popular operating systems have no idea what's inside a file, so to them, a file is a blob. Many relational databases started supporting a blob data type to hold data such as images and sound. To the database, it's just a bag of bits, which means that no meaningful query operations are possible on a blob; the only thing you can do is to store them and retrieve them.

Some database systems also support a data object called a *clob* (for character large object). Instead of being a bag of bits, this is known to contain a sequence of characters. This means it isn't quite as opaque, for example the system can safely perform operations like *transcoding* (converting from one character encoding to another). However, the general idea is much the same. It's debatable whether XML is best treated as a blob or a clob: according to the XML specification, an XML document is a sequence of octets (bytes) which makes it a blob, but because these octets all represent characters in some encoding, it's often more convenient to manipulate XML at the character level. The only thing you need to be careful of is that an XML document starts with an XML declaration that names the character encoding used, so if someone transcodes it without realizing what he is doing, the result will be parsing errors (or miscoded characters) next time you try to read the file.

There are two main variants on blob storage (this section doesn't discuss blobs and clobs further): using operating system filestore, and using the blob data type in a relational database. You might also choose to use a content-management system that might run on either of these underlying storage engines, hiding the difference from your application.

With a pure operating-system-only approach, the only way to identify a file/document is by its name in filestore, which is fairly limiting. You might have one or two other attributes to play with, such as the date and time of creation, and you can create a hierarchic directory structure, but this isn't going to solve all your retrieval problems. Even if a single identifier is all you need, this approach suffers another drawback, which is that operating systems often struggle once you try to store thousands of small files. I hesitate to say that you should never build systems this way

(I've done it myself for a system that had to store about 50,000 documents), but it's probably a mistake to do it simply because you've got an operating system handy and don't want to mess about installing a database.

With any kind of system based on blob storage, it's likely that you'll need to identify some key properties of the documents that are extracted and indexed to enable a simple search capability. Some people refer to these fields as metadata, but in practice they aren't usually extra external information, they are copies of data items held within the document such as an author, date, title, or product number. In a relational system, you can create a table with one column for each of these indexing fields, and one blob column for the document itself.

Another approach that has very similar properties (it might even be the same implementation under the covers) is to use a content-management system based on the WebDAV model. WebDAV presents itself as a file system in which the files have an extensible set of attributes alongside their filename and their content. The DAV stands for *distributed authoring and versioning*, so it's more than just a content store: there's built-in versioning and concurrency control at the sort of granularity needed in content-management applications.

Storing XML using a blob-based approach, however you implement it, can be seen as a low-tech approach. That doesn't mean it's a bad approach: it depends on your requirements. It's likely to be efficient and easy to manage. Its limitations are in the query capabilities it offers: you can't find documents based on their content, only on the values of attributes that you have chosen to pull out for indexing purposes; and you certainly can't do any kind of aggregation or *Get me the facts* type of queries.

Using Shredded Storage

The term *shredded storage* is just as picturesque in its way as *blob*. The idea is that before you can store a document, you have to rip it up into small pieces, which you then file away neatly, each in its own pigeonhole. If you want to retrieve the document as a whole, you reassemble the pieces.

This kind of approach can work well when your XML document is very tabular in its form. When you see something like this (taken from a sample file shipped with Stylus Studio):

```
<sales>
  <region name="NE">
    <product name="A">30</product>
    <product name="B">2</product>
    <product name="C">6</product>
    <product name="D">9</product>
    <product name="E">57</product>
  </region>
```

```
  <region name="NW">
    <product name="A">89</product>
    <product name="B">2</product>
    <product name="C">4</product>
    <product name="D">31</product>
    <product name="E">60</product>
  </region>
  <region name="SE">
    <product name="A">31</product>
    <product name="B">19</product>
    <product name="C">8</product>
    <product name="D">34</product>
    <product name="E">50</product>
  </region>
</sales>
```

It's a simple matter to turn this into three rows of a table with five columns each—or, if you prefer, five rows of a table with three columns, or perhaps 15 rows of a table with columns (region, product name, and sales). All of these representations make it easy to ask *Give me the facts* queries in SQL: for example, *What were the total sales of product A?* or *Which products are under-performing in the South East?*.

Furthermore, it won't be too difficult to reconstitute the original XML document, with the help of the XML export capabilities now available in most relational databases.

There's a lot of XML like this about. It's grossly under-using the capability of XML to represent richly structured data, but that's not the point. There will always be lots of mundane stuff like this in the ledger books to keep the bean counters happy; it might not be exciting, but it makes the world go around. Relational databases are good at storing this kind of data, and although it's a bit tedious to shred your XML document before storing it, and then re-assemble it when you want it back, this is probably a sensible solution for this kind of data. In practice it's likely that when you do want to reconstruct an XML representation of the data, it won't be the original document you want anyway: you'll probably want the data for a different set of products, or a different set of regions, or a different time period. SQL is good at doing that kind of slicing and dicing, so you might as well use it.

There are in fact two main varieties of shredded storage, *generic storage* and *custom storage*. With generic storage, the design of the tables is independent of the XML schema: you will have table and column names such as Element, Attribute, and Child. Custom storage by contrast produces tables that reflect the objects defined in the schema, leading to table and column names such as Customer, Product, and Order. If you want to query the data using SQL, custom storage is likely to be much more convenient. But if you plan to use XQuery, it doesn't really matter, because the XQuery processor can target either form.

With either approach, the interesting question is how far you can take this technique when the data starts to become more complex. The richer the structure, the more layers of hierarchy, the more repeating and optional fields that occur, the more you start having to design a complex database with multiple normalized tables with primary and foreign keys to represent all the relationships, and the more code you have to write to translate between the XML representation of the data and its SQL representation.

And it's not just the complexity: it's the ability to cope with variety and change. Suppose you're exchanging data with your business partners using a standard such as FpML or XBRL or UBL. These are hugely complex vocabularies, with hundreds of different element types defined. Almost certainly, you will agree to use a subset of what the standard allows (probably with your own private extensions, in my experience!). Given a certain amount of time and patience, you will be able to write code that shreds data out of these messages into a normalized relational database. Then what happens? You start to do business with someone who is using a different subset, or different extensions. You're now faced with the task of restructuring your database to hold the extra information, and worse still, of rewriting and retesting all your existing XML-to-relational mapping code to target the revised database schema.

This is work you can do without. Converting data from one representation to another doesn't create business value; it just creates costs and reduces your responsiveness to new requirements. At some stage, as the complexity increases, it becomes worth thinking about using native XML storage.

But as with blob storage, this doesn't mean that shredded storage is always bad: it all depends on your requirements. Its big advantages are the textbook benefits of relational databases and the normalization discipline: data is stored once, in a form that's independent of how it was produced and how it's going to be used; there are no update anomalies; and no bias to one access path rather than another. Moreover, you're using technology that's mature (relational databases have been around for 30 years), that's reliable, that scales well, and where it's easy to find competent staff who know how to drive the engine, or training courses if they need to be taught.

As with blob storage, there are various ways you can implement shredded storage in practice. At one extreme you can write your own code to convert between the XML representation and the SQL database representation. All the database vendors have some level of XML support these days, however, and there are also third-party tools available.

Two variations on the approach are what I call the XR and XOR models. XR stands for *XML-Relational*, and in this model you convert directly between an XML representation (typically a message received from a business partner) to the relational representation. In this case there is either no business logic, or the business logic is written in an XML-based processing language such as XSLT or XQuery. XOR stands for *XML-Object-Relational*. Here, you convert the incoming data from XML to an object representation, for example to Java or C# objects. The business logic is then performed by Java or C# code, which then fires off SQL statements to push the data into the database. In this approach you have not two but three different ways of modeling the same information: XML on the wire, Java for processing, and SQL for storage. Even though there are tools (such as Java XML binding technology) that can help, this is a lot of complexity. My preference, for the vast majority of applications, is to keep the business logic in high-level languages such as XSLT or XQuery, to avoid the extra complexity of defining a Java or C# version of the data model.

Using Native Storage

I'm slightly hesitant to use the term *native storage;* it's one of those terms like *Web services* or *ethical investment,* where everyone agrees it's a good thing, but no one agrees exactly what it means. Marketers have been playing tug-of-war with the concept, trying to claim that its true meaning coincides with whatever they happen to be offering.

I think the best definition of native XML storage is *a physical data structure that faithfully represents the full structure and information content of XML documents, as defined in the XML infoset*. The key point here is that the stored data must retain all the significant information in the original XML document, but it is not required to retain distinctions deemed to be insignificant, such as the use of tabs or newlines to separate attributes within an element start tag. Unfortunately, there isn't universal agreement about exactly which parts of an XML document are significant and which aren't. My definition appeals rather glibly to the XML infoset specification, but the XSLT and XQuery data model (XDM) is probably more likely to be followed in practice.

Generally, the information in an XML document falls into three categories:

- *Definitely significant:* This includes the elements, attributes, and their textual content.
- *Definitely insignificant:* This includes details such as whitespace within start tags, the choice of quotation marks or apostrophes to delimit attribute values, the order of attributes, the use of CRLF versus LF as a line ending, the use of decimal versus hexadecimal in character references, and the distinction between <a/> versus <a></a>.
- *Possibly significant:* This covers a wide gray area. Examples of constructs in this category include CDATA section boundaries, comments, whitespace between elements, the choice of namespace prefixes, redundant namespace declarations, and entity references.

Most people will agree that any XML storage needs to retain information in the first category. Most will also agree that the second category does not need to be faithfully retained, for example, it doesn't matter if a document goes into the database with apostrophes around an attribute value, and emerges later with quotation marks instead. The difficulty tends to be with the third category.

If the information is intended solely to be used by software applications at the receiving end, few people are likely to object if things like comments are discarded. On the other hand, if the document is going to be further edited by human authors, they will find it inconvenient if, for example the CDATA section **<![CDATA[<<<>>>]]>** has been replaced by the sequence of entity references **<<<>>>**, or if references to external entities are replaced by the content of those entities.

Generally speaking, blob and clob storage can easily retain information in all three categories. This gives it an advantage in applications such as content management where the XML documents are likely to be edited by human beings, often in their XML form. Shredded storage systems tend only to retain the essential information items (and sometimes they have difficulty even with those, for example mixed content can prove troublesome). It's not uncommon to find, if you use shredded storage, that all the comments and processing instructions in your documents get lost, as well as whitespace that you might or might not consider significant.

Native storage is typically designed to retain everything that's deemed to be significant information in the XML document. This might not be everything that human authors would like to see retained. But it will usually cope better than shredded storage with things such as mixed content, comments, and processing instructions.

The XQuery and XSLT Data Model (XDM) itself makes some compromises in this area, in the interests of allowing XQuery to be implemented with a wide variety of different storage architectures, including the option of using shredded storage in a relational database back-end. The model allows constructs in our possibly significant category to be represented, such as comments and inter-element whitespace, but it also allows products to drop such constructs if they can't represent them (or don't choose to).

Another innovation in the XDM model is that data can be either typed or untyped. This relates to the question of whether you use an XML schema, which is examined in more detail in the next section.

The Role of Schemas in XML Storage and Query

Every introductory book on XML will tell you that there are two flavors of XML: XML that is merely well-formed, and XML that is also valid. Validity is determined by reference to a description of the permitted structure of a document, which might be expressed in a variety of notations including DTDs, XML Schemas, Relax NG schemas, or other mechanisms. There's a more complete discussion of these options in Chapter 2, and I won't revisit the subject here: instead, the focus here is on the way that schemas interact with XML storage and query.

The more documents you are storing, and the larger the community that is using the documents to communicate, the more important it is to impose some standards on the structure and content of the documents. This is true whether you are defining a house style for press releases or a standard form for claiming expenses. There are several reasons for such standards, and when you design a document structure it's useful to remember why you are doing it. Document standards are a way of imposing rules on document authors to ensure that they supply the required information in the form that it's needed. Standards also help readers to recognize the documents and to find the information they need within them. Finally, standards can be used to ensure that documents are compatible with the software that's used to process them. The UK tax authorities, for example, allow value-added tax returns to be submitted over the Internet in XML form, and if these are to be processed successfully at the receiving end, they must conform to rules defined by the government.

So there are two main reasons for using schemas in conjunction with XML database systems. They provide some quality control of documents being loaded into the system, and they allow users to formulate queries with some knowledge of the structure of the documents. This applies both to *Get me the documents* and to *Get me the facts* queries: none of the example queries cited earlier in this chapter would work if the person formulating the query didn't know about the structure of the documents and the names of the fields they contain. This contrasts with free text query (exemplified by Google), where users know nothing of the structure of the documents, and search them only by their content. We're all familiar with the frustration this causes when you want to search for a company with a name such as Abbey.

But there's also a third reason for using schemas with a query language that's a little more subtle, namely to provide type information. If you want to search for properties with a price below $500,000, you don't want to get a hit for a property priced at one million dollars because $1,000,000 comes before $500,000 in alphabetical order. This implies that the system must know that price is a numeric field, and it will typically get this information from a schema. The ability to attach type information to data elements is something that distinguishes XML schema from other validation technologies (such as Relax NG), and accounts for some of its awkward restrictions. The infamous *unique particle attribution* rule (UPA), which prevents you from writing many content models that at first sight seem perfectly natural and innocuous, is there because validation against a schema must not only give an unambiguous yes/no answer as to whether the document is valid; it must also unambiguously associate each element in the source document with exactly one element definition in the schema. (It's not only query languages that need this property: it also makes data binding possible.)

The use of schemas with XQuery (and XSLT, for that matter) has attracted some controversy. It's contentious for a number of reasons. Firstly, many people don't like the W3C XML schema specification. It's big and complex, difficult to understand, and yet full of functional restrictions that reduce its capability. Until quite recently the implementations of the specification have also been notoriously buggy and incompatible with each other. It's a standard that most XML professionals are obliged to use simply because everyone else uses it, but at the same time many of those users would love to be doing something else (like RELAX NG, perhaps). Secondly, people worry that over-restricting the documents that can be stored in a database takes away some of the benefits XML brings to the party the ability to have loosely structured, semi-structured, and highly-structured data all expressed in a common way. More particularly, they feel that it's inappropriate to use a strongly-typed query language in a world where data itself isn't always strongly typed.

On the other hand, there are clear benefits to be gained by linking the query language to the schema describing the documents being searched. Anyone who has used XSLT 1.0, which has no such linkage, will recognize how hard it can be to debug a stylesheet when there is no compile-time checking that the path expressions make sense. Mistyping an element name, or forgetting to include a namespace prefix, or leaving out one of the steps in the path, simply leads to no data being selected – to blank output. Such errors can be spotted at compile time if the stylesheet or query is checked against a schema to ensure that the paths make sense. Many proponents have also argued that compiling queries and stylesheets against a schema also enables much more powerful query optimization, which is essential as the volumes of data inevitably grow.

To accommodate this spectrum of views, XQuery has been designed so that schema-awareness is optional. For vendors, it's an optional part of the language that they aren't obliged to implement; and for users, it's an optional feature that they don't have to make use of.

Schema-Awareness in XQuery

Let's look more closely at how schemas interact with XQuery at the language level. First of all, when you write a query, you can import one or more schemas. For example if you are processing FpML, you might write:

```
import schema namespace fp="http://www.fpml.org/2005/FpML-4-2"
             at "fpml/fpml-main-4-2.xsd";
```

Here, **fp** is a namespace prefix that you can use within the query any time you want to refer to the namespace whose URI is **"http://www.fpml.org/2005/FpML-4-2"**. The second URI, **"fpml/fpml-main-4-2.xsd"**, tells the system where to find a copy of the schema for this namespace. Technically, this is just a hint: if the system already knows where to find a copy of the schema (perhaps there is one stored in the database), it uses that copy instead. In practice you'll need to find out how this works in your chosen XQuery implementation, especially if you're using multiple versions of the schema at the same time (a subject that I'll return to shortly).

In the FpML example, the schema document referred to here actually contains **<xs:include>** declarations referring to a dozen further schema documents. When you import a schema into your query, all these modules are imported as well.

What does importing a schema achieve? The answer is less than you might think. All it does is to make the names defined in the schema (specifically, the names of element and attribute declarations and of global type definitions) available for use within the query. FpML has a global element declaration like this:

```
<xsd:element name="FpML" type="Document">
  <xsd:annotation>
    <xsd:documentation xml:lang="en">The FpML element forms the root for any
     conforming FpML instance document. The actual structure of the document is
     determined by setting the 'type' attribute to an appropriate derived
     subtype of the complex type Document.
    </xsd:documentation>
  </xsd:annotation>
</xsd:element>
```

So the element name **FpML** (in namespace **"http://www.fpml.org/2005/FpML-4-2"**) can be used in the query. For example, you could define a global parameter to the query like this:

```
declare variable $input as document-node(schema-element(fp:FpML)) external;
```

When the users run this query, they must supply a value for the **$input** parameter, and the value they supply must be the root of a document whose outermost element is a valid **fp:FpML** element. Here "valid" doesn't just mean that it would be valid if you ran it past the schema, it means it must already have been successfully validated against the schema and marked as valid. The important point here is that before you can refer to **fp:FpML** in a type declaration, you must first import the schema in which the name **fp:FpML** is defined.

As it happens, FPML makes rather unusual use of XML schema, in that all FPML messages use **<fp:FpML>** as the name of the outermost element, and use the attribute **xsi:type** to distinguish one type of message from another. The previous declaration allows any valid FPML message. It might well be, however, that the query is only designed to work against one particular kind of message, say the **RequestQuote** message. Then you could declare the input parameter to the query like this:

```
declare variable $input
        as document-node(element(fp:FpML, fp:RequestQuote)) external;
```

Why would you want to bother with this? It would be perfectly legal to write

```
declare variable $input external;
```

and not trouble with declaring the expected type. There are several reasons to bother:

- A maintenance programmer reading your query (perhaps you, after a few weeks on another project) can immediately see what kind of input the query is expecting.
- If someone makes an operational error by running the query on the wrong kind of input document, you'll get an immediate and explicit error message, rather than incomprehensible garbage output.

- The compiler can check that path expressions within the query make sense. If you write, for example,

```
if (year-from-date($input/fp:FpML/fp:header/fp:creationTimeStamp) = 2005) …
```

  the system can tell you that there is no such field within the header of this message type. (If you're lucky, it will tell you that the field is actually called **creationTimestamp** – spot the difference.) Without knowledge of the schema for **$input**, there's no way the query compiler can detect this error, and in fact the query will run to completion simply delivering the value **false** for this conditional.

  It's not just invalid paths that are detected in this way. When you correct the spelling of **creationTimeStamp**, you'll get another error from the compiler, saying that the argument to the **year-from-date()** function must be of type **xs:date**, but the value you have supplied is of type **xs:dateTime**. You need to change the query to use the **year-from-dateTime()** function instead. Unlike the previous error, this one would have been caught at runtime if there were no schema. Without a schema, the **fp:creationTimeStamp** element would be untyped, so the system would try at runtime to convert it to the type required by the **year-from-date()** function. This conversion would fail, because the value is written as a **dateTime** (for example 2006-10-04T17:35:00), which isn't in the right format for an **xs:date**. But, although the error would have been caught anyway, it's much better to catch errors at compile time. You get a faster turn-round in the development cycle, and you're less dependent on the availability of comprehensive test data.
- Finally, information about types enables the system to improve performance. It's expensive to do a lot of runtime data conversion, especially of data that isn't going to be selected for processing anyway. Many schema-aware XML databases are likely to store a validated date as a date, rather than as a character string, thus avoiding any runtime conversion overhead. That might seem like a small savings, but in some cases it can be quite significant. For example, if you search for properties in a particular price band, the system may well be able to take advantage of an index to speed the search. But it will only be able to construct an index if it knows that prices are decimal numbers, and this depends on knowledge of the schema.

The same argument applies to declaring types on variables or function arguments. The more specific you are about defining the types of the values handled by your query, the more robust your application will be.

All of this, however, assumes that you're creating a database to store documents that actually do conform to a small and well-defined set of schemas, for example a database of FpML messages or a database of DOCBOOK documentation. When this isn't the case, the arguments are less clear cut. The next section covers the challenges of managing change and managing variety.

They're actually different aspects of the same problem, because variety usually results from a history of change.

Managing Schema Variety and Change

Requirements change, and schemas change as a result. What happens to your database that's carefully designed to store FpML 4.2 messages when FpML 5.0 comes along?

In the conventional database world, when the schema changes all existing data is restructured to make it conform to the new version of the schema. In fact, one of the design objectives behind the relational model was to make such changes relatively painless. Compared with the problems of unloading and reloading a network database, adding a column to a table is usually very simple. Unfortunately, not all changes can be handled quite so easily.

For example, if you want to change a structure that permitted employees to have a single email address to one that allows them to have any number of email addresses, a new side table will be needed, and the existing data will need to be extracted into this side table. The worst part of the problem, of course, is that existing applications will stop working. Instead of getting the data from a single table, they will need to join two tables, and the application logic will also have to be rethought to work out what to do with the multiple email addresses. Perhaps one of them will be marked as the default or preferred address; if you're clever, you can then hide the change from existing applications (at any rate, from read-only applications) by creating a relational view that reconstructs the old table by adding the default email address back into the main employee table.

In the XML world, it's also true that some changes are relatively painless and others are more troublesome. Allowing multiple email addresses is probably one of the more straightforward changes; it simply involves changing **maxOccurs="1"** to **maxOccurs="unbounded"** in the relevant schema type definition. Existing instances won't need to change, so there's no database restructuring necessary. Existing applications may fail, however.

In XSLT 1.0, suppose an application was written like this:

```
<xsl:for-each select="employee ">
  <tr>
    <td><xsl:value-of select="name"/></td>
    <td><xsl:value-of select="email-address"/></td>
  </tr>
</xsl:for-each>
```

As it happens, this code will continue to work. If the path expression **email-address** finds more than one element, the **<xsl:value-of>** instruction will simply output the first one. XSLT 1.0 was designed on the principle of avoiding runtime errors at almost any cost, so there's a tendency for the processor to guess what you might have wanted and carry on processing. This is a style that often occurs in scripting languages like JavaScript, which uses weak typing. It's robust in the sense that you don't get many runtime failures, but it's not at all robust in the sense that it prevents you making programming mistakes. And it's certainly an approach that can lead to some surprises. Consider the following fragment:

```
<xsl:for-each select="employee[email-address=$param]">
  <tr>
    <td><xsl:value-of select="name"/></td>
    <td><xsl:value-of select="email-address"/></td>
  </tr>
</xsl:for-each>
```

You might expect that if you are searching for the email address **bgates@microsoft.com**, this will be the address displayed in the second column. But no: with multiple email addresses, the predicate in square brackets tests whether any of the addresses matches the parameter, whereas the **<xsl:value-of>** instruction always displays the first one.

> **Note**
> This changes a little in XSLT 2.0, as it happens. In 2.0, **<xsl:value-of>** displays all the email addresses, space-separated. More significantly, other operations such as the **contains()** function, which in 1.0 silently selected the first item in the list, now report a runtime error if presented with a list containing more than one item. XQuery is the same. The thinking is that if you really want to process the first email address and ignore all the others, you should say so (by writing **email-address[1]**); otherwise, there's probably a flaw in your logic that you should be told about.

So, when you make this particular change to your schema, you won't have to change your existing instance data, but it's very likely that you will have to change your applications, just as you did in the relational case. This time, there are no clever mechanisms like relational views that hide the change. It's possible, however, to adopt a similar approach if you write your applications in the form of a pipeline of processing steps. There are many benefits to breaking up a complex query or transformation into a sequence of simple steps, each of which operates on the output of the previous step. One of the advantages is that it makes it easier to manage change: you can insert transformations into the pipeline that convert from one version of a schema to another.

A common example of this is handling the different versions of the popular news syndication format RSS. Depending on how you count, there have been at least five and possibly up to nine different versions of RSS, all of them incompatible (see http://www.rssdotnet.com/documents/version_comparison.html). Writing queries and stylesheets that can process all of these variants is not easy—the code for doing anything useful with the data can quickly become buried in nested conditionals for handling the different variants. It's much better to write components that translate from one format to another, and assemble these into a pipeline as required, so that the real logic of your application only has to deal with one format.

That's fine if you are processing RSS feeds that come in on the wire. What happens if you are storing RSS to create a searchable archive of news stories in a particular subject area? In this case, it's best to try to have your database standardize on one format, because otherwise the queries will be more difficult. So the pipeline of conversion modules needs to sit on the input side, in the application that processes a news feed before loading the stories into the database.

So the first rule about managing variety is to try to minimize it if you can, by converting documents to a common standard on their way into the database. This isn't always possible, for example when you are obliged to store documents exactly as they arrived for legal or contractual reasons. Also, it doesn't help when you discover that the format you chose to standardize on last year is no longer good enough, because requirements have changed. When this happens, you have to adopt a new format, and you have to make a decision whether to convert all the old data to the new format, or leave it as it is. As I said at the beginning of this section, the conventional database approach is to restructure the existing data, but with XML, you have a choice. A number of factors will influence the decision:

- How compatible are the new version and the old? Is it realistically possible to do queries that can search across the two different formats? (If they use different namespaces, as is the case with different RSS versions, it may be surprisingly difficult.)
- Are there policy reasons that dictate that the old documents cannot be changed?
- What constraints are imposed by the database product you have chosen? Some products, for example, will only allow one schema to be present for a given namespace. Schema-aware XQuery also imposes this rule—the schema that the query knows about must be the same as the schema that was used to validate the input documents (although even here, different products will interpret this rule with different levels of strictness).

One approach that is sometimes useful is to keep the old documents in both the old and the new formats. Having two copies does no harm if they aren't being updated, which will usually be the case when old documents need to be retained. You then have an archive of documents in their original format, which you can either keep for ever, or use transitionally while applications are being upgraded; but at the same time, all documents exist in a common format that's useful for across-the-board queries.

Another situation can arise typically in workflow applications, where the documents in the database represent work in progress. For example, a company might have a process for raising and approving capital expenditure proposals. It might take a proposal several months to go through the approval process, after which it is archived. From time to time it's likely that the finance director will ask for additional information to go on the form, or for changes in the approval cycle. Generally, you will want to apply such changes to new proposals created after the introduction of the change, while keeping the old format (and schema) for those currently working their way through the system. The details of how to achieve this again depend on the capabilities of the database product you're using: if it doesn't allow coexistence of multiple versions of a schema or namespace, it might be that changing the namespace is the best approach to take.

Remember that the schema that describes all the documents in the database doesn't have to be identical to the schema that you use for validating an incoming document feed. For example, there might be elements that are mandatory for new documents, but that were not present in older documents. Or it might be that the old pre-Euro currencies such as DEM and FFR can appear in old documents, but are not permitted in new ones. The schema for the database (the one you will use for compiling queries) can describe an element as optional, whereas the schema you use for validating newly submitted documents can describe it as mandatory; similarly they can permit different lists of currency values. Of course, this works only if the schemas are compatible.

When Not to Use a Schema

There's an alternative approach to handling variety, which is not to use a schema at all. This might appear to be a recipe for chaos, but there are cases when it makes sense.

First, there's no sense trying to pretend you're in control of the document structure when you aren't. Think about what you will do if an incoming document fails validation. If the answer is that you'll fix your schema and store it anyway, perhaps you didn't need a schema in the first place. This is surprisingly common, when one application is receiving a feed of data from another. Schema validation can still be useful, just to alert you to the fact that there's been a change in the format of data you are receiving, but perhaps the schema doesn't belong in the database.

(The same rationale can be applied at a more fine-grained level: what rules should you put in your schema? Defining a rule that the minimum age of an employee is 16 is rather pointless if the first time your company employs a 15-year-old you are simply going to change the schema to match the reality. You can argue that you want to catch data entry mistakes – but shouldn't they be caught long before the data gets anywhere near the database?)

In some applications change control over the schema can be a bottleneck, preventing users from storing the data they need to store, and thus reducing the value of the system. Many such applications try to find ways of defining an extensible schema. An example is genealogy (please don't dismiss this as frivolous, it offers some of the most successful examples of paid-for content on the Internet). Genealogical data is intrinsically open-ended; you can't define a finite list of types of events that are to be recorded, or a finite list of information to be captured about each event. The last thing to do in such cases is to force users to represent the extra data as unstructured text (or perhaps worse, as a non-XML markup syntax disguised as text for the purpose of the database). The X in XML stands for eXtensible, and the right solution in these cases is to exploit the extensibility of XML to allow users to represent all their information, not just the subset that the central schema control authority has got around to modeling.

> **Note**
>
> Some XML database products work very well with schema-less data. The open source eXist product is one example, and the commercial Mark Logic product is another. Both use indexing strategies that work from the element structure they find in actual document instances, not from any structure defined a priori in a schema. Other products (such as Software AG's Tamino) are much more schema-centered.

There's no doubt that the absence of a schema makes life harder for users who want to query across the data. For that reason it's hard to imagine a database without some kind of commonality of approach to markup design. But there might well be applications where it's best to maintain standards using a fairly informal and loosely-enforced set of voluntary guidelines, rather than the traditional rigid control structure implied by a conventional database schema.

Choosing a Database Product

The first two parts of this chapter covered the different approaches to storing XML, and the role of the schema in helping you to manage document storage and helping users to formulate queries. In a sense those two sections were simply a preamble to this final part of the chapter, which discusses how you should go about choosing the database technology (or non-database technology) that's right for your application.

> **Note**
>
> I'm not going to review specific database products in this section. Any list quickly becomes out of date. The best online source at the moment is Ron Bourret's site at http://www.rpbourret.com/xml/XMLDatabaseProds.htm, which contains brief technical descriptions of a wide variety of products. The emphasis in this section is not on doing a feature-by-feature product comparison, but on helping you to identify the questions that you need to ask about the products in order to make your decisions.

It's worth starting with some general remarks about choosing the technology components in your application architecture. Different organizations have different attitudes to risk. On some projects there seems to be an unstated assumption that the lowest-risk option is the best one. But other organizations thrive on risk, recognizing that you need to innovate to stay ahead of your competitors. It's important that everyone involved in a technology evaluation shares an understanding of how much innovation and risk is appropriate.

In the context of database technology, the biggest risks come from lack of experience. Projects don't usually fail because the technology doesn't work, but they can often fail because the developers don't know its limitations. If you want to minimize risk, use a database that has already been deployed in previous projects, where you have staff on hand who know its quirks, even if it's not intrinsically the best tool for the job. Conversely, if you want to be more innovative, take extra time to familiarize yourself with the product, find a good consultant who knows it well, and plan to manage the risk.

The decision between open source versus commercial offerings is also something that typically depends on the user organization's attitude to risk. The quality of support that's available varies enormously from one open source product to another, but the same is also true from one commercial product to another. Which are you more concerned about: the contractual obligation of the supplier to provide support, or the actual ability in practice to get a quick and helpful answer to a question? The two are not necessarily correlated. Take a look at the online forums for the product to see what kind of questions users are asking and whether the answers are prompt and detailed.

The purpose of standard interfaces is to enable you to defer decisions on the choice of components as late as possible, and if necessary to change the decisions when you need to (whether before or after the project goes live). In this area, standard interfaces include XML itself, XML Schema and the specific schemas for your document types, XQuery and XSLT, and APIs such as the Java JAXP and XQJ interfaces. Take a clear view of which interfaces are critical in your application architecture. Don't just check for product conformance to these interfaces, and then forget about them. Take care to ensure that as the project develops, your own code retains adherence to these interfaces. Ideally, develop and test with more than one implementation of a given interface (for example, more than one XML parser or XSLT engine) to ensure that you haven't locked yourself in to a vendor unintentionally.

Once you have mandated the important interfaces in your application architecture, take advantage of the flexibility this gives you to delay decisions on which products to use in particular roles. It's surprising how often projects fail to do this. The longer you can delay a decision, the more information you will have at the point where you need to commit—information about the performance requirements of the application, information about the capabilities of the candidate products, information about the quality of the support available from the vendors and about the experiences of other users.

Of course some components are more easily substituted than others, and one of the reasons that database technology plays such a strategic role is that it's quite hard to avoid getting locked in to your initial choice. That's partly because conformance to standards tends to be patchy (every SQL vendor implements a different subset of the ISO language spec, plus lots of their own extensions), and it's partly because there are lots of interfaces that aren't subject to standardization, for example the database loading and recovery utilities. In the area of XML databases, such interfaces include the way in which you create and configure collections (of documents), the relationships between collections and schemas, the interaction of XML and non-XML data (for example, relational data or binary images), and indeed the interface for the "update" part of the query language (XQuery 1.0 is read-only).

Here's a suggested list, roughly in order, of the decisions you need to make about your requirements, which should result in questions that you can ask about each of the possible products:

- What kind of data will you be storing?
- Is the document structure pre-defined or do you get to design it?
- What's the volume of data over time?
- Where does it fit in the spectrum from "document-oriented" to "data-oriented"?
- Does it make sense to have a fixed set of schemas describing the documents that are stored?
- How are the schemas likely to evolve over time?
- Do you need content-management features such as the ability to hold multiple versions of the same document?
- What kind of retrieval and update will be needed?
  Get me the documents versus *Get me the facts* queries
  Retrieval using a few metadata fields, using structured XQuery, or using free-text searching
- Will it be useful for queries to be schema-aware, or will a schema only get in the way?
- Is there a need to modify documents in-situ, or is the update requirement only to add and delete documents as a whole?
- Are any particular interfaces needed (for example, XQuery, WebDAV, or X-UPDATE)?
- What are the policy constraints on the decision?
- Are there preferred suppliers of database technology?
- Is there an existing skills base that influences the choice?
- What is the attitude to open source?
- Are there budgetary constraints?
- Are there constraints imposed by other components in the system (for example, operating system platform or development language), or the need to interface with other applications?
- Who needs to be convinced and what will convince them?
- What architectural choices for data storage are technically most appropriate?
  Blob storage in operating system filestore
  Blob storage in a relational database system
  Shredded storage in a relational database, controlled by the DBMS
  Shredded storage in a relational database, controlled by the application
  Use of an XML data type in a relational database

Use of a specialized XML database
Use of a free text search engine

There might, of course, be other requirements that are important in your particular environment; for example, there might be a requirement to integrate the database access control facilities with an existing organization-wide LDAP directory.

Once you've answered these questions you will want to check that the chosen products meet your needs in areas such as backup and recovery, but in my experience such factors rarely swing a decision one way or the other.

Evaluating performance can be a significant challenge. The first stage is to know what your requirements are. It really doesn't matter if one product is twice as fast as another, if both will actually meet your response time and throughput requirements. However, at this early stage of technical maturity, there can be quite substantial performance differences between different products. Sometimes these affect operations that you didn't immediately think of as critical—for example loading the database, modifying schemas, or even deleting documents (updating indexes when documents are removed can take longer than creating the indexes when the documents are first loaded).

If you're going to run a benchmark, take the time to do it properly. It's remarkably easy to get results from performance tests that turn out to be completely spurious. (I recall a soak test on a web server that proved it could handle thousands of requests per second, but failed to notice that 99% of the responses said "system busy, please try later".) Make sure that you have access to good technical advice for the products you are testing, and make use of it. Make sure that the paths you are measuring are relevant to the actual performance requirements of your application. And make sure that you are disciplined about keeping detailed records of your performance measurements and the system changes that you make before each measurement run.

If you're using performance figures from a third party, take them with a pinch of salt. If there's a 10:1 performance difference between two products, it's probably significant. If one is 10% faster than the other, however, a slight change in system configuration, or an upgrade to the next version of one of the products, will probably tip the scales the other way.

As for performance figures supplied by a vendor, the best advice is to avoid them entirely. It's odd how vendors can always get their products to go much faster than the average user seems able to achieve – and I say that as a vendor myself.

One final piece of advice: if two products seem to be equally good, when assessed against your requirements, they probably are. Don't waste six months agonizing over which one to choose: toss a coin, and if at all possible, be prepared to change your mind later.

Summary

This chapter outlined the factors you need to take into account when deciding how to store XML for subsequent query and retrieval. There's a great deal of material that I could have covered, but I've tried to take a breadth-first view, making sure that you don't discard any options that might be right for your application even if they are wrong for another.

The first section examined at a fairly abstract level the different ways XML can be stored on disk, whether in operating system files, in a relational database, or in a specialized XML database. Your choice in this area will have a significant effect on the performance profile of different storage and retrieval operations, so it's important to get it right.

The next section discussed the role of schemas. Again, any decisions you make about the way in which schemas for stored data will be managed are likely to have a significant operational effect, for example on the ease of formulating queries or the ease of changing the system to meet new requirements.

Finally, we took a look at a broad checklist of the features you need to take into account when choosing what XML storage and retrieval technology is right for your application.

7 XQuery

by Ronald Bourret

XQuery is a language for querying XML documents. It does not require documents to be stored in any particular place. For example, it can query documents stored in a native XML database, on the file system, in a column of type XML in a relational database, or in a stream in an application. It does not even require documents to physically exist. For example, it can query virtual documents built by mapping relational data to XML. Because of its dual roots in XPath and SQL, XQuery appeals to users who are used to dealing with databases and SQL-like queries.

XQuery is being developed by the W3C. Version 1.0 was released in June 2006, but many implementations, even from large corporations, were available for years before that. Version 1.0 only provides the ability to retrieve data from XML documents and cannot be used to update XML documents. However, an update syntax is in the works and a number of implementations using prototype update syntaxes are already available. In addition, work is in progress for performing full-text queries in XQuery.

XQuery currently has implementations by most major relational database engines (IBM, Oracle, Microsoft, and so on), as well as most native XML database companies (MarkLogic, X-Hive/DB, Ipedo, Berkeley DB XML, eXist, and so on). It is also available from middleware providers (DataDirect, Saxonica, and so on).

XQuery Data Model

In order to understand XQuery, it is first necessary to understand the data model on which XQuery is built. In relational databases, the data model essentially consists of tables, rows, and columns. Queries are designed to operate on instances of this data model, and query results, as well as the results of intermediate steps, are also instances of this model. The same is true of the XQuery data model: queries operate over data model instances and both intermediate and final results are instances of the data model.

An instance of the XQuery data model is an ordered sequence of items, where items can be atomic values, such as integers, strings, and dates, or nodes, such as elements, attributes, and text nodes. Instances of the XQuery data model are not necessarily well formed and might not be legal XML values at all. For example, a sequence of element nodes (representing a forest of elements) is not well formed because it does not have a single root element. A single floating-point value is not XML, as all data in XML is text.

Atomic Values

An atomic value is a scalar value. Its datatype can be any XML Schema atomic type. For example, this might be a primitive type like **xs:string** or **xs:number**, or it might be a derived type like **shoesize**, which is any integer between 1 and 17. (Note that XML Schemas supports list and union types as well as atomic types; list and union types are not supported as valid datatypes for atomic values in XQuery.)

The datatype of an atomic value is determined from the schema associated with an XML document. If no schema is associated with a document, the datatype is effectively undefined, but it is most easily thought of as being **xs:string** and that is how I describe it in this chapter. (This isn't quite technically correct, but it is sufficient for understanding most operations.)

Examples of atomic types:

- **xs:string**
- **xs:number**
- **xs:date**
- **xs:language**
- **shoesize** (1-17)
- **dayofweek** ("Su", "Mo", "Tu", "We", "Th", "Fr", "Sa")

Nodes

The XQuery data model has seven different types of nodes. If you are familiar with the Document Object Model (DOM) or XPath 1.0, you might notice that these are very similar to the node types found in those languages.

Technically, the "nodes" in the DOM are interfaces, implemented by concrete classes, and not parts of a data model. However, if you are familiar with the DOM and not the XPath data model, they provide a very simple way to start understanding the XQuery data model. This is because an instance of the XQuery data model is likely to be represented internally in a manner that is very similar to a forest of DOM trees.

The complete list of XQuery data model nodes is as follows:

- **Document** encapsulates the entire XML document.
- **Element** represents elements in an XML document.
- **Attribute** represents attributes in an XML document.
- **Text** represents the textual content of an XML document.
- **Namespace** represents the binding of a namespace URI and namespace prefix.
- **Processing instruction** represents processing instructions in an XML document.
- **Comment** represents comments in an XML document.

```
<?xml version="1.0" encoding="UTF-8"?>
<guild:book status="draft" xmlns:guild="http://www.xmlguild.org">
<!--This is a comment -->
    <guild:title>Advanced XML</guild:title>
    <?PageBreak?>
    <guild:chapter>
          <guild:title>XQuery</guild:title>
          <guild:para>XQuery is ...<guild:para>
          <guild:section>Section 1</guild:section>
          <guild:para>Section 1 ...</guild:section>
</guild:book>
```

Figure 7.1
Example document containing all seven nodes.

Sequences

A sequence is an ordered list of items, where items are nodes or atomic values. That is, a sequence can contain nodes, atomic values, or a mixture of the two. In addition, sequences can be empty.

The XQuery data model does not support the concept of sub-sequences. For example, if you concatenate a number of sequences, the result is not a sequence of (sub)sequences. It is a single sequence consisting of the items in the concatenated sequences.

```
(1) + (2, 3) + () + (4, 5, 6) => (1, 2, 3, 4, 5, 6)
```

Here are some examples of XQuery sequences.

```
<Color>Blue</Color>
<Color>Red</Color>
<Color>Green</Color>

"Blue", "Red", "Green"

<Title>Colors</Title>,
"A few primary colors are ",
<Color>Blue</Color>,
```

```
<Color>Red</Color>, "and",
<Color>Green</Color>,"."
<!-- Just some mixed content listing colors -->
```

Constructs Not in XQuery Data Model

The XQuery data model does not model everything in the XML 1.0 recommendation. In particular, the XQuery data model does not model such things as the XML declaration (with its version number and standalone declaration), the DOCTYPE declaration (with its root element type and DTD information), the system ID and public ID of external DTDs, and physical constructs such as CDATA sections and character and entity references.

Understanding what the data model actually models is important because anything that is not in the model cannot be queried. For example, it is not possible to use XQuery to find which documents in a collection reference a particular entity.

Grammar Notes

Before discussing the main parts of XQuery, you need to understand some basic parts of the grammar, such as how to construct new elements, as well as concepts, such as expressions. The first item is simple, and that is simply that XQuery, unlike SQL, is case sensitive. That is, its keywords must be lowercase. The other concepts are discussed in the following sections.

Constructors

It is often useful for a query to construct "literal" nodes, as opposed to retrieving them from an XML document. For example, you might want to nest a set of query results inside a "literal" root node.

XQuery provides two ways to construct nodes—**direct constructors** and **computed constructors**. Direct constructors simply use XML 1.0 syntax. For example, the "document" shown next is, in fact, a valid query, albeit a rather uninteresting one. It constructs a single element node (Book) that contains three element children (Title, Author, and Price) separated by whitespace. Direct constructors are generally used when you know the names (and possibly values) of elements, attributes, comments, and so on that you want to construct.

```
<Book>
   <Title>Introduction to XML</Title>
   <Author>John Smith</Author>
   <Price Currency="USD">29.99</Price>
</Book>
```

The other way to construct nodes is with computed constructors. These use keywords to construct nodes; for example, the **element** keyword constructs an element node. The following example constructs the same result as the previous example: a single **Book** element node with three child elements. Although this example is less than useful—the direct constructor syntax is much easier to read—computed constructors are very useful when you want to construct nodes based on query results. For example, using computed constructors, it is possible to write a function that converts an element with attributes to an element with child elements containing the same values.

```
element "Book"
{
   element "Title" {"Introduction to XML"},
   element "Author" {"John Smith"},
   element "Price" {attribute "Currency" {"USD"}, 29.99}
}
```

Expressions

XQuery queries are composed of building blocks called *expressions*. Expressions take input in the form of zero or more sequences, operate on this input, and return output in the form of a sequence. This allows expressions to be nested, because the output of one expression can be used as input for the next.

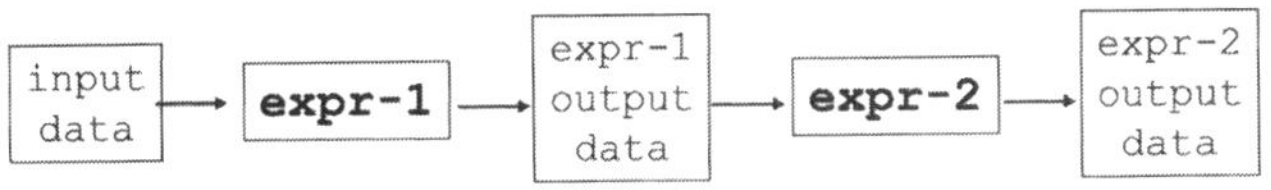

Figure 7.2
XQuery building blocks.

Consider the simple XQuery query shown in Figure 7.3.

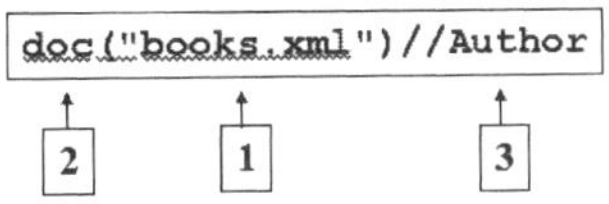

Figure 7.3
Simple XQuery query.

Table 7.1 Expressions in a Simple XQuery Query

Number	Expression	Input	Output
1	String literal	–	"books.xml"
2	doc()	"books.xml"	Document node
3	//Author	Document node	Author elements

The first expression is a literal, **"books.xml"**. This does not take any input, but constructs a sequence with a single string value as output.

The second expression is the **doc** function, which takes the string value as input, interprets it as a URI, and returns a sequence containing the document node of the specified document as output.

The third expression is the path expression **//Author**, which returns a sequence consisting of all Author elements nested inside the input node, which is the document node in this case.

Thus, the complete query opens the books.xml document and returns any Author elements found inside this document.

Enclosed Expressions

Because direct constructors use XML 1.0 syntax, and virtually any text can be placed inside a directly constructed element, it is necessary to separate literal text from XQuery expressions nested inside those elements. This is done with what is known as an **enclosed expression**, which is an expression placed inside braces (**{ }**). Such braces must be used any time an expression can be mistaken for a literal.

For example, consider the query shown next. Although it appears that this query will extract the titles of all books (in the form of Title elements) and nest these inside a Titles element, it will do no such thing. Because **doc("books.xml")//Book/Title** is nested inside a direct constructor, it will be treated as literal text and used to construct a literal text node, as is shown in the result.

```
XQuery:

<Titles>
   doc("books.xml")//Book/Title
</Titles>

Result:

<Titles>
   doc("books.xml")//Book/Title
</Titles>
```

Now consider the query shown next. This query places **doc("books.xml")//Book/Title** inside braces, so it is treated as a path expression and executed as such. In other words, it will extract the Title children of any Book elements in the current context node and return them in the query results.

```
XQuery:

<Titles>
{
   doc("books.xml")//Book/Title
```

```
}
</Titles>

Result:

<Titles>
   <Title>Introduction to XML</Title>
   <Title>XML: Real-World Solutions</Title>
   <Title>XML and Integration</Title>
</Titles>
```

The following example shows why this is useful (other than simply making life easy for query parsers, who would otherwise have to decide what is a literal and what is an expression). This example shows how you might write an XQuery tutorial using XHTML.

```
XQuery:

<p>The query:</p>
<pre>
   doc("books.xml")//Book/Title
</pre>
<p>returns the following results:</p>
{
   doc("books.xml")//Book/Title
}

Result:

<p>The query:</p>
<pre>
   doc("books.xml")//Book/Title
</pre>
<p>returns the following results:</p>
   <Title>Introduction to XML</Title>
   <Title>XML: Real-World Solutions</Title>
   <Title>XML and Integration</Title>
```

Note that top-level expressions are always treated as if they are enclosed. That is, they are never mistaken for literals.

Comma Operators

The comma operator is used to concatenate two values or sequences. For example, the following expression creates a sequence consisting of a, b, and c elements:

```
<a/>, <b/>, <c/>
```

Comma operators are important when you need to return a sequence of items that do not occur together in the document being queried. For example, the following query returns the Title and Author children of each Book element found in the books.xml document. Note the use of parentheses to enclose the sequence, because the **return** keyword can be followed only by a single expression.

```
for $b in doc("books.xml")//Book
return ($b/Title, $b/Author)
```

Path Expressions

This section discusses *path expressions,* which will be familiar to anyone who has used XPath 1.0 or XSLT. Path expressions specify a path through an XML document using the names and values of elements, attributes, and other constructs. They return the nodes (if any) at the end of each path in the document that satisfies a given path expression.

For those who are interested, XQuery path expressions are a subset of XPath 2.0 path expressions. In particular, XQuery does not support the namespace axis in path expressions. Furthermore, a number of other axes are optional, presumably because these are difficult to support in some implementations, such as over relational databases.

The following sections introduce path expressions through a number of examples that use the sample document shown next.

```
<Book>
   <Chapter Number="1">
      <Section Number="1">...</Section>
      <Section Number="2">...</Section>
   </Chapter>
   <Chapter Number="2">
      <Section Number="1">...</Section>
      <Section Number="2">...</Section>
      <Section Number="3">...</Section>
   </Chapter>
</Book>
```

Because path expressions operate on the hierarchy of a document, it is easier to illustrate them using a tree. Figure 7.4 shows the tree structure of the previous document.

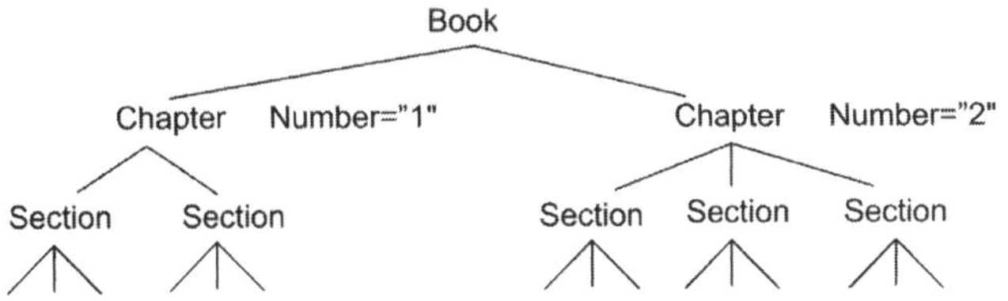

Figure 7.4
Tree structure.

Selecting the Root Element

Before discussing the first example, I need to clarify that path expressions are executed with respect to a context node. This is often the document node for a particular document. (In this case, it's assumed to be the document node for the sample document.) However, any node can be used as the context node; the query simply has to retrieve that node and then apply a path expression to it.

The first path expression is **/Book**. You can think of the slash (/) as meaning to look for child elements of the context node. (Technically, it doesn't mean this, but most people think of it this way. I'll clarify this later.) **Book** means to return any elements named "Book".

In this case, the context node is the document node of our sample document. (This node can be thought to sit "above" the root element node in our tree diagram.) Because the root element node is named "Book", this node is returned. Thus, the query returns the root element of the document. (Note that when the Book element is returned, it necessarily contains its children as well.) Figure 7.5 illustrates this concept.

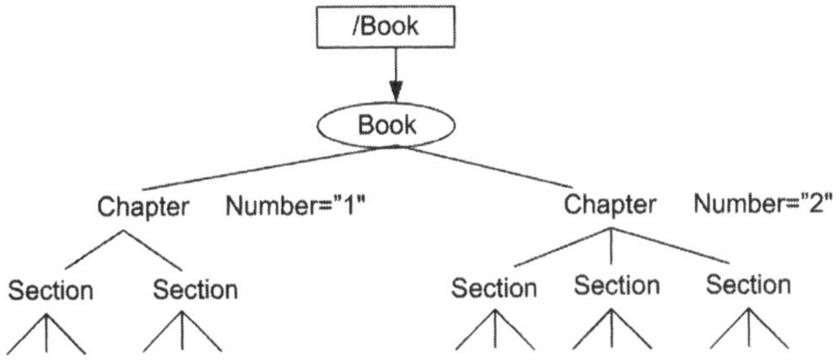

Figure 7.5
Selecting the root element.

Selecting Child Elements

The next expression is **/Book/Chapter**. This tells the query processor to start from the context node (the document node), get the Book element, and then get any children of the Book element named "Chapter". Figure 7.6 illustrates this expression.

There are a couple of things to notice here. First, this path expression is satisfied by two different physical paths in the document. Thus, it returns a sequence consisting of two different Chapter elements in document order. As before, these elements contain all of their contents (children) and their attributes.

The second thing to notice is how the expression is evaluated. Initially, the context node is the document node. The processor then evaluates the expression **/Book**, which returns a sequence consisting of a single Book element. This element becomes the context node for the next part of the expression: **/Chapter** .

That is, the **/Chapter** expression is evaluated in the context of the Book element. As you can see, this means that the process for evaluating a path expression is to evaluate it as a series of steps. The output of one step becomes the context for the next step.

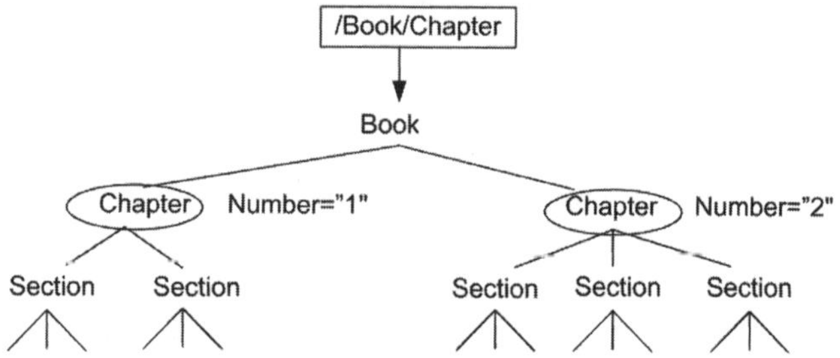

Figure 7.6
Selecting elements.

Selecting Attributes

The third expression is **/Book/Chapter/@Number**. This is interesting for two reasons. First, the @ means to look for an attribute, not a child element. Second, you will remember from the previous example that **/Book/Chapter** returned a sequence containing two Chapter elements. Figure 7.7 illustrates this expression.

Because path expressions are evaluated with respect to a context node, not a context sequence, how does the processor handle this? That is, how does the processor evaluate **/@Number** against a sequence of Chapter elements? The answer is to evaluate it against each node in the sequence in turn.

Thus, when the processor evaluates **/@Number** for the first Chapter element, it finds the Number attribute belonging to this element. And when it evaluates **/@Number** for the second Chapter element, it finds the Number attribute belonging to that element. The result is the sequence constructed by concatenating the results of each operation. In other words, it is a sequence of two Number attributes, returned in document order.

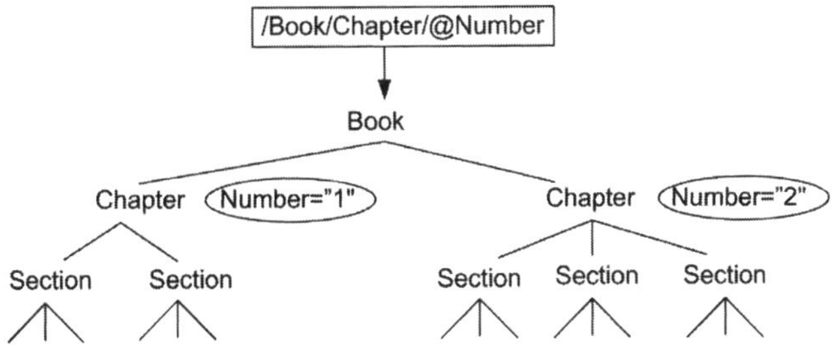

Figure 7.7
Selecting attributes.

Restricting the Selection

The final example shows how to restrict a selection. This is done with the expression **[@Number="2"]**. As before, the example uses **/Book/Chapter** to construct a sequence of two Chapter elements. It then applies the predicate **@Number="2"** to each element in turn. This predicate means that a context element satisfies it if that element has a Number attribute and that the value of that Number attribute is "2".

When the processor applies this to the first Chapter element, it finds a Number attribute, but also finds that the value of that Number attribute is "1". Therefore, the processor does not return the first Chapter element. However, it finds that the second Chapter element does have a Number attribute whose value is "2", so it returns this element. As you can see, the effect of applying a predicate to a sequence of nodes is to remove those nodes that don't satisfy that predicate.

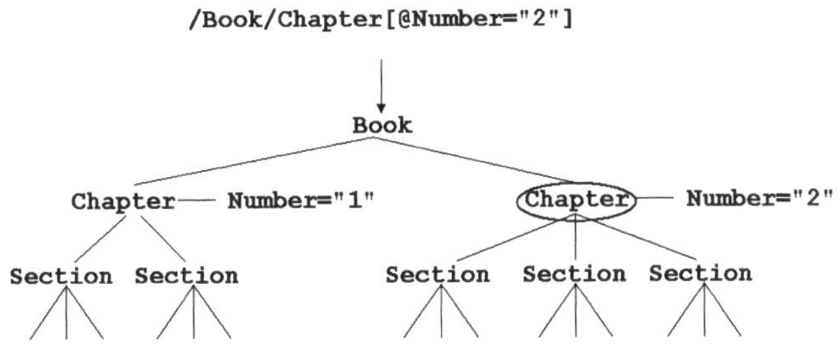

Figure 7.8
Restricting the selection.

How Do Path Expressions Work?

A path expression is a series of steps separated by slashes (see Figure 7.9). (Remember when I said that a slash didn't really mean, "Look for a child element"? That is because the default action to take in a step is to look at children. Because this is the default action, there are no other symbols telling you to do something else, and it is therefore easy to misinterpret the slash, which is really separating steps, as meaning to look for a child.)

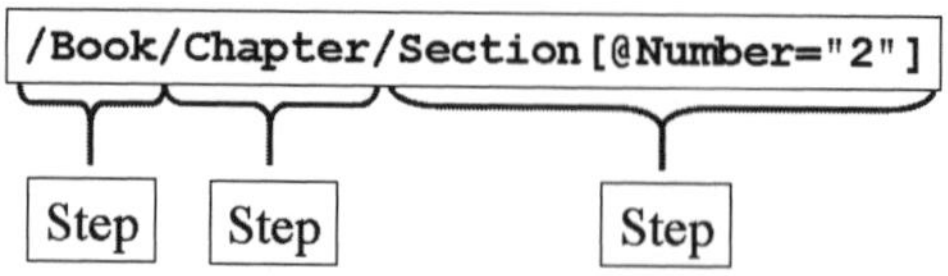

Figure 7.9
XPath steps.

As I already mentioned, steps are evaluated in the context of a particular node. (If the input sequence has more than one node, the step is evaluated over each node in the sequence in turn.) The result of evaluating a step is a sequence of nodes used as input for the next step. After the last step has been evaluated, the resulting sequence of nodes is returned.

For example, consider the expression **/Book/Chapter/Section[@Number="2"]**. This expression returns all Section elements whose Number attribute is "2". To see what actually happens, let's consider each step in turn.

The first step **(/Book)** is evaluated in the context of the document node. It returns the Book child of this node. The second step **(/Chapter)** is evaluated in the context of the Book node. It returns a sequence containing the Chapter children of the Book node. The final step (**/Section [Number="2"]**) is evaluated twice, once in the context of each Chapter element. The first part of this expression (**/Section**) retrieves all Section children of a particular Chapter element. The second part (**[@Number="2"]**) eliminates those Section elements that do not have a Number attribute whose value is "2". Thus, the complete expression returns two Section elements—those that have Number attributes whose value is "2". This is summarized in Table 7.2.

Table 7.2 Evaluating /Book/Chapter/Section[@Number="2"]

Step	Context Node	Selects Node
1	document	Book
2	Book	Chapter(s)
3a	Chapter[1]	Section[2]
3b	Chapter[2]	Section[2]

Each step has three parts: an axis, a node test, and an optional predicate. The axis tells the step which "direction" to take from the context node. For example, does it look at the children of the context node? The parent? All ancestors? The attributes? The following or preceding siblings?

The node test tells the expression how to filter nodes along a particular axis. For example, suppose you are using the child axis—that is, looking at the children of the context node—do you want just text children? Just elements? Just elements with a particular name? Just comments?

The predicate is optional and allows you to specify more complex filtering criteria. For example, the node test might have limited the results to just Section elements, but you might want to restrict this further to those Section elements that have a Number attribute whose value is "2".

A step can be expressed using either of two syntaxes. The first syntax uses a shorthand for the axis. For example, @ means to use the attribute axis. This is the most common syntax, but abbreviations do not exist for all axes. The second syntax spells out the axis name in full and uses a double colon (::) to separate this from the node test. For example, **attribute::** means to use the attribute axis.

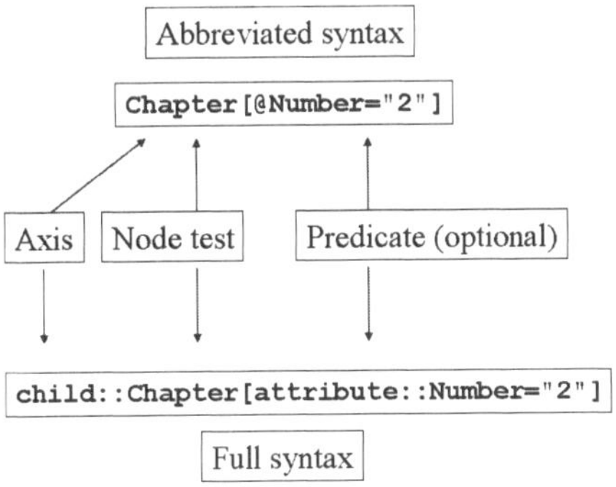

Figure 7.10
XPath steps.

Let's now take a closer look at axes.

Axes

The supported axes are listed in Table 7.3, along with the types of nodes that they can return. Most of these axes are self-explanatory—for example, the child axis looks at the children of the context node and the parent axis looks at the parent of the context node. However, a couple of notes are in order.

The preceding and following axes use document order. For example, the preceding axis looks at all nodes that precede the context node in document order (except for attributes, namespaces, and ancestors). The preceding-sibling axis looks at all siblings the precede the context node in document order.

Child nodes are those node types that can be children of an element node: elements, text, processing instructions, and comments. It is worth noting that namespace nodes and attribute nodes are not considered to be children of element nodes. (The converse is not true, the parent of an attribute or namespace node is an element node.) Also note that support for a number of axes is optional; these axes are marked with an asterisk. Presumably, this is because these axes are difficult to implement over relational databases.

Table 7.3 Axes

Direction	Axes	Return Types
Down	child, descendant, descendant-or-self	child node
Up	parent, ancestor*, ancestor-or-self*	element, document
Later	following*, following-sibling*	child node
Earlier	preceding*, preceding-sibling*	child node
None	self	all types
Attributes	attribute	attribute

Some examples of how to specify different axes are now in order.

The first example uses the child axis. This is the default axis and, in the abbreviated syntax (shown first), does not require an axis specifier. Thus, you only need to specify the name of the child element(s) you want. For the first step, this is the Book child of the document node. For the second step, these are the Chapter children of the Book element. The unabbreviated syntax (using **child::**) is also shown.

```
/Book/Chapter
/child::Book/child::Chapter
```

The second example uses the descendant-or-self axis. The abbreviated syntax (shown first) finds all Section elements that occur anywhere beneath a Book element. Note that in the unabbreviated syntax, the double slash (//) is replaced by **/descendant-or-self::node()/**.

```
/Book//Section
/child::Book/descendant-or-self::node()/child::Section
```

The next example uses the attribute axis. The abbreviation for this axis is @. Thus, **/Book/Chapter/@Number** gets the Number attributes of all Chapter elements. The unabbreviated syntax (using **attribute::**) is also shown.

```
/Book/Chapter/@Number
/child::Book/child::Chapter/attribute::Number
```

The final example looks at the parent axis, whose abbreviation is two periods (..). The expression **//comment()/..[element()]** finds all elements (as opposed to the document node) that have comment children.

```
//comment()/..[element()]
fn:root(self::node()) treat as document-node()/
   descendant-or-self::node()/child::comment()/parent::node()[element()]
```

Let's look at how this is done. In brief, **//comment()** finds all comment nodes anywhere beneath the document node and gets the parents of these nodes, which may be either the document node or element nodes. And **[element()]** filters these nodes to return only element nodes.

The unabbreviated syntax is less obvious. When **//** appears at the start of the path, it retrieves the document node in which the context node occurs. **(fn:root(self::node())** returns the root node of the context node; **treat as document-node()** raises an error at execution time if this is not a document node.) **descendant-or-self::node()/child::comment()** returns all descendant nodes that are comment nodes. **parent::node()** returns the parents of these nodes. And **[element()]** filters these nodes to return only element nodes.

Node Tests

You have undoubtedly noticed the use of things like **element()** and **comment()**. These are examples of node tests. Node tests provide an initial filter and are applied to the nodes found along the specified axis.

Node tests come in two types. The first type is a *name* test, which tests the name of a node. Element, attribute, and processing instruction nodes have names. (The name of a processing instruction is its target, which is the first token in the processing instruction.) The second type of node test is a *kind* test. This filters nodes by kind—elements, attributes, comments, and so on. These tests also allow elements and attributes of particular datatypes to be returned. The most common tests are name tests for elements and attributes.

Take a look now at some examples of node kind tests. The following example gets the text children of Section elements. **//Section** returns all Section elements. **/text()** uses the child axis, so it looks at all children (elements, text, comments, and processing instructions) of the Section elements. The **text()** test filters out everything that is not a text node.

```
//Section/text()
```

The following example gets all comments in the document. **//** looks at the document node and all its descendants—that is, all element, text, comment, and processing instruction nodes in the document. **comment()** filters out those nodes that are not comment nodes.

```
//comment()
```

The following example uses a datatype test to get all element children of Section elements whose type is **xs:integer**. **//Section** gets all Section elements in the document. The **element()** "function"—I use quotes because it isn't actually a function; it's just a keyword that is followed by parentheses—filters out nodes that aren't elements. The arguments of this "function" allow filtering by both name and type. The first argument is the element name. Because this is a wildcard (*****), it doesn't filter out any nodes. The second argument is datatype. Because this is **xs:integer**, it filters out all elements except those whose type is **xs:integer**.

```
//Section/element(*, xs:integer)
```

Predicates

A predicate is an additional test that can be used to filter out nodes that have passed the node test. It can be any XQuery expression, although the most common predicates are comparisons of the type that might be found in a WHERE clause of a SELECT statement in SQL.

Because expressions return sequences, these must be interpreted as Boolean values. This is done as follows:

- The empty sequence is interpreted as false.
- A sequence whose first item is a node is interpreted as true.
- A sequence containing a single atomic value is interpreted as follows:
  - Boolean values are interpreted as themselves. That is, the Boolean value true is (obviously) true and the Boolean value false is (obviously) false.
  - Numeric values are interpreted as sequence positions and test whether the context node occurs at the specified position. For example, if an expression returns 3 and the context node is the third node in the sequence in which it occurs, the predicate is true. If not, the predicate is false. (Because positions are positive integers, all numeric values except positive integers result in the predicate evaluating to false.)
  - Empty strings, URIs, and untyped values are interpreted as false. Non-empty strings, URIs, and untyped values are interpreted as true.
- All other values (dates, sequences of atomic values, and so on) return a type error.

Table 7.4 Evaluating Expressions in Predicates

Expression	Result	Value Treated As
Boolean value	true	true
	false	false
Numeric value	Any	Position in sequence
String, URI, untyped value	Zero length	false
	Non-zero length	true
Sequence	Starting with a node	true
	Empty	false
All others	Any	Type error

Let's now look at some sample predicates.

The first example uses the predicate **[@Number=1]**. This example filters the Chapter elements and leaves only those that have a Number attribute—remember that the context node for the predicate is the Chapter element—whose value is 1.

```
/Book/Chapter[@Number=1]
```

The second example uses a pre-defined function which tests if the value of a Title element starts with the string **"XML"**. (The **string** function returns the string value of the current node, which is the concatenation of all of the values of the text descendants of the node—in this case, the title of the book.)

```
//Title[fn:starts-with(string(), "XML")]
```

The third example uses the predicate **[2]**. This means to retrieve the second item in the sequence to which the predicate is applied. Because the sequence is the Chapter children of the Book element, this predicate returns the second Chapter element.

```
/Book/Chapter[2]
```

The fourth example uses the predicate **[./Author]**. This returns only those Chapter elements that have Author children. Let's see how this is done. Because no axis is specified in the expression Author, the child axis is used. Thus, **./Author** returns all child elements of the Chapter whose name is Author. This is a sequence of zero or more nodes. Remember that empty sequences are treated as false and sequences starting with a node are treated as true. Thus, if a Chapter element does not have any Author children, it is filtered out; if it has one or more Author children, it is retained.

```
/Book/Chapter[./Author]
```

FLWOR Expressions

This section discusses FLWOR expressions, which are one of the most common types of XQuery expressions.

FLWOR (pronounced "flower") is an acronym of for, let, where, order by, return. A FLWOR expression must have at least one for or let clause. (It may have many, including a mixture of the two.) It may have a where and/or an order by clause. And it must have a return clause.

FLWOR expressions are commonly used to transform single documents or join values from two or more documents.

Unless otherwise stated, all examples in this section use the following sample document.

```
<Books>
   <Book>
      <Title>Introduction to XML</Title>
      <Author>John Smith</Author>
      <Price Currency="USD">29.99</Price>
   </Book>
   <Book>
      <Title>XML: Real-World Solutions</Title>
      <Author>Jean Lefebvre</Author>
      <Price Currency="USD">44.99</Price>
   </Book>
   <Book>
      <Title>XML and Integration</Title>
      <Author>Joerg Schmidt</Author>
      <Author>Helga Schmidt</Author>
   </Book>
</Books>
```

For Clauses

A for clause is similar to a for loop in programming languages such as Java or C. The main difference is that, instead of incrementing the value of the loop variable, the loop variable ranges over the items in a sequence.

For example, consider the for clause shown here. This ranges over the sequence (1, 2, 3), using the variable $n. (Variables in XQuery are QNames preceded by a dollar sign $. This allows them to be easily distinguished from other uses of QNames, such as name tests.)

For each value of $n—that is, each item in the sequence (1, 2, 3)—the return clause constructs a Number element and sets its content to the value of $n. Note that an enclosed expression is used to make sure that $n is evaluated. That is, the $n in the return clause is placed inside braces so the query processor will retrieve its value instead of treating it as the string literal "$n".

```
for $n in (1, 2, 3) return <Number>{$n}</Number>

Results:

<Number>1</Number>
<Number>2</Number>
<Number>3</Number>
```

Let's now look at a somewhat more useful example. This example returns the titles of the books in the sample document as a sequence of Title elements.

The for clause in this example uses the variable **$b** to range over the sequence returned by the expression **doc("books.xml")//Book**. This expression first retrieves the document node of our sample document (books.xml). It then returns all of the Book elements that are descendants of the document node. In other words, it retrieves the Book elements in the books.xml document.

For each value of **$b**—that is, each Book element in books.xml—the return clause returns the Title child (**$b/Title**).

```
for $b in doc("books.xml")//Book
return $b/Title

Results:

<Title>Introduction to XML</Title>
<Title>XML: Real-World Solutions</Title>
<Title>XML and Integration</Title>
```

Let Clauses

Let clauses are assignment statements, like the = operator in Java or the := operator in Pascal. In particular, a let clause sets the value of a variable to be an entire sequence.

To see the difference between let clauses and for clauses, consider the following examples. The for clause in the first example uses the variable **$i** to iterate over the values in the sequence consisting of the a, b, and c elements. For each value of **$i**—that is, each element in the sequence—the return clause constructs a result element whose content is the value of **$i**. The result of this is three result elements, one for each value in the sequence.

```
for $i in (<a/>, <b/>, <c/>)
return <result>{$i}</result>

Results:

<result><a/></result>
<result><b/></result>
<result><c/></result>
```

By contrast, the let clause in the second example assigns the same sequence to the $s variable. That is, the value of **$s** is the entire sequence. The return clause of this query constructs a result element and sets its contents to the value of $s. As you can see, the result is to construct a single result element whose content is the entire sequence.

```
let $s := (<a/>, <b/>, <c/>)
return <result>{$s}</result>

Results:

<result><a/><b/><c/></result>
```

One thing that helps to understand let clauses is to remember that all values in XQuery are sequences. Even things that look like scalar values, such as 10.0 or "XML", are sequences consisting of a single atomic value. Thus, assignments in XQuery aren't very different from assignments in other languages—it's just that XQuery (effectively) views all values as arrays, rather than single values.

As an aside, there is one significant difference between variables in XQuery, which is a functional language, and variables in procedural languages such as Java or C++. This difference is that the values of variables cannot be changed. That is, once a value is assigned to a variable, that value is retained for the entire life of the variable. Unfortunately, XQuery allows you to reuse variable names in a manner that appears you are updating the variable.

For example, the following query appears to count the number of times a query loops through a for clause. In fact, this query does no such thing. Instead, the second **$count** variable masks the first **$count** variable and the query returns the sequence (1, 1, 1). That is, each time the for clause is entered, the processor creates a new **$count** variable, assigns to it the sum of the first **$count** variable (which is 0) and 1 and returns this value.

```
let $count := 0
for $i in (1, 2, 3)
let $count := $count + 1
return $count
```

It is even possible to write queries that appear to update the value of a variable and return the correct value. For example, the following query appears to update the value of **$i** and return the expected value (2). In fact, the query creates two **$i** variables, the second masking the first, with the value of the second **$i** variable being returned.

```
let $i := 1
let $i := $i + 1
return $i
```

Let clauses are often used with aggregate functions. For example, the **avg** function accepts a sequence as an argument and calculates the average of the values in the sequence. This is used in the following query to calculate the average price of books sold in US dollars.

The query first sets **$p** to a sequence containing all Price elements in the books.xml document whose Currency attribute has a value of **"USD"**. It then constructs an AveragePrice element and sets its content to the value returned by the **avg** function when called with the value of **$p**. In other words, it uses **$p** to pass the sequence of Price elements to the **avg** function, which then returns the average price.

```
let $p := doc("books.xml")//Price[@Currency="USD"]
return <AveragePrice>{avg($p)}</AveragePrice>

Results:

<AveragePrice>37.49</AveragePrice>
```

Let clauses are also commonly used to clarify what is happening in a query.

For example, the following query uses a for clause to iterate over the Book elements in the sample document. It then uses two let clauses. For each value of **$book**—that is, each Book element—it sets the value of **$title** to the Title child of the Book element and the value of **$authors** to the sequence of Author children of the Book element. Notice that the value of **$title** will be either the empty sequence or a single node (depending on whether the book has a title), whereas the value of **$authors** will be a sequence of zero or more nodes (depending on how many authors the book has).

The query references **$title** and **$authors** in the return clause, which constructs a new Book element containing the title of the book (as a Title element) and the number of authors of the book (as a NumAuthors element). The number of authors is calculated by passing the value of **$authors** to the **count** function, which counts the number of items in the sequence represented by **$authors** (the number of Author children of the Book element).

Technically, this query did not need to use the **$title** and **$authors** variables—the path expressions to which these variables were set could have been used directly in the return clause instead. However, using the variables (hopefully) helped clarify the query.

```
for $book in doc("books.xml")//Book let $title := $book/Title
let $authors := $book/Author
return
   <Book>
      {$title},
```

```
        <NumAuthors>{count($authors)}</NumAuthors>
    </Book>
```

```
Results:
```

```
<Book>
   <Title>Introduction to XML</Title>
   <NumAuthors>1</NumAuthors>
</Book>
<Book>
   <Title>XML: Real-World Solutions</Title>
   <NumAuthors>1</NumAuthors>
</Book>
<Book>
  <Title>XML and Integration</Title>
   <NumAuthors>2</NumAuthors>
</Book>
```

Where Clauses

The next part of a FLWOR expression is the where clause. Where clauses are optional, and are used to filter values according to an expression. An expression can be built from multiple sub-expressions, where the sub-expressions can be grouped with parentheses and combined with the and and or keywords.

As was the case with predicates, any expression can be used as a filter. And as was the case with predicates, expressions that return non-Boolean values must be interpreted as Booleans. This is known as *computing the effective Boolean value of a sequence*. It is the same as was done with predicates—for example, empty strings and empty sequences are interpreted as false—except that numeric values are not interpreted as positions in a sequence. Instead, **0** and **NaN** are interpreted as false and all other numeric values are interpreted as true.

The most common expressions are comparisons.

Here is a where clause that filters the output according to the value of the Author element. In particular, if the value of the Author element is **"John Smith"**, the corresponding value of **$b** is used in the return clause.

```
for $b in doc("books.xml")//Book
where $b/Author = "John Smith"
return $b/Title
```

```
Results:

<Title>Introduction to XML</Title>
```

Here is a where clause that filters the output according to whether the book has a price. In particular, if **$b/Price** is a non-empty sequence, the book's title is included in the result. If **$b/Price** is empty (there is no Price child), the book's title is omitted from the result.

```
for $b in doc("books.xml")//Book
where $b/Price
return $b/Title

Results:

<Title>Introduction to XML</Title>
<Title>XML: Real-World Solutions</Title>
```

Order By Clauses

The final part of FLWOR expressions is the order by clause. (Return clauses have been covered in the descriptions of the other clauses.) This works in conjunction with a for clause to determine the order in which the return clause is evaluated. In particular, the for clause can be thought of as sending a stream of values to the return clause; the order in which these values are sent is determined by the order by clause.

For example, in the following query, the stream is ordered by title (the value of the Title element). Although XQuery does not require any particular implementation of order by clauses, the following procedure could be used to evaluate this query. First, a sequence is constructed that contains the Book elements in the document. Second, the filtered sequence is sorted by the value of the Title child of each Book element. Third, the Book elements in the sorted sequence are passed to the return clause, which returns their Title children.

```
for $b in doc("books.xml")//Book
order by $b/Title
return $b/Title

Results:

<Title>Introduction to XML</Title>
<Title>XML and Integration</Title>
<Title>XML: Real-World Solutions</Title>
```

Note that an order by clause can have multiple sort keys and that there is no requirement that the sort keys be used in the return clause.

Joining Documents with FLWOR Expressions

As a final example of FLWOR expressions, take a look at how a FLWOR expression might be used to join two documents. The first document (authors.xml) contains a list of authors. For each author, there is an Author element with Name and Address children. The second document (books2.xml) contains a list of books. For each book, there is a Book element with Title, Author, and Publisher children.

Now suppose that, from these two documents, you want to construct a modified authors document that contains the titles of all the books that a given author has written, as well as the rest of the author information.

authors.xml

```
<Authors>
   <Author>
      <Name>John Smith</Name>
      <Address>Dryden, NY, USA</Address>
   </Author>
   <Author>
      <Name>Jean Lefebvre</Name>
      <Address>Namur, Belgium</Address>
   </Author>
</Book>
```

books2.xml

```
<Books>
   <Book>
      <Title>Introduction to XML</Title>
      <Author>John Smith</Author>
      <Publisher>Basic Press</Publisher>
   </Book>
   <Book>
      <Title>An XML Style Guide</Title>
      <Author>John Smith</Author>
      <Publisher>College Books, Inc.</Publisher>
   </Book>
```

```
    <Book>
       <Title>XML in Microsoft Office</Title>
       <Author>John Smith</Author>
       <Author>Gino Ferrari</Author>
       <Author>Juan Herrero</Author>
       <Publisher>Tam O'Shanter Books</Publisher>
    </Book>
    <Book>
       <Title>XML: A Sample-Driven Approach</Title>
       <Author>Jean Lefebvre</Author>
       <Publisher>Quizz Press</Publisher>
    </Book>
    <Book>
       <Title>XML: Real-World Solutions</Title>
       <Author>Jean Lefebvre</Author>
       <Publisher>McGeorge Publishing</Publisher>
    </Book>
</Books>
```

The FLWOR expressions shown next construct the desired document. The outer expression iterates over the Author elements in the authors document. It uses these to create new Author elements that contain all of the information in the old elements, as well as a new Titles child.

The inner FLWOR expression populates the Titles element. It retrieves all of the Book elements from the books2.xml document and filters out those Book elements whose Author child does not match the Name child of the current Author element from authors.xml. This effectively performs a join of the two documents.

(Although I stated that all Book elements are retrieved from books2.xml, it is unlikely that a query engine would actually execute the query in this manner, as it would mean retrieving all of the Book elements for each author in authors.xml. A more likely solution is that the engine would use an index to retrieve the Author elements from books2.xml that matched a given Name element in authors.xml. From these books2.xml Author elements, it would then be possible to navigate to the corresponding Title elements.)

Notice that this is a left outer join. That is, it lists all authors in the authors document, regardless of whether they have any books in the books document, and only lists books that have authors in the authors document. It is also possible to perform inner joins and right outer joins. For examples, see the XQuery recommendation at http://www.w3.org/TR/xquery/.

```
for $a in doc("authors.xml")//Author
return
<Author>
{
   $a/Name,
   $a/Address,
   <Titles>
   {
      for $b in doc("books2.xml")//Book
      where $b/Author = $a/Name
      return $b/Title
   }
   </Titles>
}
</Author>
```

Here is the output of the query. As you can see, each of the authors is listed, along with the titles of the books they have written.

```
<Author>
   <Name>John Smith</Name>
   <Address>Dryden, NY, USA</Address>
   <Titles>
      <Title>Introduction to XML</Title>
      <Title>An XML Style Guide</Title>
      <Title>XML in Microsoft Office</Title>
   </Titles>
</Author>
<Author>
   <Name>Jean Lefebvre</Name>
   <Address>Namur, Belgium</Address>
   <Titles>
      <Title>XML: A Sample-Driven Approach</Title>
      <Title>XML: Real-World Solutions</Title>
   </Titles>
</Author>
```

Other Expressions

This section briefly reviews some of the remaining types of XQuery expressions.

Arithmetic Expressions

XQuery supports the usual numeric operations of addition, subtraction, multiplication, and division. It also supports integer division, which operates only on integers and rounds toward zero, and modulus. These operate as expected on numbers, with XQuery automatically promoting values from one type to another as needed. The only thing to be aware of is that the division operators are **div** and **idiv**, because a slash (/) can be mistaken for a step separator in a path expression, and that whitespace must precede the minus sign so it can be distinguished from a minus in a QName. For example, **a-b** is a legal QName; **a - b** and **a -b** are not and can therefore be correctly interpreted as arithmetic expressions.

Arithmetic operations can also be performed on date/time values when it makes sense. For example, you can subtract one date from another, add a duration to a date, and divide a duration by a number, but cannot multiply one date by another date.

Comparison Expressions

XQuery has three types of comparison expressions: value comparisons, general comparisons, and node comparisons.

Value comparisons are the usual comparisons (equal, less than, greater than, and so on) between two atomic values. These use the **eq**, **ne**, **lt**, **le**, **gt**, and **ge** operators. Value comparisons can be performed on any values of any datatype, including user-defined datatypes. XQuery performs the necessary type promotions and subtype substitutions to make this possible. (Of course, values of completely different types, such as dates and QNames, cannot be compared and will raise an error.)

Value comparisons are useful any time you want to guarantee that only a single value is compared. For example, the following expression returns all books whose prices are less than $50. It will raise an error if a book has more than one price (more than one Price element).

```
doc("books.xml")//Book[Price lt 50.00]
```

General comparisons are set-valued comparisons and can be used to compare two sequences. They use the **=**, **!=**, **<**, **<=**, **>**, and **>=** operators.

A general comparison is successful if any value in the first sequence satisfies the comparison against any value in the second sequence. This can lead to some surprising results. For example, **(1, 2, 3)** is equal to, not equal to, less than, less than or equal to, greater than, and greater than or equal to **(0, 2, 4)**, since 2 (in the first sequence) is equal to 2 (in the second sequence), 1 (in the first sequence) is not equal to 0 (in the second sequence), and so on.

General comparisons are useful when more than one value might be present. For example, suppose you want to find the titles of all the books written by John Smith. The following expression will do this, even if a given book has more than one author—that is, even if **$b/Author** returns more than one Author element. This is because only one of the Author elements must equal **"John Smith"**.

```
for $b in doc("books.xml")//Book
where $b/Author = "John Smith"
return $b/Title
```

Node comparisons are used to compare nodes, each of which has its own unique identity. Order comparison (**<<** and **>>**) compares nodes based on document order. That is, one node is **<<** another node if it occurs before the latter node. Similarly, node identity (**is** and **isnot**) checks whether two nodes are the same node or not.

Note that having the same name and content is not sufficient to satisfy the node identity test. For example, the following expression returns false, since the two different **<a>** elements have different identities. (The **deep-equal** function can be used to determine whether two sequences have the same values.)

```
(<a/> = <a/>)
```

As might be expected, all comparison expressions can be combined with the keywords **and** and **or** and grouped with parentheses.

Conditional Expressions (if-then-else)

XQuery contains an if-then-else construct for returning different results based on the outcome of a test. (It does not, however, support case expressions for performing multiple branches in a single, easy-to-use expression.) The syntax of the if-then-else expression is as expected, although you should remember that the **else** clause is required. For example, the following expression returns the price in US dollars if one is available and the string **"N/A"** if one is not.

```
for $b in doc("books.xml")//Book
return
{
  "Title: ", $b/Title/string(),
  "Price: ", if ($b/Price/@Currency = "USD") then $b/Price/string() else "N/A"
)
```

XQuery also contains quantified expressions (using the **some** and **every** keywords) for determining if some, all, or no items in a sequence meet a particular criteria.

Set Expressions

XQuery contains three operators for joining sequences: **union, intersection**, and **except**. The function of the first two is obvious; **except** returns all nodes that are in the first sequence but not the second sequence. All of these operators return nodes in document order and remove any duplicates (based on node identity).

Functions

XQuery defines more than 100 functions, covering a wide range of functionality. To give you an idea of some of the kinds of functions that are available, a few of them are listed here:

- Numeric functions: **floor, ceiling, round**, and so on
- String functions: **concat, substring, upper-case, contains, replace**, and so on
- Date/time functions: **year-from-date, adjust-date-to-timezone**, and so on
- Sequence functions: **empty, distinct-values, insert-before**, and so on
- Aggregate functions: **count, min, max**, and so on
- QName functions: **prefix-from-QName, in-scope-prefixes**, and so on
- Node functions: **name, local-name, namespace-uri**, and so on

Although a complete description of these functions is beyond the scope of this book–check out the XQuery Functions and Operators recommendation (http://www.w3.org/TR/xpath-functions/) for complete details–this section will describe a few of the more important functions, as well as describe how users can define their own functions.

Input Functions

XQuery has two primary input functions: **doc** and **collection**.

The **doc** function accepts the URI of the document to be retrieved. It returns the document node of the specified document. For example, the following call to the **doc** function retrieves the document node of the books.xml document.

```
for $b in doc("books.xml")//Book
return $b/Title
```

The **collection** function accepts the URI of the collection to be retrieved. It returns the sequence of nodes in the collection. The definition of a collection is implementation-defined.

For example, if XQuery is implemented over a native XML database, an XQuery collection might be a native XML database collection. If XQuery is implemented over the file system, a collection might be all the XML documents in a directory. If XQuery is implemented over a relational database, it might be all the rows in a table, each of which is returned as a separate <row>

element. In the following example, the **collection** function returns all the documents in the c:/bookdocs/ directory.

```
for $d in collection("file://localhost/c|/bookdocs/")
return $d/Book/Title
```

String and Data Functions

The **string** function returns the string value of an item. The string value of an atomic value is simply that value cast as a string. The string value of a node depends on the node type, as shown in Table 7.5.

Table 7.5 String Values of Nodes

Node Type	String Value
Document	Descendant text, concatenated together
Element	Descendant text, concatenated together
Attribute	Attribute value
Text	Content
Comment	Content
Processing Instruction	Content (does not include target)
Namespace	Namespace URI

If you are accustomed to working with data-centric XML, the string values of document and element nodes may be surprising. Concatenating all the text found in a data-centric XML document or complex element type is likely to lead to an unusable result. For example, the string value of the following Book element is "Introduction to XMLJohn SmithBasic Press".

```
<Book>
   <Title>Introduction to XML</Title>
   <Author>John Smith</Author>
   <Publisher>Basic Press</Publisher>
</Book>
```

However, string values do make sense when working with document-centric XML and mixed content in particular. For example, the string content of a <p> element in XHTML will simply be the paragraph without any embedded elements, such as <a> or <b> elements.

Table 7.6 shows examples of values returned by the **string** function.

Table 7.6 string() Examples

Input Argument	Return Value
()	
123 (number)	"123"
1958-10-29 (date)	"1958-10-29"
<Name>Lopez</Name>	Lopez
<p>This is <b>bold</b></p>	This is bold
<point><x>1.0</x><y>2.5</y></point>	"1.02.5"
my_attr="This is an attribute value"	"This is an attribute value"

The **string** function is most commonly used to return the value of a node. For example, the following code assumes that the first author listed for a book is the primary author. It uses the **string** function to return the author's name in a **PrimaryAuthor** element. Note the use of the **[ ]** operator to get the first author and the use of the **string** function without any arguments to operate on the context node.

```
for $b in doc("books.xml")//Book
return
   <Book>
      {$b/Title},
      <PrimaryAuthor>{$b/Author[1]/string()}</PrimaryAuthor>,
      {$b/Author[position() > 1]},
      {$b/Price}
   </Book>
```

The **data** function is similar to the **string** function except that it returns a typed value. It accepts a sequence of items as its argument and returns a sequence of atomic values. As might be expected, atomic values in a sequence are simply returned and the values returned for a text, comment, processing instruction, or namespace node are the same as those returned by the **string** function. The value returned for a document node is the same as that returned by the **string** function, except that its type is **xs:untypedAtomic**, and the value returned for an attribute node is the typed attribute value.

The value returned for an element node depends on the content model of the element. If the element has simple type, the returned value is the content of the element, returned as a typed value. If it is untyped or has mixed content, the returned value is the same as that returned by the **string** function, except that its type is **xs:untypedAtomic**. And if the element has element-only content, an error is raised.

Table 7.7 shows examples of values returned by the **data** function.

Table 7.7 data() Examples

Input Argument	Return Value
()	
123 (number)	123 (number)
1958-10-29 (date)	1958-10-29 (date)
<Name>Lopez</Name>	"Lopez" (assumes <Name> has type xs::string)
<p>This is <b>bold</b></p>	This is bold (xs:untypedAtomic)
<point><x>1.0</x><y>2.5</y></point>	Error!
my_attr="This is an attribute value"	"This is an attribute value"

The **data** function is used in a similar fashion to the **string** function, except it is used when typed values are needed.

User-Defined Functions

XQuery allows users to define their own functions. These can have zero or more parameters and may have an implicit or explicit return type. (If no return type is declared, the return type is assumed to be an arbitrary sequence—that is, it can contain nodes or atomic values of any type.) The body of an XQuery function is simply an expression; no return keyword is needed. The function returns the result of evaluating the expression.

For example, the following function has no parameters and has a return type of a non-empty sequence of integers. It always returns the sequence **(1, 2, 3)**, since this is the expression in the body of the function.

```
declare function local:oneTwoThree()
   as xs:integer+
{
   (1, 2, 3)
};
```

Next is a somewhat more useful function, which converts attributes to child elements:

```
declare function local:attr_to_elem($e as element())
   as element()
{
   element {node-name($e)}
   {
```

```
      for $a in $e/@*
      return element {node-name($a)} {data($a)}
   }
};
```

This function accepts an element node as a parameter. It returns a new element with the same name as the input element. The output element has no attributes and its children have the same names and values as the attributes on the input elements. Note that any child elements of the input element are ignored.

The function signature is easy to understand. **declare function local:attr_to_elem** declares a function whose name is **local:attr_to_elem. ($e as element)** declares a single parameter whose type is an element node. The **as element** after the parameter list declares that the function returns a single element node.

The function body is an expression that constructs a new element using element constructors. (Direct constructors, which use XML syntax, cannot be used in this function, because the names of the new element and its children are determined at runtime.) The first call to the element constructor uses the **node-name** function to construct a new element whose name is the same as that of the input element. The content of this element is constructed with a FLWOR expression. This uses the path expression **$e/@*** to retrieve a sequence containing all of the attribute nodes of the input element. For each attribute, it uses an element constructor to construct a child element with the same name and value as the attribute. The name is retrieved with the **node-name** function and the value is retrieved with the **data** function.

It is important to note that the **return** keyword is not a return statement, as is found in functions in other languages. Instead, it is part of a FLWOR expression and simply returns elements to be used in the sequence constructed by that expression. For most people, this lack of a return statement is the most confusing part of writing XQuery functions.

XQuery functions can be recursive. That is, they can call themselves. For example, the following function calls itself in order to construct the path leading to an element node. It stops only when it reaches an element that does not have an element as a parent. (The **element()** node test ensures that the parent axis only returns element nodes, not the document node.) As in the previous function, note that the **return** keyword is part of a FLWOR expression—in this case, with two **let** keywords and no **for** keywords—and not a return statement for the function itself.

```
declare function local:element_path($e as element())
   as xs:string
{
   let $name := fn:node-name($e)
   let $parent := $e/parent::element()
```

```
    return
    (
        if ($parent)
        then fn:concat(local:element_path($parent), "/", $name)
        else $name cast as xs:string
    )
};
```

Datatypes

XQuery is a strongly typed language, a fact I've only hinted at until now. When I say that XQuery is strongly typed, I mean that each item in a sequence, whether it is an atomic value or a node, has a well-defined type, and that variables have well-defined types as well. By assigning types to values and variables, processors are able to perform static type-checking of queries—that is, catching type errors at compile time—as well as to better optimize queries. In spite of this, static type checking is optional and most processors do not currently support it, although this is likely to change as processors mature.

XQuery uses a type system based on the type system defined in XML Schemas. It automatically includes all of the datatypes defined in Part 2 of the XML Schemas recommendation and adds a few types of its own. The most important of these are **xs:untyped**, which is used for untyped element nodes, and **xs:untypedAtomic**, which is used for untyped atomic values and untyped attribute nodes. The other types are **xs:anyAtomicType**, which is similar to **xs:anySimpleType** but does not support lists or unions, and **xs:dayTimeDuration** and **xs:yearMonthDuration**, both of which support ordering. As with XML Schemas, XQuery supports user-defined simple and complex types as well.

Using XQuery without Datatypes

XQuery needs datatype information for a variety of operations, the most common of which are comparisons, ordering, and arithmetic operations. Other uses include implicit casting during function calls, checking datatypes in node tests, and so on. Because the use of datatypes in queries is optional (and XML is inherently untyped), XQuery does its best to cast untyped values as expected. In this respect, it usually succeeds.

For example, suppose a variable does not have a declared type. If it is compared to a literal with a general comparison operator (<, >, =, and so on), it is cast to the type of that literal. If it is compared to a variable whose type is unknown, both variables are treated as strings, which can lead to unexpected results in some cases.

This is illustrated by the following two queries. The first query returns **true** because **$v1** is cast to an **xs:double**, which is the type of the literal **2.0** and is compared numerically.

```
let $doc := <values>
              <value_1>2.0</value_1>
              <value_2>2</value_2>
            </values>
let $v1 := $doc//value_1
return
   if ($v1 = 2.0)
   then fn:true()
   else fn:false()
```

In contrast, the second query returns **false** because both **$v1** and **$v2** are untyped, so both are cast to and compared as strings. This might not be the expected result, depending on whether you think of the values as strings or numbers.

```
let $doc := <values>
              <value_1>2.0</value_1>
              <value_2>2</value_2>
            </values>
let $v1 := $doc//value_1, $v2 := $doc//value_2
return
   if ($v1 = $v2)
   then fn:true()
   else fn:false()
```

The easiest solution to this problem is to explicitly cast the variables when they are assigned or compared; the latter is shown in the following query. Another solution is to associate a schema for the values, value_1, and value_2 elements with the query.

```
let $doc := <values>
              <value_1>2.0</value_1>
              <value_2>2</value_2>
            </values>
let $v1 := $doc//value_1, $v2 := $doc//value_2
return
   if ($v1 cast as xs:double = $v2 cast as xs:double)
   then fn:true()
   else fn:false()
```

As was mentioned earlier, values are usually cast as needed. The main exception to this rule is when using the value comparison operators (**eq**, **ne**, **gt**, and so on). In this case, untyped values are always cast to strings, which may lead to unexpected results. For example, the following query raises an error because **$v1** is untyped and therefore cast as an **xs:string**, which can't be compared to an **xs:double**.

```
let $doc := <values>
              <value_1>2.0</value_1>
              <value_2>2</value_2>
            </values>
let $v1 := $doc//value_1
return
   if ($v1 eq 2.0)
   then fn:true()
   else fn:false()
```

Using XQuery with Datatypes

Although XQuery processors know the datatypes defined by XML Schemas, they do not know any user-defined datatypes, such as the datatypes of elements and attributes. This can lead to problems, as you saw in the previous section when the XQuery processor did not know the datatypes of the value_1 and value_2 elements. To solve this problem, queries can explicitly import XML Schemas describing the user-defined types. For example, the following schema defines the datatypes of the values, value_1 and value_2 elements.

```
<xsd:schema xmlns:xsd="http://www.w3.org/2001/XMLSchema"
   xmlns="http://www.xmlguild.org/book/xquery/values"
   targetNamespace="http://www.xmlguild.org/book/xquery/values"
   elementFormDefault="qualified">
   <xsd:element name="values">
      <xsd:complexType>
         <xsd:sequence>
            <xsd:element name="value_1" type="xsd:double"/>
            <xsd:element name="value_2" type="xsd:double"/>
         </xsd:sequence>
      </xsd:complexType>
   </xsd:element>
</xsd:schema>
```

To import this schema into a query, use an import schema statement at the start of the query. For example, the following statement imports the values.xsd schema. It specifies that **"http://www.xmlguild.org/book/xquery/values"** is the default element namespace and that the schema can be found in the values.xsd file. (The at keyword is optional and XQuery processors can define other, implementation-dependent, ways to specify the location of a schema. Furthermore, the location specified by the **at** keyword is just a hint—XQuery processors are not obligated to use it.)

```
import schema default element namespace
  "http://www.xmlguild.org/book/xquery/values" at "values.xsd";
```

Alternatively, you could have associated a prefix with the namespace by using the **namespace** keyword and the prefix, as is shown in the following statement, which associates the v prefix with the namespace.

```
import schema namespace v = http://www.xmlguild.org/book/xquery/values
   at "values.xsd";
```

It is not enough to simply import the schema. You also need to tell XQuery to use the schema. In particular, you need to tell XQuery to annotate items with their datatypes. There are a number of ways to do this, but the most common is through validation. While most people think of validation as checking that a particular XML document conforms to a schema, a side-effect of validation is that the document nodes are annotated with their datatypes—that is, a datatype is assigned to each node in the document.

There are several ways to perform validation in XQuery. The most common is to validate documents when they are retrieved with the **doc** and **collection** functions. (How the user tells these functions to perform validation is implementation dependent.) The other way to perform validation is to use a validate expression, as is shown in the following query. (Although this query uses the validate expression to validate input data, it is more commonly used to validate the results of an XQuery expression, such as in the return clause of a FLWOR expression or in the body of a function.)

If this query is executed without the validate expression—as was done previously—it returns **false**. This is because the datatypes of the value_1 and value_2 elements are not known and are therefore compared as strings. In this query, the validate expression annotates the value_1 and value_2 nodes with the type **xs:double**. Thus, **$v1** and **$v2** are compared numerically and the expression returns **true**.

```
import schema default element namespace
    "http://www.xmlguild.org/book/xquery/values"
   at "values.xsd";
let $doc := validate {<values>
                          <value_1>2.0</value_1>
                          <value_2>2</value_2>
                      </values>}
let $v1 := $doc//value_1, $v2 := $doc//value_2
```

```
return
   if ($v1 = $v2)
   then fn:true()
   else fn:false()
```

The final part of using XQuery with datatypes is to explicitly assign datatypes to variables. Although this is optional, it is a good practice, as it allows XQuery processors to perform static type checking and possibly optimize query processing, and it makes explicit to developers how a given variable is supposed to be used. For example, the following query uses the **as** keyword to specify that the **$v1** and **$v2** variables are of type **xs:double**.

```
import schema default element namespace
   "http://www.xmlguild.org/book/xquery/values"
   at "values.xsd";
let $doc := validate {<values>
                         <value_1>2.0</value_1>
                         <value_2>2</value_2>
                      </values>}
let $v1 as xs:double := $doc//value_1, $v2 as xs:double := $doc//value_2
return
   if ($v1 = $v2)
   then fn:true()
   else fn:false()
```

Expressions that Use Datatypes

You have already seen how to use a cast expression to explicitly cast a value from one type to another. XQuery provides a number of expressions for working with types. These are summarized in Table 7.8.

Table 7.8 Expressions on Types

Expression	Description
cast	Casts a value to a specified type. The expression returns a new value.
castable	Checks that a value can be cast to the specified type. This allows queries to avoid errors at evaluation time. For example, a query might use an **if-then-else** expression to check if a string can be cast as a number before casting and comparing it to another number.
treat	Specifies that a given value must be of a specified type. This is generally used when an expression, such as a variable reference, has a less specific type than the type required by another expression. For example, a variable might have type **xs:decimal**, but a function might require a

Expression	Description
	value of type **xs:integer**. Applying a treat expression to the variable tells the processor that the variable will have the correct type at evaluation time and avoids any static type checking errors. (An error is raised if the variable does not have the correct type at evaluation time.) Unlike **cast**, **treat** does not return a new value.
typeswitch	Switches processing according to type. For example, an expression for processing address elements might process each element according to its subtype (US address, Guatemalan address, Chinese address, and so on).
instanceof	Checks that a value has a specified type. This allows queries to avoid errors at evaluation time. For example, a query might use an **if-then-else** expression to check if a variable is a number before comparing it to another number. This is similar to **castable**, except that it checks the type of a value, rather than whether that value can be cast to a particular type.

Some Important Details

Until this point, I've hidden a few important details about how XQuery operates. Let's now tackle these subjects.

Atomization

The first important detail is *atomization*, which is the process of converting a sequence of items (possibly including nodes) into a sequence of atomic values. Atomization is necessary whenever atomic values are required, such as in arithmetic expressions, comparisons, ordering, and calls to functions with atomic arguments. For example, in the following query, the sequence of Author elements generated by the path expression **$b/Author** is atomized before they are compared to the string **"John Smith"**. This is because an element, which is a node, cannot be directly compared to a string, which is an atomic value.

```
for $b in doc("books.xml")//Book
where $b/Author = "John Smith"
return $b/Title
```

To atomize a sequence, XQuery processors apply the **data** function to the sequence. That is, they construct a new sequence in which each item is replaced by its typed value. As you might recall, this is the value itself for atomic values, the typed value of attribute and element nodes, and so on. In the case of element nodes with simple types, such as the Author element, the content is simply returned as a typed value.

The second example shows how a sequence containing a single element node is atomized before it is used to order the results of a FLWOR expression. In this case, the Title element is atomized into a string (or **xs:untypedAtomic** if no schema information is present), which is then used to order the results.

```
for $b in doc("books.xml")//Book
order by $b/Title
return $b/Title
```

This final example shows how a sequence containing multiple element nodes is atomized before being used in a function. In this case, the sequence of Price elements in the **$p** variable is atomized before the average price is calculated. This is because the datatype of the argument of the **avg** function is a sequence of atomic values.

```
let $p := doc("books.xml")//Price[@Currency="USD"]
return <AveragePrice>{avg($p)}</AveragePrice>
```

Effective Boolean Values

The second important detail involves calculating an *effective Boolean value*. XQuery requires Boolean values in a number of places, such as **if-then-else** expressions, the **where** clause in FLWOR expressions, predicates, and so on. However, the result of the XQuery expressions used in these places is a sequence. An effective Boolean value, then, is the Boolean value calculated from a sequence. Table 7.9 shows how these are calculated.

Table 7.9 Effective Boolean Values

Sequence	Value	Treated As
Boolean value	true	true
	false	false
Numeric value	0, NaN	false
	All others	true
String, URI, untyped value	Zero length	false
	Non-zero length	true
Sequence	Starting with a node	true
	Empty	false
All others	Any	Type error

The first example shows a trivial case of effective Boolean values. The comparison expression (in parentheses) tests if any of the Author elements returned by the path **$b/Author** are equal to the string **"John Smith"**. The result of this expression is a sequence consisting of a single atomic value whose type is Boolean. The effective Boolean value of this sequence is another Boolean value. (To understand the difference between the two Booleans, you can think about how this might be implemented. The expression might return a Sequence object, which is an array of Item objects. This might be passed to a function that computes the effective Boolean value of the Sequence object and returns a Boolean value.)

```
for $b in doc("books.xml")//Book
where ($b/Author = "John Smith")
return $b/Title
```

The second example is more interesting. It computes the effective Boolean value of the sequence returned by the path expression **$b/Price**. Because a Book element in the sample document can have either zero or one Price children, this is a sequence containing either zero or one element nodes. If it contains zero nodes—that is, it is the empty sequence—then, according to the previous table, its effective Boolean value is false. If it contains one node, then its effective Boolean value is true. In other words, the query tests for the existence of a Price element.

```
for $b in doc("books.xml")//Book
where $b/Price
return $b/Title
```

Although the books.xml document simply omits prices when they aren't known, one can also imagine a document that used the value 0.0 to indicate an unknown price. In this case, the **where** clause could test the expression **data($b/Price) cast as xs:double**, where casting is required only if no schema information is associated with the query. This would be 0.0 (false) for an unknown price and non-zero (true) for a known price.

Modules and Prologs

Queries can be broken into individual pieces called *modules*. A main module contains an expression to be evaluated, whereas library modules contain only functions and variables that can be imported by other modules. (A main module can contain functions and variables as well.) An XQuery query consists of exactly one main module.

A *prolog* is a set of statements at the start of a module that sets up the environment used by that module. For example, prologs can contain statements to declare namespaces, functions, and global variables, import schemas and modules, specify how whitespace is to be handled and what collations to use, and so on. This section discusses a few of the more important prolog statements. You can read about the rest in the XQuery recommendation.

Library Modules

Library modules are collections of functions and global variables. They allow queries to be broken into smaller pieces and also allow you to build collections of reusable functions. To create a library module, you simply declare the module, its namespace, and its associated prefix, and then declare the functions and global variables in the module.

For example, the following module contains three simple functions used to calculate an average. (XQuery already provides functions that perform these operations; I show these only as an example.) The declaration at the start of the module specifies the namespace of the module and the prefix associated with this namespace. Note that all of the functions in this module use this prefix as part of their name.

```
module namespace math = "http://www.xmlguild.org/book/xquery/math";

declare function math:average($v as xs:double+) as xs:double
{
   math:sum($v) div math:count($v)
};

declare function math:sum($v as xs:double+) as xs:double
{
   if (math:count($v) > 1)
   then $v[1] + math:sum(fn:subsequence($v, 2))
   else $v[1]
};

declare function math:count($v as item()*) as xs:double
{
   if (fn:empty($v))
   then 0
   else 1 + math:count(fn:subsequence($v, 2))
};
```

The next example shows a query (main module) that uses an import module statement to import the math module. This statement specifies the namespace of the module and the prefix associated with it, which can be different from the prefix used in the module itself. The statement also provides a hint as to where the module can be found; as with the import schema statement, this hint can be ignored by the query processor. The body of the query is a FLWOR expression that uses the average function in the math module to calculate the average price of books in the books.xml document.

```
import module namespace
   mathlib = "http://www.xmlguild.org/book/xquery/math" at "math.lib";

let $prices := doc("books.xml")//Price
return mathlib:average($prices)
```

Global Variables

Modules can also declare global variables. These are visible both in the module in which they are declared and in any modules that import that module. Global variables can either be initialized to a particular expression or specified as external. The latter case is the more useful one, as external variables can be used to parameterize queries. (How a query processor retrieves the value for an external variable is implementation-dependent.)

For example, the following query declares an external variable named **$limit** and uses it to allow the query to return a list of books whose price is less than that limit.

```
declare variable $limit as xs:double external;

for $b in doc("books.xml")//Book
where $b/Price < $limit
return $b/Title
```

Note that global variables declared in a library module must be in the namespace used by that module.

Namespaces

XQuery uses XML namespaces as a way to uniquely identify things like element, attribute, variable, and function names. Before I describe how this is done, I need to clear up a bit of terminology, which is inconsistent across W3C recommendations and common usage.

A *QName* (also known as a qualified name or a prefixed name) is a name that contains a colon, such as **math:average**, **xs:integer**, and **o:Order**. QNames consist of an optional *prefix* (the part before the colon) and a *local name* (the part after the colon); if the prefix is omitted, so is the colon. When the prefix is mapped to a *namespace name* (also known as a namespace URI), the result is an *expanded name* (also known as an expanded QName or a universal name). An expanded name consists of an optional namespace name and a local name.

As far as XQuery is concerned, the important thing is that QNames are used in a number of places, the most important of which are element and attribute names, variable names, function names, parameter names, and atomic type names. To resolve QNames, XQuery maintains a set of mappings from prefixes to namespace names. These mappings are specified in a number of ways.

First, the XQuery recommendation itself associates a number of prefixes with namespace names, as is shown in the following list. Except for the **xml** prefix, these can be overridden in a query. The first three of these should be familiar. The fourth prefix (**fn**) is used by functions defined by the XQuery recommendation and the fifth prefix (**local**) is used by user-defined functions that are not specifically placed in another namespace.

- **xml** = http://www.w3.org/XML/1998/namespace
- **xs** = http://www.w3.org/2001/XMLSchema
- **xsi** = http://www.w3.org/2001/XMLSchema-instance
- **fn** = http://www.w3.org/2005/xpath-functions
- **local** = http://www.w3.org/2005/xquery-local-functions

The second way to associate prefixes with namespace names is in the prolog. The module declaration, import schema, and import module statements all associate prefixes with namespace names. In addition, the namespace declaration and default namespace declarations can also be used to associate prefixes with namespace names. For example, the following declarations associate the **foo** prefix with the "http://www.xmlguild.org/book/xquery/foo" namespace and specify that the default element and function namespaces are "http://www.xmlguild.org/book/xquery/example" and "http://www.xmlguild.org/book/xquery/functions". A prolog can contain multiple namespace declarations, but at most one default element namespace declaration and one default function namespace declaration.

```
declare namespace foo = "http://www.xmlguild.org/book/xquery/foo";
declare default element namespace
    "http://www.xmlguild.org/book/xquery/example";
declare default function namespace
    "http://www.xmlguild.org/book/xquery/functions";
```

The default element namespace is the namespace used by unqualified element names. By default, unqualified element names are not in any namespace. The default function namespace is the namespace used by unqualified function names. By default, unqualified function names are in the "http://www.w3.org/2005/xpath-functions" namespace, which is the namespace for functions defined by XQuery. This allows you to use these functions without specifying a prefix. Note that unqualified variable and attribute names are not in any namespace.

The final way to associate prefixes with namespace names is with namespace declarations (**xmlns** attributes) in direct constructors. Unlike the other declarations, whose scope is the entire query, the scope of these declarations is the element on which they are declared.

Summary

This chapter introduced you to XQuery, a language for querying individual XML documents, collections of XML documents, and non-XML data that is mapped to XML documents. XQuery is based on a data model in which individual values are sequences of items, which can be either atomic values (scalar values) or nodes (documents, elements, attributes, and so on). The language is strongly typed, using the types defined in XML Schemas, but can be used in an untyped manner.

Queries are composed of expressions, with the result of one expression being used as input for the next. The most commonly used expressions are path expressions, FLWOR expressions, and calls to functions. Other expressions allow you to query, combine, and manipulate XML documents in almost any way imaginable. In addition, XQuery contains a large number of predefined functions and allows you to define your own functions.

Version 1.0 of XQuery is read only, but work is already being done to add update expressions to the language.

8 XML Authoring

by Betty Harvey

Long before XML became the darling of the technological age, XML was being used to develop intellectual information. Intellectual information is created by individuals. In most cases, these individuals are not technologically inclined. In some cases, the only exposure these individuals have to a computer is with a word processor.

One of the most neglected areas of XML advances is in the development of tools for creating intellectual information. Long before Web services and W3C Schemas, XML was used by major publishers, manufacturers, and so on, to create intellectual information in XML. XML authoring tools haven't advanced as far as we would have hoped. As a result of the lack of effective intuitive authoring tools, organizations are developing inventive processes to get information into XML. One organization actually used rubber stamps to include tags on a printed page to be inserted when the document was retyped—this is the extreme in inventiveness—not very productive but great for rubber stamp manufacturers.

In many cases, moving to XML results in content providers thinking about their data in different ways. There are many different approaches to moving toward developing an XML workflow. Approaches that work in one organization may not necessarily work in another organization.

In fact, one approach may not work across a single organization. Organizations should assess and define their requirements before embarking on any project. However, this is extremely important when the changes to processes and workflows impacts individuals who will migrating from a word processing or desktop publishing environment to an XML authoring environment.

Involving the authors early in decisions that will impact their way of doing business is crucial. The most elegant technical solution can fail if the content developers are not communicated to and do not feel part of the process for change. Communication will make the transition from standard desktop publishing to XML successful.

This chapter discusses various approaches and important aspects of XML that aid the content developer in developing XML efficiently.

Defining an XML Authoring Environment

It is important for organizations to determine the appropriate authoring environment when they embark on using XML for the exchange and publication of their content. There are numerous methods for determining the appropriate authoring environment. The success of an XML document project relies heavily on the appropriate authoring environment. This section describes some of the methodologies for establishing a suitable authoring environment:

- Creating XML data using a validating WYSIWYG authoring tool.
- Creating XML data using a XML Interactive Development Environment (IDE).
- Creating XML data using a standard word processing tool.
- Using form-based authoring.
- Converting data from proprietary format into XML after creation.

Using a WYSIWYG Authoring Tool

Most organizations whose business relies heavily on authors and editors who create information usually decide to provide their authors with WYSIWYG authoring tools. WYSIWYG authoring tools provide the authors a familiar environment to create information. These tools provide increased productivity in that they can start creating XML information more efficiently than with other methods of authoring.

When using a WYSIWYG authoring tool, the content creator needs less training to create information. Customized stylesheets can be created that will simulate the final product. The editor can guide the authors through the authoring experience. WYSIWYG authoring tools do not allow the authors to invalidate the structure of the schema, unless they specifically turn validation off.

The WYSIWYG editor allows the authors to put special characters into the content from the keyboard. Special characters are characters that are not normally found on an English keyboard—the characters that go beyond the 128 ASCII character set—and ensure they are either UNICODE or ISO-8859-1 compliant. This is an enormous benefit for authors who use alternate characters. Some organizations are mandated by policy to use ISO-8859-1 character sets. ISO-8859-1 character set was heavily used with SGML. The encoding of ISO-8859-1 is different than UNICODE or UTF-8 encoding. The editor will recognize the character set being used by the **encoding** attribute in the XML declaration and will use the correct encoding.

```
<?xml version="1.0" encoding="UTF-8"?>
```

```
<?xml version="1.0" encoding="ISO-8859-1"?>
```

When the authors type the percent sign (%) in the text, the editor will automatically input the character % in UTF8, or **&pct;** if the encoding is ISO-8879-1.

Some organizations have found the cost of a WYSIWYG authoring tool prohibitive. However, if the organization has a large staff, an organization can justify the cost in the savings for training a staff in XML. Providing the authors an environment they are familiar with and feel comfortable working in is worth the cost.

Using XML IDE

Another option when creating XML data is using an XML IDE. The IDE tool allows developers the capability of developing *schemas*, which are XSLT and XML documents that conform to a specific schema. These tools are used quite successfully by developers and technical people. If your content developers are technically savvy, the IDE approach may be an appropriate tool.

On the other hand, if your content creators are developers of information, these tools may be overwhelming to them. They do not support creating content with customized styles. The view they will see is an ASCII view with angle brackets. The IDE validates the XML content, but does not prevent the authors from making mistakes.

Using Standard Word Processing

Even before Microsoft Word 2003 Professional provided the capability of authoring XML directly into a word processor, many organizations were already using WordPerfect to create XML. WordPerfect provided SGML authoring in Version 8 and has continually provided the capability to author XML.

Organizations who use Microsoft Word and are moving toward XML are looking seriously at using Microsoft Word as an XML authoring environment. Large organizations that have already invested and standardized on Microsoft Office have adopted the use of Microsoft Word or are looking at adopting Microsoft Word as their XML authoring environment. There are some attractive benefits to using Microsoft Word:

- They have made a significant investment in the Microsoft Office Suite.
- Authors are already familiar with Microsoft Word.
- Training costs are less because of the familiarity with Word; no need to purchase or train on new products.

The disadvantages of using a standard word processor to produce XML are:

- Authors are unable to control the authoring environment. Even if customized schema is used, word processors are not true validating authoring tools and will allow the authors access to all functions provided by the word processor. They can change font sizes, add bold and italics, and so on.

- Organizations must rely on XSLT for conversion even when custom schemas are used.
- More quality assurance (QA) processes on the file are required. The flexibility of word processors provide inconsistency in the data. For example, every time an author clicks the mouse, a new paragraph or text node is added to the data. You may not be able to visibly see it in the word processing tool, but when the file is saved as XML, empty nodes will be scattered throughout the file.

Converting Data into XML

Many organizations convert their information into XML after it is created and finalized. Converting the data as a post process is a good solution for organizations that have many authors and the data is set in stone once it has passed through the editorial stage. Many publishers and government organizations, such as the U.S. Patent and Trademark Office, take this approach. This method works well when an organization has little or no control over intellectual information providers. Once the information has been approved, the data gets converted to XML.

There are many approaches for getting the data converted to XML. A few are as follows:

- *Convert using XSLT:* If the document is in a form such as Word, WordPerfect, or Open Office, conversion using XSLT can have good results. The document will still require QA after the conversion but XSLT can provide a reasonable conversion.
- *Off-shore conversion:* Off-shore conversion can be cost effective when there is a large volume of information to be converted. Off-shore conversion houses usually rekey the information. The conversion cost is calculated by the number of characters converted and graphics that require conversion.
- *Other programming languages:* There are other programming languages that are used for the purpose of conversion. A program called Omnimark (http://www.stilo.com/index.htm) has been used successfully for many years to convert unstructured information into structured information. Some organizations use languages such as Perl and PHP for conversion of semi-structured information to XML.

Selecting an Appropriate Schema

Selecting an appropriate schema is the most critical decision that you must make. You basically have three options for the schema(s) to use in your project:

- Select an existing schema and use it unmodified.
- Develop your own schema.
- Modify an existing schema to meet your requirements.

There aren't any hard statistics on what percentage of organizations select one of the three options. In our experience, probably 20% use a standard schema without modification, 40% develop their schema, and 40% modify an existing schema to meet their needs.

Selecting and/or creating the appropriate schema will be critical to the entire process. If the data model doesn't fit the structure and content of the data being developed, creative workarounds will happen. The workarounds may not always be consistent between authors, which will result in inconsistent tagging of data.

Schema Constructs that Affect Authors

There are some common obstacles that can make creating XML difficult for developers of information. Some of the constructs are unavoidable. However, when an organization is developing an XML application that will require individuals to create XML information, some consideration should be given to the complexity of the XML model; the organization should be aware of the impact on authors when developing the schema and authoring environment.

Too Many Options

Most validating XML authoring tools provide a mechanism for the authors to create XML components in context. This means that the authors can see the available XML elements that can be included in the document at the location where the current focus of the cursor resides.

The authors can scroll through the elements and include the element they want. When there are too many options, the authors will have a more difficult time making selections. DOCBOOK, a standard and very popular schema, provides the users many options. For example, within a paragraph element (**<para>**), the authors have the ability to choose from 60-plus elements. Figure 8.1 shows the Insert Markup window for a DOCBOOK schema. The window shows the first 16 elements. If the authors want to include an inline element that isn't in the first 16 elements, they have to scroll to the appropriate location.

Because of the flexibility of a schema like DOCBOOK, most organizations that adopt this schema for internal use will customize the schema to eliminate elements that aren't appropriate for their organization. Figure 8.2 shows the same Insert Markup window from Arbortext's Epic Editor. It shows the allowed inline elements of a paragraph from a simplified DOCBOOK schema.

It is easy to see that the scaled-down schema would ease the difficulty for making decisions in element use.

Attributes

The use of attributes is good for providing more information about the element being described. In many cases, such as inclusion of graphics, mandatory elements are essential. However, creating non-essential mandatory attributes puts an unnecessary burden on the author. Whenever the authors encounter a mandatory attribute, they must switch focus from creating content to populating attributes.

Figure 8.1
The Insert Markup window for a DOCBOOK schema.

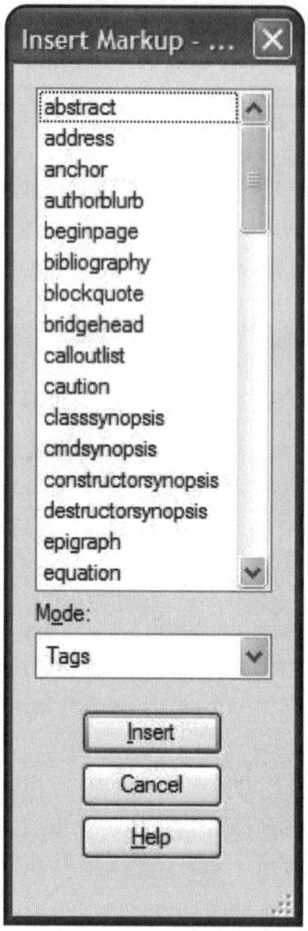

There are ways the XML authoring environments can be improved to diminish the burden on the author. Small enhancements can be made to the authoring environment that can populate mandatory attributes.

Unique Identifiers

A good example of a small enhancement but a drastic improvement to the authoring environment is the automation of unique identifiers at major structural levels—a chapter, sections, figures, tables, and so on. There are a number of ways to populate unique identifiers within a document without making the authors create a new identifier every time they start to write a structural component.

- Create a small application that creates a new identifier when the structural element is selected. Most XML authoring tools provide the capability to add custom macros.
- Develop a post-process tool that traverses the document and adds the unique identifiers. XSLT is a perfect tool for providing this functionality.

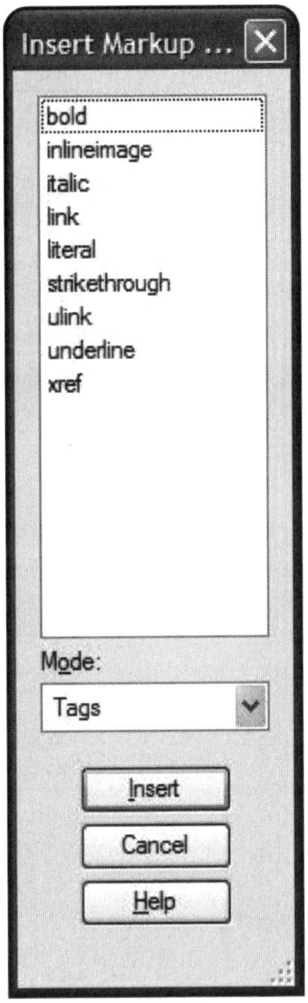

Figure 8.2
The same Insert Markup window from Arbortext's Epic Editor.

Some XML authoring tools, such BlastRadius XMetaL and Arbortext's Epic Editor, provide the capability to write small programs that can be processed during user interaction. Both XMetaL and Epic Editor support programs written in Visual Basic and JScript. Both use the DOM to support traversing the document tree. The following example shows how to create a unique identifier for section element within XMetaL. This is a Visual Basic script.

```
'Generate a random ID number
In digits between 1 To
9 Child = ActiveDocument.documentElement.nodeName Function GenID() Dim szRet
Randomize ' initialize VB's random number generator ' Get a random number szRet
= Right((Int(Rnd * 1000000000) & ""), Int(10 * Rnd)) If ((szRet = " ") Or
(Len(szRet) = 0) ) Then szRet = "0" End If GenID = szRet End Function
Selection.ElementAttribute("id", "section", 0) = "section" + GenID()
```

The following example shows a simple XSLT that creates a unique identifier for a document whose structure is Section/Subsection/Subsection1. This XSLT can be modified for use with many schemas and environments. This XSLT could be a post-process application that would add an identifier to a document.

```
<?xml version='1.0'?>
<xsl:stylesheet version="1.0" xmlns:xsl="http://www.w3.org/1999/XSL/Transform">

<xsl:template match="node() | @*">
<xsl:copy><xsl:apply-templates select="@* | node()" /></xsl:copy>
</xsl:template>

<xsl:template match="Section">
<Section>
<xsl:attribute name="id">ID-<xsl:number/></xsl:attribute>
<xsl:apply-templates/>
</Section>
</xsl:template>

<xsl:template match="Section/Subsection">
<Subsection>
<xsl:attribute name="id">ID-<xsl:number count="Section | Subsection"
level="multiple"/></xsl:attribute>
<xsl:apply-templates/>
</Subsection>
</xsl:template>

<xsl:template match="Section/Subsection/Subsection1">
<Subsection1>
<xsl:attribute name="id">ID-<xsl:number count="Section | Subsection |
Subsection1" level="multiple"/></xsl:attribute>
<xsl:apply-templates/>
</Subsection1>
</xsl:template>


</xsl:stylesheet>
```

Overuse of Attributes

Figure 8.3 shows the dialog box for inputting attributes in Arbortext Epic Editor. This example shows the attributes for a section for the MIL-PRF-38784C schema. MIL-PRF-38784C is the standard schema (DTD) for U.S. Air Force technical manuals.

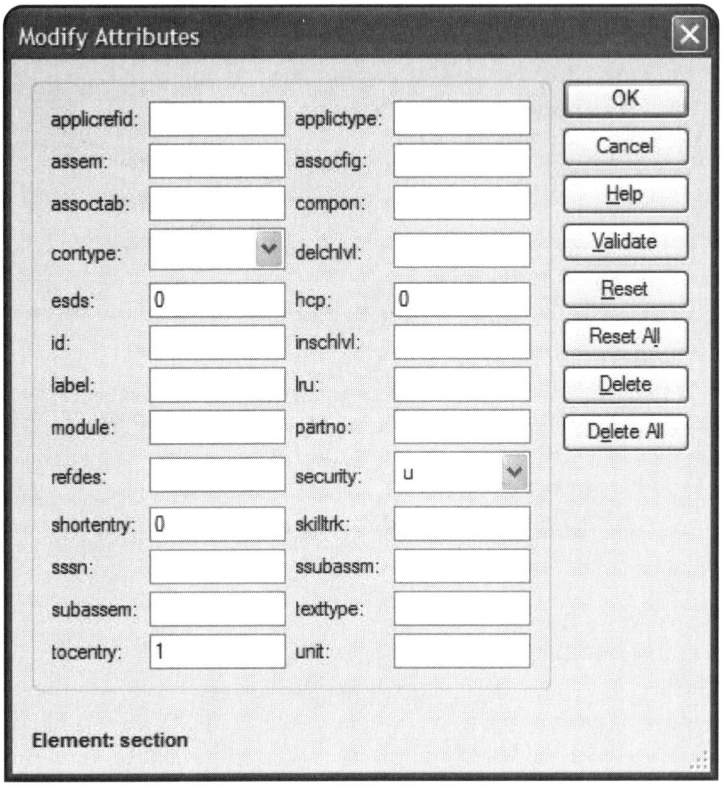

Figure 8.3
The dialog box for inputting attributes in Arbortext Epic Editor.

Approaches for Difficult Schema Structures

This section discusses some of the more difficult structures that can cause problems for XML authors. Common solutions are provided.

Tables

A *table* is a selection of information that is represented in columns and rows. There are essentially two table models that are commonly used in XML schemas.

- The *OASIS-Open Exchange table model* is the most comprehensive table model. The OASIS-Open Exchange model is a subset of the CALS (Continuous Acquisition and Lifecycle

Support) table model. The CALS table model was developed by the Defense Department in the 1980s for publication of tables.

- The *HTML table model* was developed for use with HTML. The structure of HTML table model is similar to the CALS table model in structure, but uses different elements. The CALS table model is more comprehensive than the HTML table model.

Both the HTML and OASIS-Open Exchange table models have been incorporated into most WYSYWYG authoring tools. These tools provide the XML authors the capability to create tables using visual columns and rows, similar to popular word processing software.

Table 8.1 shows how the OASIS-Open Exchange table model and HTML table model are tagged.

Table 8.1 Geneological Table

Name	Birth	Death	Father	Mother
Jasper Arnett Father	30 MAR 1838	7 FEB 1899	James Arnett	Rachel Meredeth
James Arnett Father	10 SEP 1797	22 FEB 1850	Andrew Arnett	Elizabeth Leggett
James Arnett Father	Approx. 1748	Approx. 1818	Thomas Arnett	UNKNOWN

```
<table frame="all">
    <title>Geneological Table</title>
    <tgroup cols="5" colsep="1" rowsep="1" align="center">
         <colspec colnum="1" colname="col1" colwidth="1.67*"
             align="left"/>
         <colspec colnum="2" colname="col2" colwidth="1.00*"
             align="left"/>
         <colspec colnum="3" colname="col3" colwidth="1.64*"
             align="left"/>
         <colspec colnum="4" colname="col4" colwidth="1.77*"
             align="left"/>
         <colspec colnum="5" colname="col5" colwidth="1.84*"
             align="left"/>
         <thead>
            <row valign="top">
               <entry colname="col1" align="left" rowsep="1" colsep="1"
                    valign="top">Name
```

```
        </entry>
        <entry colname="col2" align="left"
             valign="top">Birth
        </entry>
        <entry colname="col3" align="left"
             valign="top">Death
        </entry>
        <entry colname="col4" align="left"
             valign="top">Father
        </entry>
        <entry colname="col5" align="left"
             valign="top">Mother
        </entry>
    </row>
</thead>
<tbody>
    <row valign="top">
        <entry colname="col1" align="left"
             valign="top">Jasper Arnett Father:
        </entry>
        <entry colname="col2"
             align="left" valign="top">30 MAR 1838
        </entry>
        <entry colname="col3"
             align="left" valign="top">7 FEB 1899
        </entry>
        <entry colname="col4"
             align="left" valign="top">James Arnett
        </entry>
        <entry
             colname="col5" align="left" valign="top"
             >Rachel Meredeth
        </entry>
    </row>
    <row valign="top">
        <entry colname="col1" align="left"
             valign="top">James Arnett Father:
```

```
                </entry>
                <entry colname="col2"
                     align="left" valign="top">10 SEP 1797
                </entry>
                <entry
                     colname="col3" align="left" valign="top">22 FEB 1850
                </entry>
                <entry
                     colname="col4" align="left" valign="top">Andrew Arnett
                </entry>
                <entry colname="col5" align="left" valign="top">
                     Elizabeth Leggett
                </entry>
             </row>
             <row valign="top">
                <entry
                     colname="col1" align="left" valign="top"
                     >James Arnett Father:
                </entry>
                <entry colname="col2" align="left" valign="top"
                     >ABT. 1748
                </entry>
                <entry colname="col3" align="left" valign="top"
                     >ABT. 1818
                </entry>
                <entry colname="col4" align="left" valign="top"
                     >Thomas Arnett
                </entry>
                <entry colname="col5" align="left"
                     valign="top">UNKNOWN
                </entry>
             </row>
          </tbody>
     </tgroup>
</table>
```

Here is an example of an XHTML table.

```
<table border="1" width="100%">
<caption>Geneological Table</caption>
<col width="30%">
<col width="15%">
<col width="15%">
<col width="20%">
<col width="20%">
<tr valign="top">
<th valign="top" align="left"> Name </th>
<th valign="top" align="left">Birth </th>
<th valign="top" align="left"> Death </th>
<th valign="top" align="left"> Father </th>
<th valign="top" align="left"> Mother </th>
</tr>
<tr valign="top">
<td valign="top" align="left"> Jasper Arnett Father: </td>
<td valign="top" align="left"> 30 MAR 1838</td>
<td valign="top" align="left"> 7 FEB 1899 </td>
<td valign="top" align="left"> James Arnett</td>
<td valign="top" align="left"> Rachel Meredeth</td>
</tr>
<tr valign="top">
<td valign="top" align="left"> James Arnett Father: </td>
<td valign="top" align="left"> 10 SEP 1797 </td>
<td valign="top" align="left"> 22 FEB 1850</td>
<td valign="top" align="left"> Andrew Arnett</td>
<td valign="top" align="left"> Elizabeth Leggett</td>
</tr>
<tr valign="top">
<td valign="top" align="left"> James Arnett Father: </td>
<td valign="top" align="left"> ABT. 1748</td>
<td valign="top" align="left"> ABT. 1818 </td>
<td valign="top" align="left"> Thomas Arnett</td>
<td valign="top" align="left"> UNKNOWN</td>
</tr>
</table>
```

Content-Driven Tables

Information is visually formatted into tables to aid individuals into logically associating information in a concise and recognizable format. When developing schemas for use within an organization, it is beneficial to identify distinct pieces of information according to its content.

For example, let's consider a parts list, shown in Table 8.2.

Table 8.2 Content Table Example

Part Name	Part Name	Cost
My Part	A-1235	$1.00
Your Part	B-1235	$2.00

The table information in Table 8.2 can be tagged in XML using a common table model or a schema fragment could be developed that will distinctly tag each part of the table.

```
<PartsCatalog>
<Part>
<PartName>My Part</PartName>
<PartNumber>A-1235</PartNumber>
<Cost>$1.00</Cost>
</Part>
<Part>
<PartName>Your Part</PartName>
<PartNumber>B-1235</PartNumber>
<Cost>$2.00</Cost>
</Part>
</PartsCatalog>
```

Tables that are identified by their content and not by their format become more valuable and useful to an organization. Organizations should consider developing custom table formats for traditional tabular information. One can convert content tagged tables to the CALS table model, the HTML table model, or the XSL-FO table model for output into different presentations.

Appropriate stylesheets can be developed for authors who will be creating content tables natively in XML in an XML editor.

Common Standard Schemas

Table 8.3 lists some common standard schemas for your information.

Table 8.3 Examples Of Common Schemas

Schema Name	Schema Domain	Reference
DOCBOOK	Technical Documentation	
Text Encoding Initiative (TEI)	Scholorly Documents	http://www.tei-c.org/
National Library of Medicine (NLM) Journal Archiving and Interchange	Scientific Journals	http://dtd.nlm.nih.gov/publishing/

Form-Based Authoring

Form-based authoring might be the best approach for creating structured XML from structured input. Electronic commerce organizations that have data-centric content, as apposed to document-centric content, gain the most benefit from using a form-based XML authoring solution.

The advantages of this approach is the forms can be accessible over the Web. Forms are developed to ensure that the human interaction is a pleasant experience. There is a whole avocation devoted to human factors and success of the human experience in interaction with computers in general and specifically forms. Using forms as the authoring solution makes a lot of sense when the information being developed can lend itself to form-based authoring.

Forms are very hard to implement when developing document-centric information. Document-centric information are things like books, reports, manuals, and so on. These types of manuscripts rely on human creative ability to put thoughts, ideas, facts, and the like, on paper in an understandable way for consumption by other people. Although computers can process this information very easily for different purposes, in most cases the computer cannot process the ideas and concepts internally in the document, beyond the capability of indexing.

There are basically two options that support XML forms for authoring:

- HTML forms with custom programming
- XForms, an XML application defined by the W3C

HTML Custom Forms

Developing HTML instances from custom HTML forms is relatively easy. You have the option to choose your favorite programming language, such as Java, PHP, Perl, and so on. In this section, I attempt to show a very simple HTML form that takes input from the user and creates an XML document. Figure 8.4 shows a very simple input form created in HTML.

For this form, I have chosen to create the HTML using PHP for the programming language. Here is the HTML that was used to create the form in Figure 8.4:

```
<html>
<head>
  <title>Example Form</title>
</head>
  <body text='"#003366"'>
        <h1>Example Form</h1>
<hr>
<form action="create-form-xml.php" method="post">
      <table border="0" width="95%">
     <tr>
      <td>Name</td>
      <td>
            <input type="text" name="name" size="30"><br>
```

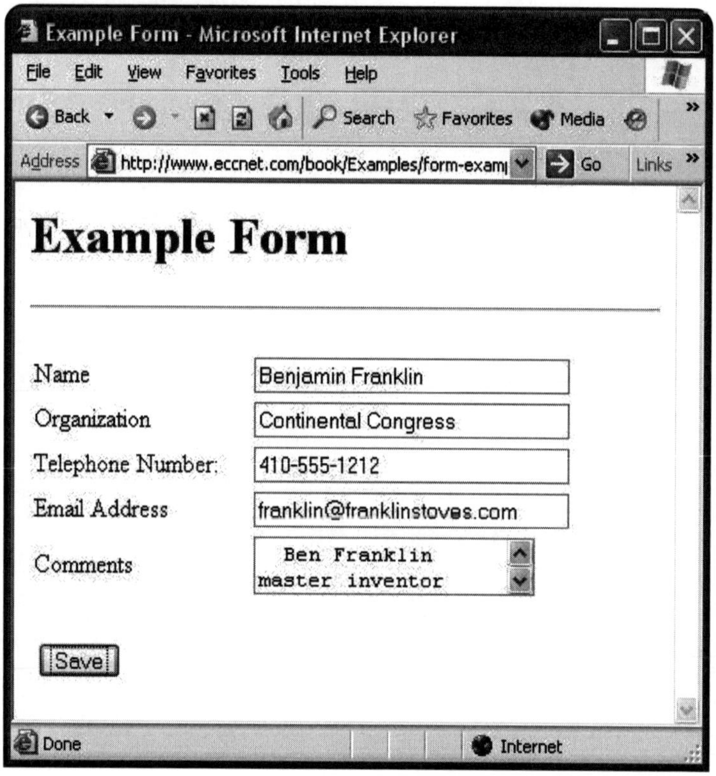

Figure 8.4
Simple HTML input form.

```
    </td>
    </tr>
    <tr>
    <td>Organization</td>
    <td>
        <input type="text" name="company" size="30" maxlength="100"><br>
    <td>
    </tr>
    <tr>
    <td>Telephone Number:</td>
    <td>
        <input type="text" name="telephone" size="30" maxlength="100"><br>
    </td>
    <tr>
    <td>Email Address</td>
    <td>
        <input type="text" name="email" size="30" maxlength="100"><br>
    </td>
    </tr>
    <tr>
      <td>Comments</td>
           <td>
           <textarea name="comments" size="30">  </textarea>
    </td>
    </tr>
    <tr>
    <td colspan="2"><input type="submit" value="Register"></td>
    </tr>
  </table>
</form>
</body>
</html>
```

For this example, I chose PHP as the mechanism to create the XML file. Obviously this is a very simple demonstration and complex forms can get tricky to create.

```
<html>
<head>
```

```
<title> Sample HTML Form to XML</title>
</head>
<body>

<?

// The next line opens a file handle to a file called xmlinstance.xml

$out = fopen("xmlinstance.xml", "a");

// if the file could not be opened for whatever reason, print
// an error message and exit the program

if (!$out) {
    print("Could not append to file");
    exit;
}

// fputs writes output to a file. the syntax is where to write
// followed by what to write

// $name is the contents of the name field in the sample form
// \t represents a tab character and \n represents a new line

fwrite($out, "<person>");
fwrite($out,"<name>$name</name>\n");
fwrite($out,"<organization>$company</organization>\n");
fwrite($out,"<telephone>$telephone</telephone>\n");
fwrite($out,"<email>$email</email>\n");
fwrite($out,"<comments>\n");
fwrite($out,"<p>$comments</p>\n");
fwrite($out,"</comments>\n");
fwrite($out,"</person>\n");
print("File successfully created");

fclose($out);
```

```
?>


</body>
</html>
```

Here's the resulting XML file:

```
<person>
     <name>Benjamin Franklin</name>
     <organization>Continental Congress</organization>
     <telephone>410-555-1212</telephone>
     <email>franklin@franklinstoves.com</email>
     <comments>
        <p> Ben Franklin master inventor</p>
     </comments>
</person>
```

Creating Forms with XForms

XForms is beginning to obtain a lot of momentum. As of the fall of 2006, the implementations of XForms is not available natively in browsers. Firefox has plug-in support for XForms. There are some server-side support for XForms, which is the way most organizations will deploy XForms, unless they have the ability to dictate user browsers.

Figure 8.5 shows the input form from an XForm for the same data being captured from the HTML form shown previously.

The XForm example does not show schema validation. One of the advantages of XForms is its capability to provide validation through XML schema. Here's the XForm source for the previous source:

```
<?xml version="1.0" encoding="ISO-8859-1"?>
<html xmlns="http://www.w3.org/1999/xhtml"
           xmlns:xforms="http://www.w3.org/2002/xforms"
           xmlns:ev="http://www.w3.org/2001/xml-events"
            xmlns:xsi="http://www.w3.org/2001/XMLSchema-instance"
           xmlns:xsd="http://www.w3.org/2001/XMLSchema">


  <head>
    <xforms:model id="form1">
```

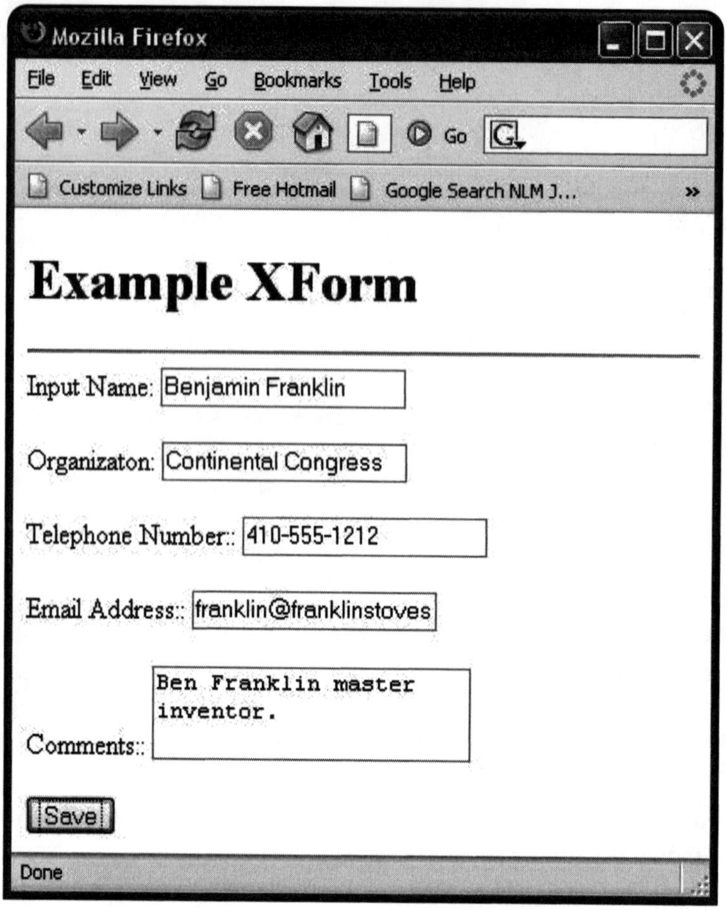

Figure 8.5
XForm input form.

```
<xforms:submission id="s01" method="put"
  action="person.xml" />
<xforms:instance id="instance1" xmlns="" >
  <person>
    <name></name>
    <organization></organization>
    <telephone></telephone>
    <email></email>
    <comment>
          <p></p>
        </comment>
```

```
        </person>
      </xforms:instance>
      <xforms:bind nodeset="/my/selectboolean" type="xsd:boolean"/>
    </xforms:model>
  </head>
<body>

<h1>Example XForm</h1>
<hr/>

<xforms:input ref="/person/name">
  <xforms:label>Input Name:  </xforms:label>
</xforms:input>
  <br/>
  <br/>
  <xforms:input ref="/person/organization">
    <xforms:label>Organization:  </xforms:label>
  </xforms:input>

  <br/>
  <br/>

  <xforms:input ref="/person/telephone">
    <xforms:label>Telephone Number::  </xforms:label>
  </xforms:input>

  <br/>
  <br/>

  <xforms:input ref="/person/email">
    <xforms:label>Email Address::  </xforms:label>
  </xforms:input>

  <br/>
  <br/>

  <xforms:textarea ref="/person/comment/p">
```

```
    <xforms:label>Comments::  </xforms:label>
  </xforms:textarea>

  <br/>
  <br/>

  <xforms:submit submission="s01">
    <xforms:label>Save</xforms:label>
  </xforms:submit>

</body>
</html>
```

The following code snippet shows the resulting XML file from the previous XForms. Notice the namespace declarations get transferred to the XML instance. The previous form creates a file called person.xml. Notice the XForms include namespace declarations in the output.

```
<?xml version="1.0" encoding="UTF-8"?>
<person xmlns:xforms="http://www.w3.org/2002/xforms"
              xmlns:ev="http://www.w3.org/2001/xml-events"
              xmlns:xsi="http://www.w3.org/2001/XMLSchema-instance"
              xmlns:xsd="http://www.w3.org/2001/XMLSchema">
          <name>Benjamin Franklin</name>
          <organization>Continental Congress</organization>
          <telephone>410-555-1212</telephone>
          <email>franklin@franklinstoves.com</email>
          <comment>
               <p>Ben Franklin master inventor.</p>
              </comment>
        </person>
```

Summary

This chapter provides the reader a basic understanding of different approaches to authoring XML information. Authoring XML is a human intellectual process. It is important for organizations that rely on intellectual content from authors and editors to understand the impact that creating XML data will have on the author. Organizations that rely on intellectual content from authors and editors will find this chapter useful in making decisions about XML authoring.

9 XSL-FO

by G. Ken Holman

Presentation-oriented markup vocabularies are designed to reflect the semantics of the medium or methodology for laying information out for the reader to access. The Web has long established the browser window as an electronic canvas onto which we lay out our information using HTML and CSS. Presentation conventions for navigation tools provided to the user allow us to identify hot spots on the page with which we interact in order to trigger behaviors in the browser.

Through the use of these HTML hyperlinks, we navigate a large corpus of information presented in a set of Web files. When we do this, we don't need to know where traversing links will take us. It is the responsibility of the browser software to do the traversing for us.

For centuries, we have been navigating corpora of information using books, in which information has been paginated into collections of *folios (pages)*. As there is no automation, it is the reader who has the responsibility to navigate the information in these many pages. The publisher, in turn, has the responsibility to equip the readers with the tools necessary to find their way around the publication.

The basic navigation tool in a book is, of course, the page number. Tables of content, indexes, and explicit citations to particular places in the book all use the page number as the mechanism to identify where in the information to find what you are looking for. This allows random access into the book by easily jumping through the (hopefully) sequential page numbers.

Other tools for finding the way around the book include headers and footers. Opening a bound book will, in our Western European writing convention of left to right, put the recto page on the right and the verso page on the left. A common convention is to place chapter titles and chapter numbers on, say, the bottom-right footer. To balance the appearance of text on the page, the lower-left footer might have the book title. This provides a coarse way of locating what you are looking for by bringing you to the chapter in which the information is found.

A finer-grained navigation mechanism might provide at the top left and top right of the open book running section numbers indicating the first of the subsections found on that particular page side. When there are no sections starting on the page, it would indicate the section that carries over from the previous page. Thus the readers can use these to find they particular subsection of the book they are seeking.

So what happens when we have a lot of information to convey electronically over the Web to a browser user? Operator interaction takes one back and forth through the information. Of course a lengthy Web page can be printed for off-line use, and indeed many people are still paper oriented and assimilate a lot of information best when it is on paper. However, these users are not well served by a large collection of numbered pages where blue and purple text indicate links to information: without the automated navigation, the readers are lost as to where they are supposed to take their attention.

What is needed, therefore, is an alternative to HTML/CSS that can be offered to browser users when they need a lot of information in printed form. Web sites can then offer a professionally formatted, composed paginated output and have the layout of the information possibly very differently organized than on the browser screen. With tables of content, headers and footers, page numbers and citations, a paginated reformatting of the information can be distributed, perhaps in a ubiquitous format such as PDF.

> **Note**
>
> This chapter assumes a basic understanding of these principles and the use of XSL-FO. Various advanced concepts and rendering issues are cited and overviewed in this chapter to help existing users of XSL-FO understand nuanced behaviors of semantic interpretation. Details are not explored for the basics of semantic interpretation that are assumed to be known to all XSL-FO stylesheet users.

This is the role that the Extensible Stylesheet Language (XSL) was developed to play: to paginate information using a vocabulary geared to the semantics of laying out information in a collection of pages using suitable navigation tools for the reader of the formatted result. The XSL Transformations (XSLT) language was originally wholly contained within the XSL specification, before being extracted and made a standalone specification. XSL still normatively refers to XSLT in a brief chapter that indicates the use of XSLT as a suitable method of constructing a tree of formatting objects. The remainder of the XSL specification describes the vocabulary of formatting objects, a collection of element and attribute labels, and a processing model and semantic interpretation of the use of those objects so labeled.

To distinguish the vocabulary directing tree construction (XSLT) from the vocabulary of formatting objects, the community of users has adopted the abbreviation XSL-FO as that part of XSL not describing XSLT. This abbreviation, however, is not used anywhere in the XSL specification itself.

XML Transformation and Rendering Using HTML

Note there is no architectural difference in working with XML to create HTML than to create a paginated result. Note in Figure 9.1 how there are three distinct steps to produce the result on the screen: the construction of an HTML result tree from the XML (transformation) creating (in this example) a standalone HTML file, the interpretation of the semantics of HTML presentation (formatting), and the visualization of the result to the screen (rendering). In fact it is not necessary to create the standalone HTML file if the entire process is built into a browser such that the semantics interpretation acts on the in-memory result tree created by transformation.

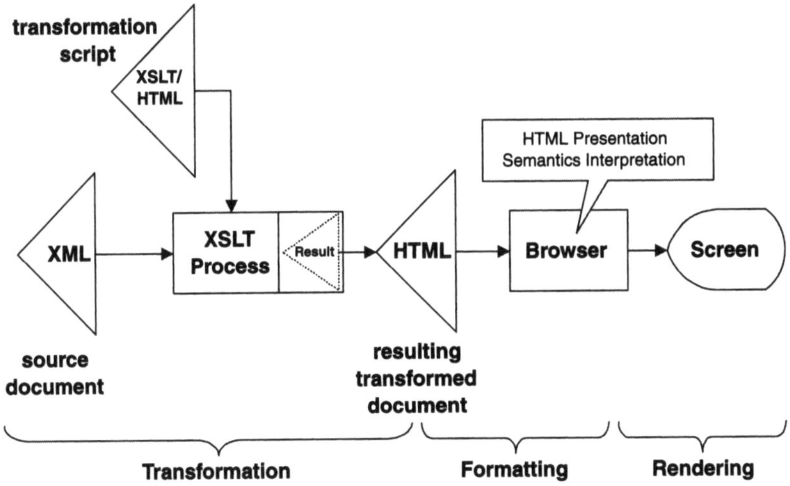

Figure 9.1
Three identifiable phases of publishing XML information to a Web screen.

XML Transformation and Pagination Using XSL-FO

The same steps are shown in Figure 9.2. The transformation constructs an XSL-FO result tree from the XML, creating a standalone XSL-FO file (when not all processes are not integral to a single application), the formatting of the presentation according to the semantics of XSL-FO, and the rendering of the formatted result to the output medium.

There are three defined media for interpreting and rendering XSL-FO: a sound-based *aural* presentation, an *electronic presentation* for interaction with an operator, and by far the most widely implemented interpretation of XSL-FO to a *static printed form*.

Note that the actual rendering is outside the scope of the XSL-FO recommendation in that vendors can choose to implement any method of rendering they wish. A very common rendering choice is to use a two-step method of creating PDF files, thus requiring users to use a PDF reader to actually print the result. Nevertheless, as noted, this intermediate PDF form is useful in and of itself for distribution.

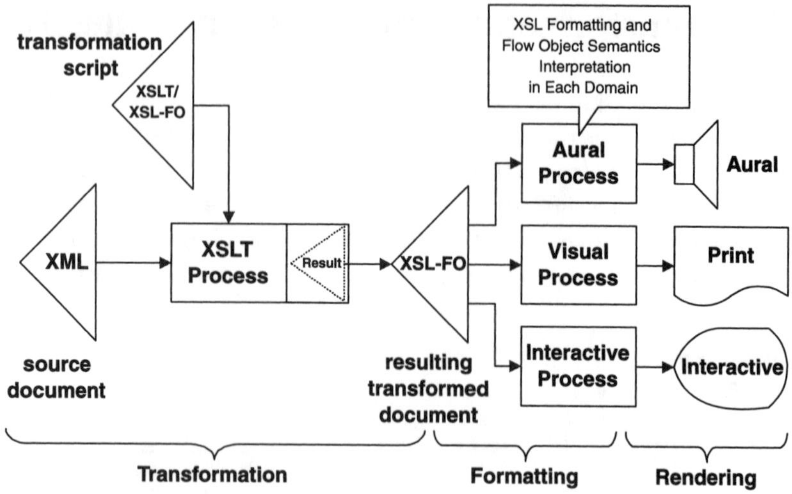

Figure 9.2
Three identifiable phases of publishing XML information to a paginated result.

The XSL-FO Processing Model

Figure 9.3 depicts the various steps encompassed by the XSL-FO recommendation. In fact, implementations are not obliged to implement their XSL-FO engines using these steps, rather, they must produce the end result *as if* they had implemented using these steps.

XSL-FO instances can be created by any means. Although XSLT is a normative way that instances may be created, in fact they can be hand-authored (making an excellent sandbox for learning the language) or created by a program (thus using XSL-FO directly as a pagination layout language).

The instance tree is created from the external file, but may have been the directly generated abstract result tree created as part of XSLT. XSLT engines offer applications to opportunity to act on the result tree created by supplying the constructs as dynamic events, such as SAX calls.

A tree of formatting objects is created by interpreting the instance tree. Element nodes become formatting objects of the corresponding name. Attribute nodes become properties of the corresponding name. Text nodes become character objects.

The process of refinement examines each of the properties on the objects and distills only those traits from properties that apply to each object. Many traits are inherited from property specifications found "higher" in the object tree. The end result is a refined *formatting object tree* with each object having all the traits and only the traits that apply to that object.

Semantic interpretation happens on the refined formatting object tree based on the objects and their traits. The XSL-FO specification goes into gory detail regarding what areas with what traits are created in the formatted result: a very large collection of areas in the area tree.

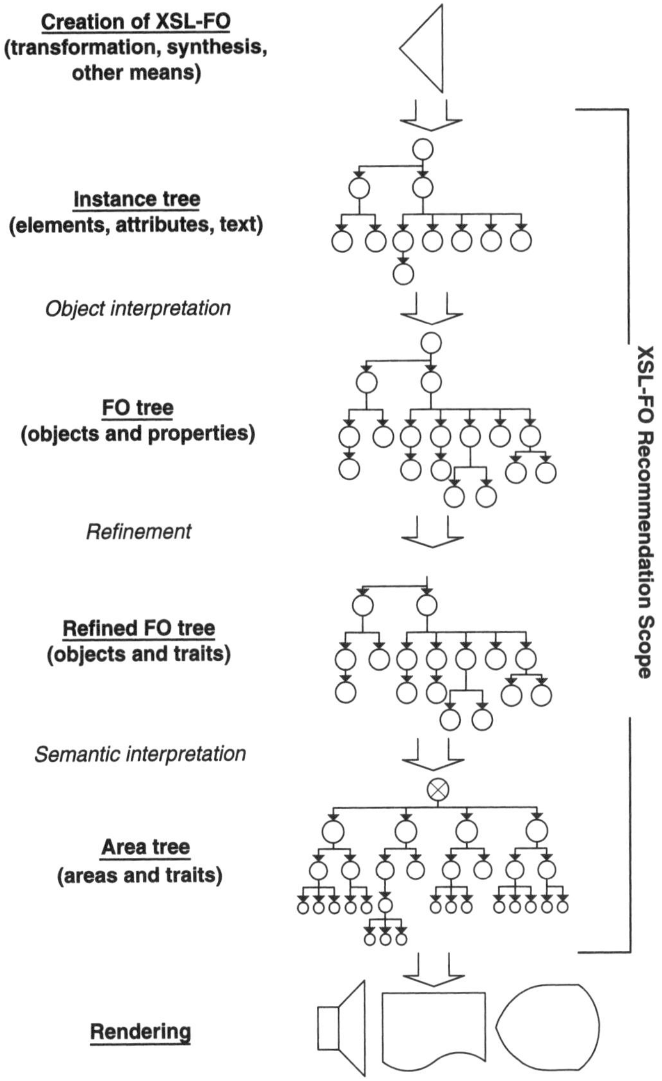

Figure 9.3
The processing model described by the XSL-FO recommendation describes a number of abstract constructs and steps in paginating information.

This area tree represents the formatted paginated interpretation of the XSL-FO instance and is the basis of the rendering of the final result. The root of the area tree has page nodes as its children, each node representing a formatted page in the result. Each area found anywhere under each page node has a location and dimension and set of traits that the rendering software uses to affect the formatted result to the target medium.

What this means to the stylesheet writers is they have to work backward along this processing model flow in order to plan their solution to their formatting problem as follows.

The end users should give a formatting specification to the stylesheet writers expressing their desired result of how they wish to *visualize the XML* that will be given to the process. This tells the stylesheet writers what areas are needed on each page, the traits that they need, their dimensions, and their locations.

Armed with this information, the stylesheet writers use their knowledge of XSL-FO semantic interpretation to divine the collection of objects and traits that are needed to produce the desired areas on the pages.

The stylesheet writers must then strategize the appropriate uses and placements of *properties* in the *formatting object tree,* such that refinement results in the desired use of objects and traits for semantic interpretation. This often requires determining the opportune locations for the specification of inherited properties, as well as the necessary locations for the specification of non-inherited properties.

At this point, this information informs the stylesheet writers of the structure and content of the instance tree, thus what the end result of the transformation should be. Thus equipped, the stylesheet writers can correspond the input XML to, say, the XSLT construction processes they need to write for generating the XSL-FO instance tree from the source content.

Bordering and Area Tree Rectangles

Stylesheet writers who know CSS sometimes get confused with the way bordering works in XSL-FO. For much of the specification, the behavior is the same, but there are nuances that require additional properties to get identical results.

Recall that during semantic interpretation of the XSL-FO objects in the *refined tree,* there are very many area-tree areas created, each one being a rectangle nested inside some other rectangle. This area tree can become very large and very detailed (and to new stylesheet writers, very scary!), although it really isn't considered complex. Each area has a defined relationship to the parent area in the tree.

Un-Bordered and Bordered Areas

Most areas are not bordered, as in there are no visual boxes drawn around the content of words or paragraphs. In this case, three of the rectangles are coincident, as shown in Figure 9.4: the padding, border, and content rectangles.

When a border is drawn, these three rectangles separate in order to define the outside and inside boundaries of the opaque border, as well as the outside boundary of the contained area content, as shown in Figure 9.5. Note there is no obligation to separate the padding and content rectangles if you want the area's content to be immediately within the border's inside. There is also no obligation that the four gaps between the edges of these rectangles be the same, thus allowing you to have more room on one or any number of the sides.

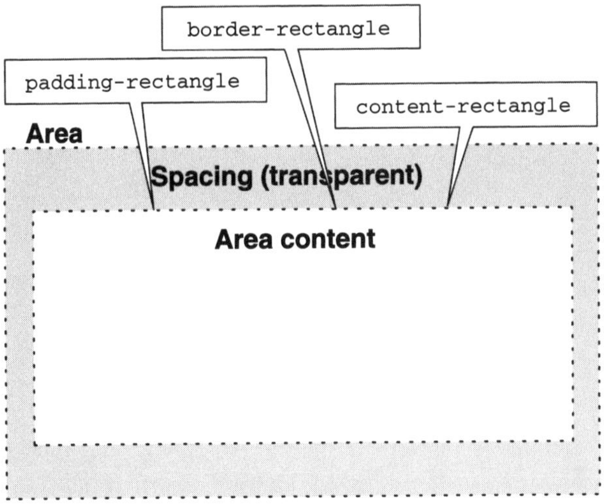

Figure 9.4
When there is no border specified, three area rectangles are co-incident.

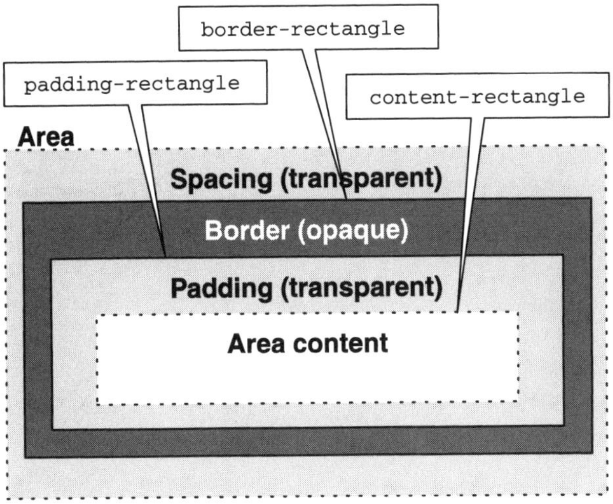

Figure 9.5
When a border is specified with padding and spacing, the rectangles are separated.

The various rectangles are specified using individual traits that, although they have their own properties, are also encapsulated in shorthand properties that make it convenient for setting all or some of the individual properties using a single property specification. For a block-level area in the area tree, see Figure 9.6 for an illustration of all of the individual properties that are in play.

Some shorthand properties specify other shorthand properties. For example, consider the following simple shorthand expression for **border**:

```
border="2pt solid green"
```

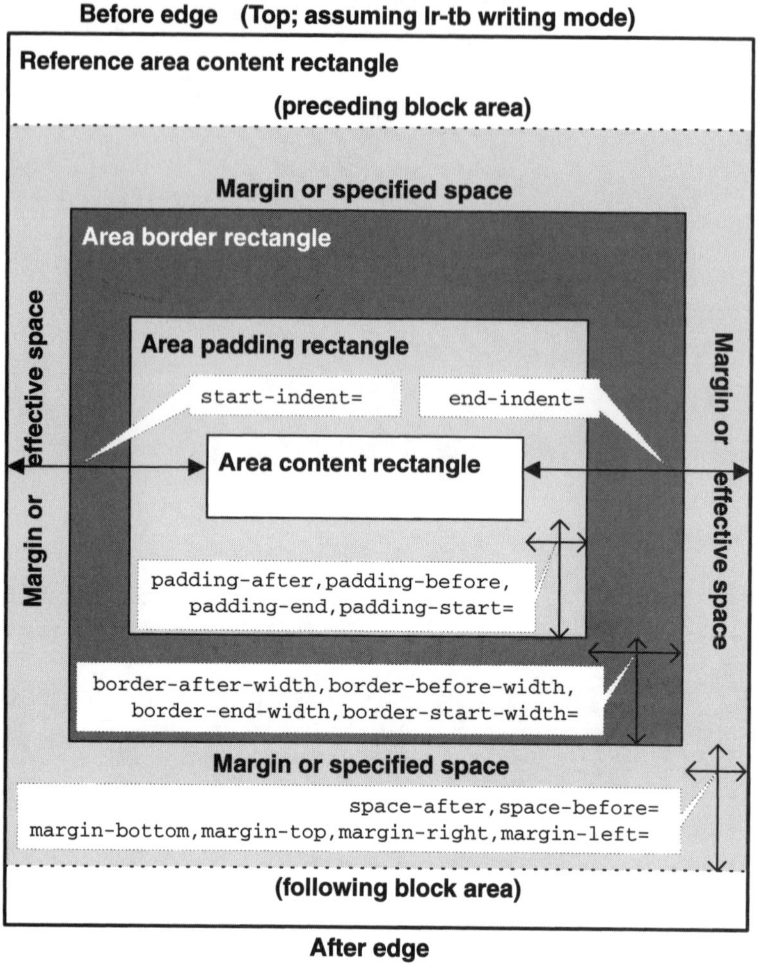

Figure 9.6
There are many properties available to be specified for a nuanced formatted result.

That is the equivalent of specifying three shorthand properties:

```
border-width="2pt"
border-style="solid"
border-color="green"
```

These are shorthand properties. Note that for all multi-valued shorthand properties for the same concept, the last specification value is repeated for all of the missing specifications. In the previous example, each single specification is repeated for all four values for which the shorthand represents.

You can specify individual values for up to four sides:

```
border-width="1pt 4pt 8pt 12pt"
border-style="solid dashed dotted double"
border-color="green blue red yellow"
```

Which can alternatively be specified using the writing-direction-dependent properties:

```
border-before-width="1pt"
border-end-width="4pt"
border-after-width="8pt"
border-start-width="12pt"
border-before-style="solid"
border-end-style="dashed"
border-after-style="dotted"
border-start-style="double"
border-before-color="green"
border-end-color="blue"
border-after-color="red"
border-start-color="yellow"
```

Although they are not portable across different writing directions, the following expressions are equivalent to using the writing-direction-dependent properties as in Western European left-to-right top-to-bottom:

```
border-top-width="1pt"
border-right-width="4pt"
border-bottom-width="8pt"
border-left-width="12pt"
border-top-style="solid"
border-right-style="dashed"
border-bottom-style="dotted"
border-left-style="double"
border-top-color="green"
border-right-color="blue"
border-bottom-color="red"
border-left-color="yellow"
```

The padding can be specified with a shorthand too, as in:

```
padding="5pt 20pt 40pt 80pt"
```

Which can alternatively be specified using the writing-direction-dependent properties:

```
padding-before="5pt"
padding-end="20pt"
padding-after="40pt"
padding-start="80pt"
```

Which, although again not portable across different writing directions, is equivalent to:

```
padding-top="5pt"
padding-right="20pt"
padding-bottom="40pt"
padding-left="80pt"
```

Margins can only be specified independent of the writing direction as in:

```
margin="5pt 20pt 40pt 80pt"
```

Which is the equivalent of:

```
margin-top="5pt"
margin-right="20pt"
margin-bottom="40pt"
margin-left="80pt"
```

Spacing is different than margins in a few of ways. Spacing can only be specified using writing-direction-dependent properties, but at all times only two of the four available specifications are respected. Indentation can also affect the effective spacing.

Examples of explicit and effective space specifications that can be used at a block level are:

```
space-before="10pt"
space-after="20pt"
start-indent="5pt"
end-indent="15pt"
```

Examples of explicit specifications that can be used at an inline level are:

```
space-start="5pt"
space-end="15pt"
```

Area Placement for Block-Level Constructs

The relation of these rectangles to parent block and line areas needs to be carefully considered before deciding which of the properties to use to create the required result. The key to remember for block-level constructs is that the placement of areas changes based on the specification of the start and end margins.

Block-Level Construct's Areas with Margins Specified

Consider Figure 9.7, where start and end margin properties are explicitly specified by the user for a block-level construct. Because of the stacking rules, the preceding block-level area is (in the Western European left-to-right top-to-bottom writing mode) above the area generated by the construct, and the following block-level area is below. Note how the margin pushes in the border rectangle defining the outside of the border. The border width (defining the padding rectangle) and the padding width further push in the definition of the content rectangle for the construct's normally flowed descendants.

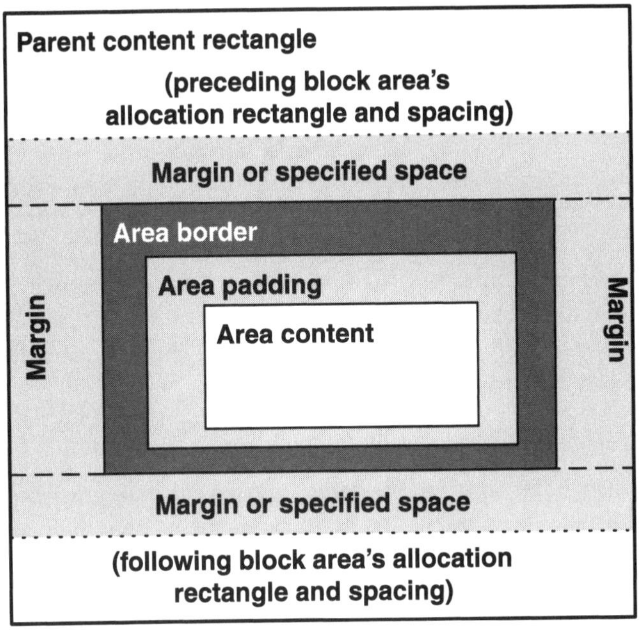

Figure 9.7
A block with margins specified is spaced from the start and end sides by the margin values.

This effect is the case even when the margin value specified is 0pt, because the determining factor is the fact that the margin has, indeed, been explicitly specified.

Block-Level Construct's Areas Without Margins Specified

The result is different when margins have not been specified, as shown in Figure 9.8. Note how there is effective space created by the **start-indent** and **end-indent** properties. This effective space is the difference after subtracting the area padding and border width from the indent's value.

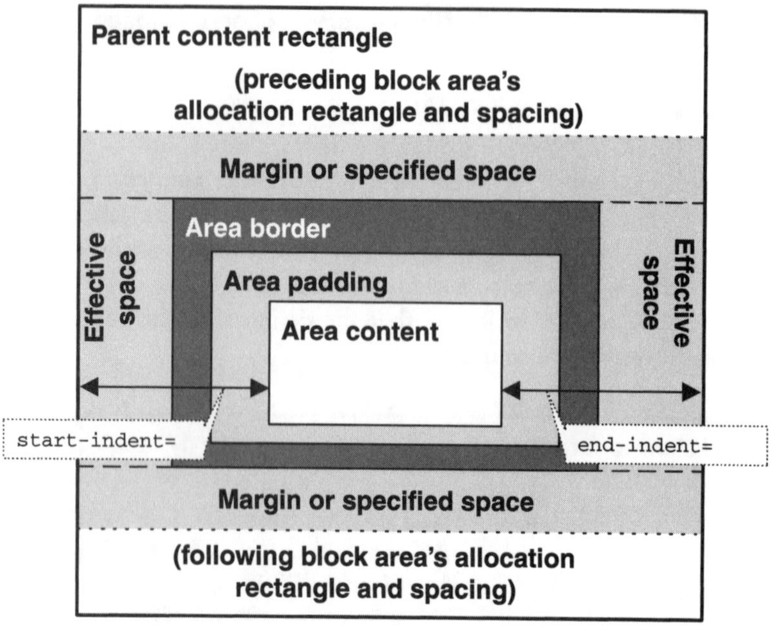

Figure 9.8
A block without margins specified is spaced from the start and end sides by an effective value considering the widths of border and padding from the indents.

Border Positions with Small Values for start-indent

But what if the indent's value is *less* than the sum of the area padding and the border width, perhaps even an inherited or explicitly specified value of 0pt? Figure 9.9 shows how, unlike CSS, the visible border is pushed out, extending beyond the parent's area.

Illustration of Use of Margin Specification

You might imagine why this behavior seems so unintuitive, yet it makes sense in paginated publishing where, unlike Web publishing, the flowed text takes precedence over the borders. Figure 9.10 shows six lines of text formatted with various properties.

Note in line (1) there are no border or margin specifications and it is a simple line of text. Drawing a border around (2), without using **margin-left**, causes the left parentheses to line up and the border to extend outside of the area containing the text. In this way, the border does not interfere with the flow of text, a common occurrence in print publishing.

To get the Web effect mimicking CSS, using a **margin-left** of 0pt in line (3) without a border does not affect the position of the text relative to the lines before. However when a border is specified in line (4), the **margin-left** of 0pt aligns the left edge of the border with the left parentheses of lines 1 through 3.

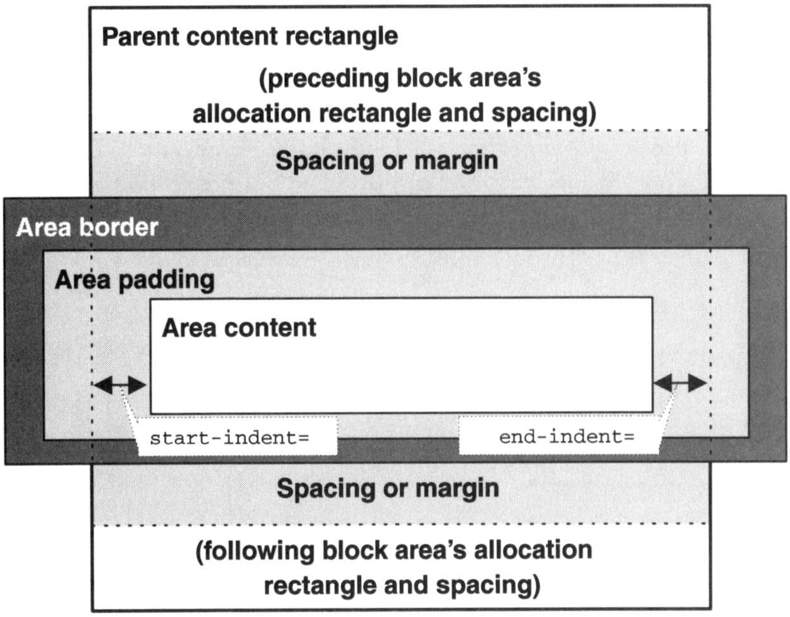

Figure 9.9
Using a start indent less than the widths of border and padding will set the edge of the border outside of the parent content rectangle.

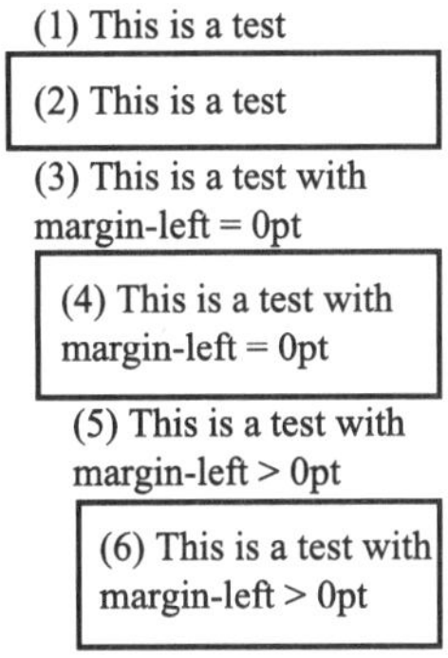

Figure 9.10
Contrasting the effect of the absence and presence of margins on the starting position of text in a block.

Specifying a non-zero margin in line (5) pushes the text away from the left parentheses of lines 1 through 3, and line (6) shows how the border is aligned with this new margin point shown as the left edge of the left parenthesis of line (5).

Area Placement for Inline-Level Constructs

The key to remember for inline-level constructs is that the placement of the areas relative to the parent line area changes based on the nature of the inline construct having either a *normal allocation rectangle* or a *large allocation rectangle*. In both inline cases, any space or margin specifications above and below are ignored, whereas whitespace and margin specifications at the start or end of the area (left or right in the Western European writing mode) are in play.

Border for Inline with Normal Allocation Rectangle
Simple text has a *normal allocation rectangle* and Figure 9.11 shows how the area's content rectangle has the same height as the parent line area, and any padding or border width is drawn outside. The allocation rectangle does not change the maximum height of the constructs on the line, thus drawing the border can possibly impact the lines stacked above and below the parent line.

Figure 9.11
The padding and border around an inline area with a normal allocation rectangle goes beyond the parent line area boundaries.

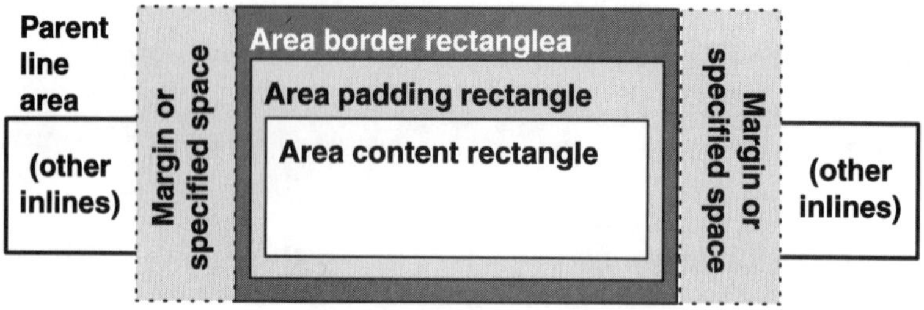

Border for Inline with Large Allocation Rectangle
Image and inline container areas have a large allocation rectangle and Figure 9.12 shows how the area's border rectangle defines the maximum height of the parent line area, thus guaranteeing there is no impact on the lines stacked above and below the parent line.

Figure 9.12
The padding and border around an inline area with a large allocation rectangle is within the parent line area boundaries.

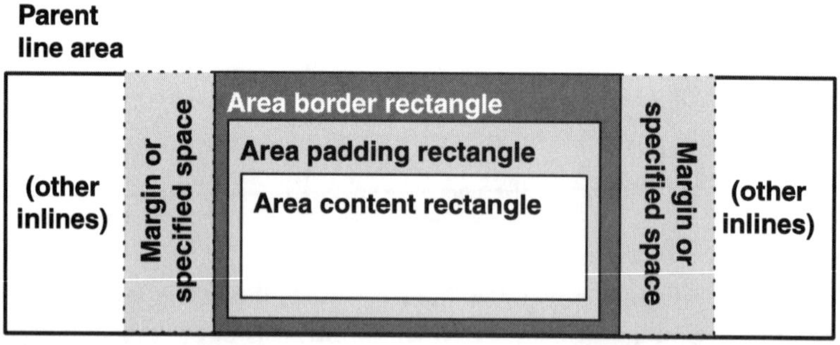

Illustration of Inline Bordered Areas
Figure 9.13 illustrates in five paragraphs the effect of specifications on lines with areas having normal and large allocation rectangles. The second line of each paragraph has the word "test" around which the tests are being affected, by placing the word in an <inline> area, thus having a normal allocation rectangle around the word. Paragraph (1) has no properties specified on the word's area.

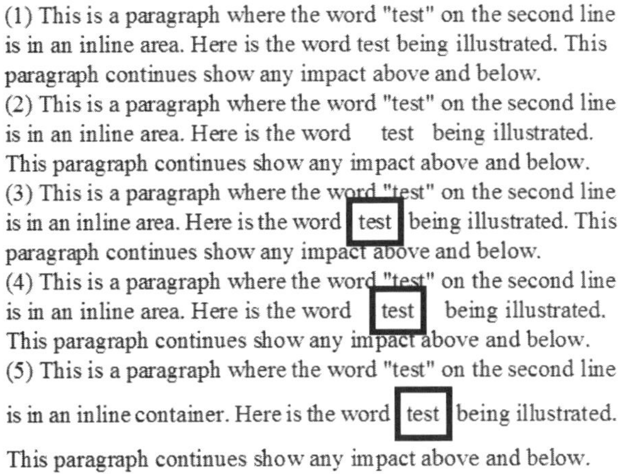
(1) This is a paragraph where the word "test" on the second line is in an inline area. Here is the word test being illustrated. This paragraph continues show any impact above and below.
(2) This is a paragraph where the word "test" on the second line is in an inline area. Here is the word test being illustrated. This paragraph continues show any impact above and below.
(3) This is a paragraph where the word "test" on the second line is in an inline area. Here is the word test being illustrated. This paragraph continues show any impact above and below.
(4) This is a paragraph where the word "test" on the second line is in an inline area. Here is the word test being illustrated. This paragraph continues show any impact above and below.
(5) This is a paragraph where the word "test" on the second line is in an inline container. Here is the word test being illustrated. This paragraph continues show any impact above and below.

Figure 9.13
Contrasting the effect of the absence and presence of properties on bordered inline areas.

Paragraph (2) has both **start-indent** and **end-indent** specified, and the gaps can be seen between the adjacent words.

Paragraph (3) introduces the use of a border, and the padding and border width are such that the line areas above and below the word's parent line area are overwritten. This paragraph has no start or end spacing specified, whereas paragraph (4) does and the gaps can be seen.

In paragraph (5), the word is in an **<inline-container>** that has a large allocation rectangle. In this case, the maximum height of the line is the height of the container and its border, thus the stacking of the lines prevents the border from overwriting the line areas above and below the word's parent line area.

Area Backgrounds

Lastly, where do background colors go when borders and padding are specified? Figure 9.14 attempts to show the shadow of the different rectangles of a given area and labels the shadows with an indication of the source of the filler. Lines joining the box corners with the shadows align the rectangles accordingly. Note how the area's parent's background fills in the space and margins and any gaps that might be in the border (such as a dotted or dashed border).

The padding rectangle defining the inside of the border is the rectangle that contains the given area's background. The area's content might have backgrounds of its own, but where the content's parent background shows through, that would be the given area's background. Figure 9.15 shows this effect.

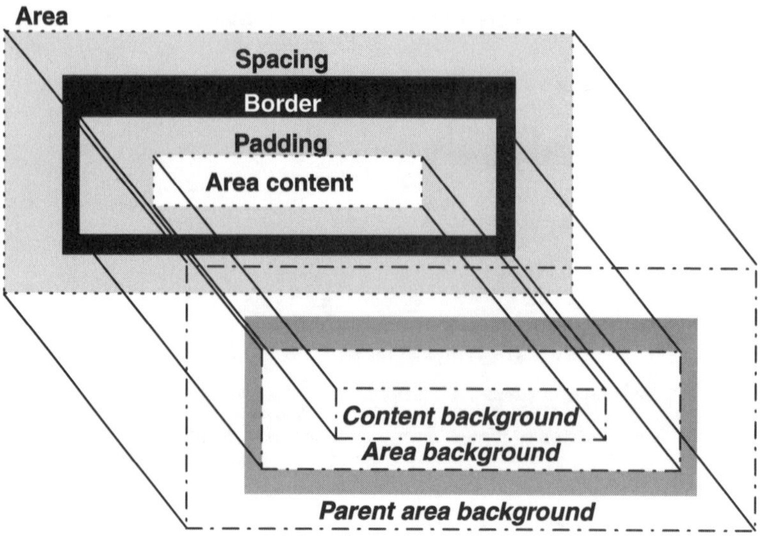

Figure 9.14
An illustration of the position of the border relative to the backgrounds of areas and their parent areas.

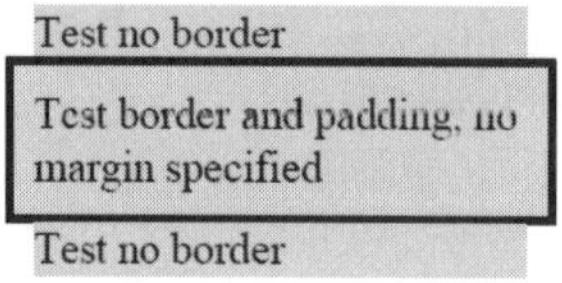

Figure 9.15
The border of an area extends beyond the parent area to the inside of the area's border.

Bidirectional Text Protection

When designing XML vocabularies for the markup of international text, no special considerations are necessary in designing markup vocabularies to accommodate the presence of or mixture of either left-to-right text (such as Western European-based languages) with right-to-left text (such as Hebrew or Arabic). It all works because XML is based on Unicode. Consider that HTML and XML vocabularies such as Open Document Format allow strings of Unicode characters in their paragraph constructs without the need for markup to wrap characters to indicate the direction of the characters.

Nevertheless, there are still important techniques that the stylesheet writers should consider when anticipating the formatting of a mixture of left-to-right and right-to-left text.

Unicode Directionality

The Unicode standard includes the Unicode Character Database that itemizes for each and every character a number of properties, one of which is the direction property. There are three strengths of direction for Unicode characters, thus each character is considered either a strong, weak, or neutral character.

Because the characters already have direction built in, there is no need to overload an XML vocabulary with direction information about the text. XML-aware processors are already obliged to respect Unicode direction information inherent in the characters (whether they do or not is a separate question).

Strong characters are from language groups with well-defined left-to-right or right-to-left character progression directions. Hebrew and Arabic characters are strong right-to-left characters.

Weak characters are digits, currency symbols, and some punctuation characters, including mirroring characters whose presentation on the canvas may be different than their representation in the data. For examples, (,), [,], <, >, { , }, «, », and so on. The mirroring characters that look like "left" brackets are considered to be "open" brackets, and the those that look like "right" brackets are considered to be "closed" brackets. In the presence of left-to-right characters, these parentheses appear as you would expect, but in the presence of right-to-left characters, the character code for the left parenthesis is presented visually as a right parenthesis, so that it opens the right-to-left flow.

Neutral characters include whitespace characters and some separator characters.

The rendering of a sequence of Unicode characters is governed by the Unicode Bidirectional Algorithm. The impact that strong characters have on weak characters can result in undesirable results, so Unicode includes a number of invisible control characters, called *marks*, that XML writers can include in their text to overcome the problems. The basic marks used to indicate a strong invisible character of the given direction are:

- **‎** for the left-to-right mark (LRM)
- **‏** for the right-to-left mark (RTM)

The concept of embedding will "push" the running direction of flow (whatever it might be), indicate a given direction, whereas a "pop" will restore the running direction of flow before the embedding. A simple embed infers a new direction but does not change the interpretation of the characters' implicit direction, whereas an overriding embed forces the characters embedded to be a specific direction regardless of their implicit directions. The marks used for this are:

- **‪** for left-to-right embed begin (LRE)
- **‫** for right-to-left embed begin (RLE)
- **‭** left-to-right override begin (LRO)
- **‮** right-to-left override begin (RLO)
- **‬** for pop directional formatting (PDF)

With all these controls, the author of a Unicode document can ensure that the text wrapped in markup is self-consistent and will appear correctly in isolation when the stream of characters is displayed. But the burden is on the author of the stream of characters to ensure the direction characters are in place to affect display.

Formatting Without Consideration for Direction

Often, however, such Unicode direction controls are not needed, such as the following example XML file that has titles in four languages. Because the individual titles are authored in isolation, there is no consideration or need for direction characters. In the following, the Hebrew characters in the title are translated to English as "Hebrew test", the Arabic characters in the title are translated to English as "Arabic test", and no direction characters are present as this is the information in the raw, rather than the information being displayed:

```
<doc>
  <section>
    <title>English Test</title>
    <subsection>Sub 1 in English</subsection>
    ...
    <subsection>Sub 15 in English</subsection>
  </section>
  <section>
    <title>&#x05D1;&#x05D3;&#x05D9;&#x05E7;&#x05D4;
           &#x05E2;&#x05D1;&#x05E8;&#x05D9;&#x05EA;</title>
    <subsection>Sub 1 in Hebrew</subsection>
    ...
    <subsection>Sub 14 in Hebrew</subsection>
  </section>
  <section>
    <title>&#x0625;&#x062e;&#x062a;&#x0628;&#x0627;&#x0631;
           &#x0639;&#x0631;&#x0628;&#x064a;</title>
    <subsection>Sub 1 in Arabic</subsection>
    ...
    <subsection>Sub 14 in Arabic</subsection>
  </section>
  <section>
    <title>Test Fran&#xe7;ais</title>
    <subsection>Sub 1 in French</subsection>
    ...
    <subsection>Sub 12 in French</subsection>
  </section>
</doc>
```

A simple presentation of the text value of the title is as follows:

```
<page-sequence master-reference="frame">
  <flow flow-name="frame-body">
    <block id="{generate-id(.)}">
      <xsl:value-of select="title"/>
    </block>
    <xsl:for-each select="subsection">
      <block space-before="1em">
        <xsl:value-of select="."/>
      </block>
    </xsl:for-each>
  </flow>
</page-sequence>
```

The resulting titles look very straightforward, as shown in Figure 9.16.

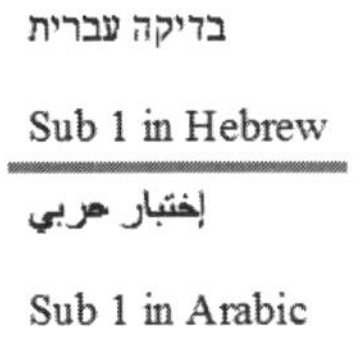

Figure 9.16
The section titles in isolation (that is, without surrounding text on the line) present right to left without influence on the before and after lines.

The author of an XSL-FO stylesheet must consider, however, what might be happening when mixing authored information from different XML files, from different places of a single XML file, or from the stylesheet and the XML file. The resulting combination of Unicode characters becomes a single stream for display and there is then an interaction between neighboring characters.

XSL-FO has awareness of Unicode directionality. Section 5.8 of the XSL-FO 1.0 Recommendation, titled "Unicode BIDI Algorithm", documents a slightly modified CSS definition. Whereas CSS assumes an unspecified initial direction, XSL-FO assumes the direction to be that of the writing-mode currently in effect. But when the stylesheet mixes text, it is the sequence in the resulting stream of characters, however obtained, that's interpreted by the Unicode bi-directionality rules.

Consider a naïve implementation of a stylesheet formatting a table of contents entry that mixes the authored XML title text with stylesheet text without thinking about the possible interactions.

The following fragment is a simple assembly of the section titles with a parenthesized count of the subsections that are included in the section:

```
<block space-after=".5cm">
  Mixing direction without using embed:
</block>
<xsl:for-each select="/doc/section">
  <block text-align-last="justify">
    <xsl:value-of select="position()"/>.
    <xsl:value-of select="title"/>
    (<xsl:value-of select="count(subsection)"/>)
    <leader leader-pattern="dots"/>
    <page-number-citation ref-id="{generate-id(.)}"/>
  </block>
</xsl:for-each>
```

The resulting display appears as in Figure 9.17. Note that the space, left parenthesis of the subsection count and the subsection count itself are all immediately following the title in the resulting character stream. For the English and French entries, there is no problem because there is no interaction with right-to-left characters. However, the strong right-to-left characters of the Hebrew title and the Arabic title have influenced the mirroring left parenthesis character as an "open" parenthesis, thus rendered as a right parenthesis on the canvas, and placed the left-to-right digits of the subsection count to the left of the title. According to the Unicode algorithm, the right parenthesis after the count stays a right parenthesis to the right of the other information due to the following content being at the current embedding level.

Figure 9.17
When mixing text of different directions without using embed, strong characters influence the weak characters.

Mixing direction without using embed:

1. English Test (15) 2
2. 14) בדיקה עברית) 3
3. 14) إختبار عربي) 4
4. Test Français (12) 5

Formatting with Consideration for Direction

XSL-FO provides abstract control to the embedding algorithm of Unicode through the **<bidi-override>** formatting object. Two properties are available to be specified:

- **unicode-bidi** indicates the nature of the embedding being done, with the possible values:
  1. **normal** to do nothing special (the initial value), thus requiring a value to be specified in order to get a new behavior
  2. **embed** to start a new level of Unicode embedding without forcing a direction
  3. **bidi-override** to start a new level of Unicode embedding forcing a given direction
- **direction** indicates the forced direction, with the possible values:
  1. **ltr** for left-to-right
  2. **rtl** for right-to-left

In the following stylesheet fragment, note how the value of the title text is wrapped in a single **<bidi-override>** formatting object:

```
<block space-before="1.5cm" space-after=".5cm">
  Mixing direction using embed:
</block>
<xsl:for-each select="/doc/section">
  <block text-align-last="justify">
    <xsl:value-of select="position()"/>.
    <bidi-override unicode-bidi="embed">
      <xsl:value-of select="title"/>
    </bidi-override>
    (<xsl:value-of select="count(subsection)"/>)
    <leader leader-pattern="dots"/>
    <page-number-citation ref-id="{generate-id(.)}"/>
  </block>
</xsl:for-each>
```

Using the transformed flow for the characters, Figure 9.18 illustrates the result where the weak-direction characters are not impacted by the neighboring strong-direction characters because of the protection offered by the embedding level.

Mixing direction using embed:

1. English Test (15) 2
2. בדיקה עברית (14) 3
3. إختبار عربي (14) 4
4. Test Français (12) 5

Figure 9.18
Protecting the weak characters from the strong characters prevents them from being influenced.

Going one step further, in the following stylesheet fragment a second level of embedding is being used to wrap the subsection count and the parentheses within the running direction of the text in the first level of embedding:

```
<block space-before="1.5cm" space-after=".5cm">
  Mixing direction using embed (alternative):
</block>
<xsl:for-each select="/doc/section">
  <block text-align-last="justify">
    <xsl:value-of select="position()"/>.
    <bidi-override unicode-bidi="embed">
      <xsl:value-of select="title"/>
      <bidi-override unicode-bidi="embed">
        (<xsl:value-of select="count(subsection)"/>)
      </bidi-override>
    </bidi-override>
    <leader leader-pattern="dots"/>
    <page-number-citation ref-id="{generate-id(.)}"/>
  </block>
</xsl:for-each>
```

Note in Figure 9.19 how the nested level of embedding correctly flows the subsection count at the end of the subsection title. For the text that reads from right to left, this would properly be at the left of the subsection title.

Mixing direction using embed
(alternative):

1. English Test (15) 2
2. (14) בדיקה עברית................................3
3. (14) إختبار عربي..................................4
4. Test Français (12) 5

Figure 9.19
When using nested levels of embedding, you can control which direction embedded text follows.

Although this behavior can be mimicked manually by inserting the Unicode marks, it requires knowledge of the writing direction of the authored text to know which marks to insert, yet the stylesheet writer is not aware of this. The XSL-FO engine is, however, aware of the direction of flow of the characters being used, thus using <bidi-override> for all of the titles produces the desired results without having the stylesheet keep track of the direction of the text.

So proper use of the XSL-FO formatting objects takes the burden away from the stylesheet writers to know the current direction of characters in order to know the correct choice in Unicode marks

that need to be made in the display stream. But it does require an awareness by the stylesheet writers to know when best to apply these formatting objects as needed.

Disambiguation and Aggregation in Area Tree References

Many formatted documents contain a number of different kinds of cross-references, some of which are the responsibility of the XML author and some of which are the responsibility of the stylesheet writer. And when formatting the aggregate of a number of separately-authored XML documents, the opportunity for problems increases when writing naïve algorithms for resolving the references in the formatted result.

References are necessary in area trees to use as identifiers of placeholders whose formatted page location needs to be known. These locations are not known before the time of formatting, because the transformation process or other process creating the instance tree completes its work before the formatting begins, and only the completion of the formatting process up to the point of the location can give the resolution of a reference to a particular page in the resulting set of pages. There are two kinds of such references that formatting objects in the stylesheet add to the area tree during the semantic interpretation of the refined formatting object tree.

A page number can be cited in the flow of the text in order to create the "see page X" kind of result. The formatter resolves the reference to the placeholder into the page number of the page of the area tree on which the placeholder itself is flowed. Using **<page-number-citation>** with **ref-id** and having some reference value for the placeholder, the stylesheet writer asks that the characters representing the formatted page number of the page in the area tree replace the citation-formatting object. Note that the formatting object is empty, and the stylesheet wraps the use of the element with whatever preamble or other formatting is desired around the page number. The actual characters of the formatted page number are determined from properties of the **<page-sequence>** element in which the placebo is found. There is no need to know, nor is there any control available over the formatting of the page number at the point of reference, since the rules are determined at the point at which the placeholder is flowed.

A page can be the target of a hyperlink reference such that when the operator interacts with a hot spot described by the stylesheet's formatting of the area tree, the viewing software navigates the operator to the page resolved for the placeholder. It is the stylesheet's responsibility to wrap the hot spot area with a *basic-link* with *internal-destination* having some reference value for the placeholder. This indicates that interaction from the operator is to take the operator either to the top of the page with the area or to the actual location on the page at which the placeholder is flowed.

In both cases, there may be many references of either kind to the same placeholder, and the references may be made either before or after the placeholder is flowed to the area tree. Therefore, the formatter must implement some kind of backtracking or caching of the formatted result of forward references to a placeholder where the placeholder flows after the reference.

The placeholder is marked in the area tree with the **id** attribute having the value that is referenced by the other constructs. Although there has been some debate about whether an **id** attribute on the **<wrapper>** element should put a placeholder in the area tree (since the wrapper doesn't itself create areas), a clarification from the development committee indicates this is indeed expected.

A Problem of Ambiguity

There are no difficulties in deciding what to do when a referencing construct names the identifier of a placeholder in the area tree and that placeholder is not found. This is an error condition and the formatter should be reporting it. For the purposes of continuing the formatting process, some formatters will replace the referencing construct with a meaningless but predictable sequence of characters. Whereas one formatter puts the digit 0 in its place, another puts the sequence **???** in its place.

When there are multiple placeholders with the identifier being used as a reference, this is not an error condition, so it is not reported, and the formatter uses the first placeholder with a given identifier found in the area tree from the start of the area tree. But this lack of reporting an error can cause unexpected results if the stylesheet writer is not careful to avoid ambiguity.

Consider two situations where ambiguities can crop up. First, when the stylesheet has to create placeholders in the area tree for its own use while at the same time incorporating placeholders from the authored content of the XML document being supplied. Second, when the stylesheet is aggregating a number of XML documents, each supplying placeholders for the area tree, and these placeholders are used verbatim.

Typical XML document uniqueness is guaranteed at validation time by using ID-typed attributes whose values must be unique. But a validated XML document is only guaranteed to have ID-typed attribute specifications unique in the context of the given document, and not related to other XML documents. Should a stylesheet need to create a placeholder, say to indicate the page number of the last page in the document, the stylesheet needs to use a placeholder value guaranteed not to be used in the XML document or documents to ensure there is no ambiguity.

The problem of ambiguity will produce incorrect results but without an error report. The stylesheet places into the area tree placeholders of its own choice, plus the placeholders of the values unique to each of the XML documents being processed. But should the same value be used by the stylesheet as is coincidentally used by the XML document, then the cited last page will get formatted as the page number of the placeholder created for the XML document. Similarly, when two aggregated XML documents coincidentally use the same placeholder value, pointers to the second and subsequent uses of a given placeholder value will all be resolved to the location of the first use of the placeholder value.

The XSLT function **generate-id()** is used to protect oneself from this issue of ambiguity, but it takes discipline to use it everywhere where it is necessary. This function returns a given value for each node of every source node tree created as part of the transformation process. Although the value itself is opaque, in that the user of the value must not make any assumptions of the value or composition, the values are guaranteed to be unique for each and every node in each and every tree. All that can be assumed is that the value generated is lexically acceptable as an XML name as defined in the standard so that it, itself, can be used as an ID value.

The lifetime of a given value returned by **generate-id()** is only guaranteed during a single run of XSLT. This means that each and every time you visit a given source tree node during a given run of XSLT, you are guaranteed to get the same value returned. The next time XSLT is run, however, the value returned for a given node is not guaranteed to be the same as the last time XSLT was run. Implementers of XSLT processors can use any means they want to generate identifier values provided they are persistent for the single run of the processor. A subsequent run may change the properties by which the XSLT processor generates these values.

Using **generate-id()**, the stylesheet writer can thus guarantee the uniqueness of references across the aggregation of multiple XML documents. Consider the situation where attributes of type ID are named **anchor** and attributes of type IDREF are named **linkend** and thus point to the elements with the attributes of **anchor**.

The following would be a typical, but naïve, approach to writing the stylesheet:

```
<block id="{@anchor}"/>
...
<block>
  See page
  <page-number-citation ref-id="{@linkend}"/>.
</block>
```

The problem is that the anchors from two different authors might be the same value. What if each author used the string "**last**" as an anchor value? This stylesheet would end up creating two placeholders in the area tree, each with the value "**last**" and all references to both would be resolved to be a reference to the first in the area tree.

The following approach would take more work but be guaranteed to provide uniqueness:

```
<block id="{generate-id(.)}"/>
...
<block>
  See page
  <page-number-citation ref-id="{generate-id(id(@linkend))}"/>.
</block>
```

The use of the XPath function **id()** requires the XML instances to have informed the XML processor of the types of attributes being ID values. Absent a DTD, this requires the XML instances to have declarations in the internal declaration subset along the lines of the following (noting there is no need to declare IDREF attributes, only ID attributes):

```
<!DOCTYPE book
[
<!ATTLIST para anchor ID #IMPLIED>
]>
<book>
  ...
```

A well-formed document can have an internal declaration subset with only **ATTLIST** declarations.

In the situation where there is no control over the authored documents, and there is no DTD, the previous example would be very difficult to police. Then the stylesheet can abandon the use of id() and use keys.

The following fragments in a stylesheet would support the previous functionality using keys:

```
<xsl:key name="ids" match="*[@anchor]" use="normalize-space(@anchor)"/>
...
<block id="{generate-id(.)}"/>
...
<block>
  See page
  <page-number-citation
    ref-id="{generate-id(key('ids',normalize-space(@linkend))[1])}"/>.
</block>
```

While supporting IDREF with keys is straightforward, it is not straightforward supporting IDREFS, although with some recursive programming techniques, this is possible.

Adding Stylesheet References

A common stylesheet task in XSLT 1.0 is to utilize **<page-number-citation>** in the fulfillment of the last page number of a publication, as in "Page 37 of 123". The page number "123" is obtained by citing an anchor placed at the end of the flow of content. A naïve implementation of this has long been advocated in some books, and that is to use a hardwired string in the stylesheet as follows:

```
<block>
  Page <page-number/>
  of <page-number-citation ref-id="last"/>
</block>
```

As indicated in the earlier example, this example would be ambiguous with authored uses of an ID value of "**last**" outside the control of the stylesheet. But what of the use of **generate-id()**? Because the values are opaque and indeterminate, there is no way to select a hardwired string value to ensure avoiding the coincidence of colliding with a generated id.

The solution is to use **generate-id()** for the last anchor in the flow for the page count, but to choose a node that is guaranteed never to be referenced by the content. The root node is such a node, and there is no reference using ID/IDREF that would ever point to the root node because the root node is not an element node. Although you can also never point to a node of any other kind (attribute, namespace, text, and so on), these are candidates; they are not guaranteed to be present, thus pointing to the root node is entirely acceptable as in:

```
<block>
  Page <page-number/>
  of <page-number-citation ref-id="{generate-id(/)}"/>
</block>
```

Making Numerous References

There are times when writing stylesheets that two-way references need to be made, where a single concept on the input or from the stylesheet requires two placeholders for that concept to be used in the area tree.

Consider the requirement where end notes are displayed for chapters of a book. At some arbitrary point within the XML content of a chapter, an end note is defined. Producing end notes flowing a citation to the end note at that point in the flow, continuing the flowing of the remainder of the content (possibly encountering other notes along the way), and then at the end of the chapter aggregating the notes together into an enumerated list indexed by their citations.

A bidirectional link is desirable for this presentation. Making the citation in the middle of the flow hot through a hyperlink using **<basic-link>** to the collection of end notes allows the reader to jump to the end of the chapter to read the cited content while going through the content of the chapter. Likewise, **<basic- link>** can be used in the formatting of the end note aggregation and point to the location of the citation so that the reader can, on review of the set of end notes for a chapter, click on an end note to be brought to the middle of the chapter where the note is cited.

In this situation, two placeholders are needed in the area tree, one to anchor the end note so that it can be pointed to from the citation, and one to anchor the citation so that it can be pointed to from the end note. But there is only one source tree node that has created the need for two anchors, that being the note itself, so using **generate-id()** alone in both placeholders will introduce an ambiguity without reporting an error.

In this situation prefixing the value returned from **generate-id()** with two different prefixes disambiguates the two placeholders, but there are ramifications of doing this. If only the end note anchors are being prefixed and not, say, cross-reference anchors, there is an infinitesimal (but not zero) chance for an ambiguity with the use of **generate-id()** for an authored identifier. Thus, if *any* use of **generate-id()** needs to be prefixed, then *every* use of **generate-id()** needs to be prefixed to absolutely guarantee uniqueness.

As an example, you might choose the prefixes **x_** for cross reference anchors, **e_** for end note anchors, and **c_** for end note citation anchors throughout the stylesheet and be assured of no ambiguities in the result.

```
<xsl:template match="chapter">
  <block id="x_{generate-id(.)}">
    ...
  </block>
  <xsl:for-each select="note">
    <!--aggregate set of chapter end notes-->
    <block id="e_{generate-id(.)}">
      <!--point to citation-->
      <basic-link internal-destination="c_{generate-id(.)}">
      ...
...
<xsl:template match="note">
  <!--render citation-->
  <inline id="c_{generate-id(.)}" baseline-shift="super">
    <!--point to end note-->
    <basic-link internal-destination="e_{generate-id(.)}">
      <xsl:number level="any"/>
      ...
...
```

Retrieve-Marker Arbitration

A marker in XSL-FO is a construct placed in the flow of paginated information. This construct holds arbitrary formatting objects that can be retrieved and placed into static content defined for a page. The retrieval is parameterized such that the stylesheet writer can control which marker in the flow is retrieved when needed. In this fashion, the static content for publishing constructs such as headers and footers can reflect changes found throughout the flow, provided the changed values are embedded in the flow in the markers that are retrieved.

Consider that at transformation time, the stylesheet writer has no idea on which page any given content is going to flow. Therefore, there is no detection of when to arbitrarily change the pagination to use new content. Moreover, defining a new heading in pagination can only be done when starting a new page sequence, which will trigger the start of a new page, thus not flowing the content immediately after the preceding content on the same page. When the static content is defined to retrieve a marker, the definition does not change even though the marker retrieved changes. The rendered content changes because it contains a new set of retrieved formatting objects, but because the definition of the static content doesn't change, the seamless flow continues without interrupting the page.

A common use of simple markers is to render running section numbers in a header or footer of a publication. Typically, whenever a section's content begins, the flow is created with a number of marker definitions, each one suitable to a particular use when retrieved in static content. For example, two markers could be defined for each section, one with the heading suitably formatted for use in a recto header and one with the heading suitably formatted for use in a verso header. The static content for each header would only retrieve the marker suitable for its use and would ignore the other marker defined for each section.

Another common use of markers is for dictionary headings. Think about how in a Western dictionary the verso page on the left has a highlighted word at the top left of the page indicating either the word starting on a previous page whose definition is overflowing to the given page, or the word at the start of the page if the page begins with a word. Similarly, the recto page on the right has a highlighted word at the top right of the page indicating the last word whose definition begins on that page.

Such are the simple publishing problems for which the markers as defined in XSL-FO 1.0 are used.

There is, however, no arbitration for markers. Arbitration is required when it is necessary to choose between multiple markers that might be available to be retrieved from a page, rather than directly retrieving a given marker by its name (called its "class"). A requirement arises for retrieved marker arbitration when it is necessary to reflect "the highest value" of a semantic group of values that might not be available on the page. For example, the publishing of security-sensitive information might need to reflect for a given page the value of most sensitive classification of content, where content might be considered "confidential", "secret", or "top secret". The publishing objective is to indicate on every page the security level of the most sensitive content found on the page.

A marker for each kind of classification can accompany the affected flowed text, thus reflecting the nature of each portion of content. Retrieving each of these markers for a given page in a simple flow of formatting objects would, in some cases, retrieve a number of markers from the same page. This would reflect all levels of classification found on the page, rather than just the highest classification, thus not meeting the publishing requirement.

But there is, in fact, an XSL-FO construct in which a sense of "priority" is reflected numerically, and with this control one can mimic the required arbitration of retrieval. Absolutely positioned block containers can be specified with a z-index property to indicate priority and visibility within a stacking context relative to other absolutely positioned block containers. Formatting objects with a higher z-index appear in front of formatting objects with a lower z-index in the stacking context and could thus be considered as having higher priority. Transparent formatting objects (those without a specified background) that have a higher z-index will reveal those formatting objects that have a lower z-index that are behind.

The publishing requirement is then implemented by collocating the retrieved formatting objects for each level of classification, each with an opaque background that obscures any retrieved formatting objects of a lesser priority. The end result, therefore, reveals only the highest priority classification by exposing only those formatting objects with the highest z-index in the stacking context in the static content.

Consider the following example, where the static content positions three collocated absolutely positioned block containers, each with a different z-index:

```
<static-content flow-name="frame-before">
  <block-container z-index="1" absolute-position="absolute"
                   height="12pt" width="3cm" right="0cm">
    <block background-color="white" text-align="end"
           font-family="Courier" font-size="12pt">
      <retrieve-marker retrieve-class-name="confidential"
                       retrieve-boundary="page"/>
    </block>
  </block-container>
  <block-container z-index="2" absolute-position="absolute"
                   height="12pt" width="3cm" right="0cm">
    <block background-color="white" text-align="end"
           font-family="Courier" font-size="12pt">
      <retrieve-marker retrieve-class-name="secret"
                       retrieve-boundary="page"/>
    </block>
  </block-container>
  <block-container z-index="3" absolute-position="absolute"
                   height="12pt" width="3cm" right="0cm">
    <block background-color="white" text-align="end"
           font-family="Courier" font-size="12pt">
      <retrieve-marker retrieve-class-name="topsecret"
                       retrieve-boundary="page"/>
    </block>
  </block-container>
</static-content>
```

The following text has a number of short blocks, some with a specified marker identifying the classification of the block. The marker supplies the actual text that is to be rendered on the page, thus indicating the classification to the reader:

```
<block space-before="4em">
  <marker marker-class-name="confidential">CONFIDENTIAL</marker>
  This is a confidential test</block>
<block space-before="4em">This is a test</block>
<block space-before="4em">
  <marker marker-class-name="secret">SECRET</marker>
  This is a secret test</block>
<block space-before="4em">This is a test</block>
<block space-before="4em">
  <marker marker-class-name="topsecret">TOP SECRET</marker>
  This is a top secret test</block>
<block space-before="4em">This is a test</block>
```

Although the retrieved content found in the markers of the flowed text may contain the block containers and their specified z-index level, the previous approach is very compact, requiring only the presence of the text of each block that is placed in the block container at each level. When no text is retrieved for a particular block container, the block has no dimension and the block container does not obscure lower z-index levels. When text is retrieved for a particular block container, the block has dimension, and the background fills the block to the width of the block container.

Summary

Using XSL-FO for paginating XML documents can produce nicely nuanced presentations of the content. Building on the basics, you can use advanced techniques to create the desired effects. It is also important to remember the basic differences between the XSL-FO and CSS rendering of borders, so that the CSS effect can be mimicked if needed.

Appendix A

XML Tools and Implementations

The following sections provide a snapshot of current implementations of some of the applications described in the previous chapters. This is not necessarily a complete list. Check the websites listed to get an updated status for each product.

XSLT Implementations

Product	Company	URL	Description	Type
DataPower Products	IBM	http://www.ibm.com/us/	DataPower's products have now been incorporated into IBM's Web-related offerings. The XI50 is a hardware-based data transformation appliance. The XS40 is a hardware-based XML and Web services security appliance. The XA35 is a hardware-based XML accelerator that speeds XSLT, XPath, and XSD (Schema validation) by 30X or more.	Commercial
XF Rendering Server	Ecrion Software	http://www.ecrion.com/	Uses XSL formatting objects to dynamically create customized PDF, POSTSCRIPT, HTML, GIF, JPEG, or PNG files from XML data.	Commercial
libxslt		http://xmlsoft.org/XSLT/	XSLT C library developed for the Gnome project.	Open source, MIT
MDC-XSL		http://mdc-xsl.sourceforge.net/	XSLT processor written in C++.	Open source, GPL
Microsoft XML Downloads	Microsoft	http://msdn.microsoft.com/XML/XMLDownloads/	Contains an XSLT engine, which fully implements the XSLT standard.	Freeware
PassiveTeX	Text Encoding Initiative Consortium	http://www.tei-c.org/Software/passivetex/index.html	A library of TeX macros that can be used to process an XML document that results from an XSL transformation to FO (formatting objects).	LaTex
Sablotron	gingerall.org	http://www.gingerall.org/sablotron.html	Sablotron is an attempt to develop a fast, compact, and portable XSLT processor. Supported platforms include Linux, Windows NT, and Solaris.	Open source, GPL
SAXON XSLT Processor (free version)		http://saxon.sourceforge.net/	Java XSLT processor developed by Michael Kay.	Open source, MPL
SAXON XSLT Processor	Saxonica	http://www.saxonica.com/	Java XSLT processor developed by Michael Kay.	Commercial
Scriptura	Inventive Designers	http://www.inventivedesigners.com/products/scriptura.html	A letter, report, and output generator for XSLT/XSLFO documents. GUI designer for stylesheets, plus an engine to create XSLT, XSLFO, PDF, XHTML, and PCL5.	Commercial
ShoXS: a Shorter XSL Syntax	Xtal Mountain	http://www.xm.co.nz/ShoXS.htm	ShoXS is a Shorter Syntax for XSL and this site provides some tools to read XSL files, convert and edit in ShoXS and then convert back and save in XSL.	Open source, GPL
4Suite XML Tools	4suite.org	http://4suite.org/index.xhtml	Includes an XSLT Processor written in Python by FourThought LLC.	Open source
Tiger XSLT Mapper	Axizon	http://www.axizon.com/	Drag and drop XSLT editor that doesn't require knowledge of XSLT syntax. Developer edition is free.	Commercial

Product	Company	URL	Description	Type
Unicorn XSLT Processor	Unicorn Enterprises SA	http://www.unicorn-enterprises.com/products_uxt.html	XSLT processor for Windows written in C++.	Freeware
Xalan-C++		http://xml.apache.org/xalan-c/index.html	XSLT Processor written in C++. A part of Apache's XML project.	Open source
XML::XSL		http://xmlxslt.sourceforge.net/	A server-side XSLT processor written in Perl.	Open source, GPL
XML/XSL Portal		http://www.bayes.co.uk/xml/index.xml?/xml/main.xml	Utilities and downloads for XSLT and related developers.	
XSet		http://www.openhealth.org/XSet/	An XML property set description of XML 1.0 and XML namespaces that enables XPath-based indexing and addressing of the full fidelity grove of an XML document.	
XSL Processor for ColdFusion	activSoftware	http://www.activsoftware.com/xml/xslt/	CFX Tag allows you to perform XSL Transformations with ColdFusion.	Free developer edition; commercial sites must purchase a license per server.
XSL Report Designer	Antenna House	http://www.antennahouse.com/product/designer/	Includes a Windows GUI that simplifies designing layouts for complex XML forms and a runtime engine that merges a layout with XML data to produce a PDF via XSL-FO.	Commercial
XSL Transformations (XSLT) in Mozilla		http://www.mozilla.org/projects/xslt/	Information about Mozilla's native XSLT processor. Includes a FAQ and a list of known bugs.	
xsl:easy	SoftProject GmbH	http://xsl-easy.com/	Transformation tool using a built-in graphical XSLT editor to create XML out of arbitrary data and save the transformation result back to other formats.	Commercial
XSLScript		http://pault.com/XSLScript/	Terse notation for writing complex XSLT stylesheets.	
Xsltp.pl	DOPS	http://www.dopscripts.com/doc/description.html	Perl CGI XSLT processor.	Open source

XSL-FO Implementations

Reprinted with permission from the W3C (www.w3.org).

Product	Company	URL	Description	Type/ Platform
Ibex PDF Creator	Visual Programming	http://www.xmlpdf.com/	Ibex is a .NET component or Java JAR file that can be used in command line, thick client Web server (ASP.NET,Tomcat) applications.	(Java, .NET; free downloads)
DOPE/ compose	Compart Systemhaus GmbH	http://www.compart.net/cms/ index.php?page=dope-compose_en	High performance formatter.	Commercial (Win/Linux/ Solaris/Other, Java)
XSL Formatter	Antenna House	http://www.antennahouse.com/	XML and XSL-FO to PDF with high-quality SVG, MathML, and multilingual support for over 50 languages.	Commercial (Win/Linux, free evaluation versions)
Scriptura XBOS: Output Solution (Java, evaluation on request)	Inventive Designers	http://www.inventivedesigners.com/ scriptura/what.htm	An intuitive, what-you-see-is-what-you-get design interface.	Commercial
XSLFast	jCatalog Software AG	http://www.xslfast.com/	Drag and drop, WYSIWYG editor.	Commercial (Java, free evaluation version)
XEP	RenderX	http://www.renderx.com/		Commercial (Java, free evaluation version)
Apache FOP PassiveTeX		http://xmlgraphics.apache.org/fop/	Open source formatter.	Java, open source (TeX, open source)
Apoc XSL-FO,	Chive	http://www.chive.com/	A rendering engine for the XSL-FO layout language for integration with .NET.	Commercial (free evaluation version)
Unicorn FOs	Unicorn Enterprises SA	http://www.unicorn-enterprises.com/ products_ufo.html	A standalone command-line XML formatter.	(TeX, free Windows binaries)
REXP		http://www.esng.dibe.unige.it/REXP/	Early implementation based on Apache FOP.	Open source
X-smiles		http://www.xsmiles.org/		Java, open source

Product	Company	URL	Description	Type/ Platform
Novosoft RT-F2FO:		http://rtf2fo.com/	RTF to FO converter.	Java, Free evaluation version
html2fo		http://sourceforge.net/projects/html2fo/		C, open source
FOA:		http://foa.sourceforge.net/	XSL authoring tool.	Java, open source
JFO	Northbit	http://www.northbit.de/	RTF to XSL-FO converter, XSL-FO API, reporting tool.	Commercial (Java, free evaluation version available)
Adobe Live-Cycle Assembler :	Adobe	http://www.adobe.com/products/livecycle/assembler/	Document production framework.	Commercial, Win/Solaris
WH2FO:		http://wh2fo.sourceforge.net/	Word HTML to formatting objects converter.	Open source
Infoprint XML Extender for z/OS	IBM	http://www.printers.ibm.com/internet/wwsites.nsf/vwweb published/ipxmlsupt_ww	From IBM: document printing application.	Commercial, z/OS

XML Authoring Tools

Editor	Company	Website	Platforms	Free
<alt> Mobile	<alt> Mobile	http://altmobile.com/Home.html	All (Java)	No
Authentic	Altova	http://www.altova.com/	Win	Yes
Conglomerate		http://www.conglomerate.org/	Linux	Yes
EditLive! For XML	Ephox	http://www.ephox.com/products/editliveforxml/	All (browser-based)	No
Emacs/nXML		http://hacks.oreilly.com/pub/h/2044	All	Yes
Emacs/PSGML		http://www.lysator.liu.se/~lenst/about_psgml/	All	Yes
epcEdit		http://www.epcedit.com/	Linux, Win, Solaris	No
Epic/Arbortext	PTC/Arbortext	http://www.ptc.com/company/arbortext/index.htm	Win, Solaris	No
eWebEditPro+XML	ektron	http://www.ektron.com/ewebeditproxml.aspx		
Exchanger XML Editor	cladonia	http://www.exchangerxml.com/	All (Java)	No
Excosoft XML Client	Excosoft	http://www.excosoft.se/site/notfound.html	Win, Solaris, Linux	No
FrameMaker 7	Adobe	http://www.adobe.com/products/framemaker/index.html	Win, Mac, Unix (no Linux)	No
jEdit (with XML plugin)		http://www.jedit.org/	All (Java)	Yes
Lyx		http://www.lyx.org/	*nix, Win, Mac	Yes
oXygen XML Editor		http://www.oxygenxml.com/	All (Java)	No

Editor	Company	Website	Platforms	Free
Pollo		http://pollo.sourceforge.net/	All (Java)	Yes
Serna	Syntext	http://www.syntext.com/products/serna/index.htm	Win, Linux, Mac OS X	No
Stylus Studio	Stylus Studio	http://www.stylusstudio.com/xml/editor/	Microsoft Windows XP, 2000 Service Pack 2	No
SwiXAT Swing-XML Authoring	SwiXAT	http://www.swixat.org/docs/index.html	All (Java)	Yes
TurboXML	Tibco	http://www.tibco.com/	All (Java)	No
Topologi Collaborative Markup Editor	topologi	http://www.topologi.com/	Win, Mac, Linux	No
Vex		http://vex.sourceforge.net/	All (Java)	Yes
Vim XML Edit FtPlugin		http://www.vim.org/scripts/script.php?script_id=301	All	Yes
Xerlin		http://www.xerlin.org/	All (Java)	Yes
XMetaL	JUSTSYSTEMS	http://www.xmetal.com/index.x	Win	No
XML Spy	Altova	http://www.altova.com/	Win	No
XML Suite 2007	Altova	http://www.altova.com/	Win	No
xmlBlueprint XMLEditor		http://www.xmlblueprint.com/	Win	No
XMLwriter	Wattle	http://xmlwriter.net/g2_index.shtml?xmlauthoring		
Xopus		http://xopus.com/	Win	No
Xpress Author for MS Word XML	In.vision	http://www.invisionresearch.com/		
XXE	XMLmind	http://www.xmlmind.com/xmleditor/	All	No
XXE Standard Edition	XMLmind	http://www.xmlmind.com/xmleditor/	All (Java)	Yes

XQuery Implementations

Reprinted with permission from the W3C (www.w3.org).

- **Abacus Systems' *Relational XQuery* (http://216.154.221.184/) supports both relational data (via JDBC) and other sources, including XML files, and also claims XQJ (XQuery for Java API) conformance. Includes a GUI for creating and editing queries. 30 day evaluation.**
- **Altova GmbH *XMLSpy 2006* (http://www.altova.com/features_xslxpath.html) includes an XQuery Debugger, a code generator for mapping between Schemas, and AltovaXML Query Processor (http://www.altova.com/altovaxml.html), which handles both XSLT 2 and XML Query 1.0. 30 day free trial.**
- **Apple's *Sherlock* (http://developer.apple.com/macosx/sherlock/) for Mac OS X; see also their XML Query Extension functions (http://developer.apple.com/documentation/AppleApplications/Conceptual/Sherlock/Concepts/ ScriptExtensions.html#//apple_ref/doc/uid/20001085-160986-BAJFIAGE).**
- **ATS' *BizQuery* (http://www.atssoft.com/products/bizquery.htm) 30 day free trial.**

- Axyana Software's *Qizx/Open* (http://www.axyana.com/qizxopen/). Java, open source under the Mozilla public license.
- BEA's *AquaLogic Data Services Platform* (http://www.bea.com/framework.jsp?CNT=index.htm&FP=/content/products/aqualogic/data_services/). 90 day free trial.
- Berkeley Lab's *Nux* (http://dsd.lbl.gov/nux/), an open source Java toolkit for XML, XQuery, XPath, schema validation, fuzzy fulltext similarity search and related technologies using Saxon, XOM, Xerces, and JAXB. Open source under a BSD-style license.
- Bluestream Database Software Corp.'s *XStreamDB* (http://www.bluestream.com/products/xstreamdb32) Java; includes a native XML database and full text support. Commercial with trial download.
- David Carlisle's *xq2xml* (http://monet.nag.co.uk/xq2xml//index.html) converts XQuery to XML, to XQueryX, and to XSLT.
- webMethods' *Cerebra* (http://www.webmethods.com/cerebra) supports XQuery, OWL-DL, and RDF, and can connect to external databases.
- Cognetic Systems's *XQuantum* (http://www.cogneticsystems.com/) implements a subset of XML Query in an XML-native data store. They have a Web page demonstrating the XQuery use cases, and support static typing as well as the full text extensions. Windows and Linux; 30 day evaluation.
- DataDirect's *DataDirect XQuery (tm)* (http://www.datadirect.com/products/xquery/index.ssp), an embeddable component for XQuery that implements the XQuery for Java, API (XQJ) Java; 15 day trial download.
- DataDirect's *Stylus Studio 5.0* (http://www.stylusstudio.com/). XQuery, XML Schema, and XSLT IDE.
- *eXist* (http://exist.sourceforge.net/) has a Java-based native XML database with an XQuery interface. Open source; GNU LGPL.
- Fatdog Software's *XQEngine* (http://xqengine.sourceforge.net/). Java, with full-text support. Open source; GPL or as negotiated.
- GAEL's *Derby* (http://www.gael.fr/derby/) provides a Java API via their Data Request Broker.
- *Galax* (http://www.galaxquery.org/). Open source (in OCAML), with a Galatex (http://www.galaxquery.com/galatex/) full text search implementation.
- GNU's Qexo *(Kawa-Query)* (http://www.gnu.org/software/qexo/) by Per Bothner. Compiles XQuery on-the-fly to Java bytecodes. Based on and part of the Kawa (http://www.gnu.org/software/kawa/) framework. An online sandbox (http://www.cocoonhive.org/xquery/xqueryform.html) is available too. Open source under the GPL-like Kawa License.
- Ipedo's *XIP* (http://www.ipedo.com/html/products.html) includes a "dual core" SQL + XML QuQery engine.

- IBM's *xqnsta* (http://www.alphaworks.ibm.com/tech/xqnsta). XQuery Normalizer and Static Analyzer (XQNSTA) is a Java API and GUI for normalizing and computing the static type of XQuery expressions.
- IBM's *DB2 Content Manager* (http://www-306.ibm.com/software/data/cm/) has an "Xpath- based query language"; in addition, the DB2 Viper (http://www-306.ibm.com/software/data/db2/xml/) release will have XQuery support.
- IPSI's *IPSI-XQ* (http://www.ipsi.fraunhofer.de/i-info/en/content/view/74/0//index_e.html). Java; free download.
- Ispras Modis' *Sedna* (http://modis.ispras.ru/sedna/index.htm). Native XML DBMS in C/C++ and Scheme; partial support for XML Query. Includes an Apache HTTP module and APIs for .NET, Python, and Chicken Scheme. Open source under the Apache license.
- Mark Logic's *Content Interaction Server* (http://xqzone.marklogic.com/). There is also a technical overview document (http://xqzone.marklogic.com/howto/tutorials/technical-overview.xqy). Commercial, with free download restricted to 50MB of data.
- Microsoft's *SQL Server 2005 Express* (http://www.microsoft.com/sql/editions/express/default.mspx), with XML Schema, XPath 2, and XML Query support.
- The MonetDB/XQuery group's *MonetDB/XQuery* (http://monetdb.cwi.nl/XQuery/) is an independent compiler producing code for the MonetDB server backend. Open source (adapting the Mozilla public license).
- The Mono Project (http://www.mono-project.com/Main_Page) implements a draft of XML Query (open source).
- OpenLink Software's *Virtuoso Universal Server* (http://www.openlinksw.com/) supports XSLT, XQuery, and SQLX.
- Oracle's *Oracle XQuery* (http://www.oracle.com/technology/tech/xml/xquery/index.html) is part of the Oracle Database 10g Release2. Multi-platform; seems to be a free binary download.
- *PHP XML Classes* (http://sourceforge.net/projects/phpxmlclasses/) includes Xquery-Lite, a PHP implementation from 2002. Open source.
- Politecnico di Milano's *XQBE* and other XQuery products (http://dbgroup.elet.polimi.it/xquery/).
- QuiLogic's *SQL/XML-IMDB* (http://www.quilogic.cc/) supports a mixure of SQL statements and XQuery expressions. Free trial requires a restart every hour.
- RainingData's *TigerLogic XDMS XML Data Management Server* (http://www.rainingdata.com/products/tl/) for Sun Solaris and Microsoft Windows; free trial.
- Renmin University of China's *OrientX* (http://idke.ruc.edu.cn/), a native XML database system in C/C++ developed under Renmin University of China. Open source.
- Saarland University Database Group's *FluXQuery* (http://www.infosys.uni-sb.de/~scherzin/FluXQuery.html), an extension of the XQuery language, FluX, that supports event-based query processing and the conscious handling of main memory buffers.

- Saxonica's *Saxon* (http://saxonica.com/) implements both XML Query and XSLT 2.0. Available in a schema-aware version as a commercial product, and without schema support as open source.
- Oracle's *Berkeley DB XML 2.0* (http://www.oracle.com/database/berkeley-db/index.html), an embeddable native XML database with support for XQuery 1.0 (July 2004 draft), implemented in C++, with interfaces for Java, Python, Perl, and PHP. Open source.
- Software AG's *Tamino XML Server* (http://www.softwareag.com/corporate/products/tamino/default.asp) and *Tamino XML Query Demo* (http://tamino.demozone.softwareag.com/demoXQuery/index.html).
- Sonic Software's *Sonic XML Server* (http://www.sonicsoftware.com/products/sonic_xml_server/index.ssp). 30 day trial.
- The University of Texas at Arlington Computer Science Department has people working on *XQP* (http://lambda.uta.edu/xqp/): XQuery Processing on a P2P System. Java; open source.
- Worcester Polytechnic Institute's *RainbowCore* (http://davis.wpi.edu/~dsrg/rainbow/). Java; available at no charge and without warranty.
- The Univerisity of Antwerp's *blixem LiXQuery engine* (http://adrem.ua.ac.be/~blixem/) implements a subset of XQuery intended for teaching.
- X-Hive's *XQuery demo* (http://support.x-hive.com/xquery/index.html).
- Xpriori's *NeoCore XMS* (http://www.xpriori.com/) native XML database, with XPath2.0/XQuery access language support. .Net on Linux and MS Windows; free unlimited download for development purposes.
- XQuare Group and Universite' de Versailles Saint-Quentin's: *XQuare Fusion and XQuare Bridge* (http://forge.objectweb.org/projects/xquare/). Open source; used to be called xQuark (see also the *Xquare home page*: http://xquare.objectweb.org/).
- Xyleme's *Xyleme Server* (http://www.xyleme.com/page/62476/); commercial.

XML Databases

Reprinted with permission from Ronald Bourret (http://www.rpbourret.com/). For a more extensive list of products you can use with XML and databases, see http://www.rpbourret.com/xml/XMLDatabaseProds.htm.

Middleware

Middleware is software that "XML-enables" a database. That is, it helps the database import data from an XML document or export data to an XML document.

Product	Developer	License	URL
ADO	Microsoft	Commercial	http://www.microsoft.com/
Alliance XML/400	Patrick Townsend & Associates	Commercial	http://www.patownsend.com/
Allora	HiT Software	Commercial	http://www.hitsw.com/
Altova MapForce	Altova	Commercial	http://www.altova.com/
Connect for SQL/XML	DataDirect Technologies	Commercial	http://www.datadirect.com/
Connect XML-2-DB	Skyhawk Systems	Commercial	http://www.skyhawksystems.com/
DataDirect XQuery	DataDirect Technologies	Commercial	http://www.datadirect.com/
dbsql2xml	Stepan RYBAR	Open source	http://dbsql2xml.sourceforge.net/
DBIx::XMLMessage	Andrei Nossov	Open source	http://cpan.uwinnipeg.ca/htdocs/DBIx-XMLMessage/DBIx/XMLMessage.html
DBIx::XMLServer	Martin Bright	Open source	http://search.cpan.org/dist/DBIx-XMLServer/XMLServer.pm
DB/XML Transform	DataMirror Corp.	Commercial	http://www.datamirror.com/
Hyperjaxb	Aleksei Valikov	Open source	https://hyperjaxb2.dev.java.net/
JSQLMapper	jNetDirect	Commercial	http://www.jnetdirect.com/
Oracle XML Developer's Kit (XDK)	Oracle	Free	https://www.oracle.com/
truExchange XML	nuBridges	Commercial	http://www.nubridges.com/
XML-DBMS	Ronald Bourret, et al	Open source	http://www.rpbourret.com/
XML Gateway	SPI Ltd.	Commercial	http://www.xmlgateway.co.uk/
XQuare Bridge, XQuare Fusion	Odonata	Open source	http://xquare.objectweb.org/

IDEs and Editors

The following XML IDEs support data transfer between XML and databases and may also provide support for XQuery and SQL/XML.

Product	Developer	License	URL
Alchemist XML IDE	Mentat Technologies	Commercial	http://www.mentattech.com/
<oXygen/>	SyncRO Soft Ltd.	Commercial	http://www.oxygenxml.com/
Stylus Studio	DataDirect Technologies	Commercial	http://www.stylusstudio.com/
XML Spy	Altova	Commercial	http://www.altova.com/

XML-Enabled Databases

XML-enabled databases contain features for importing data from XML documents and for exporting data to XML documents.

Product	Developer	License	Database Type	URL
Access	Microsoft	Commercial	Relational	http://www.microsoft.com/
Cache	InterSystems Corp.	Commercial	Post relational	http://www.intersystems.com/
DB2	IBM	Commercial	Relational	http://www.ibm.com/
FileMaker	FileMaker	Commercial	FileMaker	http://www.filemaker.com/
FoxPro	Microsoft	Commercial	Relational	http://www.microsoft.com/
Matisse	Matisse Software	Commercial	Post relational	http://www.matisse.com/
Objectivity/DB	Objectivity	Commercial	Object oriented	http://www.objectivity.com/
OpenInsight	Revelation Software	Commercial	Multi-valued	http://www.revelation.com/
Oracle	Oracle	Commercial	Relational	http://www.oracle.com/
SQL Server	Microsoft	Commercial	Relational	http://www.microsoft.com/
Sybase	Sybase	Commercial	Relational	http://www.sybase.com/
UniData	IBM	Commercial	Nested relational	http://www.ibm.com/
UniVerse	IBM	Commercial	Nested relational	http://www.ibm.com/

Native XML Databases

Native XML databases are databases that use the XML data model.

Product	Developer	License	URL
4Suite	FourThought	Open source	http://4suite.org/
Berkeley DB XML	Oracle	Open source	http://www.oracle.com/
eXist	Wolfgang Meier	Open source	http://exist.sourceforge.net/
Infonyte DB	Infonyte	Commercial	http://www.infonyte.com/
Ipedo	Ipedo	Commercial	http://www.ipedo.com/
MarkLogic Server	Mark Logic Corp.	Commercial	http://www.marklogic.com/
Neocore XMS	Xpriori	Commercial	http://www.xpriori.com/
Sedna XML DBMS	ISP RAS MODIS	Free	http://modis.ispras.ru/sedna/
Sonic XML Server	Sonic Software	Commercial	http://www.sonicsoftware.com/
Tamino	Software AG	Commercial	http://www.softwareag.com/
TeraText DBS	TeraText Solutions	Commercial	http://www.teratext.com/
TEXTML Server	IXIASOFT, Inc.	Commercial	http://www.ixiasoft.com/
TigerLogic XDMS	Raining Data	Commercial	http://www.rainingdata.com/
X-Hive/DB	X-Hive Corporation	Commercial	http://www.x-hive.com/
Xindice	Apache Software Foundation	Open source	http://xml.apache.org/
XQuantum XML Database Server	Cognetic Systems	Commercial	http://www.cogneticsystems.com/
XStreamDB Native XML Database	Bluestream Database Software Corp.	Commercial	http://www.bluestream.com/
Xyleme Zone Server	Xyleme SA	Commercial	http://www.xyleme.com/

Content (Document) Management Systems

Content-management systems are systems designed for managing XML documents or fragments of XML documents. (The term "content-management system" is actually very broad; it

is used here in a limited sense. Most products in this table can manage non-XML documents as well.)

Product	Developer	License	URL
Amaxus XML CMS	Box UK	Commercial	http://www.boxuk.com/
Astoria	LightSpeed Software	Commercial	http://www.astoriasoftware.com/
Content@XML	XyEnterprise	Commercial	http://www.xyenterprise.com/
Documentum	Documentum, Inc.	Commercial	http://software.emc.com/
EXPLOit	Document Solutions	Commercial	http://www.documentsolutions.it/
GEMt	X.Systems, Inc.	Commercial	http://www.xsystemsinc.com/
Ingeniux CMS	Ingeniux Corporation	Commercial	http://www.ingeniux.com/
Life*CMS, Life*CDM	Corena	Commercial	http://www.corena.de/en/
SCHEMA ST4	SCHEMA GmbH	Commercial	http://www.schema.de/eds/en/
SiberSafe	SiberLogic	Commercial	http://www.siberlogic.com/
TeraText DMS	TeraText	Commercial	http://www.teratext.com/
Vasont	Vasont Systems	Commercial	http://www.vasont.com/
XDocs	Bluestream Database Software Corp.	Commercial	http://www.bluestream.com/
X-Hive/Docato	X-Hive Corporation	Commercial	http://www.x-hive.com/

Index

A

X–Z